Data-Centric Systems and Applications

For further volumes:
http://www.springer.com/series/5258

Zohra Bellahsene · Angela Bonifati
Erhard Rahm
Editors

Schema Matching and Mapping

 Springer

Editors

Zohra Bellahsene
LIRMM CNRS/Univ. Montpellier 2
Rue Ada 161
34392 Montpellier
France
bella@lirmm.fr

Angela Bonifati
Consiglio Nazionale delle
Ricerche (CNR)
Via P. Bucci 41/C
87036 Rende
Italy
bonifati@icar.cnr.it

Erhard Rahm
Universität Leipzig
Inst. Informatik
Augustusplatz 10-11
04109 Leipzig
Germany
rahm@informatik.uni-leipzig.de

ISBN 978-3-642-26717-8   ISBN 978-3-642-16518-4 (eBook)
DOI 10.1007/978-3-642-16518-4
Springer Heidelberg Dordrecht London New York

ACM Computing Classification (1998): H.2, I.2, F.4

Cover design: KuenkelLopka GmbH

Printed on acid-free paper

Springer is part of Springer Science+Business Media (www.springer.com)

Preface

This book provides an overview about the state-of-the-art solutions and the most recent advances in schema matching and mapping, both recognized as key areas of metadata management. Tasks involving metadata are indeed pervasive in databases and information systems and include schema evolution, schema and ontology integration and matching, XML message mapping, as well as data migration and data exchange. While research on these complex problems has been performed since several decades, we have witnessed significant progress especially in the last decade. In particular, research addressed the metadata problems in a more abstract and generic way rather than focusing on specific applications and data models. A cornerstone of this new line of research is the notion of *schema mappings*, i.e., expressive mappings interrelating schemas (or other metadata models such as ontologies). Furthermore, powerful operators to manipulate schemas and mappings (e.g., matching and merging of schemas or composition of mappings) have been investigated for solving various kinds of metadata-related tasks. Raising the level of abstraction for metadata management was a vision first articulated by Phil Bernstein et al. in *A vision for management of complex models, ACM Sigmod Record 2000*. Since then, many steps have been performed towards the various goals of matching and mapping different kinds of design artifacts (i.e., a relational schema, a web site, or a data mart), thus motivating a flurry of recent research, which we survey in this book. The book consists of ten comprehensive chapters grouped within three parts: large-scale and knowledge-driven schema matching, quality-driven schema mapping and evolution and evaluation and tuning of matching tasks.

The first part deals with schema matching, i.e., the semi-automatic finding of semantic correspondences between elements of two schemas or two ontologies. Schema matching implements a Match operator that is often the first step to determine schema mappings, e.g., for schema evolution, data integration and data exchange. The typically high semantic heterogeneity of the schemas makes schema matching an extremely difficult problem. The separation of Match from other metadata management tasks such as Merge helped to address the match problem better than in the past. Numerous powerful prototypes for schema and ontology matching have been developed in the last decade and automatic match functionality found already its way into commercial products. The four chapters in the first part cover the achieved state of the art and point out areas where more work is needed, in particular support for large-scale match problems and improved user interaction. Further chapters deal with proposed extensions to enhance the semantic power of match correspondences and to deal with the uncertainty of match decisions.

The second part of the book also consists of four chapters and focuses on schema mappings and their use for schema evolution and schema merging. The first chapter of the second part surveys the existing schema mapping algorithms and the most recent developments towards realizing efficient, optimized and correct schema mapping transformations. Two further chapters deal with the use of schema mappings for schema evolution. One of these introduces the requirements for effective schema evolution support and provides an overview of proposed evolution approaches for diverse kinds of schemas and ontologies. The other evolution-related chapter focuses on the automatic adaptation of mappings after schema changes by presenting two first-class operators on schema mappings, namely composition and inversion. The final chapter surveys the state of the art on mapping-based merging of schemas by discussing the key works in this area and identifying their commonalities and differences.

The third part of the book consists of two chapters devoted to the evaluation and tuning of schema matching and mapping systems. The first of these chapters provides a comprehensive overview of existing evaluation efforts for data transformation tasks, by providing a brand-new perspective under which the various approaches are being/have been evaluated. Such perspective allows the authors to identify the pitfalls of current evaluations and brings them to discuss open problems for future research in this area. The last chapter deals with the complex problem of tuning schema matching tools to optimize their quality and efficiency with a limited amount of configuration effort. An overview of proposed tuning efforts including the use of machine learning techniques is provided.

To the best of our expectations, this book provides:

1. A comprehensive survey of current and past research on schema matching and mapping.
2. An up-to-date source of reference about schema and ontology evolution and schema merging.
3. Scholarly written chapters enabling a learning experience to both experts and non-experts whenever they would like to enhance their knowledge or build it from the scratch; the chapters have been conceived in such a way to be readable individually or altogether by following the book table-of-contents.

As such, we hope that the book proves to be a useful reference to researchers as well as graduate students and advanced professionals. We thank the editors of the DCSA book series, Mike Carey and Stefano Ceri, for their support of our book project and all authors for preparing their chapters and revisions within a few months. Without them, this project would not have been possible. Further thanks go the referees of the individual chapters for their insightful comments and to Ralf Gerstner from Springer-Verlag for his professional assistance during all the stages of the book production.

September 2010   *Zohra Bellasehne*
                                                                                Angela Bonifati
                                                                                   Erhard Rahm

Contents

Part III   Evaluating and Tuning of Matching Tasks

Contributors

Zohra Bellahsène LIRMM – CNRS/Université Montpellier II, 161 Rue Ada, 34095 Montpellier Cedex 5, France, bella@lirmm.fr

Angela Bonifati ICAR-CNR, Rende, Italy
bonifati@icar.cnr.it

Xin Luna Dong Data Management Department, AT&T Labs – Research, Bld 103, Rm B281, 180 Park Ave., Florham Park, NJ 07932, USA, lunadong@research.att.com

Fabien Duchateau CWI, Amsterdam, The Netherlands
fabien@cwi.nl

Ronald Fagin IBM Almaden Research Center, Dept. K53/B2, 650 Harry Road, San Jose, CA 95120, USA, fagin@almaden.ibm.com

Sean Falconer Stanford University, Stanford, CA 94305-5479, USA
sean.falconer@stanford.edu

Avigdor Gal Faculty of Industrial Engineering and Management, Technion – Israel Institute of Technology, Technion City, Haifa 32000, Israel, avigal@ie.technion.ac.il

Alon Halevy Google Inc., 1600 Amphitheatre Blvd, Mountain View, CA 94043, USA, halevy@google.com

Michael Hartung Department of Computer Science, University of Leipzig, P.O. Box 100920, 04109 Leipzig, Germany, hartung@informatik.uni-leipzig.de

Phokion Kolaitis IBM Almaden Research Center, 650 Harry Road, San Jose, CA 95120, USA
and
University of California Santa Cruz, 1156 High Street, Santa Cruz, CA 95064, USA, kolaitis@cs.ucsc.edu

Giansalvatore Mecca Dipartimento di Matematica e Informatica, Università della Basilicata, c.da Macchia Romana, 85100 Potenza, Italy, giansalvatore.mecca@unibas.it

Natalya Noy Stanford University, Stanford, CA 94305-5479, USA
and
Medical School Office Building, Room X-215, 251 Campus Drive, Stanford, CA
94305-5479, USA, noy@stanford.edu

Paolo Papotti Dipartimento di Informatica e Automazione, Università Roma Tre,
Via della Vasca Navale 79, 00146 Rome, Italy, papotti@dia.uniroma3.it

Lucian Popa 8CC/B1, IBM Almaden Research Center, 650 Harry Road,
San Jose, CA 95120, USA, lucian@almaden.ibm.com

Rachel Pottinger Department of Computer Science, University of British
Columbia, 201-2366 Main Mall, Vancouver, BC, Canada V6T 1Z4, rap@cs.ubc.ca

Erhard Rahm Department of Computer Science, University of Leipzig, P.O. Box
100920, 04109 Leipzig, Germany, rahm@informatik.uni-leipzig.de

Anish Das Sarma Yahoo! Research, 2-GA 2231, Santa Clara, CA 95051, USA,
anish@yahoo-inc.com

Wang-Chiew Tan E3-406, IBM Almaden Research Center, 650 Harry Road,
San Jose, CA 95120, USA
and
University of California Santa Cruz, 1156 High Street, Santa Cruz, CA 95064,
USA, wctan@cs.ucsc.edu

James F.Terwilliger Microsoft Research, Redmond, WA, USA, James.
Terwilliger@microsoft.com

Yannis Velegrakis DISI – University of Trento, Via Sommarive 14, 38123 Trento,
Italy, velgias@disi.unitn.eu

Part I
Large-Scale and Knowledge-Driven Schema Matching

Schema matching is the task of finding semantic correspondences between elements of two schemas. It is needed in many metadata-intensive applications, such as XML message mapping, integration of web data sources, catalogue integration, data warehouse loading and peer-to-peer data management. The typically high semantic heterogeneity of the schemas make schema matching an extremely difficult problem.

Currently, such matching tasks are largely performed manually by domain experts, at best supported by some GUI, and therefore they are time consuming, tedious and error prone. Approaches for automating the schema and ontology matching tasks as much as possible are needed to simplify and speed up the development, maintenance and use of metadata-intensive applications.

In the last decade semi-automatic schema matching and related variants such as ontology matching have attracted a huge amount of research effort and considerable progress has been achieved. In particular, powerful schema matching prototypes have been developed and successfully applied to a large variety of match problems. These prototypes typically allow the combined execution of multiple match algorithms to improve overall match quality. Furthermore, initial schema matching capabilities found their way into middleware platforms from IBM, Microsoft (Biztalk) and SAP (Neteaver). Still, the current solutions are not yet sufficient but need improvements to deal with large scale match problems, to improve user interaction and to enhance the semantic power of mappings.

The introductory part of the book reviews the current state of the art and recent research efforts in these directions. Chapter 1 written by Erhard Rahm describes approaches to match large schemas and ontologies. He discusses advanced strategies and techniques for improving the match quality and the runtime efficiency for such large-scale match tasks.

Chapter 2 by Sean Falconer and Natasha Noy deals with recent approaches for improving the crucial user interaction for schema matching. They present visualization techniques for assisting users with mapping generation and discuss wiki-based techniques for collaborative schema matching.

Chapter 3 by Avi Gal focuses on the generation of enhanced match results that are not limited to simple 1:1 attribute correspondences. In particular, he considers semantically refined correspondences by taking the context of schema elements and ontological relationships into account.

Das Sarma, Dong and Halevy discuss in Chap. 4 recent work on supporting probabilistic mappings to deal with the inherent uncertainty of data integration. They focus on dataspace-oriented environments for which probabilistic mappings and probabilistic mediated schemas can help minimize the amount of upfront modelling effort for data integration.

Chapter 1
Towards Large-Scale Schema and Ontology Matching

Erhard Rahm

Abstract The purely manual specification of semantic correspondences between schemas is almost infeasible for very large schemas or when many different schemas have to be matched. Hence, solving such large-scale match tasks asks for automatic or semiautomatic schema matching approaches. Large-scale matching needs especially to be supported for XML schemas and different kinds of ontologies due to their increasing use and size, e.g., in e-business and web and life science applications. Unfortunately, correctly and efficiently matching large schemas and ontologies are very challenging, and most previous match systems have only addressed small match tasks. We provide an overview about recently proposed approaches to achieve high match quality or/and high efficiency for large-scale matching. In addition to describing some recent matchers utilizing instance and usage data, we cover approaches on early pruning of the search space, divide and conquer strategies, parallel matching, tuning matcher combinations, the reuse of previous match results, and holistic schema matching. We also provide a brief comparison of selected match tools.

1 Introduction

Schema matching aims at identifying semantic correspondences between metadata structures or models, such as database schemas, XML message formats, and ontologies. Solving such match problems is a key task in numerous application fields, particularly to support data exchange, schema evolution, and virtually all kinds of data integration. Unfortunately, the typically high degree of semantic heterogeneity reflected in different schemas makes schema matching an inherently complex task. Hence, most current systems still require the manual specification of semantic correspondences, e.g., with the help of a GUI. While such an approach is appropriate for

E. Rahm
University of Leipzig, Ritterstraße 26, 04109 Leipzig, Germany
e-mail: rahm@informatik.uni-leipzig.de

Z. Bellahsene et al. (eds.), *Schema Matching and Mapping*, Data-Centric Systems and Applications, DOI 10.1007/978-3-642-16518-4_1,
© Springer-Verlag Berlin Heidelberg 2011

matching a few small schemas, it is enormously time-consuming and error-prone for dealing with large schemas encompassing thousands of elements or to match many schemas. Therefore, automatic or semiautomatic approaches to find semantic correspondences with minimal manual effort are especially needed for large-scale matching. Typical use cases of large-scale matching include:

- Matching large XML schemas, e.g., e-business standards and message formats (Rahm et al. 2004; Smith et al. 2009)
- Matching large life science ontologies describing and categorizing biomedical objects or facts such as genes, the anatomy of different species, diseases, etc. (Kirsten et al. 2007; Zhang et al. 2007)
- Matching large web directories or product catalogs (Avesani et al. 2005; Nandi and Bernstein 2009)
- Matching many web forms of deep web data sources to create a mediated search interface, e.g., for travel reservation or shopping of certain products (He and Chang 2006; Su et al. 2006).

Schema matching (including its ontology matching variant) has been a very active research area, especially in the last decade, and numerous techniques and prototypes for automatic matching have been developed (Rahm and Bernstein 2001; Euzenat and Shvaiko 2007). Schema matching has also been used as a first step to solve data exchange, schema evolution, or data integration problems, e.g., to transform correspondences into an executable mapping for migrating data from a source to a target schema (Fagin et al. 2009). Most match approaches focus on *2-way* or *pairwise schema matching* where two related input schemas are matched with each other. Some algorithms have also been proposed for *n-way* or *holistic schema matching* (He and Chang 2006), to determine the semantic overlap in many schemas, e.g., to build a mediated schema. The result of pairwise schema matching is usually an equivalence mapping containing the identified semantic correspondences, i.e., pairs of semantically equivalent schema elements. Some ontology matching approaches also try to determine different kinds of correspondences, such as is-a relationships between ontologies (Spiliopoulos et al. 2010). Due to the typically high semantic heterogeneity of schemas, algorithms can only determine approximate mappings. The automatically determined mappings may thus require the inspection and adaptation by a human domain expert (deletion of wrong correspondences, addition of missed correspondences) to obtain the correct mapping.

Despite the advances made, current match systems still struggle to deal with large-scale match tasks as those mentioned above. In particular, achieving both good effectiveness and good efficiency are two major challenges for large-scale schema matching. *Effectiveness* (high match quality) requires the correct and complete identification of semantic correspondences, and the larger the search space, the more difficult it is to achieve. For pairwise schema matching, the search space increases at least quadratically with the number of elements. Furthermore, the semantic heterogeneity is typically high for large-scale match tasks, e.g., the schemas may largely differ in their size and scope, making it difficult to find all correspondences. Furthermore, elements often have several equivalent elements in the other schema that

are more difficult to identify than 1:1 correspondences that are more likely for small
match tasks. Some large-scale problems in the ontology alignment evaluation initiative (OAEI) contest on ontology matching are still not satisfactorily solved after
several years. For example, the best F-measure[1] result for the catalog test to match
web directories (71%) was achieved in 2007; in 2009, the best participating system achieved merely 63%; the average F-measure was around 50% (Euzenat et al.
2009).

Efficiency is another challenge for large-scale matching. Current match systems
often require the schemas and intermediate match results to fit in main memory,
thereby limiting their applicability for large-scale match tasks. Furthermore, evaluating large search spaces is time consuming, especially if multiple matchers need
to be evaluated and combined. For some OAEI match tasks and systems, execution
times in the order of several hours or even days are observed (Euzenat et al. 2009).
For interactive use of schema matching systems, such execution times are clearly
unacceptable.

In this book chapter, we provide an overview of recent approaches to improve
effectiveness and efficiency for large-scale schema and ontology matching. We only
briefly discuss further challenges such as support for sophisticated user interaction
or the evaluation of match quality, but these are treated in more detail in other chapters of this book (Falconer and Noy 2011; Bellahsene et al. 2011). For example,
advanced GUIs should be supported to visualize large schemas and mappings, to
specify automatic match strategies (selection of matchers, parameter tuning), to
incrementally start automatic schema matching and adapt match results, etc.

In the next section, we introduce the kinds of matchers used in current match
systems as well as a general workflow to combine the results of multiple matchers for improved match quality. We also discuss performance optimizations for
single matchers and present recently proposed approaches for instance-based and
usage-based matching. In Sect. 3, we present several match strategies that we consider as especially promising for large-scale matching: early pruning of the search
space, partition-based matching, parallel matching, self-tuning match workflows,
and reuse-based matching. We also discuss briefly approaches for *n*-way (holistic)
schema matching. Section 4 contains a short discussion of match support in commercial systems and a comparison of selected research prototypes that have been
applied to large match problems.

2   Matchers and Match Workflows

The developed systems for schema and ontology matching typically support several
match algorithms (or matchers) and combine their results for improved match quality. There exists a large spectrum of possible matchers and different implementations

---

[1] F-Measure combines Recall and Precision, two standard measures to evaluate the effectiveness
of schema matching approaches (Do et al. 2003).

as surveyed in (Rahm and Bernstein 2001; Euzenat and Shvaiko 2007), particularly metadata-based and instance-based matchers. Metadata-based matchers are most common and exploit characteristics of schema or ontology elements such as their names, comments, data types, as well as structural properties. Instance-based matchers determine the similarity between schema elements from the similarity of their instances; this class of matchers has recently been studied primarily for matching large ontologies and will be discussed in more detail below.

Further matching techniques exploit different kinds of auxiliary (background) information to improve or complement metadata- and instance-based matchers. For example, name matching for both schema elements and instance values can be enhanced by general thesauri such as Wordnet or, for improved precision, domain-specific synonym lists and thesauri (e.g., UMLS as a biomedical reference). Furthermore, search engines can be used to determine the similarity between names, e.g., by using the relative search result cardinality for different pairs of names as a similarity indicator (Gligorov et al. 2007). At the end of this section, we will briefly discuss a further kind of match technique, the recently proposed consideration of usage information for matching.

Efficiently matching large schemas and ontologies implies that every matcher should impose minimal CPU and memory requirements. For improving linguistic matching, many techniques for efficiently computing string similarities can be exploited, e.g., for tokenization and indexing (Koudas et al. 2004). Structural matching can be optimized by precollecting the predecessors and children of every element, e.g., in database tables, instead of repeatedly traversing large graph structures (Algergawy et al. 2009). Such an approach can also avoid the need of keeping a graph representation of the schemas in memory that can become a bottleneck with large schemas. The results of matchers are often stored within similarity matrices containing a similarity value for every combination of schema elements. With large schemas, these matrices may require millions of entries and thus several hundreds of MB memory. To avoid a memory bottleneck, a more space-efficient storage of matcher results becomes necessary, e.g., by using hash tables (Bernstein et al. 2004). In Sect. 3, we will discuss further performance techniques such as parallel matcher execution.

In the following, we first describe a general workflow-like approach to apply multiple matchers and to combine their results. We then discuss approaches for instance-based ontology matching and usage-based matching.

2.1 Match Workflows

Figure 1.1a shows a general workflow for automatic, pairwise schema matching as being used in many current match systems. The schemas are first imported into an internal processing format. Further preprocessing may be applied such as analysis of schema features or indexing name tokens to prepare for a faster computation of name similarities. The main part is a subworkflow to execute several matchers each

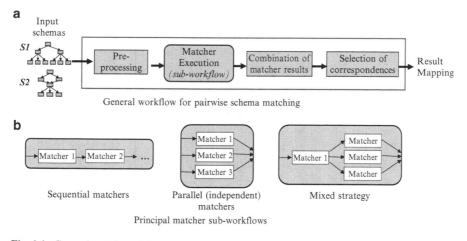

Fig. 1.1   General match workflows

of which determines a preliminary set of correspondences. After the execution of the matcher subworkflow, there are typically several postprocessing steps, particularly the combination of the individual matcher results and finally the selection of the correspondences from the combined result.

As indicated in Fig. 1.1b, the individual matchers may either be executed sequentially, independently (in parallel), or in some mixed fashion. In the sequential approach, the matchers are not executed independently, but the results of initial matchers are used as input by subsequent matchers. A common strategy, e.g., used in Cupid (Madhavan et al. 2001), is to first execute a linguistic matcher to compare the names of schema elements and then use the obtained similarities as input for structure-based matching. In the parallel matcher strategy, individual matchers are autonomous and can be independently executed from other matchers. This supports a high flexibility to select matchers for execution and combination. Furthermore, these matchers may also physically be executed in parallel, e.g., on multicore or multiserver hardware. On the other hand, the autonomy of individual matchers may introduce redundant computations, e.g., of name similarities to be used for structural matching. The mixed strategy combines sequential and parallel matcher execution and is thus most complex.

There are different methods to combine match results of individual matchers, e.g., by performing a union or intersection of the correspondences or by aggregating individual similarity values, e.g., by calculating a weighted average of the individual similarities. Similarly, there are different methods to finally select the correspondences. Typically, correspondences need to exceed some predetermined threshold but may also have to meet additional constraints for improved precision. So it is reasonable for 1:1 mappings to enforce the so-called stable marriages, i.e., a correspondence $c1 - c1'$ is only accepted if $c1'$ is the most similar element for $c1$ and vice versa. Some ontology matching systems such as ASMOV enforce additional constraints regarding is-a relationships (see Sect. 4.2).

For interactive schema matching, the user may interact with the system and the match workflow in different ways (not shown in Fig. 1.1), preferably via a user-friendly GUI. She typically has to specify the workflow configuration, e.g., which matchers should be executed and which strategy/parameters should be applied for the final combination and selection steps. The final results are typically only suggested correspondences that the user can confirm or correct. The match workflow itself could be executed on the whole input schemas or *incrementally* for selected schema parts or even individual elements (Bernstein et al. 2006). The latter approach is a simple but reasonable way to better deal with large schemas as it reduces the performance requirements compared to matching the whole schemas. Furthermore, the determined correspondences can better be visualized avoiding that the user is overwhelmed with huge mappings. Shi et al. (2009) propose an interesting variation for interactive matching where the system asks the user for feedback on specific correspondences that are hard to determine automatically and that are valuable as input for further matcher executions.

2.2 Instance-Based and Usage-Based Matching

2.2.1 Instance-Based Ontology Matching

Instance-based ontology matching determines the similarity between ontology concepts from the similarity of instances associated to the concepts. For example, two categories of a product catalog can be considered as equivalent if their products are largely the same or at least highly similar. One can argue that instances can characterize the semantics of schema elements or ontology concepts very well and potentially better than a concept name or comment. Therefore, instance-based matching holds the promise of identifying high-quality correspondences. On the other hand, obtaining sufficient and suitable instance data for all ontologies and all ontology concepts to be matched is a major problem, especially for large ontologies. Hence, we consider instance-based approaches primarily as a complementary, albeit significant, match approach to be used in addition to metadata-based matchers.

As indicated in Fig. 1.2, two main cases for instance-based ontology matching can be distinguished depending on whether or not the existence of common instances is assumed. The existence of the same instances for different ontologies (e.g., the same web pages categorized in different web directories, the same products offered in different product catalogs, or the same set of proteins described in different life science ontologies) simplifies the determination of similar concept. In this case, two concepts may be considered as equivalent when their instances overlap significantly. Different set similarity measures can be used to measure such an instance overlap, e.g., based on Dice, Jaccard, or cosine similarity. The instance overlap approach has been used to match large life science ontologies (Kirsten et al. 2007) and product catalogs (Thor et al. 2007).

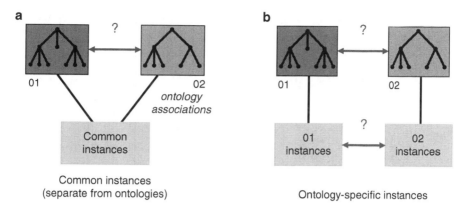

Fig. 1.2 Two cases for instance-based ontology matching

The more broadly applicable case is when only similar but potentially different instances are used to determine correspondences (Fig. 1.2b). In this case, determining concept similarity requires determining the similarity between sets of instances, which is a variation of the well-studied problem of object matching or entity resolution (Elmagarmid et al. 2007; Koepcke and Rahm 2010). One approach for addressing this task is to combine all instances of a concept into a *virtual document*. Matching is then implemented by comparing such virtual documents with each other based on some document similarity measure, e.g., TF/IDF. This approach is supported in several match prototypes including Rimom and Coma++ (see Sect. 4.2). Massmann and Rahm (2008) evaluate instance-based matching for web directories utilizing a virtual document approach for website names and descriptions as well as an instance overlap approach for website URLs. The approaches achieve an average F-measure of about 60% (79% in combination with metadata-based matching) for different match tasks; the largest directory had more than 3,000 categories. The OAEI contest also includes a web directory match task, however, without providing instance data, thereby limiting the achievable match quality (as mentioned in the introduction, the participating systems could not improve on this task in recent years; the best F-measure in 2009 was 63%).

An alternate approach for instance-based matching using machine learning has been implemented in the GLUE and SAMBO systems (Doan et al. 2003; Lambrix et al. 2008). The SAMBO approach focuses on matching life science ontologies based on the similarity of publications (Pubmed abstracts) referring to the ontology concepts. Both GLUE and SAMBO perform a training phase per ontology to learn concept classifiers for the available instances. These classifiers are then mutually applied to the instances from the other ontology to determine the concepts an instance is predicted to belong to. The instance-concept associations are aggregated, e.g., by a Jaccard-based set similarity measure, to derive concept similarities and concept correspondences. The approaches do not require shared instances but only similar ones for classification. Furthermore, they can utilize many existing instances in applications such as matching product catalogs or web directories. On the other hand, the classification problem becomes inherently more difficult to solve for increasing numbers of concepts. The GLUE evaluation in Doan et al. (2003) was restricted to comparatively small match tasks with ontology sizes between 31 and 331 concepts. The SAMBO approach was evaluated for even smaller (sub-) ontologies (10–112 concepts). Effectiveness and efficiency of the machine learning approaches to large-scale match tasks with thousands of concepts is thus an open issue.

2.2.2 Usage-Based Matching

Two recent works propose the use of query logs to aid in schema matching. In Elmeleegy et al. (2008), SQL query logs are analyzed to find attributes with similar usage characteristics (e.g., within join conditions or aggregations) and occurrence frequencies as possible match candidates for relational database schemas. The Hamster approach (Nandi and Bernstein 2009) uses the click log for keyword queries of an entity search engine to determine the search terms, leading to instances of specific categories of a taxonomy (e.g., product catalog or web directory). Categories of different taxonomies sharing similar search queries are then considered as match candidates. Different search terms referring to the same categories are also potential synonyms that can be utilized not only for matching but also for other purposes such as the improvement of user queries.

A main problem of usage-based matching is the difficulty to obtain suitable usage data, which is likely more severe than the availability of instance data. For example, the click logs for the Hamster approach are only available to the providers of search engines. Furthermore, matching support can primarily be obtained for categories or schema elements receiving many queries.

3 Techniques for Large-Scale Matching

In this section, we provide an overview about recent approaches for large-scale pairwise matching that go beyond specific matchers but address entire match strategies. In particular, we discuss approaches in four areas that we consider as especially promising and important:

- Reduction of search space for matching (early pruning of dissimilar element pairs, partition-based matching)
- Parallel matching
- Self-tuning match workflows
- Reuse of previous match results

We also discuss proposed approaches for holistically matching n schemas.

3.1 Reduction of Search Space

The standard approach for pairwise schema matching is to compare every element of the first schema with every element with the second schema to determine matching schema elements, i.e., evaluation of the cross join. Such an approach has at least a quadratic complexity with respect to schema size and does not scale well. There are not only efficiency problems for large schemas but the large search space makes it also very difficult to correctly identify matching element pairs. Hence, it is important for large match tasks to reduce the search space in order to improve at least efficiency and, potentially, match quality.

To reduce the search space for matching, we can adopt similar approaches as in the area of entity resolution (or object matching), where the number of objects and thus the search space is typically much larger than for schema matching. The initial step to reduce the search space for entity matching has been called blocking, and there exist numerous approaches for this task, e.g., based on clustering on selected object attributes (Elmagarmid et al. 2007).

For schema and ontology matching, two main types of approaches have been considered to reduce the search space that we discuss in the following:

- Early pruning of dissimilar element pairs
- Partition-based matching

3.1.1 Early Pruning of Dissimilar Element Pairs

The idea is to limit the evaluation of the cartesian product to at most a few initial steps in the match workflow, e.g., one matcher, and to eliminate all element pairs with very low similarity from further processing since they are very unlikely to match. This idea is especially suitable for workflows with sequential matchers where the first matcher can evaluate the cartesian product, but all highly dissimilar element pairs are excluded in the evaluation of subsequent matchers and the combination of match results.

Quick ontology matching (QOM) was one of the first approaches to implement this idea (Ehrig and Staab 2004). It iteratively applies a sequence of matchers and can restrict the search space for every matcher. The considered approaches to restrict the search space include focusing on elements with similar names (labels) or similar structural properties. The authors showed that the runtime complexity of QOM can be reduced to $(O(n \cdot \log(n))$ instead of $O(n^2)$ for ontologies of size n.

Peukert et al. (2010a) propose the use of filter operators within match workflows to prune dissimilar element pairs (whose similarity is below some minimal threshold) from intermediate match results. The threshold is either statically predetermined or dynamically derived from the similarity threshold used in the match workflow to finally select match correspondences. Peukert et al. (2010a) also propose a rule-based approach to rewrite match workflows for improved efficiency, particularly to place filter operators within sequences of matchers.

3.1.2 Partition-Based Matching

Partition-based matching is a divide-and-conquer strategy to first partition the input schemas/ontologies and then perform a partition-wise matching. The idea is to perform partitioning in such a way that every partition of the first schema has to be matched with only a subset of the partitions (ideally, only with one partition) of the second schema. This results in a significant reduction of the search space and thus improved efficiency. Furthermore, matching the smaller partitions reduces the memory requirements compared to matching the full schemas. To further improve performance, the partition-based match tasks may be performed in parallel.

There are many possible ways to perform partitioning, and finding the most effective approaches is still an open research problem. COMA++ was one of the first systems to support partition-based schema matching by a so-called *fragment matching* (Aumueller et al. 2005; Do and Rahm 2007). Fragment matching works in two phases. In the first phase, the fragments of a specified type (e.g., user-specified fragments or subschemas such as relational tables or message formats in large XML schemas) are determined and compared with each other to identify the most similar fragments from the other schema worth to be fully matched later. The search for similar fragments is some kind of light-weight matching, e.g., based on the similarity of the fragment roots. In the second phase, each pair of similar fragments is independently matched to identify correspondences between their elements. The fragment-based match results are finally merged to obtain the complete output mapping. In the evaluation for large XML schemas in (Do and Rahm 2007), fragment matching not only improved execution times significantly but also led to a slight improvement of match quality.

The ontology matching system *Falcon-AO* also supports partition-based matching to reduce the search space (Hu et al. 2008). The approach is similar to fragment matching but uses a structural clustering to initially partition the ontologies into relatively small, disjoint blocks. Matching is then restricted to the most similar blocks from the two ontologies. To determine the block similarity, Falcon-AO utilizes the so-called *anchors*. Anchors are highly similar element pairs that are determined before partitioning by a combined name/comment matcher. Figure 1.3 illustrates the idea to limit matching to pairs of similar partitions sharing at least one anchor. In the shown example, only partitions of the same color are matched with each other (e.g., B_{S2} with B_{T2}), while partitions without shared anchor (B_{T3}) are excluded from matching. An extension of the Falcon approach has been proposed for the *Taxomap* system (Hamdi et al. 2009). They first partition only one of the ontologies like in Falcon and then try to partition the second ontology accordingly. In particular, it is tried to achieve that the anchors per partition can be localized in few partitions of the other ontology to reduce the number of pairs to be matched.

The taxonomy matching system *AnchorFlood* implements a dynamic partition-based matching that avoids the a-priori partitioning of the ontologies (Hanif and Aono 2009). It also utilizes anchors (similar concept pairs) but takes them as a starting point to incrementally match elements in their structural neighborhood until no further matches are found or all elements are processed. Thus the partitions (called

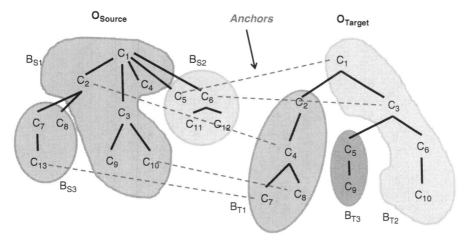

Fig. 1.3 Partition-based matching in Falcon-AO and Taxomap (from Hamdi et al. (2009))

segments) are located around the anchors, and their size depends on the continued success of finding match partners for the considered elements.

Zhong et al. (2009) focus on the case when a small ontology is matched with a much larger one, e.g., one that is obtained from merging several others. They determine the subontology (partition) from the larger ontology that is most similar to the smaller ontology and consider only this subontology for matching to improve efficiency. Finding the subontology is performed in two steps. First, a name matcher is applied on the Cartesian product of elements to determine the most similar ontology elements from the large ontology. Then, the subontology is determined by evaluating the subgraphs around the similar elements found in the first step.

3.2 Parallel Matching

A relatively straight forward approach to reduce the execution time of large-scale matching is to run match processes in parallel on several processors. As discussed in Gross et al. (2010), two main kinds of parallel matching are applicable: inter- and intra-matcher parallelization. *Inter-matcher parallelization* enables the parallel execution of independently executable (parallel) matchers in match workflows. This kind of parallelism is easy to support and can utilize multiple cores of a single computing node or multiple nodes. However, inter-matcher parallelization is limited by the number of independent matchers and not applicable for sequential matchers. Furthermore, matchers of different complexity may have largely different execution times limiting the achievable speedup (the slowest matcher determines overall execution time). Moreover, the memory requirements for matching are not reduced since matchers evaluate the complete ontologies.

Intra-matcher parallelization is more versatile and deals with internal parallelization of matchers, typically based on a partitioning of the schemas or ontologies to
be matched. Partitioning leads to many smaller match tasks that can be executed
in parallel with reduced memory requirements per task. By choosing appropriate partition sizes, the approach becomes very flexible and scalable. Furthermore,
intra-matcher parallelism can be applied for sequential as well as independently
executable matchers, i.e., it can also be combined with inter-matcher parallelism.

The partition-based matching discussed in Sect. 3.1 inherently supports intra-
matcher parallelization as well as a reduction of the search space by limiting
matching to pairs of similar partitions. However, intra-matcher parallelization could
also be applied without reduced search space by matching all partition pairs, i.e., to
evaluate the Cartesian product in parallel. As discussed in Gross et al. (2010), such
a simple, generic parallelization is applicable for virtually all element-level matchers (e.g., name matching) but can also be adapted for structural matching. In this
case, one can also choose a very simple, size-based partitioning (same number of
elements per partition) supporting good load balancing.

3.3 Self-Tuning Match Workflows

The match workflows in most current systems need to be manually defined and con-
figured. This affects the choice of matchers to be applied and specification of the
methods to combine matcher results and to finally select match correspondences.
Obviously, these decisions have a significant impact on both effectiveness and efficiency and are thus especially critical for large-scale match tasks. Unfortunately,
the huge number of possible configurations makes it very difficult even for expert
users to define suitable match workflows. Hence, the adoption of semi-automatic
tuning approaches becomes increasingly necessary and should especially consider
the challenges of matching large schemas.

The companion book chapter (Bellahsene and Duchateau 2011) provides an
overview of recent approaches including tuning frameworks such as Apfel and
eTuner (Ehrig et al. 2005; Lee et al. 2007). Most previous approaches for automatic
tuning apply supervised machine learning methods. They use previously solved
match tasks as training to find effective choices for matcher selection and parameter settings such as similarity thresholds and weights to aggregate similarity values,
e.g., Duchateau et al. (2009). A key problem of such approaches is the difficulty of
collecting sufficient training data that may itself incur a substantial effort. A further
problem is that even within a domain, the successful configurations for one match
problem do not guarantee sufficient match quality for different problems, especially
for matching large schemas. Therefore, one would need methods to preselect suitable and sufficient training correspondences for a given match task, which is an open
challenge.

Tan and Lambrix (2007) propose an alternative approach that recommends a
promising match strategy for a given match problem. They first select a limited

number of pairs of small segments from the schemas to be matched (e.g., subgraphs with identically named root concepts) and determine the perfect match result for these segments. These results are used to comparatively evaluate the effectiveness and efficiency of a predetermined number of match strategies from which the best performing one is recommended for the complete match task. The approach thus requires manual "training" for matching the preselected segment pairs; this effort pays off if it helps to avoid a larger amount of manual postprocessing. On the other hand, the number of reasonable match strategies can be very high (many combinations of available matchers, many possible similarity thresholds, etc.), so that likely only a small subset of them can be evaluated (in the evaluation merely 30 strategies are considered).

Several match systems first analyze the schemas to be matched and determine their linguistic and structural similarity. These similarity characteristics are then used to select matchers or to weigh the influence of different matchers in the combination of matcher results (Pirrò and Talia 2010). The Rimom system (Li et al. 2009) uses such similarity factors for dynamically selecting matchers for a specific match task. For example, they use string measures for name matching only if the input schemas have highly similar names; otherwise, they rely on thesauri such as Wordnet. Similarly, they apply structural matching only if the input schemas are deeply structured and structurally similar. Falcon-AO uses the linguistic and structural similarities to combine matcher results, particularly to optimize individual similarity (cutoff) thresholds (Hu et al. 2008). For example, if the linguistic similarity is high, Falcon-AO uses lower thresholds for linguistic matchers so that more of their correspondences are considered.

A versatile approach to combine the results of individual matchers is to determine a weighted average of the individual matcher similarities per correspondence and to accept a correspondence if the combined similarity exceeds some threshold. Several approaches try to tune matcher combination by applying task-specific weights and combination methods, e.g., by favoring higher similarity values (Ehrig and Staab 2004; Mao et al. 2008; Mork et al. 2008). For example, the approach of Mao et al. (2008), used in the PRIOR+ match prototype, combines similarity values according to the matchers' so-called harmony value that is defined as the ratio of element pairs for which a matcher achieved the top similarity values. The comparative analysis in Peukert et al. (2010b) showed that such combination approaches can be effective in some cases but that they are mostly less effective and less robust than generic approaches such as taking the average matcher similarity.

Optimizing complete match workflows is so far an open challenge, especially since most match systems prescribe workflows of a fixed structure, e.g., regarding which matchers can be executed sequentially or in parallel. As discussed in Sect. 3.1, (Peukert et al. 2010a) propose a first approach for tuning match workflows focusing on reducing the search space for improved efficiency.

3.4 Reuse of Previous Match Results

A promising approach to improve both the effectiveness and efficiency of schema matching is the reuse of previous match results to solve a new but similar match task (Rahm and Bernstein 2001). An ideal situation for such a reuse is the need to adapt a mapping between two schemas after one of them evolves to a new schema version. By reusing the previous match mapping for the unchanged schema parts, a significant amount of match effort can likely be saved. The reuse of previously determined correspondences and match results may also be applicable in other cases, especially when different schemas share certain elements or substructures, such as standardized address information. Exploiting the reuse potential requires a comprehensive infrastructure, particularly a repository to maintain previously determined correspondences and match results. Furthermore, methods are necessary to determine the schema elements and fragments for which match reuse is applicable. Reuse can be exploited at three mapping granularities: for individual element correspondences, for mappings between common schema fragments, and for complete mappings and schemas.

Coma and its successor Coma++ support the reuse of complete match mappings (Do and Rahm 2002). They apply a so-called MatchCompose operator for a join-like combination of two or more match mappings to indirectly match schemas. For example, a mapping between schemas $S1$ and $S3$ can be obtained by combining preexisting $S1$–$S2$ and $S2$–$S3$ mappings involving another schema $S2$. For two schemas to be matched, the reuse matcher of Coma searches the repository for all applicable mapping paths connecting the two schemas and combines the composition results just like other matcher results. The reuse matcher can also be combined with regular matchers. Furthermore, the compose approach allows the adaptation of an old mapping after one of the schema evolves. Figure 1.4 shows a Coma++ screenshot for such a reuse scenario where the target schema (shown on the right) has been slightly changed. The mapping between the source schema and the old target schema (shown in the middle) can be reused by composing it with the mapping between the old and the new target schema. The latter mapping has to be newly determined, but this is easy when the two schema versions are highly similar as in the example. The evaluations in (Do and Rahm 2002) and (Do 2006) showed the high effectiveness and efficiency of the reuse approach even when only completely automatically determined match results are composed.

The corpus-based match approach of Madhavan et al. (2005) uses a domain-specific corpus of schemas and match mappings and focuses on the reuse of element correspondences. They augment schema elements with matching elements from the corpus and assume that two schema elements match if they match with the same corpus element(s). They use a machine learning approach to find matches between schema and corpus elements. In particular, for each corpus element c, a model based on several matchers is learned to decide whether schema elements s match c. The approach thus requires a substantial effort for learning the models and applying the models to determine the matches, especially for a large corpus and large schemas.

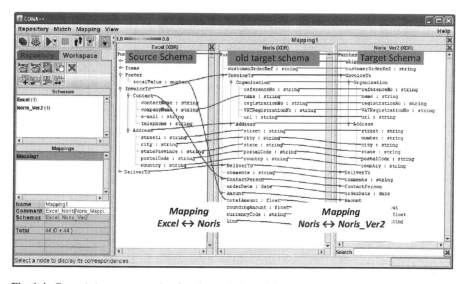

Fig. 1.4 Coma++ reuse scenario after the evolution of the target schema

There are several other attempts to provide repositories of schemas and mappings for matching or information integration, in general. For example, the OpenII project is developing an infrastructure for information integration that includes a repository of schemas and mappings to permit their reuse (Seligman et al. 2010). While the OpenII schema matcher, Harmony, does not yet exploit this reuse potential, there are several other tools to explore and visualize the schemas and mappings. In particular, the Schemr search tool determines a ranked list of schemas in the repository that are similar to a given schema fragment or list or keywords (Chen et al. 2009). For this purpose, Schemr uses an index on schema element names to first find repository schemas that are linguistically similar to the search input. In a second step, the candidate schemas are matched with the input schema to obtain refined schema similarities used for ranking. The search tool could thus be useful to determine relevant schemas for reuse.

A new project at the IBM Almaden research center investigates the repository-based reuse of schema fragments and mappings, particularly for enhancing schema matching (Alexe et al. 2009). The repository stores conceptual schema fragments called unified famous objects (UFOs) such as address or employee structures that are in use or relevant for different applications and schemas. By maintaining mappings between similar UFOs in the repository, these mappings may be reused when matching schemas that contain the respective UFOs. Successfully implementing such an idea is promising but also highly complex and apparently not yet finished. First, the repository has to be built and populated; a first design is sketched in Gubanov et al. (2009). For schema matching, the schemas to be matched have to be analyzed whether they include schema fragments from the repository for which mappings exist. Finally, the fragment mappings need to be properly assembled (and combined with the results of other matchers) in order to obtain a complete schema mapping. Saha et al. (2010) focuses on the second step and describes an approach called *schema covering* to partition the input schemas such that the partitions can be matched to schema fragments in the repository. They first apply a filter step to determine relevant repository fragments with some similarity with the schemas to be matched. Then for each of the remaining repository fragments, the maximal subgraphs in the schemas are determined that can be covered by the fragment. To speed-up the similarity computations, filtering and subgraph identification utilize a predetermined index of the schema element names and their positions in the repository schemas and the schemas to be matched.

SAP also works on an ambitious project called Warp10 to exploit the reuse of XML schemas and mappings for business integration including improved schema matching (SAP 2010). As indicated in Fig. 1.5, the key idea is to maintain a central repository maintaining a global schema (called consolidated data model) that includes semantically consolidated versions of individual schemas or schema fragments. Consolidation is based on the UN/CEFACT core component technical specification (CCTS) rules for uniformly naming and structuring concepts. The global schema is initially populated by standard business schemas and data types (e.g., from SAP) and can be semiautomatically and collaboratively extended by integrating specific schemas. The correct integration of such schemas is likely a complex merge operation needing the control by domain experts. Once mappings between schemas and the global schema are established, they can be reused for quickly solving new integration tasks, particularly for matching between schemas (to match schemas *S1* with *S2*, one has to compose their mappings with the global schema *G, S1–G* and *G–S2*). Unfortunately, the details about how the global schema is maintained are not yet published.

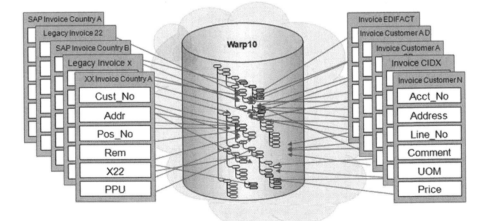

Fig. 1.5 Mappings between schemas and the consolidated data model in Warp10 (from SAP (2010))

3.5   Holistic Schema Matching

While most of the previous match work focuses on pairwise matching, there has also been some work on the generalized problem of matching n schemas. Typically, the goal is to integrate or merge the n schemas such that all matching elements of the n schemas are represented only once in the integrated (mediated) schema. N-way matching can be implemented by a series of 2-way match steps, and some systems such as Porsche follow such an approach and incrementally merge schemas (Saleem et al. 2008). The alternative is a holistic matching that clusters all matching schema elements at once.

The holistic approach has primarily been considered for the use case of matching and integrating web forms for querying deep web sources (He et al. 2004; He and Chang 2006; Su et al. 2006). While there are typically many web forms to integrate in a domain, the respective schemas are mostly small and simple, e.g., a list of attributes. Hence, the main task is to group together all similar attributes. Matching is primarily performed on the attribute names (labels) but may also use additional information such as comments or sample values. A main observation utilized in holistic schema matching is the correlation of attribute names, particularly that similar names between different schemas are likely matches but similar names within the same schema are usually mismatches. For example, the attribute's *first name* and *last name* do not match if they co-occur in the same source.

The dual correlation mining (DCM) approach of He and Chang (2006) utilizes these positive and negative attribute correlations for matching. It also utilizes negative correlations to derive complex relationships, e.g., that attribute *name* matches the combination of both *first name* and *last name*. The HSM approach of Su et al. (2006) extends the DCM scheme for improved accuracy and efficiency. HSM also utilizes that the vocabulary of web forms in a domain tends to be relatively small and that terms are usually unambiguous in a domain (e.g., *title* in a book domain). A main idea is to first identify such shared attributes (and their synonyms) in the input schemas and exclude such attributes from matching the remaining attributes for improved efficiency and accuracy.

Das Sarma et al. (2008) propose to determine a so-called *probabilistic mediated schema* from n input schemas, which is in effect a ranked list of several mediated schemas. The approach observes the inherent uncertainty of match decisions but avoids any manual intervention by considering not only one but several reasonable mappings. The resulting set of mediated schemas was shown to provide queries with potentially more complete results than with a single mediated schema. The proposed approach only considers the more frequently occurring attributes for determining the different mediated schemas, i.e., sets of disjoint attribute clusters. Clustering is based on the pairwise similarity between any of the remaining attributes exceeding a certain threshold as well as the co-occurrence of attributes in the same source. The similarity between attributes can also be considered as uncertain by some error margin, which leads to different possibilities to cluster such attributes within different mediated schemas. The probabilistic mapping approach is further described in the companion book chapter (Das Sarma et al. 2011).

We finally note that some of the partition-based and reuse-based match approaches discussed above dealt with multiple subschemas, so they also implement some form of n-way schema matching. An important building block in such advanced match strategies is to search a collection of n (sub) schemas for the schema that is most similar to a given schema. There are many other applications for the schema search problem, e.g., finding similar peer schemas in P2P data integration or the discovery of suitable web services (Dong et al. 2004; Algergawy et al. 2010).

4 Selected Match Systems

To further illustrate the state of the art, we discuss in this section the schema matching capabilities in commercial tools as well as in selected research prototypes. For better comparability, we restrict ourselves on systems for pairwise schema matching.

4.1 Commercial Match Tools

In commercial tools, schema matching is typically a first step for generating executable mappings (e.g., for data transformation) between schemas, particularly XML schemas or relational database schemas. Systems such as IBM Infosphere Data Architect, Microsoft Biztalk server, SAP Netweaver Process Integration, or Altova MapForce provide a GUI-based mapping editor but still require a largely manual specification of the match correspondences. In recent years, support for automatic matching has improved and all mentioned systems can present users equally named schema elements (typically within preselected schema fragments) as match candidates. The Infosphere mapping editor also supports approximate name matching and the use of external thesauri for linguistic matching. The mapping tool of Microsoft Biztalk server 2010 has significantly improved for better matching large schemas (www.microsoft.com/biztalk). It supports an enhanced user interface to better visualize complex mappings similar as described in Bernstein et al. (2006). Furthermore, it supports approximate name matching by a new search functionality called "indicative matching."

The increasing support in commercial tools underlines the high practical importance of automatic schema matching. However, the tools need much further improvement to reduce the manual mapping effort especially for large match tasks. For example, commercial tools do neither support structural matching nor any of the advanced techniques discussed in Sect. 3.

4.2 Research Prototypes

As already discussed in the previous sections, in research, more advanced approaches for semiautomatic schema and ontology matching have been developed. In fact, hundreds of prototypes and algorithms for schema and ontology matching have been developed in the last decade, many of which are surveyed in Euzenat and Shvaiko (2007). To illustrate the state of the art in current tools, we briefly compare a few recent prototypes that have successfully been applied to large-scale match problems, particularly within the OAEI benchmark competition (http://oaei. ontologymatching.org). Table 1.1 provides a rough comparison between six match prototypes. All of them are capable of matching (OWL) ontologies, and two systems (Coma++, Harmony) can also match relational and XML schemas. The shown years of introduction are estimates based on the oldest publication found per system.

The table indicates that all systems include linguistic and structural matchers. Linguistic matching can always be performed either on element names and comments; furthermore, external dictionaries such as synonym lists or thesauri can be utilized. Most systems (except Falcon and Harmony) also support instance-based matching. A comprehensive GUI for interactive matching is provided by Coma++, AgreementMaker, and Harmony; for the other systems, no specific details on this issue could be found. The individual matchers may either be executed independently or sequentially within a predetermined, fixed match workflow (not mentioned in Table 1.1). Partitioning of large schemas is currently supported by two of the considered systems (Coma++, Falcon), a self-tuning by dynamically selecting the matchers to execute only by Rimom. Coma++ is the only system supporting the reuse of previous mappings for matching. All systems except Harmony have

Table 1.1 Comparison of match prototypes (*AM* AgreementMaker)

	COMA++	Falcon	Rimom	Asmov	AM	Harmony
Year of introduction	2002/2005	2006	2006	2007	2007	2008
Input						
relational schemas	√	–	–	–	–	√
XML schemas	√	–	–	–	(√)	√
ontologies	√	√	√	√	√	√
Compreh. GUI	√	(√)	?	?	√	√
Matchers						
Linguistic	√	√	√	√	√	√
structure	√	√	√	√	√	√
Instance	√	–	√	√	√	–
Use of ext.dictionaries	√	?	√	√	√	√
Schema partitioning	√	√	–	–	–	–
Parallel matching	–	–	–	–	–	–
Dyn. matcher selection	–	–	√	–	–	–
Mapping reuse	√	–	–	–	–	–
OAEI participation	√	√	√	√	√	–

successfully participated in OAEI ontology matching contests; some systems even implemented specific extensions to better solve certain contest tasks. Not shown in the table is that most systems focus on 1:1 correspondences, although the elements of a schema may participate in several such correspondences (the fact that element Name in one schema matches to the combination of Firstname and Lastname in the second schema can thus not directly be determined). Parallel matching (Sect. 3.2) is also not yet supported in the tools.

In the following, we provide some specific details for the considered prototypes.

4.2.1   Coma++

Coma++ (Aumueller et al. 2005; Do and Rahm 2007) and its predecessor Coma (Do and Rahm 2002) are generic prototypes for schema and ontology matching developed at the University of Leipzig, Germany. They were among the first systems to successfully support the multimatcher architecture and match workflows as introduced in Sect. 2. Initially, the focus was on a metadata-based matching; instance-based matching was added in 2006. Coma++ supports the partitioning and reuse approaches discussed in the previous section.

Coma++ is available for free for research purposes, and hundreds of institutes worldwide have used and evaluated the prototype. Surprisingly, the default match workflow of Coma++ (combining four metadata-based matchers) proved to be competitive in many diverse areas, particularly for matching XML schemas (Algergawy et al. 2009), web directories (Avesani et al. 2005), or even meta-models derived from UML (Kappel et al. 2007). Coma++ successfully participated in the ontology matching contest OAEI 2006.

4.2.2   Falcon

Falcon-AO is an ontology matching prototype developed at the Southeast University in Nanjing, China (Hu et al. 2008). As discussed in Sect. 3.1, it supports a partitioning approach to reduce the search space and uses coefficients of the linguistic and structural schema similarity to control the combination of matcher results. Instance-based matching is not yet provided. In the OAEI contests from 2005–2007, it was among the best performing systems.

4.2.3   Rimom

Rimom is an ontology matching prototype developed at Tsinghua University in Beijing, China (Li et al. 2009). It was one of the first systems implementing a dynamic selection of matchers, as discussed in Sect. 3.3. The schema elements and their instances are first linguistically matched; structural matching is only applied if the schemas exhibit sufficient structural similarity. There are several methods for linguistic matching including one that uses a virtual document per element consisting of the name, comments, and instance values of the element. Rimom is among the best performing prototypes in the OAEI contests until 2009.

4.2.4 Asmov

Automated semantic matching of ontologies with verification (ASMOV) prototype (Jean-Mary et al. 2009) is among the best performing systems at the recent OAEI match contests. Its most distinctive feature is an extensive postprocessing of the combined matcher results to eliminate potential inconsistencies among the set of candidate correspondences. Five different kinds of inconsistencies are checked including the avoidance of the so-called crisscross correspondences, e.g., to prevent that for a correspondence between classes $c1$ and $c1'$, there is another correspondence mapping – a child of $c1$ to a parent of $c1'$.

4.2.5 AgreementMaker

This ontology matching prototype is developed at the University of Illinois at Chicago (Cruz et al. 2009). It provides a sophisticated GUI so that the user can control the iterative execution of matchers. AgreementMaker was among the best performing systems in the OAEI 2009 contest.

4.2.6 Harmony

Harmony is the match component within the Open Information Integration project on developing a publicly available infrastructure for information integration (Seligman et al. 2010). It provides many of the known features of previous match prototypes as well as a GUI. Instance-based matching is not yet supported. The combination of matcher results uses a nonlinear combination of similarity values to favor matchers with higher similarity values (Mork et al. 2008) as briefly discussed in Sect. 3.3. According to Smith et al. (2009), Harmony is able to match larger schemas with about 1,000 elements each. However, so far, no detailed evaluation of Harmony's effectiveness and efficiency has been published.

5 Conclusions

We have provided an overview of selected approaches and current implementations for large-scale schema and ontology matching. Commercial systems increasingly support automatic matching but still have to improve much to better handle large schemas. The current research prototypes share many similarities, particularly a multimatcher architecture with support for combining linguistic, structural, and instance-based matching. We discussed first approaches in several areas that seem promising for large-scale matching, particularly partition-based matching, parallel matching, self-tuning of match workflows, and reuse of previously determined match mappings. Such techniques are not yet common in current match systems, and more research is needed in all these areas.

Research on holistic (n-way) schema matching mostly focused on very simple schemas such as web forms. More research is therefore needed for n-way matching (clustering) of more complex schemas. An important variation of this problem is searching the most similar schemas for a given schema. Within advanced match strategies for large schemas, such search approaches are also needed for finding relevant subschemas.

Fully automatic schema matching is possible and may provide sufficient match quality for simple schemas such as web forms. This is especially the case for the idea of probabilistic mediated schemas considering several alternatives for clustering attributes. For large schemas and ontologies, on the other hand, user interaction remains necessary to configure match workflows, perform incremental matching on selected schema portions, and to provide feedback on the correctness of match candidates. Integrating the various match techniques within a usable and effective data integration infrastructure is challenging and also requires much more work.

References

Alexe B, Gubanov M, Hernandez MA, Ho H, Huang JW, Katsis Y, Popa L, Saha B, Stanoi I (2009) Simplifying information integration: Object-based flow-of-mappings framework for integration. In: Proceedings of BIRTE08 (business intelligence for the real-time enterprise) workshop. Lecture Notes in Business Information Processing, vol 27. Springer, Heidelberg, pp 108–121

Algergawy A, Schallehn E, Saake G (2009) Improving XML schema matching performance using Prüfer sequences. Data Knowl Eng 68(8):728–747

Algergawy A et al. (2010) Combining schema and level-based matching for web service discovery. In: Proceedings of 10th international conference on web engineering (ICWE). Lecture Notes in Computer Science, vol 6189. Springer, Heidelberg, pp 114–128

Aumueller D, Do HH, Massmann S, Rahm E (2005) Schema and ontology matching with COMA++. In: Proceedings of ACM SIGMOD conference, demo paper. ACM, NY, pp 906–908

Avesani P, Giunchiglia F, Yatskevich M (2005) A large scale taxonomy mapping evaluation. In: Proceedings of international conference on semantic web (ICSW). LNCS, vol 3729. Springer, Heidelberg, pp 67–81

Bellahsene Z, Duchateau F (2011) Tuning for schema matching. In: Bellahsene Z, Bonifati A, Rahm E (eds) Schema matching and mapping, Data-Centric Systems and Applications Series. Springer, Heidelberg

Bellahsene Z, Bonifati A, Duchateau F, Velegrakis Y (2011) On evaluating schema matching and mapping. In: Bellahsene Z, Bonifati A, Rahm E (eds) Schema matching and mapping, Data-Centric Systems and Applications Series. Springer, Heidelberg

Bernstein PA, Melnik S, Petropoulos M, Quix C (2004) Industrial-strength schema matching. ACM SIGMOD Rec 33(4):38–43

Bernstein PA, Melnik S, Churchill JE (2006) Incremental schema matching. In: Proceedings of VLDB, demo paper. VLDB Endowment, pp 1167–1170

Chen K, Madhavan J, Halevy AY (2009) Exploring schema repositories with Schemr. In: Proceedings of ACM SIGMOD Conference, demo paper. ACM, NY, pp 1095–1098

Cruz IF, Antonelli FP, Stroe C (2009) AgreementMaker: Efficient matching for large real-world schemas and ontologies. In: PVLDB, vol 2(2), demo paper. VLDB Endowment, pp 1586–1589

Das Sarma A, Dong X, Halevy AY (2008) Bootstrapping pay-as-you-go data integration systems. In: Proceedings of ACM SIGMOD conference. ACM, NY, pp 861–874

Das Sarma A, Dong X, Halevy AY (2011) Uncertainty in data integration and dataspace support platforms. In: Bellahsene Z, Bonifati A, Rahm E (eds) Schema matching and mapping, Data-Centric Systems and Applications Series. Springer, Heidelberg

Do HH (2006) Schema Matching and Mapping-based Data Integration. Dissertation, Dept of Computer Science, Univ. of Leipzig

Do HH, Rahm E (2002) COMA – A System for Flexible Combination of Schema Matching Approaches. Proceedings VLDB Conf., pp 610–621

Do HH, Rahm E (2007) Matching large schemas: Approaches and evaluation. Inf Syst 32(6): 857–885

Do HH, Melnik S, Rahm E (2003) Comparison of schema matching evaluations. In: web, web-services, and database systems, LNCS, vol 2593. Springer, Heidelberg

Doan A, Madhavan J, Dhamankar R, Domingos P, Halevy AY (2003) Learning to match ontologies on the semantic web. VLDB J 12(4):303–319

Dong X, Halevy AY, Madhavan J, Nemes E, Zhang J (2004) Similarity search for web services. In: Proceedings of VLDB conference. VLDB Endowment, pp 372–383

Duchateau F, Coletta R, Bellahsene Z, Miller RJ (2009) (Not) yet another matcher. In: Proceedings of CIKM, poster paper. ACM, NY, pp 1537–1540

Ehrig M, Staab S (2004) Quick ontology matching. In: Proceedings of international conference semantic web (ICSW). LNCS, vol 3298. Springer, Heidelberg, pp 683–697

Ehrig M, Staab S, Sure Y (2005) Bootstrapping ontology alignment methods with APFEL. In: Proceedings of international conference on semantic web (ICSW). LNCS, vol 3729. Springer, Heidelberg, pp 1148–1149

Elmagarmid AK, Ipeirotis PG, Verykios VS (2007) Duplicate record detection: A survey. IEEE Trans Knowl Data Eng 19(1):1–16

Elmeleegy H, Ouzzani M, Elmagarmid AK (2008): Usage-based schema matching. In: Proceedings of ICDE conference. IEEE Computer Society, Washington, DC, pp 20–29

Euzenat J, Shvaiko P (2007) Ontology matching. Springer, Heidelberg

Euzenat J et al. (2009) Results of the ontology alignment evaluation initiative 2009. In: Proceedings of the 4th international workshop on Ontology Matching (OM-2009)

Fagin R, Haas LM, Hernández MA, Miller RJ, Popa L, Velegrakis Y (2009) Clio: Schema mapping creation and data exchange. In: Conceptual modeling: Foundations and applications. LNCS, vol 5600. Springer, Heidelberg

Falconer SM, Noy NF (2011) Interactive techniques to support ontology mapping. In: Bellahsene Z, Bonifati A, Rahm E (eds) Schema matching and mapping. Data-Centric Systems and Applications Series. Springer, Heidelberg

Gligorov R, ten Kate W, Aleksovski Z, van Harmelen F (2007) Using Google distance to weight approximate ontology matches. In: Proceedings WWW Conf., pp 767–776

Gross A, Hartung M, Kirsten T, Rahm E (2010) On matching large life science ontologies in parallel. In: Proceedings of 7th international conference on data integration in the life sciences (DILS). LNCS, vol 6254. Springer, Heidelberg

Gubanov M et al (2009) IBM UFO repository: Object-oriented data integration. PVLDB, demo paper. VLDB Endowment, pp 1598–1601

Hamdi F, Safar B, Reynaud C, Zargayouna H (2009) Alignment-based partitioning of large-scale ontologies. In: Advances in knowledge discovery and management. Studies in Computational Intelligence Series. Springer, Heidelberg

Hanif MS, Aono M (2009) An efficient and scalable algorithm for segmented alignment of ontologies of arbitrary size. J Web Sem 7(4):344–356

He B, Chang KC (2006) Automatic complex schema matching across Web query interfaces: A correlation mining approach. ACM Trans. Database Syst 31(1):346–395

He H, Meng W, Yu CT, Wu Z (2004) Automatic integration of Web search interfaces with WISE-Integrator. VLDB J 13(3):256–273

Hu W, Qu Y, Cheng G (2008) Matching large ontologies: A divide-and-conquer-approach. Data Knowl Eng 67(1):140–160

Jean-Mary YR, Shironoshita EP, Kabuka MR (2009) Ontology matching with semantic verification. J Web Sem 7(3):235–251

Kappel G et al. (2007) Matching metamodels with semantic systems – An experience report. In: Proceedings of BTW workshop on model management, pp 1–15

Kirsten T, Thor A, Rahm E (2007) Instance-based matching of large life science ontologies. In: Proceedings of data integration in the life sciences (DILS). LNCS, vol 4544. Springer, Heidelberg, pp 172–187

Koepcke H, Rahm E (2010) Frameworks for entity matching: A comparison. Data Knowl Eng 69(2):197–210

Koudas N, Marathe A, Srivastava D (2004) Flexible string matching against large databases in practice. In: Proceedings of VLDB conference. VLDB Endowment, pp 1078–1086

Lambrix P, Tan H, Xu W (2008) Literature-based alignment of ontologies. In: Proceedings of the 3rd International Workshop on Ontology Matching (OM-2008)

Lee Y, Sayyadian M, Doan A, Rosenthal A (2007) eTuner: Tuning schema matching software using synthetic scenarios. VLDB J 16(1):97–122

Li J, Tang J, Li Y, Luo Q (2009) RiMOM: A dynamic multistrategy ontology alignment framework. IEEE Trans Knowl Data Eng 21(8):1218–1232

Madhavan J, Bernstein P A, Rahm E (2001) Generic Schema Matching with Cupid. In: Proceedings VLDB Conf., pp 49–58

Madhavan J, Bernstein PA, Doan A, Halevy AY (2005) Corpus-based schema matching. In: Proceedings of ICDE conference. IEEE Computer Society, Washington, DC, pp 57–68

Mao M, Peng Y, Spring M (2008) A harmony based adaptive ontology mapping approach. In: Proceedings of international conference on semantic web and web services (SWWS), pp 336–342

Massmann S, Rahm E (2008) Evaluating instance-based matching of web directories. In: Proceedings of 11th international Workshop on the Web and Databases (WebDB 2008)

Mork P, Seligman L, Rosenthal A, Korb J, Wolf C (2008) The harmony integration workbench. J Data Sem 11:65–93

Nandi A, Bernstein PA (2009) HAMSTER: Using search clicklogs for schema and taxonomy matching. PVLDB, vol 2(1), pp 181–192

Peukert E, Berthold H, Rahm E (2010a) Rewrite techniques for performance optimization of schema matching processes. In: Proceedings of 13th international conference on extending database technology (EDBT). ACM, NY, pp 453–464

Peukert E, Massmann S, König K (2010b) Comparing similarity combination methods for schema matching. In: Proceedings of 40th annual conference of the German computer society (GI-Jahrestagung). Lecture Notes in Informatics 175, pp 692–701

Pirrò G, Talia D (2010) UFOme: An ontology mapping system with strategy prediction capabilities. Data Knowl Eng 69(5):444–471

Rahm E, Bernstein PA (2001) A survey of approaches to automatic schema matching. VLDB J 10(4):334–350

Rahm E, Do, HH, Massmann S (2004) Matching large XML schemas. SIGMOD Rec 33(4):26–31

Saha B, Stanoi I, Clarkson KL (2010) Schema covering: A step towards enabling reuse in information integration. In: Proceedings of ICDE conference, pp 285–296

Saleem K, Bellahsene Z, Hunt E (2008) PORSCHE: Performance oriented SCHEma mediation. Inf Syst 33(7–8):637–657

SAP (2010) Warp10 community-based integration. https://cw.sdn.sap.com/cw/docs/DOC-120470 (white paper), https://cw.sdn.sap.com/cw/community/esc/cdg135. Accessed April 2010

Seligman L, Mork P, Halevy AY et al (2010) OpenII: An open source information integration toolkit. In: Proceedings of ACM SIGMOD conference. ACM, NY, pp 1057–1060

Shi F, Li J et al (2009) Actively learning ontology matching via user interaction. In: Proceedings of international conference on semantic web (ICSW). Springer, Heidelberg, pp 585–600

Smith K, Morse M, Mork P et al (2009) The role of schema matching in large enterprises. In: Proceedings of CIDR

Spiliopoulos V, Vouros GA, Karkaletsis V (2010) On the discovery of subsumption relations for the alignment of ontologies. J Web Sem 8(1):69–88

Su W, Wang J, Lochovsky FH (2006) Holistic schema matching for web query interfaces. In: Proceedings of international conference on extending database technology (EDBT). Springer, Heidelberg, pp 77–94

Tan H, Lambrix P (2007) A method for recommending ontology alignment strategies. In: Proceedings of international conference on semantic web (ICSW). LNCS, vol 4825. Springer, Heidelberg

Thor A, Kirsten T, Rahm E (2007) Instance-based matching of hierarchical ontologies. In: Proceedings of 12th BTW conference (Database systems for business, technology and web). Lecture Notes in Informatics 103, pp 436–448

Zhang S, Mork P, Bodenreider O, Bernstein PA (2007) Comparing two approaches for aligning representations of anatomy. Artif Intell Med 39(3):227–236

Zhong Q, Li H et al. (2009) A gauss function based approach for unbalanced ontology matching. In: Proceedings of ACM SIGMOD conference. ACM, NY, pp 669–680

Chapter 2
Interactive Techniques to Support Ontology Matching

Sean M. Falconer and Natalya F. Noy

Abstract There are many automatic approaches for generating matches between ontologies and schemas. However, these techniques are far from perfect and when the use case requires an accurate matching, humans must be involved in the process. Yet, involving the users in creating matchings presents its own problems. Users have trouble understanding the relationships between large ontologies and schemas and their concepts, remembering what they have looked at and executed, understanding output from the automatic algorithm, remembering why they performed an operation, reversing their decisions, and gathering evidence to support their decisions. Recently, researchers have been investigating these issues and developing tools to help users overcome these difficulties. In this chapter, we present some of the latest work related to human-guided ontology matching. Specifically, we discuss the cognitive difficulties users face with creating ontology matchings, the latest visual tools for assisting users with matching tasks, Web 2.0 approaches, common themes, challenges, and the next steps.

1 Introduction

As ontologies become more commonplace and their number grows, so does their diversity and heterogeneity. As a result, research on ontology matching has become a prominent topic in the Semantic Web and ontology communities. There are rigorous evaluations that compare the effectiveness of different algorithms [Euzénat et al., 2009], and researchers have proposed a standard matching language [Euzénat, 2006]. As the results of the evaluations show, ontology matching is far from being a fully automated task. In most cases where high precision is required, manual intervention will be necessary to verify or fine-tune the matchings produced by the automatic algorithms.

S.M. Falconer (✉) and N.F. Noy
Stanford University, Stanford, CA 94305, USA
e-mail: sean.falconer@stanford.edu, noy@stanford.edu

Z. Bellahsene et al. (eds.), *Schema Matching and Mapping*, Data-Centric Systems and Applications, DOI 10.1007/978-3-642-16518-4_2,
© Springer-Verlag Berlin Heidelberg 2011

In many areas of science, researchers are investigating how best to pair human input with automated procedures. For example, in the area of intelligent robot design, some researchers believe that the future of the field lies not in the development of fully automated robots, but in the development of partially automated ones [Coradeschi and Saffiotti, 2006]. Some tasks, such as classification and pattern recognition, are very difficult and robots need help from humans in performing these tasks. At the same time, robots can help humans with tedious and repetitive tasks. Similarly, in ontology matching, humans have access to vast amounts of background knowledge, which they can use to help make inductive judgments about potential correspondences.

In general, potential matching correspondences produced by a matching tool must be examined by a domain or ontology expert. The expert must determine the correspondences that are correct, remove false positives, and create additional correspondences missed by the automated procedure. This process is both time consuming and cognitively demanding. It requires understanding of both ontologies that are being mapped and how they relate to each other. Furthermore, both the ontologies and the number of candidate matching correspondences that the tools produce can be very large. Researchers have largely focused on improving the performance of the algorithms themselves. However, recently there has been a growing trend toward a more human-centered approach to ontology matching.

Examining and supporting the symbiosis between tool and user has been gaining more prominence and more tools that support a *semiautomatic* process are becoming available. Shvaiko et al. discuss ten challenges for ontology matching, three of which directly relate to the user: *user involvement, explanation of matching results,* and *social and collaborative ontology matching* [Shvaiko and Euzénat, 2008]. One approach researchers have been exploring to help support user involvement is information visualization techniques, such as those used by AlViz [Lanzenberger and Sampson, 2006] and CoGZ [Falconer and Storey, 2007b]. The *International Workshop on Ontology Alignment and Visualization*[1] was created as a platform for researchers to share and explore new visual techniques to support the matching process. Another growing trend is the use of Web 2.0 approaches to help support the social and collaborative matching process. Researchers are exploring the utility of *crowdsourcing* to help facilitate the process of generating many matching correspondences [Noy et al., 2008, Zhdanova, 2005].

These new trends in ontology matching research offer an exciting and interesting alternative to completely manual or completely automated processes. The research emphasis is shifting. New research is investigating how to gain a better understanding of the cognitive demands placed on the user during a matching procedure, how communities of users can work together to create more comprehensive and precise matchings, and how to make the most effective use of automation. Research on these topic areas is still in its infancy, but the future of the field lies in a joint effort between human and machine.

---

[1] http://www.ifs.tuwien.ac.at/?mlanzenberger/OnAV10/.

In this chapter, we explore research and tools that support the visual and interactive ontology matching process. We begin by discussing the cognitive difficulties with creating an ontology matching (Sect. 2). In Sects. 3–5, we discuss interactive tools for ontology matching, schema matching, and Web 2.0 approaches. In Sect. 6, we present several user-oriented evaluations and experiments that researchers in this area have carried out. We discuss common themes in Sect. 7, challenges and future directions for this field in Sect. 8. We conclude the chapter in Sect. 9.

2 Why is Ontology Matching Difficult?

Reconciling different ontologies and finding correspondences between their concepts is likely to be a problem for the foreseeable future. In fact, every self-assessment of database research has listed interoperability of heterogeneous data as one of the main research problems [Bernstein and Melnik, 2007]. Despite years of research on this topic, ontology and schema matching is far from being a fully automated task. In general, a user must interact with an ontology-matching tool to examine *candidate matchings* produced by the tool and to indicate which ones are correct, which ones are not, and to create additional correspondences that the tool has missed. However, this validation process is a difficult cognitive task. It requires tremendous patience and an expert understanding of the ontology domain, terminology, and semantics.

Obtaining this understanding is very difficult. Languages are known to be *locally ambiguous*, meaning that a sentence may contain an ambiguous portion that is no longer ambiguous once the whole sentence is considered [PPP, 2006]. Humans use detailed knowledge about the world to infer unspoken meaning [NLP, 2002]. However, an ontology often lacks sufficient information to infer the intended meaning. The concepts are largely characterized by a term or a small set of terms, which may be ambiguous.

The underlying data format that is used for specifying the ontology also introduces potential problems. The language used (e.g., OWL, RDF, XSD) constrains the expressiveness of the data representation. For example, many formats lack information relating to units of measure or intended usage [Bernstein and Melnik, 2007].

Ontologies are also developed for different purposes and by users with potentially opposing world views or different requirements. As a result, two ontologies may describe the same concept with different levels of granularity or the same concept with different intended application or meaning. All of these issues make discovering and defining matchings a very challenging problem for both man and machine.

As a consequence, to create accurate matchings in a reasonable amount of time, users and tools must be paired together. This process, usually referred to as *semi-automatic ontology matching*, typically follows an iterative process that is similar to the one that we describe in Fig. 2.1. Recently, this approach has received greater attention and an increasingly larger number of semiautomatic tools are becoming

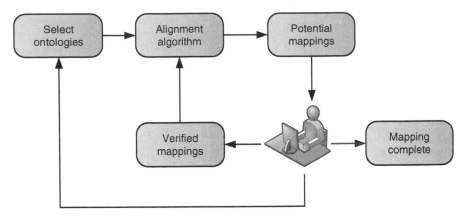

Fig. 2.1 Example of semiautomatic matching process. A user is involved in iteration with the tool. As the user evaluates potential matching correspondences, their decisions are used by the tool to make other suggestions about correspondences. This iteration continues until the user determines the matching is complete

available (more discussion in Sect. 3). Beyond tool design, some researchers have started to carry out behavioral studies in an attempt to identify the cognitive difficulties with validating matching correspondences.

Falconer and Storey have used results from several studies to propose a "cognitive support framework" [Falconer and Storey, 2007b, Falconer, 2009] that helps guide the design of ontology matching tools. They also used their experiments to uncover several themes that describe human and tool limitations: human memory limitations, decision-making difficulty, problems searching and filtering for information, issues with navigating the ontologies, understanding the progress of the task, and trusting the results from the automated procedure [Falconer and Storey, 2007a].

In another study, Yamauchi demonstrated that humans tend to bias their inductive judgments based on class-inclusion labels [Yamauchi, 2007]. In this work, Yamauchi carried out several studies examining how human subjects classify properties and class-labels for randomly generated cartoon images. Using the results from these experiments, he drew several interesting conclusions directly relating to ontology construction and matching. For example, because people tend to overuse class-labels for comparison, even when other information is available, the impact between the similarity of concept labels between two ontological concepts may bias the decision made by user of an ontology matching tool.

Research exploring the cognitive challenges of resolving data heterogeneity is still very new. Such research provides theoretical foundations for the design and evaluation of ontology matching tools. In the next three sections, we provide a short survey of different tools and approaches for ontology and schema matching.

3 Existing Tools

Researchers have developed a number of tools that enable users to find matching correspondences between ontologies. For example, Euzenat et al. discuss more than 20 different algorithms and tools [Euzénat et al., 2004b]. In this section, we focus our discussion on semiautomatic tools that follow an iterative process that is similar to the one shown in Fig. 2.1. The user selects the ontologies to be mapped, an algorithm runs to compute an initial set of correspondences, the user interacts with the tool to validate the matching correspondences, and the tool uses this information to provide other possible matches. Some of the projects that we discuss in this chapter are no longer under active development; and some of the projects are still in the early research prototype phase and are not available for public use. However, each system provides an interesting example of the variety of approaches available for supporting semiautomatic ontology matching.

COMA++ [Do, 2006] automatically generates matchings between source and target schemas (XML or OWL), and draws lines between potentially matching terms (see Fig. 2.2). Users can define their own term matches by interacting with the schema trees. Hovering over a potential correspondence displays a confidence level about the match as a numerical value between zero and one. COMA++

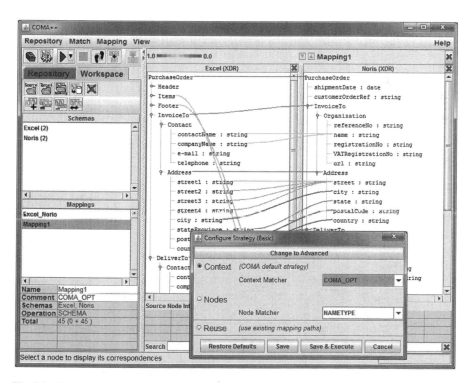

Fig. 2.2 Screenshot of COMA++ interface

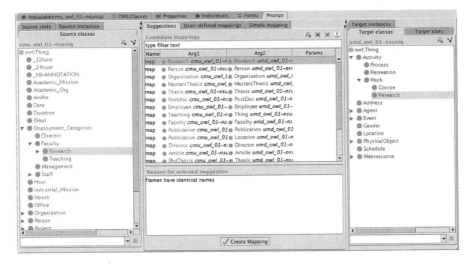

Fig. 2.3 Screenshot of PROMPT plugin while matching two university ontologies

contains several different matching algorithms in its library and the library is extensible. It also assumes interaction with a user: as a user approves of certain matches, COMA++ uses this information to make further suggestions.

PROMPT [Noy and Musen, 2003] (see Fig. 2.3) is a plugin for the popular ontology editor Protégé.[2] The plugin supports tasks for managing multiple ontologies including ontology differencing, extraction, merging, and matching. PROMPT begins the matching procedure by allowing the user to specify a source and target ontology. It then computes an initial set of candidate correspondences based largely on lexical similarity between the ontologies. The user then works with this list of correspondences to verify the recommendations or to create correspondences that the algorithm missed. Once a user has verified a correspondence, PROMPT's algorithm uses this information to perform structural analysis based on the graph structure of the ontologies. This analysis usually results in further correspondence suggestions. This process is repeated until the user determines that the matching is complete. PROMPT saves verified correspondences as instances in a *matching ontology* [Crubézy and Musen, 2003]. The matching ontology provides a framework for expressing transformation rules for ontology matchings. The transformation rule support depends on the matching plugin and ontology used. In the default matching plugin, the matching ontology simply describes the source and target correspondence components and metadata, such as the date, who created the correspondence, and a user-defined comment.

Like COMA++, PROMPT is extensible via its own plugin framework [Falconer et al., 2006]. However, while COMA++ supported extensibility only at the

---

[2] http://protege.stanford.edu.

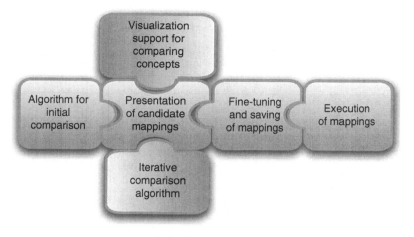

Fig. 2.4 Configurable steps in the PROMPT framework. Developers can replace any component in the figure with their own implementation

algorithm level, PROMPT supports a much more comprehensive set of extensions. It decomposes the matching process into several steps: an algorithm for comparison, the presentation of matching correspondences, fine-tuning and saving of correspondences, and execution of a matching (see Fig. 2.4). These steps represent plugin extension points in PROMPT: a new plugin can replace or augment any of these steps.

COGZ is an interactive visual plugin for PROMPT. Figure 2.5 presents the main COGZ interface. Like COMA++, COGZ uses a visual metaphor for the representation of matching correspondences. Candidate correspondences are represented by dotted, red arcs, while validated correspondences are represented by solid, black arcs. The tool supports incremental search and filtering of both source and target ontologies and generated correspondences. For example, as a user types in a search term for the source ontology, after each keystroke, the tree representation of the ontology is filtered to show only terms and hierarchy that matches the search criteria. Other filtering is available that allow a user to focus on certain parts of the hierarchy or help hide unwanted information from the display.

COGZ uses highlight propagation to assist users with understanding and navigating matching correspondences. When a user selects an ontology term, all matchings except those relevant to the selected term are semitransparent, while the relevant matchings are highlighted. To support navigation of large ontologies, a fish-eye zoom is available. The fish-eye zoom creates a distortion effect on the source and target trees such that selected terms are shown in a normal font size while other terms are shown progressively smaller depending on their relevance to the selected values (see Fig. 2.6).

Similar to PROMPT, AlViz [Lanzenberger and Sampson, 2006] is a plugin for Protégé, however the tool is primarily in an early research phase. AlViz was developed specifically for visualizing ontology alignments. It applies multiple-views

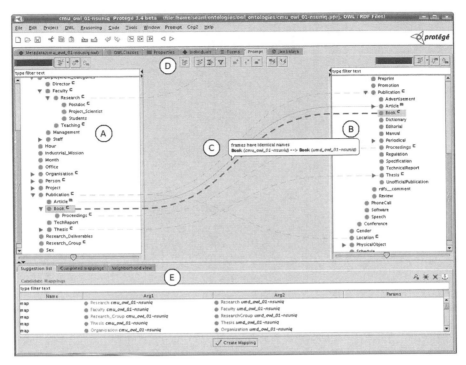

Fig. 2.5 The COGZ perspective in PROMPT. (A) and (B) show the source and target ontologies. Concepts with "C" icons represent terms with candidate correspondences that were discovered automatically, while concepts with "M" icons (e.g., Article) are terms that have been validated and mapped. (C) shows a visual representation of correspondences. (D) shows the main toolbar. Each ontology has a set of buttons for applying filters, moving through the correspondences, and representing the overall progress. Finally, (E) shows three tabs. The first tab displays all the candidate or suggested correspondences found automatically. The second tab displays only the correspondences validated by the user. The final tab displays a side by side visual comparison between the concepts selected in the source and target ontologies

through a cluster graph visualization along with synchronized navigation within standard tree controls (see Fig. 2.7). The tool attempts to facilitate user understanding of the ontology matching results [Lanzenberger and Sampson, 2006] by providing an overview of the ontologies in the form of clusters. The clusters represent an abstraction of the original ontology graph; moreover, clusters are colored based on their potential concept similarity with the other ontology.

OWL Lite Alignment (OLA) is a tool for automated matching construction as well as an environment for manipulating matching correspondences [Euzénat et al., 2004a]. The tool supports parsing and visualization of ontologies, automated computing of similarities between ontology entities, manual construction, visualization, and comparison of matching correspondences (see Fig. 2.8). OLA supports only OWL Lite ontologies and uses the Alignment API specified in Euzénat [2006] to describe a matching. The matching algorithm finds correspondences by analyzing

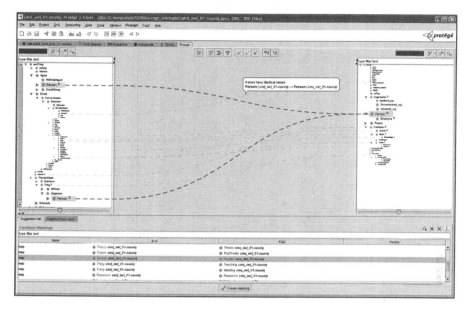

Fig. 2.6   Example of COGZ fisheye distortion effect

the structural similarity between the ontologies using graph-based similarity techniques. This information is combined with label similarity measures (e.g., Euclidean
distance, Hamming distance, substring distance) to produce a list of matching
correspondences.

Muse is a matching design wizard that uses data examples to help guide a user
through the matching design process [Alexe et al., 2008]. Like AlViz, Muse is still
in the early research phase and is not available for public download. The Muse tool
takes a different approach to user support by attempting to compile a small set of
yes/no questions that a designer can answer. The answers allow Muse to infer the
desired semantics of a potential matching correspondence. Muse also constructs
examples based on ontology instance data to help a user disambiguate a potential
correspondence with multiple interpretations.

The NeOn toolkit [Le Duc et al., 2008], developed as an Eclipse plugin,[3] is an
environment for managing ontologies within the NeOn project.[4] NeOn supports run
time and design time ontology matching support and can be extended via plugins.
The toolkit includes a matching editor called OntoMap, which allows a user to create
and edit matchings (see Fig. 2.9). Similar to the previously mentioned tools, NeOn
supports OWL ontologies; however it also supports RDF and F-Logic. The toolkit
can convert a variety of sources (e.g., databases, file systems, UML diagrams) into
an ontology to be used for matching.

---

[3] http://www.eclipse.org.

[4] http://www.neon-project.org.

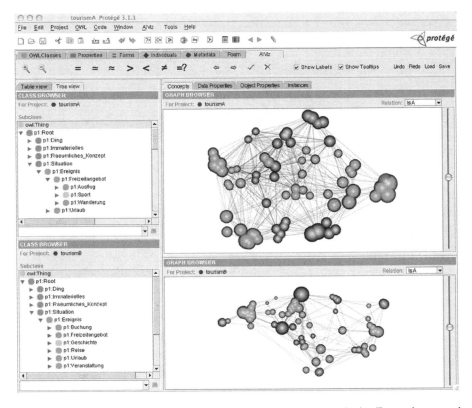

Fig. 2.7 Screenshot of AlViz plugin while matching two tourism ontologies [Lanzenberger and Sampson, 2006]

These are just a few of the visual and interactive tools available for ontology matching. In the next section, we discuss similar tools that have been developed to support the related problem of schema matching.

4 Schema Matching

Typically in schema matching the goal is to map entities from relational database schemas, XML schemas, Web catalogs, or directories rather than entities of an ontology. While the process of schema matching is very similar to the process of ontology matching, there are some significant differences. For example, there are fundamental differences in terms of the representational semantics of a database schema versus an ontology. An ontology is a representation of the concepts for a domain of discourse, which is often developed independent from an application. A database or XML schema is usually modeled to represent data with a particular application in mind. Moreover, ontologies are often constructed and published

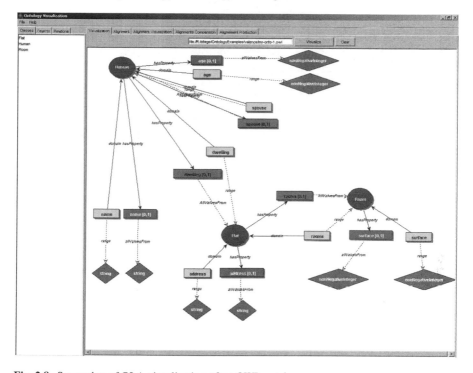

Fig. 2.8 Screenshot of OLA visualization of an OWL ontology

publicly with sharing in mind. In contrast, schemas are often internal to a particular application and are not available for others to consume or re-use. In terms of matching, the focus in ontology matching is usually to create semantic links between two independent ontologies that can later be used for various applications. With data-specific schemas, data translation or integration is often the focus. Thus, a lot of schema-matching tools support sophisticated methods for constructing transformation rules to translate data from a source schema to a target. Finally, while ontology matching has primarily been confined to research laboratories, there is a number of commercial tools available for schema matching. Microsoft, IBM, and Oracle are just a few of the companies that have commercial tools available.

Many of these tools have been developed through successful collaborations between researchers and industry. Clio, one of the first and most sophisticated schema matching tools, was a research prototype developed through a collaboration at IBM's Almaden Research Center and the University of Toronto [Miller et al., 2001]. Clio can automatically generate a view to reformulate queries from one schema to another or transform data from one representation to another to facilitate data exchange.

Like the previously discussed ontology matching tools, Clio proposes a semi-automatic approach and supports a visual matching representation similar to COMA++, CoGZ, and OntoMapper (see Fig. 2.10). Users can draw arrows

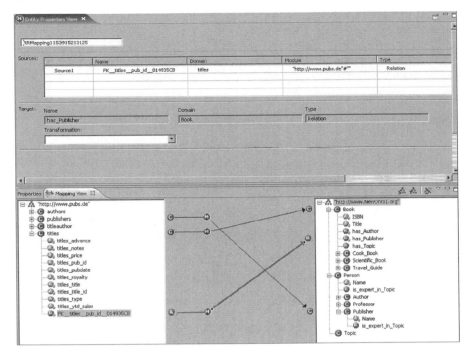

Fig. 2.9 Screenshot of NeOn toolkit matching editor [NE08, 2008]

between the source and target schema elements and these arrows are interpreted as matchings and translated into a query. The heart of Clio is its incremental matching engine, which uses information about the matching that is input from a user to infer and re-rank correspondences. The Clio project has been in development since 1999, and a product version is now available as part of the Rational Data Architect.[5]

MapForce is part of Altova's XML suite of tools.[6] Similar to Clio, users can draw matching correspondences between the source and target schemas and these are used to automatically generate queries to support data integration. For XML and database matchings, the matching can be saved as XSLT, XQuery, or generated as programming language code (e.g., Java). MapForce supports a feature to "auto connect matching children." When a parent element is manually connected, children with the same name are automatically mapped.

Similar to MapForce, the Stylus Studio contains an XML matching tool that supports visual matching between XML, relational databases, and web service data.[7] Users can drag and drop lines between source and target elements and matching

---

[5] http://www-01.ibm.com/software/data/optim/data-architect/.

[6] http://www.altova.com/mapforce.html.

[7] http://www.stylusstudio.com/xml_to_xml_mapper.html.

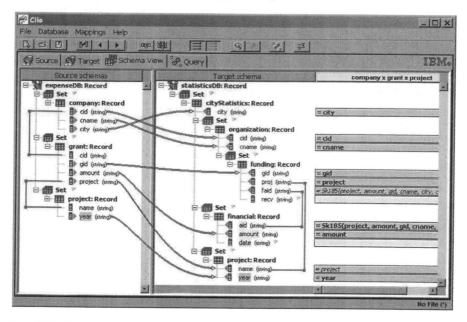

Fig. 2.10 Screenshot of the Schema Viewer from http://www.almaden.ibm.com/cs/projects/criollo/(2009)

correspondences can be interpreted as XSLT or XQuery code. This tool also only supports manual creation of matching correspondences.

Finally, like the Clio project, Microsoft's BizTalk mapper[8] has had both a research and commercial focus. BizTalk mapper provides similar functionality as MapForce and the matching tools in the Stylus Studio, however, work from Microsoft's Research has been incorporated to allow the matching tool to work more effectively for large schemas.

Robertson et al. discuss visual enhancements that were made to BizTalk mapper as well as a user evaluation [Robertson et al., 2005]. The tool uses the same visual metaphor for matching as many of the previously mentioned tools (see Fig. 2.11) and many of the visual enhancements are similar to features of the COGZ tool.

One of the problems with such a visual metaphor is that the interface can quickly become unmanageable as the number of matchings increases. To help alleviate this issue, Robertson et al. made several small enhancements to the interface that led to great impact in terms of usability. First, like COGZ, highlight propagation was incorporated to make it easier to follow the correspondences for a particular schema entity. This feature simply highlights all the relevant correspondences for a selected entity, while all other correspondences are made semitransparent. Moreover, auto-scrolling was incorporated so that when a user selects a source entity, the target

---

[8] http://www.microsoft.com/biztalk/en/us/product-documentation.aspx.

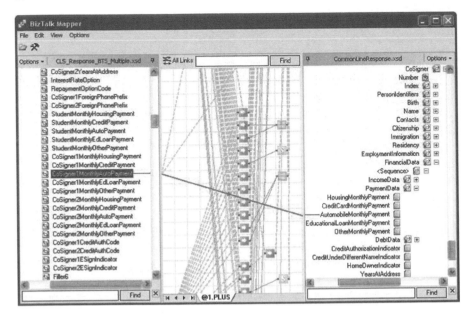

Fig. 2.11 Screenshot of the BizTalk mapper [Bernstein et al., 2006]

schema tree is automatically scrolled to display the area of the target most likely to have a correspondence of interest. As with the COGZ tool, features were introduced to help users deal with a large number of entities in the schema. Instead of zooming or distortion effects, tree coalescing is used to automatically collapse and hide entities deemed to be nonrelevant to the current selected and highlighted elements. Finally, search enhancements were incorporated to support incremental search. Unlike COGZ's incremental search that filters to display results, BizTalk mapper uses scrollbar highlighting. The scrollbar highlighting is used to mark areas of the tree that have search hits.

Besides visualization research, the BizTalk mapper developers have incorporated research for workflow enhancements [Bernstein et al., 2006]. In this research, Bernstein et al. argued that presenting all schema matching correspondences to a user at once is too overwhelming and in fact annoys the user as they become frustrated sifting through all the false positives. Alternatively, the authors suggest that an incremental approach is necessary, where a user can select an entity of interest and then be presented with just the candidate correspondences for that entity. The correspondences are ranked based on their match likelihood, and the user can easily navigate between the candidates. Once a decision is reached and committed by the user, this information can be incorporated into further incremental suggestions.

Each of these tools uses similar visual interaction techniques as the ontology matching tools that we discussed in Sect. 3. However, there is more focus on data translation rule construction than with the ontology-related tools. In the next section, we discuss a different interaction approach, one based on creating matchings by harnessing the power of a community of users.

5 Web 2.0 Approaches

Besides interactive desktop tools, researchers have started to explore how to use communities of users to develop ontology matchings collaboratively and to share them. *Crowdsourcing* – outsourcing of a task to a community of motivated individuals – has had huge success in projects such as Wikipedia and social bookmarking sites such as Digg. Similar wisdom of the crowd approaches are beginning to gain traction in the matching community.

Zhdanova and Shvaiko developed an online application to support and collect community-driven matchings [Zhdanova, 2005]. The web application allowed users to upload ontologies and to use online tools to perform an automatic matching between the ontologies. Once the users generated the matching, they could save and share it with other members of the community. Realizing that matchings can often be subjective, the authors designed their application to collect information about the users of the community in terms of their expertise, experience levels with particular ontologies, and their goals for a particular matching. Other members of the community could therefore make informed decisions about whether or not to rely on an uploaded matching. The application also stored information about the relationship between users of the community.

Similarly, the OntoMediate Project, as part of their research initiative, has been exploring to what extent collaborative online environments can help to facilitate the specification of ontology matchings [Correndo et al., 2008b]. The prototype system supports the matching of local ontologies to already uploaded ontologies and matchings. Furthermore, the automated procedures make use of the existing matchings to improve the quality of suggested matchings. The tools exploit social interaction to help improve matching quality. Users of the community that work with similar data can socially interact with each other to help validate matchings, spot errors, provide feedback, and propose alternatives [Correndo et al., 2008a].

McCann et al. have also been exploring Web 2.0 approaches. They have proposed an interesting approach to engage the user community [Robert McCann et al., 2008]. In their research, they have been investigating how to gather feedback from users in the form of simple questions in which the answers are used to improve the accuracy of the underlying algorithms. The goal is to pose questions to users that will have a significant impact on the tool's accuracy, as well as be questions that are easy for a human to answer but difficult for a machine. For example, an automated procedure may guess that a particular attribute is of type date, but may not be completely confident about the choice. User-expertise can be exploited in this circumstance to clarify whether the particular attribute is a date or not, leading to significant improvement in the algorithm choices.

In BioPortal,[9] an online tool for accessing and sharing biomedical ontologies, researchers have been exploring the impact of supporting matchings as a form of ontology metadata. Users can upload matchings that are generated offline as well as

---

[9] http://bioportal.bioontology.org/.

create matchings interactively through the web application. The online community can comment on the matchings, discuss and refine them. There is currently more than 30,000 such matchings available [Noy et al., 2008].

One important aspect of BioPortal's matching support is that both the ontologies and the matchings are available via web services. This is an important distinction from the early work of Zhdanova and Shvaiko. By making the consumption of these resources readily available to anyone that wishes to make use of this information, it greatly lowers the barrier of entry for applications that need matchings. The consuming applications do not need to be concerned with updates to the ontologies or matchings, as those are handled by BioPortal and immediately available via the services. The services also potentially help promote feedback and improvement about the matchings in BioPortal as it is in consuming application's best interest to improve the matchings. However, without the services, if the matchings were simply downloaded, consumers could make local changes without contributing those back to the community.

There is great potential with a community web-based approach for collecting and sharing matchings. However, this area of study is still very new. To the best of our knowledge, researchers have not yet performed any evaluation to determine whether users can be motivated to contribute to such projects and whether such an approach is feasible. In the next section, we survey existing user-based evaluations and experiments that have been carried out in the ontology matching community. These experiments have mostly been focused on the differences between two tools or how users interpret the automatic suggestions computed by the underlying algorithms.

6   Experiments and Evaluation

As our survey of tools in this chapter demonstrates, the development of semi-automatic tools for ontology matching has been gaining momentum. However, evaluation of such tool is still very much in its infancy. There has been only a handful of user-based evaluations carried out in this area. All of these experiments have involved the PROMPT system.

The first experiment was led by the authors of the PROMPT tool. The experiment concentrated on evaluating the correspondence suggestions provided by the tool by having several users merge two ontologies. The researchers recorded the number of steps, suggestions followed, suggestions that were not followed, and what the resulting ontologies looked like. Precision and recall were used to evaluate the quality of the suggestions: precision was the fraction of the tool's suggestions that the users followed and recall was the fraction of the operations performed by the users that were suggested by the tool. The experiment only involved four users, which was too small to draw any meaningful conclusions. The authors stated that, "[w]hat we really need is a larger-scale experiment that compares tools with similar sets of pragmatic criteria [Noy and Musen, 2002, p. 12]."

Lambrix and Edberg [Lambrix and Edberg, 2003] performed a user evaluation of the matching tools PROMPT and Chimaera [McGuinness et al., 2000] for the specific use case of merging ontologies in bioinformatics. The user experiment involved eight users, four with computer science backgrounds and four with biology backgrounds. The participants were given a number of tasks to perform, a user manual on paper, and the software's help system for support. They were also instructed to "think aloud" and an evaluator took notes during the experiment. Afterward, the users were asked to complete a questionnaire about their experience. The tools were evaluated with the same precision and recall measurements as used in the previously described PROMPT experiment [Noy and Musen, 2002], while the user interfaces were evaluated using the REAL (Relevance, Efficiency, Attitude, and Learnability) [Löwgren, 1994] approach. Under both criteria, PROMPT outperformed Chimaera, however, the participants found learning how to merge ontologies in either tool was equally difficult. The participants found it particularly difficult to perform non-automated procedures in PROMPT, such as creating user-defined merges.

The third experiment evaluated PROMPT and the alternative user-interface CoGZ. The experiment focused on evaluating the cognitive support provided by the tools in terms of their effectiveness, efficiency, and satisfaction [Falconer, 2009]. Researchers assigned eighteen matching and comprehension tasks to participants that they had to perform using each tool (nine per tool). The evaluators then measured the time that it took a participant to complete the task and accuracy with which they performed the task. They measured the participant satisfaction via exit interviews and the System Usability Scale [Brooke, 1996].

This last experiment was significantly more comprehensive than the previous studies. Researchers used quantitative analysis to analyze the differences in participant performance across the tasks. They used qualitative approaches to help explain the differences in participant task performance. Furthermore, the design of the experiment was guided by an underlying theory that the authors previously proposed [Falconer and Storey, 2007b].

7 Discussion

In this section, we return to the ontology tools discussed in our survey. We provide a brief summary of these tools in terms of their visual paradigms, plugins, and algorithm support (see Table 2.1).

Table 2.1 provides a high-level comparison between the surveyed tools. However, more details of comparison and evaluation are needed. In the next section, we discuss this need more deeply as well as other challenges facing the area of interactive techniques for ontology matching.

Table 2.1 Tool comparison

Tool	Visual and interaction paradigm	Pluggable	Algorithm support
COMA++	*Line-based* representation of matchings. *Tree-based* representation of ontologies. *Strength* of correspondence (number between zero and one). Line color indicates similarity strength	Plugin support for matching algorithms	A variety of automatic matchers
PROMPT	*List* representation of matchings. *Tree-based* representation of ontologies. Interaction is *synchronized* with the source and target ontology trees. *Strength* of correspondence (description of the "reason for suggestion")	Extensive plugin architecture	Default algorithm is lexical based. Verification of a correspondence is used to infer new suggestions
CoGZ	*Line-based* representation of matchings. *Tree-based* representation of ontologies. Interaction is *synchronized* between search, ontology browsing, and correspondence browsing. *Strength* of correspondence (description of the "reason for suggestion")		
AlViz	*Tree-based* representation of ontologies. *Small world graphs* representation of matchings. Interaction *synchronized* with Protégé class browser. Color is used to represent the types of correspondences (e.g., equal, similar, broader than). The cluster display can be filtered by selecting particular entities in the source	No pluggable architecture	FOAM algorithm
OLA	*Graph-based* visualization of ontologies. The source and target ontologies can be compared side by side. Interaction *synchronized* between the two ontology displays	No pluggable architecture	A custom algorithm that combines similarity metrics based on lexical similarity, neighbor node similarity, and descriptive features
Muse	Interaction based on *wizards* that help a user disambiguate matching correspondences	No pluggable architecture	A custom algorithm that incorporates user feedback and automatically generates questions and examples for the user
OntoMap	*Drag and drop, line-based* representation for matchings. *Filters for data transformation* can be created interactively based on a particular matching correspondence	No pluggable architecture	Does not support automatic generation of matchings

8 Challenges and Next Steps

As our survey in this chapter demonstrates, workers are developing more and more interactive approaches for supporting semiautomatic ontology matching. Many desktop tools for both ontology and schema matching make use of a similar visual representation of matchings – the line-based metaphor for representing a correspondence. This approach is attractive because it is easy to understand what the visualization is attempting to convey. However, previous studies have indicated large variation in the usability of such an approach [Falconer and Storey, 2007a, Falconer, 2009]. It appears that visual support for matching is not as simple as copying this particular interface style. It is a combination of features and support techniques that assist with a user's workflow that is ultimately needed to help matching users make efficient and effective matching decisions.

Most of the tools in this research area have not been based on theoretical findings from behavioral user studies. They have instead often evolved from a need for some level of interaction with the underlying algorithm. However, without tool evaluations or underlying theories, it is impossible to pinpoint the exact features that lead to a more usable tool. Researchers must address this lack of evaluation and theoretical foundations.

In 2005, a group of researchers started the Ontology Alignment Evaluation Initiative (OAEI)[10] to help provide a standard platform for developers to compare and evaluate their ontology matching approaches. OAEI provides benchmark matching datasets that enable developers of different matching systems to compare their results. At the moment, OAEI evaluates only automatic approaches. We must extend this evaluation framework to compare and contrast interactive tools as well.

Such evaluation will require the development of a standardized comparison framework and evaluation protocols. Comparing interactive tools is more challenging than comparing automatic tools for several reasons: First, the evaluation of interactive tools is more expensive because it requires participation of domain experts in creating the matchings. Second, participation of humans in the evaluation introduces the inevitable bias and differences in the level of expertise and interests of those users who perform the matchings. Familiarity with some tools might bias users toward particular approaches and paradigms. Third, as our survey shows, the tools vary significantly in the types of input that they take and the types of analysis that they perform during the interactive stages. To compare the tools, we must not only characterize these differences but also develop protocols that would allow us to evaluate unique aspects of the tools, while keeping the comparison meaningful. There will need to be common interfaces that would enable evaluators to provide similar initial conditions for the tools, such as the initial set of matchings and to compare the results, such as the matchings produced by the users.

This evaluation would also face some of the same challenges that OAEI faces. For example, there are many strong tools from both industry and research, yet many are not publicly available, making even informal comparisons challenging.

---

[10] http://oaei.ontologymatching.org.

One of the contributions of OAEI was the development of a framework that identified various features of the tools, and enabled researchers to understand which tools works best under which circumstances. We hope that a similar framework can be developed for interactive tools, where there is an even greater variability in capabilities and workflows supported by the tools. Some interaction and visual paradigms only work well for small-scale ontologies, however, depending on a particular use case, these approaches may be appropriate. It would be useful to evaluate this criteria and make such information publicly available.

The criteria for evaluation of matching tools needs to be specified. This should include usability features, technical details about what ontologies are supported, as well as criteria for evaluating the scalability of the approach.

Besides desktop tools, researchers are exploring web applications that make use of crowdsourcing techniques. This paradigm introduces new directions in interaction, such as social interactions between users, interactions to upload and share ontologies, and services for consuming the matchings. This is a growing research direction and it will take time to determine how to motivate users to contribute to such projects. Also, evaluation will be important to help determine the quality of matchings that are contributed in this way, compared to more closed settings.

Such an approach is very attractive given the success of many existing crowdsourcing applications. This technique is one possible approach for helping deal with the scalability issue of generating a matching. It is a difficult and time-consuming process for a single individual to create the entire matching between two large ontologies. Crowdsourcing potentially alleviates some of this burden by allowing any Web user to contribute.

Researchers who work on the tools for interactive ontology matching, must focus more attention on the issues of scalability of the tools. As the sizes of the ontologies grows (e.g., some biomedical ontologies have tens of thousands of classes), so do the computational demands on the tools: they must be able to work with ontologies that may not load into memory or may take huge computational resources to process. Scalability of visualization techniques is another issue that must be addressed by the tools. As the ontologies become larger, some of the visualization paradigms that worked very well for small ontologies, with all the classes fitting on a single computer screen, simply may not work for ontologies where only a small fraction of the classes will fit on the screen. Both incremental matching [Bernstein et al., 2006] and ontology modularization [Stuckenschmidt et al., 2009] are approaches that potentially address this problem. They have the potential to help reduce cognitive overload during the matching process by restricting the focus of the user to particular areas of the ontology.

Finally, we still must explore new questions in interactive ontology matching, such as how to match the expertise of the user with particular areas of the ontology, where the best location to begin a matching process is, and how to best locate candidate-heavy areas of two ontologies.

9 Conclusion

There are many exciting questions to address in the growing research field of interactive techniques for matching. Industry and research has been attempting to address problems of data heterogeneity for many years, yet this problem is ever more prevalent. When precision is necessary, we must rely on human reasoning and domain expertise to help contribute to the matching process. Yet, it is important that we assist users with the process by designing tools that give them access to the information they require to make good decisions, by not hindering the process with overwhelming information, and by automating parts of the procedure when possible. From a research perspective, it is important that we address the lack of tool evaluation by carrying out more user-based evaluations. Heuristic evaluation procedures could also be useful for comparing feature sets of matching tools. There also needs to be more effort to make such findings and tools publicly available to help with evaluation.

We need evaluation to help distinguish what features and approaches are useful for particular use cases. We need theories to help explain these differences. Tools encode a workflow process and this process must align with the user's own internal process. By aligning these processes, we will be able to assist rather than hinder the user. We must incorporate a "human in the loop," where the human is an essential component in the matching process. Helping to establish and harness this symbiotic relationship between human processes and the tool's automated process will allow people to work more efficiently and effectively, and afford them the time to concentrate on difficult tasks that are not easily automated.

References

Alexe et al. (2008) Muse: Mapping understanding and design by example. In: international conference on data engineering, Cancun, 7–12 April 2008, pp 10–19

Bernstein PA, Melnik S (2007) Model management 2.0: Manipulating richer mappings. In: ACM special interest group on management of data (SIGMOD), Beijing, China, September 2007. ACM, NY, pp 1–12

Bernstein et al. (2006) Incremental schema matching. In: VLDB '06: Proceedings of the 32nd international conference on very large databases, Seoul, Korea, September 2006. VLDB Endowment, pp 1167–1170

Brooke J (1996) Usability evaluation in industry. In: Jordan PW, Thomas B, Weerdmeester BA, McClelland IL (eds) SUS: A quick and dirty usability scale. Taylor & Francis, London, pp 184–194

Coradeschi S, Saffiotti A (2006) Symbiotic robotic systems: Humans, robots, and smart environments. IEEE Intell Syst 21(3):82–84. doi:http://doi.ieeecomputersociety.org/10.1109/MIS.2006.59

Correndo et al. (2008a) Collaborative support for community data sharing. In: 2nd workshop on collective intelligence in semantic web and social networks, Sydney, Australia, 12 December 2008

Correndo et al. (2008b) A community based approach for managing ontology alignments. In: Ontology matching workshop, Karlsruhe, Germany, 26–30 October 2008

Crubézy M, Musen MA (2003) Ontologies in support of problem solving. In: Staab S, Studer R (eds) Handbook on ontologies. Springer, Heidelberg, pp 321–342

Do HH (2006) Schema matching and mapping-based data integration. PhD thesis, Department of Computer Science, Universität Leipzig

Euzénat J (2006) An API for ontology alignment (version 2.1). http://gforge.inria.fr/docman/view. php/117/251/align.pdf

Euzénat et al. (2004a) Ontology alignment with OLA. In: Proceedings of the 3rd evaluation of ontologies for the web (EON) workshop. CEUR-WS, pp 59–68

Euzénat et al. (2004b) State of the art on ontology alignment. deliverable d2.2.3. Tech. Rep. IST Knowledge Web NoE

Euzénat et al. (2009) Results of the ontology alignment evaluation initiative 2009. In: Proceedings of the 4th international workshop on Ontology Matching (OM-2009)

Falconer SM (2009) Cognitive support for semi-automatic ontology mapping. PhD thesis, University of Victoria

Falconer SM, Noy NF, Storey MA (2006) Towards understanding the needs of cognitive support for ontology mapping. In: International workshop on ontology matching at ISWC-2006, Athens, GA

Falconer SM, Storey MA (2007a) Cognitive support for human-guided mapping systems. Tech. Rep. DCS-318-IR, University of Victoria, Victoria, BC, Canada

Falconer SM, Storey MA (2007b) A cognitive support framework for ontology mapping. In: Proceedings of international semantic web conference, Busan, Korea, November 2007. Springer, Heidelberg, pp 114–127

Lambrix P, Edberg A (2003) Evaluation of ontology merging tools in bioinformatics. In: Proceedings pacific symposium on biocomputing, pp 589–600

Lanzenberger M, Sampson J (2006) Alviz – a tool for visual ontology alignment. In: Proceedings of the conference on information visualization (IV), London, July 2006. IEEE Computer Society, Washington, DC, pp 430–440. doi:http://dx.doi.org/10.1109/IV.2006.18

Le Duc et al. (2008) Matching ontologies for context: The neon alignment plug-in. Tech. Rep. Deliverable 3.3.2, IST NeOn IP, NeOn. ftp://ftp.inrialpes.fr/pub/exmo/reports/neon-332.pdf

Löwgren J (1994) Human-computer interaction. What every system developer should know. Chartwell-Bratt, England

McGuinness et al. (2000) The chimaera ontology environment. In: Proceedings of the 17th national conference on artificial intelligence and 12th conference on innovative applications of artificial intelligence, Austin, TX, 30 July–3 August 2000. AAAI, CA, pp 1123–1124

Miller et al. (2001) The clio project: Managing heterogeneity. SIGMOD Record 30(1):78–83

NE08 (2008) Neon wiki. http://www.neon-toolkit.org/wiki/index.php

NLP (2002) An introduction to NLP. http://www.cs.bham.ac.uk/ pxc/nlpa/2002/AI-HO-IntroNLP.html, http://www.cs.bham.ac.uk/~pxc/nlpa/2002/AI-HO-IntroNLP.html

Noy NF, Musen MA (2002) Evaluating ontology-mapping tools: Requirements and experience. In: Proceedings of OntoWeb-SIG3 workshop, Siguenza, Spain, October 2002, pp 1–14

Noy NF, Musen MA (2003) The PROMPT suite: Interactive tools for ontology merging and mapping. Int J Hum Comput Stud 59(6):983–1024

Noy et al. (2008) Collecting community-based mappings in an ontology repository. Tech. Rep. BMIR-2008-1310, Stanford Center For Biomedical Informatics Research

PPP (2006) Performance, Parsing and Pragmatics. http://www.phon.ucl.ac.uk/home/marco/ Principles of Linguistics Handout2006-2007.htm

Robert McCann et al. (2008) Matching schemas in online communities: A web 2.0 approach. In: Proceedings of the 2008 IEEE 24th international conference on data engineering. IEEE Computer Society, Washington, DC, pp 110–119

Robertson et al. (2005) Visualization of mappings between schemas. In: CHI '05: Proceedings of the SIGCHI conference on human factors in computing systems, Portland, OR, April 2005. ACM, NY, pp 431–439. doi:http://doi.acm.org/10.1145/1054972.1055032

Shvaiko P, Euzénat J (2008) Ten challenges for ontology matching. In: ODBASE, Monterrey, Mexico, November 2008. Springer, Heidelberg, pp 1164–1182

Stuckenschmidt et al. (2009) Modular ontologies – Concepts, theories, and techniques for knowledge modularization. Springer, Heidelberg

Yamauchi T (2007) The semantic web and human inference: A lesson from cognitive science. In: Proceedings of ISWC/ASWC, Busan, Korea, 13 November 2007. Springer, Heidelberg, pp 609–622

Zhdanova AV (2005) Towards a community-driven ontology matching. In: K-CAP '05, Banff, AB, Canada, October 2005. ACM, NY, pp 221–222. doi:http://doi.acm.org/10.1145/1088622.1088678

http://www.almaden.ibm.com/cs/projects/criollo/ (2009). Website on Clio and schema management

Chapter 3
Enhancing the Capabilities of Attribute Correspondences

Avigdor Gal

Abstract In the process of schema matching, attribute correspondence is the association of attributes in different schemas. Increased importance of attribute correspondences led to new research attempts that were devoted to improve attribute correspondences by extending their capabilities. In this chapter, we describe recent advances in the schema matching literature that attempt to enhance the capabilities of attribute correspondences. We discuss contextual schema matching as a method for introducing conditional correspondences, based on context. The use of semantic matching is proposed to extend attribute correspondences to results in an ontological relationship. Finally, probabilistic schema matching generates multiple possible models, modeling uncertainty about which one is correct by using probability theory.

1 Introduction

In the process of schema matching, attribute correspondence is the association of attributes in different schemas. Creating attribute correspondences is considered a basic step in schema matching. Attribute correspondences serve the community well. For example, they are useful as input to a manual refinement, especially if not limited to 1 : 1 constraint matching. Also, in ontology matching, attribute correspondences are used to express the relatedness of product categories or bioinformatics concepts. Finally, attribute correspondences can be used for recommending schema matchings for restricting query search space or as input for ontology merging.

Given two schemas, a matcher first evaluates the level of confidence in the correspondence of any pair of attributes. Then, decisions are made as to which attribute correspondences should be retained as part of a schema matching outcome. In recent years, new applications have emerged, putting more and more emphasis on the

A. Gal
Technion – Israel Institute of Technology, Haifa 32000, Israel
e-mail: avigal@ie.technion.ac.il

Z. Bellahsene et al. (eds.), *Schema Matching and Mapping*, Data-Centric Systems
and Applications, DOI 10.1007/978-3-642-16518-4_3,
© Springer-Verlag Berlin Heidelberg 2011

attribute correspondence selection process. Such applications involve data exchange in data spaces and integration in the Semantic Web. Matching requires more automation, as the time frame for reaching matching decisions shrinks. Also, the role of the human designer is changing, as data is being scraped from sources to which no human designer is available for evaluating the matching correctness. Finally, the sheer amount of data integration decisions that need to be taken require the development of methods for nonexperts.

As a result of this setting change, several research attempts were devoted to improve attribute correspondences by extending their capabilities, as illustrated in Fig. 3.1. In this chapter, we describe recent advances in the schema matching literature that attempt to enhance the capabilities of attribute correspondences. We discuss contextual schema matching (Sect. 3) that can express that attribute correspondences hold under certain instance conditions. For example, a code attribute in one schema may refer to an ISBN attribute in another schema only if the sold item is a book. Semantic matching is introduced in Sect. 4, extending attribute correspondences to support ontological constructs. Traditionally, attribute correspondences are limited to the ontological construct known as *synonym*. However, correspondences may be of various types. For example, a pair of attributes may correspond through a *hyperonym* relationship, where one attribute represents a more general concept than another. As a concrete example, consider two databases for selling electronic products. The correspondence between an attribute digitalCamera and an attribute PhotoAndCamera is that of subsumption and not equivalence. Finally, probabilistic schema matching (Sect. 5) extends attribute correspondences to concurrently assume the validity of attribute correspondences, which were considered conflicting in the past. For example, a 1 : 1 matching constraint may hold valid, yet under the probabilistic approach an attribute may (probabilistically) be associated

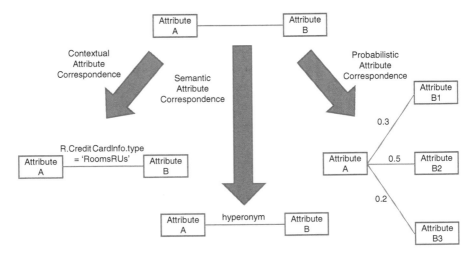

Fig. 3.1 Extensions to attribute correspondences

with more than one attribute from another schema. We conclude with a discussion of how to combine these three directions into a new, more powerful model of attribute correspondences.

2 A Model for Attribute Correspondences

In this section, we present a simple model of attribute correspondences as a basis for the proposed extensions. The model is based on Marie and Gal [2008]. We shall accompany the description with a specific simplified case study that will assist us in demonstrating the three extensions to the basic attribute correspondence model. The case study is about the design of a hotel reservation portal. The portal merges various hotel information databases, adding a mashup applications that assists in positioning hotels on a geographical map.

We consider three relational databases, and we now provide a partial description of the databases, as illustrated in Table 3.1. Database R contains three relations, CardInfo, HotelInfo, and reservation information in the relation Reservations. Database S stores data of a hotel chain RoomsRUs that separates information of a store credit card from information of major credit cards. Therefore, S contains the following two relations, CardInformation and HotelCardInformation. It also contains reservation information in the relation ReserveDetails. Finally, a database T contains urban information with two relations, CityInfo and Subway. CityInfo provides information about neighborhoods in cities and their approximate GPS positioning whereas Subway provides similar information for subway stations.

In what follows, we use a path representation. An attribute A of a given relation R in a given database D is referred to as $D.R.A$. For example, R.CardInfo.cardNum.

Table 3.1 Sample database schema description

Database R					
CardInfo	type	cardNum	lastName	firstName	securityCode
	expiryMonth	expiryYear			
HotelInfo	hotelName	neighborhood	city		
Reservations	lastName	firstName	arrivalDate	numberOfDays	
Database S					
CardInformation	type	cardNum	securityCode	expiryMonth	expiryYear
HotelCardInformation	clientNum	expiryMonth	expiryYear		
ReserveDetails	clientNum	name	checkInDay	checkOutDay	
Database T					
CityInfo	city	neighborhood	GPSPosition		
Subway	city	station	GPSPosition		

2.1 Model

Let *schema* $S = \{A_1, A_2, \ldots, A_n\}$ be a finite set of *attributes*. Attributes can be both simple and compound, compound attributes should not necessarily be disjoint, etc. For example, an attribute in a schema of a hotel reservation Web site may be lastName and firstName. A compound attribute may be creditCardInfo combining four other attributes, type, cardNum, securityCode, and expiry (which could also be a compound attribute, representing month and year of expiration). We define an attribute to be *categorical* if its domain contains a closed set of categories, e.g., a type attribute.

This model captures the essence of schema matching, namely matching of attributes, and therefore a richer representation of data models is not needed. Therefore, if we aim at matching simple attributes (such as lastName and firstName) we need not represent their composition into a compound attribute called name. If the goal of our schema matching process is to match XML paths (see, e.g., Vinson et al. 2007), then XML paths are the elements we define as attributes in our schemata.

For any schemata pair S and S', let $\mathcal{S} = S \times S'$ be the set of all possible *attribute correspondences* between S and S'. $\mathcal{S}$ is a set of attribute pairs (e.g., (arrivalDate, checkInDay)). Let $M(S, S')$ be an $n \times n'$ *similarity matrix* over $\mathcal{S}$, where $M_{i,j}$ represents a degree of similarity between the ith attribute of S and the jth attribute of S'. The majority of works in the schema matching literature define $M_{i,j}$ to be a real number in $[0, 1]$. $M(S, S')$ is a *binary similarity matrix* if for all $1 \le i \le n$ and $1 \le j \le n'$, $M_{i,j} \in \{0, 1\}$. That is, a binary similarity matrix accepts only 0 and 1 as possible values.

Similarity matrices are generated by schema matchers. *Schema matchers* are instantiations of the schema matching process [Euzenat and Shvaiko, 2007, Gal and Shvaiko, 2009]. They differ mainly in the measures of similarity they employ, yielding different similarity matrices. These measures can be arbitrarily complex, and may use various techniques for, e.g., name matching and structure matching (such as XML hierarchical representation). Schema matchers use the application semantics in many different ways. Some matchers (e.g., He and Chang 2003, Su et al. 2006) assume similar attributes are more likely to have similar names. Other matchers (e.g., Gal et al. 2005b, Madhavan et al. 2001) assume similar attributes share similar domains. Others yet (e.g., Berlin and Motro 2001, Doan et al. 2001) take instance similarity as an indication to attribute similarity.

Example 1. To illustrate our model and for completeness sake, we now present a few examples of schema matchers, representative of many other, similar matchers. Detailed description of these matchers can be found in Gal et al. [2005b] and Marie and Gal [2007]:

Term: Term matching compares attribute names to identify syntactically similar attributes. To achieve better performance, names are preprocessed using several techniques originating in IR research. Term matching is based on either complete words or string comparison. As an example, consider the attributes CreditCardInfo and HotelCardInformation. The maximum common substring is CardInfo, and the similarity of the two terms is $\frac{\text{length(CardInfo)}}{\text{length(HotelCardInfomation)}} = \frac{8}{20} =$ 40%.

Value: Value matching utilizes domain constraints (e.g., drop lists, check boxes, and radio buttons). It becomes valuable when comparing two attributes that do not exactly match through their names. For example, consider attributes arrivalDate and checkInDay. These two attributes have associated value sets {(*Select*), 1, 2, . . . , 31} and {(*Day*), 1, 2, . . . , 31} respectively, and thus their content-based similarity is $\frac{31}{33} = 94\%$, which improves significantly over their term similarity ($\frac{2(\text{Da})}{11(\text{arrivalDate})} = 18\%$).

Let the power-set $\Sigma = 2^S$ be the set of all possible *schema matchings* between the schema pair and let $\Gamma : \Sigma \rightarrow \{0, 1\}$ be a Boolean function that captures the application-specific constraints on schema matchings, for example, cardinality constraints and inter-attribute correspondence constraints (see Miller et al. [2000] and Popa et al. [2002] for constraint enforcing mechanisms). Given a constraint specification Γ, the set of all *valid* schema mappings in Σ is given by $\Sigma_\Gamma = \{\sigma \in \Sigma \mid \Gamma(\sigma) = 1\}$. We define Γ here as a general constraint model, where $\Gamma(\sigma) = 1$ means that the mapping σ can be accepted by a designer.

To conclude this section, we introduce schema mappings. Let $\overline{S}$ and $\overline{T}$ be relational schemas. A relation mapping M is a triple (S, T, m), where S is a relation in $\overline{S}$, T is a relation in $\overline{T}$, and m is a set of attribute correspondences between S and T. A *schema mapping* $\overline{M}$ is a set of one-to-one relation mappings between relations in $\overline{S}$ and in $\overline{T}$, where every relation in either $\overline{S}$ or $\overline{T}$ appears at most once.

2.2 Monotonicity: Tying Expert Opinion with Automatic Matching

The evaluation of schema matchings is performed with respect to an *exact matching*, based on expert opinions. The most common evaluation metrics are *precision*, *recall*, and their derivations such as *F-measure* and *overall*. Depending of the matching task at hand, one may wish to measure a matching using a combined metric of *precision* and *recall*, such as *F-mesaure*, or optimize to one metric, possibly constraining the other to some minimal threshold.

The monotonicity measure, first presented in Gal et al. [2005a], aims at identifying a general principle that can differentiate good from bad matchers. It is based not only on the evaluation metric itself, but rather observes the ability of a matcher to assign an increasingly better performance to more accurate schema matchings. The monotonicity principle serves as a basis for improvements to attribute correspondences and we therefore demonstrate it here. As a metric of choice we use *precision*. We note that a similar analysis can be done using *precision* with bounded *recall*, *recall*, *F-Measure*, and any other measure a designer deems suitable for assessing matcher performance.

The monotonicity principle refers to the performance of complete schema matchings from which the performance of individual attribute correspondences can be derived. Assume that out of the $n \times n'$ attribute matchings, there are $c \leq n \times n'$ correct attribute matchings, with respect to the exact matching. Also, let $t \leq c$ be the number of matchings, out of the correct matchings, that were chosen by the matching algorithm and $f \leq n \times n' - c$ be the number of incorrect attribute matchings. Then, precision is computed to be $\frac{t}{t+f}$ and recall is computed as $\frac{t}{c}$. Clearly, higher values of both precision and recall are desired. From now on, we shall focus on the precision measure, where $p(\sigma)$ denotes the precision of a schema matching σ.

We first create equivalence schema matching classes on 2^S. Two matchings σ' and σ'' belong to a class p if $p(\sigma') = p(\sigma'') = p$, where $p \in [0, 1]$. For each two matchings σ' and σ'', such that $p(\sigma') < p(\sigma'')$, we can compute their schema matching level of certainty, $\Omega(\sigma')$ and $\Omega(\sigma'')$. We say that a matching algorithm is *monotonic* if for any two such matchings $p(\sigma') < p(\sigma'') \rightarrow \Omega(\sigma') < \Omega(\sigma'')$. Intuitively, a matching algorithm is monotonic if it ranks all possible schema matchings according to their precision level.

A monotonic matching algorithm easily identifies the exact matching. Let σ^* be the exact matching, then $p(\sigma^*) = 1$. For any other matching σ', $p(\sigma') < p(\sigma^*)$. Therefore, if $p(\sigma') < p(\sigma^*)$, then from monotonicity $\Omega(\sigma') < \Omega(\sigma^*)$. All one has to do then is to devise a method for finding a matching σ^* that maximizes Ω.[1]

Figure 3.2 provides an illustration of the monotonicity principle using a matching of a simplified version of two Web forms. Both schemata have nine attributes, all of which are matched under the exact matching. Given a set of matchings, each value

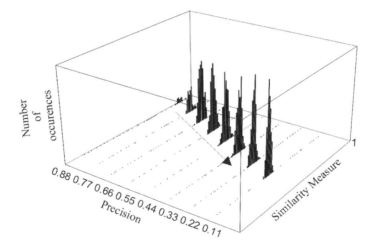

Fig. 3.2 Illustration of the monotonicity principle

---

[1] In Gal et al. [2005a], where the monotonicity principle was originally introduced, it was shown that while such a method works well for fuzzy aggregators (e.g., weighted average) it does not work for t-norms such as min.

on the x-axis represents a class of schema matchings with a different precision. The z-axis represents the similarity measure. Finally, the y-axis stands for the number of schema matchings from a given precision class and with a given similarity measure.

Two main insights are available from Fig. 3.2. First, the similarity measures of matchings within each schema matching class form a "bell" shape, centered around a specific similarity measure. Such a behavior indicates a certain level of robustness of a schema matcher, assigning close similarity measures to matchings within each class. Second, the "tails" of the bell shapes overlap. Therefore, a schema matching from a class of a lower precision may receive a higher similarity measure than a matching from a class of a higher precision. This, of course, contradicts the monotonicity definition. However, the first observation serves as a motivation for a definition of a statistical monotonicity, first introduced in Gal et al. [2005a], as follows:

Let $\Sigma = \{\sigma_1, \sigma_2, \ldots, \sigma_m\}$ be a set of matchings over schemata S_1 and S_2 with n_1 and n_2 attributes, respectively, and define $n = \max(n_1, n_2)$. Let $\Sigma_1, \Sigma_2, \ldots, \Sigma_{n+1}$ be subsets of Σ such that for all $1 \leq i \leq n + 1$, $\sigma \in \Sigma_i$ iff $\frac{i-1}{n} \leq p(\sigma) < \frac{i}{n}$. We define M_i to be a random variable, representing the similarity measure of a randomly chosen matching from Σ_i. Σ is *statistically monotonic* if the following inequality holds for any $1 \leq i < j \leq n + 1$:

$$\bar{\Omega}(M_i) < \bar{\Omega}(M_j),$$

where $\bar{\Omega}(M)$ stands for the expected value of M.

Intuitively, a schema matching algorithm is statistically monotonic with respect to given two schemata if the expected certainty level increases with precision. Statistical monotonicity can assist us in explaining certain phenomena in schema matching (e.g., why schema matcher ensembles work well [Gal and Sagi, 2010]) and also to serve as a guideline in finding better ways to use schema matching algorithms.

3 Contextual Attribute Correspondences

Attribute correspondences may hold under certain instance conditions. With contextual attribute correspondences, selection conditions are associated with attribute correspondences. Therefore, a contextual attribute correspondence is a triplet of the form (A_i, A_j, c), where A_i and A_j are attributes and c is a condition whose structure is defined in Sect. 3.1.

Example 2. With contextual attribute correspondences, we could state that R.CardInfo.cardNum is the same as S.HotelCardInfo.clientNum if R.CardInfo.type is assigned with the value RoomsRUs. For all other type values, R.CardInfo.cardNum is the same as S.CardInfo.cardNum. These contextual attribute correspondences are given as follows.

(R.CardInfo.cardNum, S.HotelCardInfo.clientNum, R.CardInfo.type = 'RoomsRUs')
(R.CardInfo.cardNum, S.CardInfo.cardNum, R.CardInfo.type ≠ 'RoomsRUs')

Contextual attribute correspondences are useful in overcoming various aspects of structural heterogeneity. A typical example of such heterogeneity involves designer's decision regarding the interpretation of subtypes. In the example above, database R was designed to include all credit card subtypes in a single relation, with type as a differentiating value. Database S refines this decision by allocating a separate relation to one of the subtypes.

In Bohannon et al. [2006], a selection condition is defined as a logical condition, with the added benefit of serving as a basis for the schema mapping process [Barbosa et al., 2005, Bohannon et al., 2005, Fagin, 2006, Fagin et al., 2007].

At the basis of contextual attribute correspondences is the use of instance values as a differentiator between possible correspondences. Therefore, the ability of identifying contextual attribute correspondences depends on the ability of a matcher to take into account instance values. For example, the Term matching technique, given earlier as an example, will not change its estimation of the amount of similarity of two attributes based on context. Instance values are used in many of the methods that apply machine learning techniques to schema matching. Autoplex [Berlin and Motro, 2001], LSD [Doan et al., 2001], and iMAP [Dhamankar et al., 2004] use a naïve Bayes classifier to learn attribute correspondence probabilities using instance training set. Also, sPLMap [Nottelmann and Straccia, 2007] use naïve Bayes, kNN, and KL-distance as content-based classifiers.

3.1 Modeling Contextual Attribute Correspondences

Contextual attribute correspondences are specified in terms of a condition on the value assignments of attributes. A k-context of an attribute correspondence is a condition that involves k database attributes. For $k = 0$, a contextual attribute correspondence becomes a common attribute correspondence. For $k = 1$, the condition is simple, of the form $a = v$, where a is an attribute and v is a constant in a's domain. For example, R.CardInfo.type='RoomsRUs'. Disjunctive, conjunctive, and general k-contexts generalize simple conditions in the usual way. For example, *simple disjunctive k-context* for $k = 1$ is a condition of the form $a \in \{v_1, v_2, \ldots, v_k\}$.

Contextual attribute correspondences can be modeled with similarity matrices. An entry in the similarity matrix $M_{i,j}$ is extended to be a tuple $\langle v, c \rangle$, where $v \in [0, 1]$ is a similarity value and c is a context as defined above. This modeling allows a smooth extension of contextual attribute correspondences to matcher ensembles [Domshlak et al., 2007, He and Chang, 2005], in which matchers are combined to improve the quality of the outcome of the matching process. For example, Do et al. [2002] and Domshlak et al. [2007] proposed several ways to combine similarity matrices, generated by different matchers, into a single matrix. Such combination, which was based solely on aggregating similarity scores, can be extended to also handle condition algebra as proposed in Bohannon et al. [2006]. For example, assume that matcher A matches

(R.CardInfo.cardNum, S.HotelCardInformation.clientNum, R.CardInfo.type = 'RoomsRUs')

with a certainty of 0.8 and matcher B matches

(R.CardInfo.cardNum, S.HotelCardInformation.clientNum, Null)

with a certainty of 0.5. If we use max as the aggregation function, then the entry

(R.CardInfo.cardNum, S.HotelCardInformation.clientNum)

in the combined similarity matrix will contain the tuple $\langle 0.8, \text{R.CardInfo.type} = \text{'RoomsRUs'}\rangle$.

Both context conditions and the constraint function Γ serve in constraining the possible space of correct matchings. Traditionally, Γ was assumed to be given by the designer (e.g., a 1 : 1 matching constraint or a user feedback after an iteration of the matching process). Context, on the other hand, is learned from the domain. However, there is no dichotomy here. One can assume that certain context conditions are given by the designer while some matching constraints are learned from the application. A decision on whether a constraint should be specified in the similarity matrix or as part of the constraint function can be based on the following two observations:

1. The similarity matrix captures information that is inherently uncertain while Γ is defined to be deterministic. Therefore, a context provided by a designer can be considered deterministic and become part of Γ while learned contexts can be embedded at the matrix level.
2. The similarity matrix inherently captures attribute correspondence information while Γ can handle schema level constraints. For example, using only the similarity matrix, one can assume that the contextual attribute correspondence

(R.CardInfo.cardNum, S.HotelCardInformation.clientNum, R.CardInfo.type = 'RoomsRUs')

can coexist with the attribute correspondence

(R.CardInfo.cardNum, S.CardInformation.cardNum)

simply because both entries have a nonzero similarity measure. It is only at the constraint function level Γ that such coexistence can be explicitly forbidden. Therefore, schema level contextual constraint should be modeled using Γ while attribute level constraints are modeled as part of the similarity matrix.

3.2   Finding Contextual Attribute Correspondences

A few challenges arise when designing an algorithm for finding contextual attribute correspondences. First, one may risk overfitting the correspondences to the training data. For example, it is possible that one could find a contextual attribute correspondence stating

(R.CardInfo.expiryMonth, S.HotelCardInformation.expiryMonth, R.CardInfo.securityCode > 333) ,

which is clearly inappropriate, since the security code is associated with the card number and not with its expiry. A naïve classifier may fall into this trap simply by some bias in the training dataset that assigns more cards with higher values of the securityCode attribute.

A second challenge involves situations in which the contextual attribute correspondences are not specializations of (noncontextual) attribute correspondences and therefore, cannot be identified as refinements of the outcome of existing matchers. As an example, consider our case study application. R.HotelInfo.neighborhood provides neighborhood information for medium-size cities. However, for bigger cities, it prefers a more accurate positioning of the hotel, using subway station names as the neighborhood information. Therefore, a possible contextual attribute correspondence may be

(R.HotelInfo.neighborhood, T.Subway.station, R.HotelInfo.city = 'Moscow').

However, this is not a refinement of an attribute correspondence (R.HotelInfo.neighborhood, T.Subway.station).

An approach for discovering contextual matches was introduced in Bohannon et al. [2006]. Let $M_{i,j}$ be the score of matching attributes $S.A_i$ with $S.A_j$. Given a condition c, a matcher can use the subset of the instance problem that satisfies c to provide a new score $M_{i,j}^c$. The difference $M_{i,j}^c - M_{i,j}$ is the *improvement* of the contextual attribute correspondence. Given the set of conditions C, we can create a contextual attribute correspondence using the condition c^* that maximizes the improvement measure. Using an improvement threshold can solve the overfitting challenge. However, thresholds are always tricky. A threshold that is set too low introduces false positives while a threshold that is too high may introduce false negatives. Using machine learning techniques to tune thresholds has proven to be effective in schema matching [Lee et al., 2007]. However, as was shown in Gal [2006], it is impossible to set thresholds that will avoid this false negative/false positive trade-off.

It has been proposed in Bohannon et al. [2006] that k-contexts with $k > 1$ will yield more trustworthy contextual attribute correspondences. The algorithm first determines an initial list of 1-context conditions. Then, it creates and evaluates disjunctive conditions that are generated from the original 1-context conditions. The generation of conditions is carried out using view selection. Views are chosen as promising whenever the data values of some non-categorical attributes are well classified by a categorical attribute. Example 2 provides such a case, where values of R.CardInfo.cardNum have many identical values in S.HotelCardInfo.clientNum whenever the categorical attribute R.CardInfo.type is assigned with the value RoomsRUs.

To avoid false positives, the measure $M_{i,j}^c - M_{i,j}$ is tested for significance against a naïve classifier, which chooses the most common value of a categorical attribute. The number of correct classifications between instances of matched attributes, given a categorical value v, is distributed binomially, with an estimated parameter

$$p = \frac{|v|}{n_{tr}}$$

the ratio is the percentage of occurrences of the value v in the training set. The expected score of such a correspondence is

$$\mu = n_{ts} p$$

(with n_{ts} being the size of the test set) and its standard deviation is

$$\sigma = \sqrt{n_{ts} p(1 - p)}$$

A threshold for the significance of a correspondence is commonly set to be

$$\Phi\left(\frac{c - \mu}{\sigma}\right)$$

(the complementary value of the probability of the null hypothesis), with c being the actual score of the contextual correspondence.

3.3 Identifying Candidate Attributes

A major performance concern is the determination of candidate attributes for contextual attribute correspondences. The approach above is based on context identification using categorical attributes. Clearly, with more categorical attributes, an exhaustive search of all categorical values becomes more expensive. However, even with a small set of categorical values, the attribute candidates for correspondences depends on the number of attributes in the target database.

To improve the run-time of an algorithm for identifying candidate attributes, we propose the use of an algorithm for finding top-K attribute correspondences. Such algorithms were proposed in the literature [Bernstein et al., 2006, Domshlak et al., 2007, Gal et al., 2005a, Gal, 2006], offering a ranked set of attribute correspondences and schema matchings. Empirical results showed the top-K list to be a quality set of candidates for schema matching. Therefore, by taking the top-K

matchings, one can generate a quality, restricted set of candidate attributes against which the algorithm for finding contextual candidate attributes can be tested.

3.4 Discussion

Contextual correspondences improve on noncontextual correspondences in two main aspects. First, it allows the specification of alternative correspondences for the same attribute, under different conditions. Second, its refined definition of a correspondence allows it to connect attributes via correspondences in cases where a common correspondence is too "weak" to be considered valid.

The way contextual correspondences are defined, they are deterministic, not allowing a probabilistic interpretation of a correspondence. Therefore, contextual correspondences are meant to resolve an issue of uncertainty by finding a more refined, yet deterministic, correspondence. It is worth noting, however, that an introduction of stochastic analysis already exists in the form of statistical significance, which can be extended to handle probabilistic mappings as well.

4 Semantic Attribute Correspondences

Traditionally, attribute correspondences are limited to the ontological construct known as *synonym*. The model of semantic matching, introduced in the realm of the semantic Web [Euzenat and Shvaiko, 2007], extends attribute correspondences in that pairwise matching results in an ontological relationship (e.g., equivalence and subsumption) between attributes. Therefore, a semantic attribute correspondence is a triplet of the form (a_i, a_j, r), where a_i and a_j are attributes and r is an ontological relationship. The S-Match system [Giunchiglia et al., 2005] defines four types of such relationships, equivalence ($=$), subsumption ($\sqsubseteq$), disjointness ($\perp$), and unknown (idk). The latter was referred to as intersection ($\cap$) in Magnani et al. [2005]. We shall use S-Match to illustrate the semantic extension to attribute correspondences.

S-Match separates labels from concepts. A label (referred to as *concept at label* in Magnani et al. [2005]) represents its meaning in the real world while a concept is a composite term that considers the label within its path in the semantic graph (e.g., ontology, classification tree). To illustrate the difference, consider the case study and Fig. 3.3. The relational model schema can be interpreted as a semantic graph, in which a relation name is linked with its attribute through a part-of relationship and a primary key is related to its foreign key through a special, foreign-key, relationship. We note here that in Giunchiglia et al. [2005] the type of the semantic link is ignored when computing semantic attribute correspondences. In our case study example, the label city appears multiple times and is considered to have the same real world meaning(s). However, the concept city is different when part of HotelInfo or part of Subway.

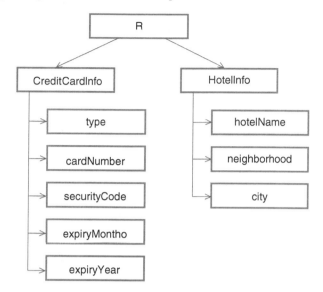

Fig. 3.3 A partial example of a semantic relationship graph

4.1 Finding Semantic Attribute Correspondence

S-Match takes two trees as input and provides for any pair of nodes from the two trees the strongest semantic relation that holds between concepts. A lattice of relationship strength is introduced in Giunchiglia et al. [2005], where for example, equivalence is considered stronger than subsumption. This is performed in four stages, the first two can be performed once for each schema, while the last two are performed whenever two schemas are matched.

The first step identifies the concept of a node. It starts with the node label, which is tokenized and lemmatized. Then, using a thesaurus, such as Wordnet,[2] all senses of the processed label (termed synsets in Wordnet) are retrieved. Finally, after some filtering, a formal statement that defines the node concept is built using disjunctions to separate senses and multiple word labels. For example, consider the relation name HotelInfo. Assume that we can separate this label into Hotel and Info, using capitalization as a hint. Using Wordnet, *Hotel* has senses such as *resort* (hyponym) and *building* (hypernym). *Info* is recognized as a synonym for *information* with senses such as *fact* (hyponym), and *message* (hypernym), creating the following concept:

hotel ∨ resort ∨ building ∨ info ∨ information ∨ fact ∨ message ∨ ...

In the second step, a node is recognized within its path in the graph. Its concept is extended to be a conjunction of all the node concepts leading from the root to

---

[2] http://wordnet.princeton.edu/.

the node. Therefore, the concept of the node HotelInfo.city is the conjunction of the concept HotelInfo and the concept city.

The third step involves the creation of a semantic relationship matrix for each pair of atomic concepts, based on node information only. This can be done either by using common string matching techniques or by using a thesaurus such as Wordnet. For the latter, equivalence is determined if there is at least one sense that is defined as a synonym. Subsumption is determined if a sense in one concept is a hypernym or holonym of a sense in the other concept. Disjointness is defined if two senses of the two concepts are different hyponyms of the same synonym set or if they are antonyms. For example, assume the use of string matching and Wordnet. HotelInfo and HotelCardInformation will be (mistakenly) considered to be equivalent, both because of the identical Hotel label and because Info and Information are synonyms.

The fourth step takes all pairs of nodes and computes a semantic relationship matrix based on the positioning of nodes within their own ontologies. Semantic relations are translated into propositional connectives, with equivalence being translated into equivalence, subsumption into implication, and disjointness into negation. Then, the following formula is checked for satisfiability:

$$C \rightarrow \text{rel}(C_i, C_j).$$

C_i and C_j are the concepts of nodes i and j in the two schemas, as generated in the first step and C is the conjunction of all the relations that hold between concepts of labels mentioned in C_i and C_j (this includes all nodes on the path to nodes i and j). This is done by using a SAT solver to test unsatisfiability. It is worth noting that the unsatisfiability problem is known to be CO-NP, yet modern SAT solvers have shown very good performance in solving such problems. To reason about relations between concepts of nodes, a set of premises (axioms) is built as a conjunction of the concepts of labels computed in the third step. For example, R.CardInfo.type will be defined to be subsumed by S.CardInformation while an equivalence semantic relationship is defined between R.CardInfo.type and S.CardInformation.type.

4.2 Discussion

A few other methods for finding semantic attribute correspondences were suggested in the literature. For example, Chimaera [McGuinness et al., 2000] finds equivalences, subsumptions, and disjointness among attributes (ontology terms in this case). As another example, FCA-Merge [Stumme and Maedche, 2001] identifies subsumptions using a natural language document corpus.

Semantic attribute correspondences can be modeled using the similarity matrix model (see Sect. 2). Each ontological relationship is modeled as a separate matrix (one matrix for equivalence, one for subsumption, etc.). These matrices represent the confidence level in an ontological relationships, as generated in the first two steps of the S-Match algorithm. Steps 3 and 4 of S-Match generate a set of binary matrices, where 1 represents relationship existence and 0 represents no relationship, using some thresholds. During this process, and as part of a constraint enforcer, if the same entry in two matrices is computed to be 1, a lattice of relationships strength determines which values are to remain 1 and which will be lowered to 0. As a final step, any entry for which a 0 value is recorded in all matrices, is assigned 1 for the *idk* matrix. We observe that such modeling may be of much practical value, especially if semantic matching is combined with quantity-based methods (e.g., based on string matching) to create matcher ensembles.

5 Probabilistic Attribute Correspondences

There are many scenarios where a precise schema mapping may not be available. For instance, a comparison search "bot" that tracks comparative prices from different web sites has – in real time – to determine which attributes at a particular location correspond to which attributes in a database at another URL. In many cases, users querying two databases belonging to different organizations may not know what is the right schema mapping. The common model of attribute correspondences assumes a unique and deterministic possible correspondence to each attribute and thus incapable of modeling multiple possibilities.

Probabilistic attribute correspondences extend attribute correspondences by generating multiple possible models, modeling uncertainty about which one is correct by using probability theory. Such probabilities can then be combined to represent possible schema mappings, based on which query processing can be performed.

Example 3. For illustration purposes, consider the case study from Sect. 2. We now describe a scenario, which we dub *semantic shift*, according to which a relation in a database, which was intended for one semantic use, changes its semantic role in the organization database over the years. For example, the relation HotelCardInformation was initially designed to hold information of RoomsRUs credit cards. Over the years, the hotel chain has outsourced the management of its credit cards to an external company, and as a result, the differentiation between hotel credit cards and other credit cards became vague, and new credit cards may be inserted in some arbitrary way to the two relations CardInformation and HotelCardInformation.

Probabilistic attribute correspondences can state that R.CardInfo.cardNum matches S.CardInformation.cardNum with a probability of 0.7 and S.HotelCardInformation.clientNum with a probability of 0.3.

This robust model allows the provision, in the case of aggregate queries, not only a ranking of the results, but also the expected value of the aggregate query outcome and the distribution of possible aggregate values.

The model of probabilistic attribute correspondences is based on the model of probabilistic schema mapping [Dong et al., 2007], extending the concept of schema mapping with probabilities. Let $\overline{S}$ and $\overline{T}$ be relational schemas. A *probabilistic mapping* pM is a triple $(S, T, \mathbf{m})$, where $S \in \overline{S}$, $T \in \overline{T}$, and $\mathbf{m}$ is a set $\{(m_1, Pr(m_1)), \ldots, (m_l, Pr(m_l))\}$, such that

- For $i \in [1, l]$, m_i is a one-to-one relation mapping between S and T, and for every $i, j \in [1, l]$, $i \neq j \Rightarrow m_i \neq m_j$.
- $Pr(m_i) \in [0, 1]$ and $\sum_{i=1}^{l} Pr(m_i) = 1$.

A schema probabilistic mapping $\overline{pM}$ is a set of probabilistic mappings between relations in $\overline{S}$ and in $\overline{T}$, where every relation in either $\overline{S}$ or $\overline{T}$ appears in at most one probabilistic mapping.

A probabilistic attribute correspondence (A_i, A_j, p) is any attribute correspondence in a probabilistic schema mapping.

The intuitive interpretation of a probabilistic schema mapping is that there is uncertainty about which of the mappings is the *right one*. Such uncertainty was justified [Miller et al., 2000] by the fact that "the syntactic representation of schemas and data do not completely convey the semantics of different databases," i.e., the description of a concept in a schema can be semantically misleading. As proposed in Dong et al. [2007], there are two ways in which this uncertainty can be interpreted: either a single mapping should be applied to the entire set of tuples in the source relation, or a choice of a mapping should be made for each of these tuples. The former is referred to as the *by-table* semantics, and the latter as the *by-tuple* semantics. The *by-tuple* semantics represents a situation in which data is gathered from multiple sources, each with a potentially different interpretation of a schema. An example that can illustrate the *by-tuple* semantics is presented in Sect. 3.2. There, R.HotelInfo.neighborhood provides neighborhood information for medium-size cities and subway stations for bigger cities. Here, the semantics is clearly *by-tuple* and not *by-table*.

5.1 Finding Probabilistic Attribute Correspondences

Uncertainty in schema matching gives rise to alternative matchings. It was argued (e.g., Gal et al. 2005a, Heß and Kushmerick 2003) that under certain conditions (e.g., monotonicity [Gal et al., 2005a], see Sect. 2.2), top-K matchings, the K matchings with the highest similarity measures, are the preferred choice of alternative matchings. Intuitively speaking, a schema matcher is *monotonic* if its ranking of all possible matchings is "similar" to that of some oracle, ranking matchings according to the Num of correct attribute correspondences in a matching. Therefore, if the top-K matchings contain many correct attribute correspondences while matchings with lower similarities do not contain as many correct attribute correspondences, the matcher performs monotonically.

As already mentioned earlier, algorithms for identifying top-K correspondences and matchings were proposed in the literature (see Bernstein et al. 2006,

Domshlak et al. 2007, Gal et al. 2005a, Gal 2006), offering a ranked set of attribute correspondences and schema matchings.

We argue that the probability that can be assigned to an attribute correspondence depends on two main factors. First, it depends on the amount of similarity that the matcher(s) of choice assign with this attribute correspondences. This is a natural assumption that lies at the basis of all matching techniques. Second, such probability also depends on the ability of the two attributes to be matched together given the constraints of the matching task (modeled using the Γ function, see Sect. 2). To illustrate this point, consider Example 3. R.CardInfo.cardNum can match well with both S.CardInformation.cardNum and S.HotelCardInformation.clientNum. However, if the application enforces 1 : 1 matching, then despite the high similarity that is assigned with both matches, they will have to "share" the same probability space when matched with R.CardInfo.cardNum.

We use the work of Domshlak et al. [2007] to demonstrate a method for computing probabilistic attribute correspondences. A generic computational framework, *Schema Meta-Matching* was introduced in Domshlak et al. [2007]. This framework computes the top-K matchings using a "consensus" ranking of matchers in an ensemble. The similarity of attribute correspondences is provided by members of a schema matching ensemble and combined to generate a consensus ranking. For example, an ensemble may include a string-matching matcher (e.g., Term) and a domain-based matcher (e.g., Value).

Each member in an ensemble uses a local aggregation function (such as average) to generate a schema matching similarity measure from the similarity measures of the attribute correspondences. Local similarity measures can then be aggregated using a global similarity measure (e.g., max) to become the ensemble similarity measure.

A *Meta-Matching* algorithm is used to generate the Top-K schema matchings according to this similarity measure. The work in Domshlak et al. [2007] supports four algorithms for top-K schema matching alternative generation. The Threshold algorithm, originally proposed in the context of database middleware [Fagin et al., 2003], is applied almost as is, yet may require time exponential in the size of the matched schemata. For a certain wide class of problems, the Matrix-Direct algorithm, a simple variation of the COMA algorithm [Do and Rahm, 2002], was introduced. The time complexity of the Matrix-Direct algorithm is polynomial in the size of the matched schemata and the required K. Subsequently, the Matrix-Direct-with-Bounding algorithm was introduced, which draws upon both the Matrix-Direct and the Threshold algorithms, addressing matching scenarios where the Matrix-Direct algorithm is inapplicable. It was shown in Domshlak et al. [2007] that the Threshold and Matrix-Direct-with-Bounding algorithms are (complexity-wise) mutually undominated – that is, there exist problem instances in which one algorithm performs dramatically better than the other. To enjoy the best of both worlds and even to improve upon them, the CrossThreshold algorithm was introduced, a hybrid version of these two algorithms, based on their in-parallel, mutually enhancing execution.

Given a user defined K or a threshold on the minimum certainty, the system can produce alternative matchings and assign a probability estimate of correctness to each of them. The probability is based on the similarity measure, as assigned by an ensemble of matchers. To justify this method, we use the monotonicity principle, as discussed before.

Equipped with the monotonicity principle, one can generate a probability space over a set of K matchings, as follows. Let $(\mu_1, \mu_2, \ldots, \mu_k)$ be the similarity measures of the top-K matchings $(\sigma_1, \sigma_2, \ldots, \sigma_k)$ and $\mu_1 > 0$. The probability assigned with matching i is computed to be:

$$p_i = \frac{\mu_i}{\sum_{j=1}^{k} \mu_j}$$

p_i is well defined (since $\mu_1 > 0$). Each p_i is assigned with a value in $[0, 1]$ and $\sum_{j=1}^{k} p_i = 1$. Therefore, $(p_1, p_2, \ldots, p_k)$ forms a probability space over the set of top-K matchings. For completeness, we argue that an appropriate interpretation of this probability space is to consider it to be the conditional probability, given that the exact matching is known to be within the top-K matchings.

We can create the probability that is assigned with an attribute correspondence (A_i, A_j) by summing all probabilities of schema matchings in which (A_i, A_j) appears. That is, for a probabilistic attribute correspondence (A_i, A_j, p) we compute p to be:

$$p = \sum_{\sigma_l | (A_i, A_j) \in \sigma_l} p_l$$

It is worth noting that methods for assigning attributes to alternative schema mappings were also suggested by other researchers, such as Magnani et al. [2005].

6 Conclusions

This chapter introduces three recent advances to the state-of-the-art, extending the abilities of attribute correspondences. *Contextual attribute correspondences* associate selection conditions with attribute correspondences. *Semantic matching* extends attribute correspondences to be specified in terms of ontological relationship. Finally, *probabilistic attribute correspondences* extend attribute correspondences by generating multiple possible models, modeling uncertainty about which one is correct by using probability theory.

These three extensions are individually powerful in extending the expressive power of attribute correspondences. However, combining them together can generate an even more powerful model. For example, combining all the three, one can declare that attribute A subsumes attribute B if the condition $C = c$ holds true. If $C \neq c$, then there is a 70% chance that attribute A is actually subsumed by attribute B and 30% chance that they are disjoint. Therefore, we conclude by identifying the challenges and benefits of putting these extensions together.

The first observation is that top-K schema matchings play a pivotal role in identifying attribute correspondences. We have shown that top-K matchings can serve in identifying both good candidates for contextual attribute correspondences and probabilistic attribute correspondences. In this research direction, there are still many open questions, first of which is the ability to identify top-K matchings in polynomial time.

A model was proposed in Magnani et al. [2005] for combining semantic and probabilistic attribute correspondences using constructs of uncertain semantic relationships in an ER model. An uncertain semantic relationship is a distribution of beliefs over the set of all possible semantic relationships, using belief functions [Shafer, 1976]. The set of possible semantic relations serve as the *frame of discernment* (marked Θ), based on which two functions are defined, namely *belief* and *plausability*. Both functions assign a value to a subset of the frame of discernment, starting from the basic probability mass that is assigned with each element in the frame of discernment. Belief of a set $A \in \Theta$ sums the probability mass of all subsets $B \subseteq A$. Plausability of a set A is the sum of all subsets that intersect with A, i.e., all B such that $A \cap B \neq \varnothing$.

Combining semantic and probabilistic attribute correspondences (as proposed in Magnani et al. [2005], for example) can be easily captured by the matrix abstraction. In Sect. 4.2, we have outlined the way semantic attribute correspondences can be captured using similarity matrices. When using the model proposed in Magnani et al. [2005], the aggregator can be Dempster's combination rule [Shafer, 1976]. Consider now that entries in each such matrix are in [0, 1], reflecting probability (or plausability) of this semantic attribute correspondence to hold. This will open a new challenge of querying a database that uses probabilistic semantic attribute correspondences. First, the notion of querying using semantic attribute correspondences should be examined carefully. Then analysis, similar to the analysis done in Dong et al. [2007] and Gal et al. [2009], where possible worlds semantics was carefully defined for probabilistic schema mapping, can be extended to the case of probabilistic semantic attribute correspondences. It is worth noting that the analysis in Magnani et al. [2005] described a de-facto set of possible worlds, each world represented by a different ER schema.

Contextual and by-tuple probabilistic attribute correspondences seem to be complementary. A by-tuple probabilistic attribute correspondence represents a situation in which there is uncertainty as to whether a given tuple should be interpreted using one correspondence or the other. Contextual attribute correspondences models exactly such knowledge. Therefore, By-tuple probabilistic attribute correspondence is needed whenever no information regarding the contextual attribute correspondence is available. Whenever contextual attribute correspondence is gathered automatically, using statistical methods as described in Sect. 3.2, another layer of uncertainty is added to the modeling. Therefore, contextual attribute correspondences should also be extended to provide probabilistic alternative versions.

Acknowledgments I thank Wenfei Fan, Pavel Shvaiko, Luna Dong, and Tomer Sagi for useful comments. The views and conclusions contained in this chapter are those of the author.

References

Barbosa D, Freire J, Mendelzon A (2005) Designing information-preserving mapping schemes for xml. In: Proceedings of the international conference on very large data bases (VLDB), Trondheim, Norway, August 2005. VLDB Endowment, pp 109–120

Berlin J, Motro A (2001) Autoplex: Automated discovery of content for virtual databases. In: Batini C, Giunchiglia F, Giorgini P, Mecella M (eds) Cooperative information systems, 9th international conference, CoopIS 2001, Trento, Italy, 5–7 September 2001. Proceedings, Lecture Notes in Computer Science, vol 2172. Springer, Heidelberg, pp 108–122

Bernstein P, Melnik S, Churchill J (2006) Incremental schema matching. In: Proceedings of the international conference on very large data bases (VLDB), Seoul, Korea, September 2006. VLDB Endowment, pp 1167–1170

Bohannon P, Fan W, Flaster M, Narayan P (2005) Information preserving xml schema embedding. In: Proceedings of the international conference on very large data bases (VLDB), Trondheim, Norway, August 2005. VLDB Endowment, pp 85–96

Bohannon P, Elnahrawy E, Fan W, Flaster M (2006) Putting context into schema matching. In: Proceedings of the international conference on very large data bases (VLDB), Seoul, Korea, September 2006. VLDB Endowment, pp 307–318

Dhamankar R, Lee Y, Doan A, Halevy A, Domingos P (2004) iMAP: Discovering complex mappings between database schemas. In: Proceedings of the ACM-SIGMOD conference on management of data (SIGMOD), Paris, France, June 2004. ACM, NY, pp 383–394

Do H, Rahm E (2002) COMA – a system for flexible combination of schema matching approaches. In: Proceedings of the international conference on very large data bases (VLDB), Hong Kong, China, August 2002. VLDB Endowment, pp 610–621

Do H, Melnik S, Rahm E (2002) Comparison of schema matching evaluations. In: Proceedings of the 2nd international workshop on web databases, German Informatics Society, 2002. citeseer.nj.nec.com/do02comparison.html

Doan A, Domingos P, Halevy A (2001) Reconciling schemas of disparate data sources: A machine-learning approach. In: Aref WG (ed) Proceedings of the ACM-SIGMOD conference on management of data (SIGMOD), Santa Barbara, CA, June 2001. ACM, CA, pp 509–520

Domshlak C, Gal A, Roitman H (2007) Rank aggregation for automatic schema matching. IEEE Trans Knowl Data Eng (TKDE) 19(4):538–553

Dong X, Halevy A, Yu C (2007) Data integration with uncertainty. In: Proceedings of the international conference on very large data bases (VLDB), Vienna, Austria, September 2007. VLDB Endowment, pp 687–698

Euzenat J, Shvaiko P (2007) Ontology matching. Springer, Heidelberg

Fagin R (2006) Inverting schema mappings. In: Proceedings of the ACM SIGACT-SIGMOD-SIGART symposium on principles of database systems (PODS), Chicago, IL, June 2006. ACM, NY, pp 50–59

Fagin R, Lotem A, Naor M (2003) Optimal aggregation algorithms for middleware. J Comput Syst Sci 66:614–656

Fagin R, Kolaitis P, Popa L, Tan W (2007) Quasi-inverses of schema mappings. In: Proceedings of the ACM SIGACT-SIGMOD-SIGART symposium on principles of database systems (PODS), Beijing, China, June 2007. ACM, NY, pp 123–132

Gal A (2006) Managing uncertainty in schema matching with top-k schema mappings. J Data Semant 6:90–114

Gal A, Sagi T (2010) Tuning the ensemble selection process of schema matchers. Inform Syst 35(8):845–859

Gal A, Shvaiko P (2009) Advances in ontology matching. In: Dillon TS, Chang E, Meersman R, Sycara K (eds) Web services and applied semantic web. Springer, Heidelberg, pp 176–198

Gal A, Anaby-Tavor A, Trombetta A, Montesi D (2005a) A framework for modeling and evaluating automatic semantic reconciliation. VLDB J 14(1):50–67

Gal A, Modica G, Jamil H, Eyal A (2005b) Automatic ontology matching using application semantics. AI Mag 26(1):21–32

Gal A, Martinez M, Simari G, Subrahmanian V (2009) Aggregate query answering under uncertain schema mappings. In: Proceedings of the IEEE CS international conference on data engineering, Shanghai, China, March 2009. IEEE Computer Society, Washington, DC, pp 940–951

Giunchiglia F, Shvaiko P, Yatskevich M (2005) Semantic schema matching. In: Proceedings of the 10th international conference on cooperative information systems (CoopIS 2005), pp 347–365

He B, Chang KC (2005) Making holistic schema matching robust: An ensemble approach. In: Proceedings of the 11th ACM SIGKDD international conference on knowledge discovery and data mining, Chicago, IL, 21–24 August 2005. ACM, NY, pp 429–438

He B, Chang KCC (2003) Statistical schema matching across Web query interfaces. In: Proceedings of the ACM-SIGMOD conference on management of data (SIGMOD), San Diego, CA, June 2003. ACM, NY, pp 217–228

Heß A, Kushmerick N (2003) Learning to attach semantic metadata to web services. In: Proceedings of the 2nd semantic web conference, Sanibel Island, FL, 2003. Springer, Heidelberg, pp 258–273

Lee Y, Sayyadian M, Doan A, Rosenthal A (2007) eTuner: Tuning schema matching software using synthetic scenarios. VLDB J 16(1):97–122

Madhavan J, Bernstein P, Rahm E (2001) Generic schema matching with cupid. In: Proceedings of the international conference on very large data bases (VLDB), Rome, Italy, September 2001. Morgan Kaufmann, CA, pp 49–58

Magnani M, Rizopoulos N, McBrien P, Montesi D (2005) Schema integration based on uncertain semantic mappings. In: Delcambre LML, Kop C, Mayr HC, Mylopoulos J, Pastor O (eds) ER. LNCS, vol 3716. Springer, Heidelberg, pp 31–46

Marie A, Gal A (2007) On the stable marriage of maximumweight royal couples. In: Proceedings of AAAI workshop on information integration on the web (IIWeb'07), Vancouver, BC, Canada

Marie A, Gal A (2008) Boosting schema matchers. In: Proceedings of the 13th international conference on cooperative information systems (CoopIS 2008), Monterrey, Mexico, November 2008. Springer, Heidelberg, pp 283–300

McGuinness D, Fikes R, Rice J, Wilder S (2000) An environment for merging and testing large ontologies. In: Proceedings of the 7th international conference on principles of knowledge representation and reasoning (KR2000), Breckenridge, CO, April 2000. Morgan Kaufmann, CA, pp 483–493

Miller R, Haas L, Hernández M (2000) Schema mapping as query discovery. In: Abbadi AE, Brodie M, Chakravarthy S, Dayal U, Kamel N, Schlageter G, Whang KY (eds) Proceedings of the international conference on very large data bases (VLDB), September 2000. Morgan Kaufmann, CA, pp 77–88

Nottelmann H, Straccia U (2007) Information retrieval and machine learning for probabilistic schema matching. Inform Process Manag 43(3):552–576

Popa L, Velegrakis Y, Miller R, Hernández M, Fagin R (2002) Translating web data. In: Proceedings of the international conference on very large data bases (VLDB), Hong Kong, China, August 2002. VLDB Endowment, pp 598–609

Shafer G (ed) (1976) A mathematical theory of evidence. Princeton University Press, NJ

Stumme G, Maedche A (2001) Ontology merging for federated ontologies in the semantic web. In: Proceedings of the international workshop for foundations of models for information integration (FMII-2001), Viterbo, Italy, pp 413–418

Su W, Wang J, Lochovsky F (2006) Aholistic schema matching for web query interfaces. In: Advances in database technology – EDBT 2006, 10th international conference on extending database technology, Munich, Germany, 26–31 March 2006. Proceedings, pp 77–94

Vinson A, Heuser C, da Silva A, de Moura E (2007) An approach to xml path matching. In: WIDM '07: Proceedings of the 9th annual ACM international workshop on Web information and data management. ACM, NY, pp 17–24. doi:http://doi.acm.org/10.1145/1316902.1316906

Chapter 4
Uncertainty in Data Integration and Dataspace Support Platforms

Anish Das Sarma, Xin Luna Dong, and Alon Y. Halevy

Abstract Data integration has been an important area of research for several years. However, such systems suffer from one of the main drawbacks of database systems: the need to invest significant modeling effort upfront. Dataspace support platforms (DSSP) envision a system that offers useful services on its data without any setup effort and that improves with time in a pay-as-you-go fashion. We argue that to support DSSPs, the system needs to model uncertainty at its core. We describe the concepts of probabilistic mediated schemas and probabilistic mappings as enabling concepts for DSSPs.

1 Introduction

Data integration and exchange systems offer a uniform interface to a multitude of data sources and the ability to share data across multiple systems. These systems have recently enjoyed significant research and commercial success (Halevy et al. 2005, 2006b). Current data integration systems are essentially a natural extension of traditional database systems in that queries are specified in a structured form and data are modeled in one of the traditional data models (relational, XML). In addition, the data integration system has exact knowledge of how the data in the sources map to the schema are used by the data integration system.

A.D. Sarma (✉)
Yahoo! Research, 2-GA 2231, Santa Clara, CA 95051, USA
e-mail: anish@yahoo-inc.com

X.L. Dong
AT&T Labs – Research, 180 Park Ave., Florham Park, NJ 07932, USA
e-mail: lunadong@research.att.com

A.Y. Halevy
Google Inc., 1600 Amphitheatre Blvd, Mountain View, CA 94043, USA
e-mail: halevy@google.com

Z. Bellahsene et al. (eds.), *Schema Matching and Mapping*, Data-Centric Systems and Applications, DOI 10.1007/978-3-642-16518-4_4,
© Springer-Verlag Berlin Heidelberg 2011

In this chapter, we argue that as the scope of data integration applications broadens, such systems need to be able to model uncertainty at their core. Uncertainty can arise for multiple reasons in data integration. First, the semantic mappings between the data sources and the mediated schema may be approximate. For example, in an application like Google Base (GoogleBase 2005) that enables anyone to upload structured data, or when mapping millions of sources on the deep Web (Madhavan et al. 2007), we cannot imagine specifying exact mappings. In some domains (e.g., bioinformatics), we do not necessarily know what the exact mapping is. Second, data are often extracted from unstructured sources using information extraction techniques. Since these techniques are approximate, the data obtained from the sources may be uncertain. Third, if the intended users of the application are not necessarily familiar with schemata, or if the domain of the system is too broad to offer form-based query interfaces (such as Web forms), we need to support keyword queries. Hence, another source of uncertainty is the transformation between keyword queries and a set of candidate structured queries. Finally, if the scope of the domain is very broad, there can even be uncertainty about the concepts in the mediated schema.

Another reason for data integration systems to model uncertainty is to support *pay-as-you-go* integration. Dataspace Support Platforms (Halevy et al. 2006a) envision data integration systems where sources are added with no effort and the system is constantly evolving in a pay-as-you-go fashion to improve the quality of semantic mappings and query answering. This means that as the system evolves, there will be uncertainty about the semantic mappings to its sources, its mediated schema, and even the semantics of the queries posed to it.

This chapter describes some of the formal foundations for data integration with uncertainty. We define probabilistic schema mappings and probabilistic mediated schemas and show how to answer queries in their presence. With these foundations, we show that it is possible to completely automatically bootstrap a pay-as-you-go integration system.

This chapter is largely based on previous papers (Dong et al. 2007; Sarma et al. 2008). The proofs of the theorems we state and the experimental results validating some of our claims can be found there in. We also place several other works on uncertainty in data integration in the context of the system we envision. In the next section, we describe an architecture for data integration system that incorporates uncertainty.

2 Overview of the System

This section describes the requirements from a data integration system that supports uncertainty and the overall architecture of the system.

2.1   Uncertainty in Data Integration

A data integration system needs to handle uncertainty at four levels.

Uncertain mediated schema: The mediated schema is the set of schema terms in which queries are posed. They do not necessarily cover all the attributes appearing in any of the sources, but rather the aspects of the domain that the application builder wishes to expose to the users. Uncertainty in the mediated schema can arise for several reasons. First, as we describe in Sect. 4, if the mediated schema is automatically inferred from the data sources in a pay-as-you-go integration system, there will be some uncertainty about the results. Second, when domains get broad, there will be some uncertainty about how to model the domain. For example, if we model all the topics in Computer Science, there will be some uncertainty about the degree of overlap between different topics.

Uncertain schema mappings: Data integration systems rely on schema mappings for specifying the semantic relationships between the data in the sources and the terms used in the mediated schema. However, schema mappings can be inaccurate. In many applications, it is impossible to create and maintain precise mappings between data sources. This can be because the users are not skilled enough to provide precise mappings, such as in personal information management (Dong and Halevy 2005), since people do not understand the domain well and thus do not even know what correct mappings are, such as in bioinformatics, or since the scale of the data prevents generating and maintaining precise mappings, such as in integrating data of the Web scale (Madhavan et al. 2007). Hence, in practice, schema mappings are often generated by semiautomatic tools and not necessarily verified by domain experts.

Uncertain data: By nature, data integration systems need to handle uncertain data. One reason for uncertainty is that data are often extracted from unstructured or semistructured sources by automatic methods (e.g., HTML pages, emails, blogs). A second reason is that data may come from sources that are unreliable or not up to date. For example, in enterprise settings, it is common for informational data such as gender, racial, and income level to be dirty or missing, even when the transactional data are precise.

Uncertain queries: In some data integration applications, especially on the Web, queries will be posed as keywords rather than as structured queries against a well-defined schema. The system needs to translate these queries into some structured form so that they can be reformulated with respect to the data sources. At this step, the system may generate multiple candidate structured queries and have some uncertainty about which is the real intent of the user.

2.2 System Architecture

Given the previously discussed requirements, we describe the architecture of a data integration system we envision that manages uncertainty at its core. We describe the system by contrasting it to a traditional data integration system.

The first and most fundamental characteristic of this system is that it is based on a probabilistic data model. This means that we attach probabilities to the following:

- Tuples that we process in the system
- Schema mappings
- Mediated schemas
- Possible interpretations of keyword queries posed to the system

In contrast, a traditional data integration system includes a single mediated schema and a single (and supposed to be correct) schema mapping between the mediated schema and each source. The data in the sources are also assumed to be correct.

Traditional data integration systems assume that the query is posed in a structured fashion (i.e., can be translated to some subset of SQL). Here, we assume that queries can be posed as keywords (to accommodate a much broader class of users and applications). Hence, whereas traditional data integration systems begin by reformulating a query onto the schemas of the data sources, a data integration system with uncertainty needs to first reformulate a keyword query into a set of candidate structured queries. We refer to this step as *keyword reformulation*. Note that keyword reformulation is different from techniques for keyword search on structured data (e.g., Agrawal et al. 2002; Hristidis and Papakonstantinou 2002) in that (a) it does not assume access to all the data in the sources or that the sources support keyword search and (b) it tries to distinguish different structural elements in the query to pose more precise queries to the sources (e.g., realizing that in the keyword query "Chicago weather," "weather" is an attribute label and "Chicago" is an instance name). That being said, keyword reformulation should benefit from techniques that support answering keyword search on structured data.

The query answering model is different. Instead of necessarily finding *all* answers to a given query, our goal is typically to find the top-k answers and rank these answers most effectively.

The final difference from traditional data integration systems is that our query processing will need to be more adaptive than usual. Instead of generating a query answering plan and executing it, the steps we take in query processing will depend on results of previous steps. We note that adaptive query processing has been discussed quite a bit in data integration (Alon Levy 2000), where the need for adaptivity arises from the fact that data sources did not answer as quickly as expected or that we did not have accurate statistics about their contents to properly order our operations. In our work, however, the goal for adaptivity is to get the answers with high probabilities faster.

The architecture of the system is shown in Fig. 4.1. The system contains a number of data sources and a mediated schema (we omit probabilistic mediated schemas from this figure). When the user poses a query Q, which can be either a structured

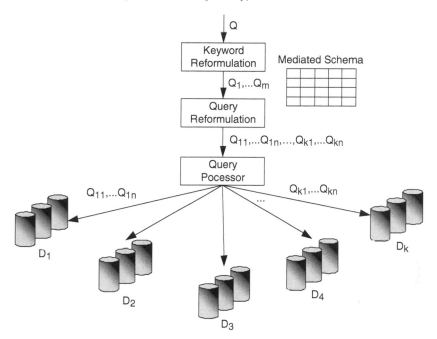

Fig. 4.1   Architecture of a data-integration system that handles uncertainty

query on the mediated schema or a keyword query, the system returns a set of answer tuples, each with a probability. If Q is a keyword query, the system first performs keyword reformulation to translate it into a set of candidate structured queries on the mediated schema. Otherwise, the candidate query is Q itself.

2.3   Source of Probabilities

A critical issue in any system that manages uncertainty is whether we have a reliable source of probabilities. Whereas obtaining reliable probabilities for such a system is one of the most interesting areas for future research, there is quite a bit to build on. For keyword reformulation, it is possible to train and test reformulators on large numbers of queries such that each reformulation result is given a probability based on its performance statistics. For information extraction, current techniques are often based on statistical machine learning methods and can be extended to compute probabilities of each extraction result. Finally, in the case of schema matching, it is standard practice for schema matchers to also associate numbers with the candidates they propose (e.g., Berlin and Motro 2002; Dhamankar et al. 2004; Do and Rahm 2002; Doan et al. 2002; He and Chang 2003; Kang and Naughton 2003; Rahm and Bernstein 2001; Wang et al. 2004). The issue here is that the numbers are meant only as a ranking mechanism rather than true probabilities. However, as schema matching techniques start looking at a larger number of schemas, one can imagine ascribing probabilities (or estimations thereof) to their measures.

2.4 Outline of the Chapter

We begin by discussing probabilistic schema mappings in Sect. 3. We also discuss how to answer queries in their presence and how to answer top-k queries. In Sect. 4, we discuss probabilistic mediated schemas. We begin by motivating them and showing that in some cases they add expressive power to the resulting system. Then, we describe an algorithm for generating probabilistic mediated schemas from a collection of data sources.

3 Uncertainty in Mappings

The key to resolving heterogeneity at the schema level is to specify schema mappings between data sources. These mappings describe the relationship between the contents of the different sources and are used to reformulate a query posed over one source (or a mediated schema) into queries over the sources that are deemed relevant. However, in many applications, we are not able to provide all the schema mappings upfront. In this section, we describe how we use probabilistic schema mappings (p-mappings, defined in Definition 3 in Chap. 3) to capture uncertainty on mappings between schemas.

We start by presenting a running example for this section that also motivates p-mappings (Sect. 3.1). Then, Sect. 3.2 formally defines its semantics in query answering. After that, Sect. 3.3 describes algorithms for query answering with respect to probabilistic mappings and discusses the complexity. Next, Sect. 3.4 shows how to leverage previous work on schema matching to automatically create probabilistic mappings. In the end, Sect. 3.5 briefly describes various extensions to the basic definition, and Sect. 3.6 describes other types of approximate schema mappings that have been proposed in the literature.

3.1 Motivating Probabilistic Mappings

Example 1. Consider a data source S, which describes a person by her email address, current address, and permanent address, and the mediated schema T, which describes a person by her name, email, mailing address, home address, and office address:

```
S=(pname, email-addr, current-addr, permanent-addr)
T=(name, email, mailing-addr, home-addr, office-addr)
```

A semiautomatic schema-mapping tool may generate three possible mappings between S and T, assigning each a probability. Whereas the three mappings all map pname to name, they map other attributes in the source and the target differently. Figure 4.2a describes the three mappings using sets of attribute correspondences. For example, mapping m_1 maps pname to name, email-addr to email, current-addr to mailing-addr, and permanent-addr to home-addr. Because of the uncertainty about which mapping is correct, we consider all of these mappings in query answering.

Suppose the system receives a query Q composed on the mediated schema and asking for people's mailing addresses:

```
Q: SELECT mailing-addr FROM T
```

Using the possible mappings, we can reformulate Q into different queries:

```
Q1: SELECT current-addr FROM S
Q2: SELECT permanent-addr FROM S
Q3: SELECT email-addr FROM S
```

If the user requires all possible answers, the system generates a single aggregation query based on Q_1, Q_2, and Q_3 to compute the probability of each returned tuple and sends the query to the data source. Suppose the data source contains a table D_S as shown in Fig. 4.2b, the system will retrieve four answer tuples, each with a probability, as shown in Fig. 4.2c.

If the user requires only the top-1 answer (i.e., the answer tuple with the highest probability), the system decides at runtime which reformulated queries to execute. For example, after executing Q_1 and Q_2 at the source, the system can already conclude that ("Sunnyvale") is the top-1 answer and can skip query Q_3.   □

Possible Mapping	Prob
$m_1 =$ {(pname, name), (email-addr, email), (current-addr, mailing-addr), (permanent-addr, home-addr)}	0.5
$m_2 =$ {(pname, name), (email-addr, email), (permanent-addr, mailing-addr), (current-addr, home-addr)}	0.4
$m_3 =$ {(pname, name), (email-addr, mailing-addr), (current-addr, home-addr)}	0.1

(a)

pname	email-addr	current-addr	permanent-addr
Alice	alice@	Mountain View	Sunnyvale
Bob	bob@	Sunnyvale	Sunnyvale

(b)

Tuple (mailing-addr)	Prob
('Sunnyvale')	0.9
('Mountain View')	0.5
('alice@')	0.1
('bob@')	0.1

(c)

Fig. 4.2 The running example: (**a**) a probabilistic schema mapping between S and T; (**b**) a source instance D_S; (**c**) the answers of Q over D_S with respect to the probabilistic mapping

3.2 Definition and Semantics

3.2.1   Schema Mappings and p-Mappings

We begin by reviewing nonprobabilistic schema mappings. The goal of a schema mapping is to specify the semantic relationships between a *source schema* and a *target schema*. We refer to the source schema as $\bar{S}$, and a relation in $\bar{S}$ as $S = \langle s_1, \ldots, s_m \rangle$. Similarly, we refer to the target schema as $\bar{T}$, and a relation in $\bar{T}$ as $T = \langle t_1, \ldots, t_n \rangle$.

We consider a limited form of schema mappings that are also referred to as *schema matching* in the literature. Specifically, a schema matching contains a set of *attribute correspondences*. An attribute correspondence is of the form $c_{ij} = (s_i, t_j)$, where s_i is a *source attribute* in the schema S and t_j is a *target attribute* in the schema T. Intuitively, c_{ij} specifies that there is a relationship between s_i and t_j. In practice, a correspondence also involves a function that transforms the value of s_i to the value of t_j. For example, the correspondence (c-degree, temperature) can be specified as temperature=c-degree $*1.8 + 32$, describing a transformation from Celsius to Fahrenheit. These functions are irrelevant to our discussion, and therefore, we omit them. This class of mappings are quite common in practice and already expose many of the novel issues involved in probabilistic mappings. In Sect. 3.5, we will briefly discuss extensions to a broader class of mappings.

Formally, relation mappings and schema mappings are defined as follows.

Definition 1 (Schema Mapping). Let $\bar{S}$ and $\bar{T}$ be relational schemas. A *relation mapping M* is a triple (S, T, m), where S is a relation in $\bar{S}$, T is a relation in $\bar{T}$, and m is a set of attribute correspondences between S and T.

When each source and target attribute occurs in at most one correspondence in m, we call M a *one-to-one relation mapping*.

A *schema mapping* $\overline{M}$ is a set of one-to-one relation mappings between relations in $\bar{S}$ and in $\bar{T}$, where every relation in either $\bar{S}$ or $\bar{T}$ appears at most once. □

A pair of instances D_S and D_T *satisfies* a relation mapping m if for every source tuple $t_s \in D_S$, there exists a target tuple $t_t \in D_t$, such that for every attribute correspondence $(s, t) \in m$, the value of attribute s in t_s is the same as the value of attribute t in t_t.

Example 2. Consider the mappings in Example 1. The source database in Fig. 4.2b (repeated in Fig. 4.3a) and the target database in Fig. 4.3b satisfy m_1. □

Intuitively, a probabilistic schema mapping describes a probability distribution of a set of *possible* schema mappings between a source schema and a target schema. For completeness, we repeat its definition as follows (also see Definition 3 in Chap. 3).

Definition 2 (Probabilistic Mapping). Let $\bar{S}$ and $\bar{T}$ be relational schemas. A *probabilistic mapping (p-mapping)*, pM, is a triple $(S, T, \mathbf{m})$, where $S \in \bar{S}, T \in \bar{T}$, and $\mathbf{m}$ is a set $\{(m_1, Pr(m_1)), \ldots, (m_l, Pr(m_l))\}$, such that

pname	email-addr	current-addr	permanent-addr
Alice	alice@	Mountain View	Sunnyvale
Bob	bob@	Sunnyvale	Sunnyvale

(a)

name	email	mailing-addr	home-addr	office-addr
Alice	alice@	Mountain View	Sunnyvale	office
Bob	bob@	Sunnyvale	Sunnyvale	office

(b)

name	email	mailing-addr	home-addr	office-addr
Alice	alice@	Sunnyvale	Mountain View	office
Bob	email	bob@	Sunnyvale	office

(c)

Tuple (mailing-addr)	Prob
('Sunnyvale')	0.9
('Mountain View')	0.5
('alice@')	0.1
('bob@')	0.1

(d)

Tuple (mailing-addr)	Prob
('Sunnyvale')	0.94
('Mountain View')	0.5
('alice@')	0.1
('bob@')	0.1

(e)

Fig. 4.3 Example 3: (**a**) a source instance D_S; (**b**) a target instance that is by-table consistent with D_S and m_1; (**c**) a target instance that is by-tuple consistent with D_S and $< m_2, m_3 >$; (**d**) $Q^{\text{table}}(D_S)$; (**e**) $Q^{\text{tuple}}(D_S)$

- For $i \in [1, l]$, m_i is a one-to-one mapping between S and T, and for every $i, j \in [1, l], i \neq j \Rightarrow m_i \neq m_j$.
- $Pr(m_i) \in [0, 1]$ and $\sum_{i=1}^{l} Pr(m_i) = 1$.

A *schema p-mapping*, $\overline{pM}$, is a set of p-mappings between relations in $\bar{S}$ and in $\bar{T}$, where every relation in either $\bar{S}$ or $\bar{T}$ appears in at most one p-mapping.   □

We refer to a nonprobabilistic mapping as an *ordinary mapping*. A schema p-mapping may contain both p-mappings and ordinary mappings. Example 1 shows a p-mapping (see Fig. 4.2a) that contains three possible mappings.

3.2.2 Semantics of Probabilistic Mappings

Intuitively, a probabilistic schema mapping models the uncertainty about which of the mappings in pM is the correct one. When a schema matching system produces a set of candidate matches, there are two ways to interpret the uncertainty: (1) a single mapping in pM is the correct one, and it applies to all the data in S, or (2) several mappings are partially correct, and each is suitable for a subset of tuples in S, though it is not known which mapping is the right one for a specific tuple. Figure 4.3b illustrates the first interpretation and applies mapping m_1. For the same example, the second interpretation is equally valid: some people may choose to use their current address as mailing address, while others use their permanent address as mailing address; thus, for different tuples, we may apply different mappings so that the correct mapping depends on the particular tuple.

We define query answering under both interpretations. The first interpretation is referred to as the *by-table* semantics, and the second one is referred to as the *by-tuple* semantics of probabilistic mappings. Note that one cannot argue for one interpretation over the other; the needs of the application should dictate the appropriate semantics. Furthermore, the complexity results for query answering, which will show advantages to by-table semantics, should not be taken as an argument in the favor of by-table semantics.

We next define query answering with respect to p-mappings in detail, and the definitions for schema p-mappings are the obvious extensions. Recall that given a query and an ordinary mapping, we can compute *certain answers* to the query with respect to the mapping. Query answering with respect to p-mappings is defined as a natural extension of certain answers, which we next review.

A mapping defines a relationship between instances of S and instances of T that are *consistent* with the mapping.

Definition 3 (Consistent Target Instance). Let $M = (S, T, m)$ be a relation mapping and D_S be an instance of S.

An instance D_T of T is said to be *consistent with D_S and M*, if for each tuple $t_s \in D_S$ there exists a tuple $t_t \in D_T$, such that for every attribute correspondence $(a_s, a_t) \in m$ the value of a_s in t_s is the same as the value of a_t in t_t.   □

For a relation mapping M and a source instance D_S, there can be an infinite number of target instances that are consistent with D_S and M. We denote by $Tar_M(D_S)$ the set of all such target instances. The set of answers to a query Q is the intersection of the answers on all instances in $Tar_M(D_S)$.

Definition 4 (Certain Answer). Let $M = (S, T, m)$ be a relation mapping. Let Q be a query over T and let D_S be an instance of S.

A tuple t is said to be a *certain answer of Q with respect to D_S and M*, if for every instance $D_T \in Tar_M(D_S), t \in Q(D_T)$.   □

By-table semantics: We now generalize these notions to the probabilistic setting, beginning with the by-table semantics. Intuitively, a p-mapping pM describes a set of possible worlds, each with a possible mapping $m \in pM$. In by-table semantics, a source table can fall in one of the possible worlds, that is, the possible mapping associated with that possible world applies to the whole source table. Following this intuition, we define target instances that are *consistent with* the source instance.

Definition 5 (By-table Consistent Instance). Let $pM = (S, T, \mathbf{m})$ be a p-mapping and D_S be an instance of S.

An instance D_T of T is said to be *by-table consistent with D_S and pM*, if there exists a mapping $m \in \mathbf{m}$ such that D_S and D_T satisfy m.   □

Given a source instance D_S and a possible mapping $m \in \mathbf{m}$, there can be an infinite number of target instances that are consistent with D_S and m. We denote by $Tar_m(D_S)$ the set of all such instances.

In the probabilistic context, we assign a probability to every answer. Intuitively, we consider the certain answers with respect to each possible mapping in isolation. The probability of an answer t is the sum of the probabilities of the mappings for which t is deemed to be a certain answer. We define by-table answers as follows:

Definition 6 (By-table Answer). Let $pM = (S, T, \mathbf{m})$ be a p-mapping. Let Q be a query over T and let D_S be an instance of S.

Let t be a tuple. Let $\bar{m}(t)$ be the subset of $\mathbf{m}$, such that for each $m \in \bar{m}(t)$ and for each $D_T \in Tar_m(D_S), t \in Q(D_T)$.

Let $p = \sum_{m \in \bar{m}(t)} Pr(m)$. If $p > 0$, then we say (t, p) is a *by-table answer* of Q with respect to D_S and pM. $\qquad\square$

By-tuple semantics: If we follow the possible-world notions, in by-tuple semantics, different tuples in a source table can fall in different possible worlds, that is, different possible mappings associated with those possible worlds can apply to the different source tuples.

Formally, the key difference in the definition of by-tuple semantics from that of by-table semantics is that a consistent target instance is defined by a mapping *sequence* that assigns a (possibly different) mapping in $\mathbf{m}$ to each source tuple in D_S. (Without losing generality, to compare between such sequences, we assign some order to the tuples in the instance.)

Definition 7 (By-tuple Consistent Instance). Let $pM = (S, T, \mathbf{m})$ be a p-mapping and let D_S be an instance of S with d tuples.

An instance D_T of T is said to be *by-tuple consistent with D_S and pM*, if there is a sequence $\langle m^1, \ldots, m^d \rangle$ such that d is the number of tuples in D_S and for every $1 \le i \le d$,

- $m^i \in \mathbf{m}$, and
- For the ith tuple of D_S, t_i, there exists a target tuple $t_i' \in D_T$ such that for each attribute correspondence $(a_s, a_t) \in m^i$, the value of a_s in t_i is the same as the value of a_t in t_i'. $\qquad\square$

Given a mapping sequence $seq = \langle m^1, \ldots, m^d \rangle$, we denote by $Tar_{seq}(D_S)$ the set of all target instances that are consistent with D_S and seq. Note that if D_T is by-table consistent with D_S and m, then D_T is also by-tuple consistent with D_S and a mapping sequence in which each mapping is m.

We can think of every sequence of mappings $seq = \langle m^1, \ldots, m^d \rangle$ as a separate event whose probability is $Pr(seq) = \Pi_{i=1}^d Pr(m^i)$. (Section 3.5 relaxes this independence assumption and introduces *conditional mappings*.) If there are l mappings in pM, then there are l^d sequences of length d, and their probabilities add up to 1. We denote by $\mathbf{seq}_d(pM)$ the set of mapping sequences of length d generated from pM.

Definition 8 (By-tuple Answer). Let $pM = (S, T, \mathbf{m})$ be a p-mapping. Let Q be a query over T and D_S be an instance of S with d tuples.

Let t be a tuple. Let $\overline{seq}(t)$ be the subset of $\mathbf{seq}_d(pM)$, such that for each $seq \in \overline{seq}(t)$ and for each $D_T \in Tar_{seq}(D_S), t \in Q(D_T)$.

Let $p = \sum_{seq \in \overline{seq}(t)} Pr(seq)$. If $p > 0$, we call (t, p) a *by-tuple answer* of Q with respect to D_S and pM. □

The set of by-table answers for Q with respect to D_S is denoted by $Q^{table}(D_S)$ and the set of by-tuple answers for Q with respect to D_S is denoted by $Q^{tuple}(D_S)$.

Example 3. Consider the p-mapping pM, the source instance D_S, and the query Q in the motivating example.

In by-table semantics, Fig. 4.3b shows a target instance that is consistent with D_S (repeated in Fig. 4.3a) and possible mapping m_1. Figure 4.3d shows the by-table answers of Q with respect to D_S and pM. As an example, for tuple $t =$ ("Sunnyvale"), we have $\bar{m}(t) = \{m_1, m_2\}$, so the possible tuple ("Sunnyvale," 0.9) is an answer.

In by-tuple semantics, Fig. 4.3c shows a target instance that is by-tuple consistent with D_S and the mapping sequence $< m_2, m_3 >$. Figure 4.3e shows the by-tuple answers of Q with respect to D_S and pM. Note that the probability of tuple t = ("Sunnyvale") in the by-table answers is different from that in the by-tuple answers. We describe how to compute the probabilities in detail in the next section. □

3.3 Query Answering

This section studies query answering in the presence of probabilistic mappings. We start with describing algorithms for returning all answer tuples with probabilities, and discussing the complexity of query answering in terms of the size of the data (*data complexity*) and the size of the p-mapping (*mapping complexity*). We then consider returning the top-k query answers, which are the k answer tuples with the top probabilities, and answering aggregate queries.

3.3.1 By-table Query Answering

In the case of by-table semantics, answering queries is conceptually simple. Given a p-mapping $pM = (S, T, \mathbf{m})$ and an SPJ query Q, we can compute the certain answers of Q under each of the mappings $m \in \mathbf{m}$. We attach the probability $Pr(m)$ to every certain answer under m. If a tuple is an answer to Q under multiple mappings in $\mathbf{m}$, then we add up the probabilities of the different mappings.

Algorithm BYTABLE takes as input an SPJ query Q that mentions the relations $T_1, \ldots, T_l$ in the FROM clause. Assume that we have the p-mapping pM_i associated with the table T_i. The algorithm proceeds as follows.

Step 1: We generate the possible reformulations of Q (a reformulation query computes all certain answers when executed on the source data) by considering every combination of the form $(m^1, \ldots, m^l)$, where m^i is one of the possible mappings in pM_i. Denote the set of reformulations by $Q'_1, \ldots, Q'_k$. The probability of a reformulation $Q' = (m^1, \ldots, m^l)$ is $\Pi_{i=1}^l Pr(m^i)$.

Step 2: For each reformulation Q', retrieve each of the unique answers from the sources. For each answer obtained by $Q'_1 \cup \ldots \cup Q'_k$, its probability is computed by summing the probabilities of the Q''s in which it is returned.

Importantly, note that it is possible to express both steps as an SQL query with grouping and aggregation. Therefore, if the underlying sources support SQL, we can leverage their optimizations to compute the answers.

With our restricted form of schema mapping, the algorithm takes time polynomial in the size of the data and the mappings. We, thus, have the following complexity result.

Theorem 1. *Let $\overline{pM}$ be a schema p-mapping and let Q be an SPJ query.*
Answering Q with respect to $\overline{pM}$ in by-table semantics is in PTIME in the size of the data and the mapping. □

3.3.2 By-tuple Query Answering

To extend the by-table query-answering strategy to by-tuple semantics, we would need to compute the certain answers for every *mapping sequence* generated by pM. However, the number of such mapping sequences is exponential in the size of the input data. The following example shows that for certain queries, this exponential time complexity is inevitable.

Example 4. Suppose that in addition to the tables in Example 1, we also have U(city) in the source and V(hightech) in the target. The p-mapping for V contains two possible mappings: $(\{(city, hightech)\}, 0.8)$ and $(\emptyset, 0.2)$.

Consider the following query Q, which decides if there are any people living in a high-tech city.

```
Q: SELECT 'true'
   FROM T, V
   WHERE T.mailing-addr = V.hightech
```

An incorrect way of answering the query is to first execute the following two subqueries Q_1 and Q_2 and then join the answers of Q_1 and Q_2, and summing up the probabilities.

```
Q1: SELECT mailing-addr FROM T
Q2: SELECT hightech FROM V
```

Now, consider the source instance D, where D_S is shown in Fig. 4.2a, and D_U has two tuples ("Mountain View") and ("Sunnyvale"). Figure 4.4a,b show $Q_1^{tuple}(D)$

Tuple (mailing-addr)	Pr
('Sunnyvale')	0.94
('Mountain View')	0.5
('alice@')	0.1
('bob@')	0.1

(a)

Tuple (mailing-addr)	Pr
('Sunnyvale')	0.8
('Mountain View')	0.8

(b)

Fig. 4.4 Example 4: (a) $Q_1^{tuple}(D)$ and (b) $Q_2^{tuple}(D)$

and $Q_2^{tuple}(D)$. If we join the results of Q_1 and Q_2, we obtain for the true tuple the following probability: $0.94 * 0.8 + 0.5 * 0.8 = 1.152$. However, this is incorrect. By enumerating all consistent target tables, we in fact compute 0.864 as the probability. The reason for this error is that on some target instance that is by-tuple consistent with the source instance, the answers to both Q_1 and Q_2 contain tuple ("Sunnyvale") and tuple ("Mountain View"). Thus, generating the tuple ("Sunnyvale") as an answer for both Q_1 and Q_2 and generating the tuple ("Mountain View") for both queries are not independent events, and so simply adding up their probabilities leads to incorrect results.

Indeed, it is not clear if there exists a better algorithm to answer Q than by enumerating all by-tuple consistent target instances and then answering Q on each of them.   □

In fact, it is proved that in general, answering SPJ queries in by-tuple semantics with respect to schema p-mappings is hard.

Theorem 2. *Let Q be an SPJ query and let $\overline{pM}$ be a schema p-mapping. The problem of finding the probability for a by-tuple answer to Q with respect to $\overline{pM}$ is #P-complete with respect to data complexity and is in PTIME with respect to mapping complexity.*   □

Recall that #P is the complexity class of some hard counting problems (that is, e.g., counting the number of variable assignments that satisfy a Boolean formula). It is believed that a #P-complete problem cannot be solved in polynomial time, unless $P = NP$.

Although by-tuple query answering in general is hard, there are two restricted but common classes of queries for which by-tuple query answering takes polynomial time. The first class of queries are those that include only a single subgoal being the target of a p-mapping; here, we refer to an occurrence of a table in the FROM clause of a query as a *subgoal* of the query. Relations in the other subgoals are either involved in ordinary mappings or do not require a mapping. Hence, if we only have uncertainty with respect to one part of the domain, our queries will typically fall in this class. The second class of queries can include multiple subgoals involved in p-mappings but return the join attributes for such subgoals. We next illustrate these two classes of queries and query answering for them using two examples.

Example 5. Consider rewriting Q in the motivating example, repeated as follows:

```
Q: SELECT mailing-addr FROM T
```

To answer the query, we first rewrite Q into query Q' by adding the id column:

```
Q': SELECT id, mailing-addr FROM T
```

We then invoke BYTABLE and generate the following *SQL* query to compute by-table answers for Q':

```
Qa: SELECT id, mailing-addr, SUM(pr)
    FROM (
      SELECT DISTINCT id, current-addr
            AS mailing-addr, 0.5 AS pr
      FROM S
      UNION ALL
      SELECT DISTINCT id, permanent-addr
            AS mailing-addr, 0.4 AS pr
      FROM S
      UNION ALL
      SELECT DISTINCT id, email-addr
            AS mailing-addr, 0.1 AS pr
      FROM S)
    GROUP BY id, mailing-addr
```

Finally, we generate the results using the following query.

```
Qu:  SELECT mailing-addr, NOR(pr) AS pr
     FROM Qa
     GROUP BY mailing-addr
```

where for a set of probabilities $pr_1, \ldots, pr_n$, *NOR* computes $1 - \Pi_{i=1}^{n}(1 - pr_i)$.

$\square$

Example 6. Consider the schema p-mapping in Example 4. If we revise Q slightly by returning the join attribute, shown as follows, we can answer the query in polynomial time.

```
Q': SELECT V.hightech
    FROM T, V
    WHERE T.mailing-addr = V.hightech
```

We answer the query by dividing it into two subqueries, Q_1 and Q_2, as shown in Example 4. We can compute Q_1 with query Q_u (shown in Example 5) and compute Q_2 similarly with a query Q'_u. We compute by-tuple answers of Q' as follows:

```
SELECT Qu'.hightech, Qu.pr*Qu'.pr
FROM Qu, Qu'
WHERE Qu.mailing-addr = Qu'.hightect
```

$\square$

3.3.3 Top-*k* Query Answering

The main challenge in designing the algorithm for returning top-*k* query answers is to only perform the necessary reformulations at every step and halt when the top-*k* answers are found. We focus on top-*k* query answering for by-table semantics, and the algorithm can be modified for by-tuple semantics.

Recall that in by-table query answering, the probability of an answer is the sum of the probabilities of the reformulated queries that generate the answer. Our goal is to reduce the number of reformulated queries we execute. The algorithm we describe next proceeds in a greedy fashion: it executes queries in descending order of probabilities. For each tuple t, it maintains the upper bound $p_{max}(t)$ and lower bound $p_{min}(t)$ of its probability. This process halts when it finds k tuples whose p_{min} values are higher than p_{max} of the rest of the tuples.

TOPKBYTABLE takes as input an SPJ query Q, a schema p-mapping $\overline{pM}$, an instance D_S of the source schema, and an integer k, and outputs the top-*k* answers in $Q^{table}(D_S)$. The algorithm proceeds in three steps.

Step 1: Rewrite Q according to $\overline{pM}$ into a set of queries $Q_1, \ldots, Q_n$, each with a probability assigned in a similar way as stated in Algorithm BYTABLE.

Step 2: Execute $Q_1, \ldots, Q_n$ in descending order of their probabilities. Maintain the following measures:

- The highest probability, $PMax$, for the tuples that have not been generated yet. We initialize $PMax$ to 1; after executing query Q_i and updating the list of answers (see third bullet), we decrease $PMax$ by $Pr(Q_i)$;
- The threshold th determining which answers are potentially in the top-*k*. We initialize th to 0; after executing Q_i and updating the answer list, we set th to the kth largest p_{min} for tuples in the answer list;
- A list L of answers whose p_{max} is no less than th, and bounds p_{min} and p_{max} for each answer in L. After executing query Q_i, we update the list as follows: (1) for each $t \in L$ and $t \in Q_i(D_S)$, we increase $p_{min}(t)$ by $Pr(Q_i)$; (2) for each $t \in L$ but $t \notin Q_i(D_S)$, we decrease $p_{max}(t)$ by $Pr(Q_i)$; (3) if $PMax \geq th$, for each $t \notin L$ but $t \in Q_i(D_S)$, insert t to L, set p_{min} to $Pr(Q_i)$, and set $p_{max}(t)$ to $PMax$.
- A list T of k tuples with top p_{min} values.

Step 3: When $th > PMax$ and for each $t \notin T$, $th > p_{max}(t)$, halt and return T.

Example 7. Consider Example 1 where we seek for top-1 answer. We answer the reformulated queries in order of Q_1, Q_2, Q_3. After answering Q_1, for tuple ("Sunnyvale") we have $p_{min} = 0.5$ and $p_{max} = 1$, and for tuple ("Mountain View") we have the same bounds. In addition, $PMax = 0.5$ and $th = 0.5$.

In the second round, we answer Q_2. Then, for tuple ("Sunnyvale"), we have $p_{min} = 0.9$ and $p_{max} = 1$, and for tuple ("Mountain View"), we have $p_{min} = 0.5$ and $p_{max} = 0.6$. Now $PMax = 0.1$ and $th = 0.9$.

Because $th > PMax$ and th is above the p_{max} for the ("Mountain View") tuple, we can halt and return ("Sunnyvale") as the top-1 answer.   □

3.3.4 Answering Aggregate Queries

Finally, we discuss queries with aggregate operators: COUNT, SUM, AVG, MAX, and MIN based on results from Gal et al. (2009). We consider three common extensions to semantics with aggregates and probabilistic information: the *range* semantics returns the range of the aggregate (*i.e.*, the minimum and the maximum value); the *expected-value* semantics returns the expected value of the aggregate, and the *distribution* semantics returns all possible values with their probabilities. Note that the answer under the former two semantics can be derived from that under the last semantics; in other words, the *distribution* semantics is the richest one. We next formally define the three semantics.

Definition 9 (Semantics of Aggregate Query). Let $pM = (S, T, \mathbf{m})$ be a p-mapping, Q be an aggregate query over T, and D_S be an instance of S. Let $\bar{V}$ be the set of result values of evaluating Q on D_S w.r.t. pM under by-table (resp. by-tuple) semantics and $Pr(v)$ be the probability of value $v \in \bar{V}$.

1. *Range semantics*: The result is the interval $[\min(\bar{V}), \max(\bar{V})]$.
2. *Expected-value semantics*: The result is $\sum_{v \in \bar{V}} Pr(v) \cdot v$.
3. *Distribution semantics*: The result is a random variable X, s.t. for each distinct value $v \in \bar{V}$, $Pr(X = v) = Pr(v)$. □

According to the definition, there are six combinations of semantics for aggregate queries w.r.t. a p-mapping. Since results under the range or expected-value semantics can be derived from the results under the distribution semantics in polynomial time, the complexity of query answering w.r.t. to the former two semantics is no higher than that w.r.t. to the distribution semantics; in fact, in some cases, query answering w.r.t. to the former two semantics can be computed more efficiently without obtaining the distribution. Table 4.1 summarizes the complexity results for each aggregate operator, and we now explain them briefly.

- In by-table query answering, we can enumerate all answers and compute their probabilities in polynomial time; thus, query answering is in PTIME for all semantics.
- In by-tuple query answering, we can enumerate all answers (without computing their probabilities) in polynomial time; thus, query answering under the range semantics (where we do not need to know the probabilities of each answer) is in PTIME.

Table 4.1 Complexity of answering aggregate queries under different semantics

Semantics	Operator	Range	Expected-value	Distribution
By-table	COUNT, SUM, AVG, MIN, MAX	PTIME	PTIME	PTIME
By-tuple	COUNT	PTIME	PTIME	PTIME
	SUM	PTIME	PTIME	?
	AVG, MIN, MAX	PTIME	?	?

- We can prove that under the expected-value semantics, the answer for the SUM operator under by-table and by-tuple semantics is the same; thus, query answering for SUM under the by-tuple and expected-value semantics is in PTIME.
- For the COUNT operator, even query answering under the by-tuple semantics is PTIME for the distribution semantics and thus also for other semantics. We next illustrate this using an example.
- For the rest of the combinations, we conjecture that query answering cannot be finished in polynomial time and the complexity of query answering remains open.

Example 8. Continue with the running example (Fig. 4.2) and consider the following query.

```
Qc: SELECT COUNT(*) FROM S
    WHERE mailing-addr = 'Sunnyvale'
```

Table 4.2 shows how the probability of each answer value changes after we process each source tuple under the by-tuple semantics. After processing the first tuple, the probability of $COUNT = 0$ is $0.5+0.1 = 0.6$ (m_1, m_3) and that of $COUNT = 1$ is 0.4 (m_2). After processing the second tuple, the probability of $COUNT = 0$ is the probability that $COUNT = 0$ after the first tuple times the probability of applying m_3 to the second tuple, so $0.6 * 0.1 = 0.06$. That of $COUNT = 1$ is $0.6 * (0.5+0.4) + 0.4 * 0.1 = 0.58$, that is, either $COUNT = 0$ after we process the first tuple and we apply m_1 or m_2 to the second tuple, or $COUNT = 1$ after the first tuple and we apply m_3 to the third tuple. Similarly, the probability of $COUNT = 2$ is $0.4 * (0.5 + 0.4) = 0.36$. □

3.4 Creating p-Mappings

We now address the problem of generating a p-mapping between a source schema and a target schema. We begin by assuming that we have a set of weighted correspondences between the source attributes and the target attributes. These weighted correspondences are created by a set of schema matching modules. However, as we explain shortly, there can be *multiple* p-mappings that are consistent with a given set of weighted correspondences, and the question is which of them to choose. We describe an approach to creating p-mappings that is based on choosing the mapping that maximizes the *entropy* of the probability assignment.

Table 4.2 Trace of query answering in Example 8

TupleID	$COUNT = 0$	$COUNT = 1$	$COUNT = 2$
1	0.6	0.4	–
2	0.06	0.58	0.36

3.4.1 Computing Weighted Correspondences

A *weighted correspondence* between a pair of attributes specifies the degree of semantic similarity between them. Let $S(s_1, \ldots, s_m)$ be a source schema and $T(t_1, \ldots, t_n)$ be a target schema. We denote by $C_{i,j}, i \in [1, m], j \in [1, n]$, the weighted correspondence between s_i and t_j and by $w_{i,j}$ the weight of $C_{i,j}$. The first step is to compute a weighted correspondence between every pair of attributes, which can be done by applying existing schema-matching techniques.

Although weighted correspondences tell us the degree of similarity between pairs of attributes, they do not tell us *which* target attribute a source attribute should map to. For example, a target attribute mailing-address can be both similar to the source attribute current-addr and to permanent-addr, so it makes sense to map either of them to mailing-address in a schema mapping. In fact, given a set of weighted correspondences, there could be a *set* of p-mappings that are consistent with it. We can define the one-to-many relationship between sets of weighted correspondences and p-mappings by specifying when a p-mapping is *consistent with* a set of weighted correspondences.

Definition 10 (Consistent p-mapping). A p-mapping pM is *consistent with* a weighted correspondence $C_{i,j}$ between a pair of source and target attributes if the sum of the probabilities of all mappings $m \in pM$ containing correspondence (i, j) equals $w_{i,j}$; that is,

$$w_{i,j} = \sum_{m \in pM, (i,j) \in m} \Pr(m).$$

A p-mapping is *consistent with* a set of weighted correspondences **C** if it is consistent with each weighted correspondence $C \in \mathbf{C}$. □

However, not every set of weighted correspondences admits a consistent p-mapping. The following theorem shows under which conditions a consistent p-mapping exists, and it establishes a normalization factor for weighted correspondences that will guarantee the existence of a consistent p-mapping.

Theorem 3. *Let* **C** *be a set of weighted correspondences between a source schema* $S(s_1, \ldots, s_m)$ *and a target schema* $T(t_1, \ldots, t_n)$.

- *There exists a consistent p-mapping with respect to* **C** *if and only if (1) for every* $i \in [1, m]$, $\sum_{j=1}^{n} w_{i,j} \leq 1$ *and (2) for every* $j \in [1, n]$, $\sum_{i=1}^{m} w_{i,j} \leq 1$.
- *Let*

$$M' = max\{max_i\{\sum_{j-1}^{n} w_{i,j}\}, max_j\{\sum_{i=1}^{m} w_{i,j}\}\}.$$

Then, for each $i \in [1, m]$, $\sum_{j=1}^{n} \frac{w_{i,j}}{M'} \leq 1$ *and for each* $j \in [1, n]$, $\sum_{i=1}^{m} \frac{w_{i,j}}{M'} \leq 1$. □

Based on Theorem 3, we normalize the weighted correspondences we generated as described previously by dividing them by M', that is,

$$w'_{i,j} = \frac{w_{i,j}}{M'}.$$

3.4.2 Generating p-Mappings

To motivate our approach to generate p-mappings, consider the following example. Consider a source schema (A, B) and a target schema (A', B'). Assume that we have computed the following weighted correspondences between source and target attributes: $w_{A,A'} = 0.6$ and $w_{B,B'} = 0.5$ (the rest are 0).

As we explained above, there are an infinite number of p-mappings that are consistent with this set of weighted correspondences and below we list two of them: pM_1:

```
m1:  (A,A'),  (B,B'):  0.3 m2:  (A,A'):  0.3 m3:
     (B,B'):  0.2 m4:  empty:  0.2
```

pM_2:

```
m1:  (A,A'),  (B,B'):  0.5
m2:  (A,A'):  0.1
m3:  empty:  0.4
```

In a sense, pM_1 seems better than pM_2 because it assumes that the similarity between A and A' is independent of the similarity between B and B'.

In the general case, among the many p-mappings that are consistent with a set of weighted correspondences **C**, we choose the one with the *maximum entropy*, that is, the p-mappings whose probability distribution obtains the maximum value of $\sum_{i=1}^{l} -p_i * \log p_i$. In the above example, pM_1 obtains the maximum entropy.

The intuition behind maximum entropy is that when we need to select among multiple possible distributions on a set of exclusive events, we choose the one that does not favor any of the events over the others. Hence, we choose the distribution that does not *introduce new information* that we did not have a priori. The principle of maximum entropy is widely used in other areas such as natural language processing.

To create the p-mapping, we proceed in two steps. First, we enumerate all possible one-to-one schema mappings between S and M that contain a subset of correspondences in **C**. Second, we assign probabilities on each of the mappings in a way that maximizes the entropy of our result p-mapping.

Enumerating all possible schema mappings given **C** is trivial: for each subset of correspondences, if it corresponds to a one-to-one mapping, we consider the mapping as a possible mapping.

Given the possible mappings $m_1, \ldots, m_l$, we assign probabilities $p_1, \ldots, p_l$ to $m_1, \ldots, m_l$ by solving the following constraint optimization problem (OPT):

maximize $\sum_{k=1}^{l} -p_k * \log p_k$ subject to:

1. $\forall k \in [1, l], 0 \leq p_k \leq 1$,
2. $\sum_{k=1}^{l} p_k = 1$, and
3. $\forall i, j : \sum_{k \in [1,l],(i,j) \in m_k} p_k = w_{i,j}$.

We can apply existing technology in solving the OPT optimization problem. Although finding maximum-entropy solutions in general is costly, the experiments described in Sarma et al. (2008) show that the execution time is reasonable for a one-time process.

3.5   Broader Classes of Mappings

In this section, we describe several practical extensions to the basic mapping language. The query answering techniques and complexity results we have described carry over to these techniques.

GLAV mappings: The common formalism for schema mappings, GLAV (a.k.a. tuple-generating dependencies), is based on expressions of the form

$$m : \forall \mathbf{x}(\varphi(\mathbf{x}) \rightarrow \exists \mathbf{y}\psi(\mathbf{x}, \mathbf{y})).$$

In the expression, φ is the body of a conjunctive query over $\bar{S}$, and ψ is the body of a conjunctive query over $\bar{T}$. A pair of instances D_S and D_T *satisfies* a GLAV mapping m if for every assignment of $\mathbf{x}$ in D_S that satisfies φ there exists an assignment of $\mathbf{y}$ in D_T that satisfies ψ.

We define *general p-mappings* to be triples of the form $pGM = (\bar{S}, \bar{T}, \mathbf{gm})$, where $\mathbf{gm}$ is a set $\{(gm_i, Pr(gm_i)) \mid i \in [1, n]\}$, such that for each $i \in [1, n]$, gm_i is a general GLAV mapping. The definition of by-table semantics for such mappings is a simple generalization of Definition 6, and query answering can be conducted in PTIME. Extending by-tuple semantics to arbitrary GLAV mappings is much trickier than by-table semantics and would involve considering mapping sequences whose length is the product of the number of tuples in each source table, and the results are much less intuitive.

Theorem 4. *Let pGM be a general p-mapping between a source schema $\bar{S}$ and a target schema $\bar{T}$. Let D_S be an instance of $\bar{S}$. Let Q be an SPJ query with only equality conditions over $\bar{T}$. The problem of computing $Q^{table}(D_S)$ with respect to pGM is in PTIME in the size of the data and the mapping.*   ⊔

Complex mappings: Complex mappings map a set of attributes in the source to a set of attributes in the target. For example, we can map the attribute **address** to the concatenation of **street**, **city**, and **state**.

Formally, a *set correspondence* between S and T is a relationship between a subset of attributes in S and a subset of attributes in T. Here, the function associated with the relationship specifies a single value for each of the target attributes given a value for each of the source attributes. Again, the actual functions are irrelevant to our discussion. A *complex mapping* is a triple (S, T, cm), where cm is a set of set correspondences, such that each attribute in S or T is involved in at most one set correspondence. A *complex p-mapping* is of the form $pCM = \{(cm_i, Pr(cm_i)) \mid i \in [1, n]\}$, where $\sum_{i=1}^{n} Pr(cm_i) = 1$.

Theorem 5. *Let $\overline{pCM}$ be a complex schema p-mapping between schemas $\bar{S}$ and $\bar{T}$. Let D_S be an instance of $\bar{S}$. Let Q be an SPJ query over $\bar{T}$. The data complexity and mapping complexity of computing $Q^{table}(D_S)$ with respect to $\overline{pCM}$ are PTIME. The data complexity of computing $Q^{tuple}(D_S)$ with respect to $\overline{pCM}$ is #P-complete. The mapping complexity of computing $Q^{tuple}(D_S)$ with respect to $\overline{pCM}$ is in PTIME.* □

Union mapping: Union mappings specify relationships such as both attribute home-address and attribute office-address can be mapped to address. Formally, a *union mapping* is a triple $(S, T, \bar{m})$, where $\bar{m}$ is a set of mappings between S and T. Given a source relation D_S and a target relation D_T, we say D_S and D_T are consistent with respect to the union mapping if for each source tuple t and $m \in \bar{m}$ there exists a target tuple t', such that t and t' satisfy m. A *union p-mapping* is of the form $pUM = \{(\bar{m}_i, Pr(\bar{m}_i)) \mid i \in [1,n]\}$, where $\sum_{i=1}^{n} Pr(\bar{m}_i) = 1$.

Both by-table and by-tuple semantics apply to probabilistic union mappings.

Theorem 6. *Let $\overline{pUM}$ be a union schema p-mapping between a source schema $\bar{S}$ and a target schema $\bar{T}$. Let D_S be an instance of $\bar{S}$. Let Q be a conjunctive query over $\bar{T}$. The problem of computing $Q^{table}(D_S)$ with respect to $\overline{pUM}$ is in PTIME in the size of the data and the mapping; the problem of computing $Q^{tuple}(D_S)$ with respect to $\overline{pUM}$ is in PTIME in the size of the mapping and #P-complete in the size of the data.* □

Conditional mappings: In practice, our uncertainty is often conditioned. For example, we may want to state that daytime-phone maps to work-phone with probability 60% if age $\leq$ 65, and maps to home-phone with probability 90% if age $>$ 65.

We define a *conditional p-mapping* as a set $cpM = \{(pM_1, C_1), \ldots, (pM_n, C_n)\}$, where $pM_1, \ldots, pM_n$ are p-mappings, and $C_1, \ldots, C_n$ are pairwise disjoint conditions. Intuitively, for each $i \in [1,n]$, pM_i describes the probability distribution of possible mappings when condition C_i holds. Conditional mappings make more sense for by-tuple semantics. The following theorem shows that the complexity results carry over to such mappings.

Theorem 7. *Let $\overline{cpM}$ be a conditional schema p-mapping between $\bar{S}$ and $\bar{T}$. Let D_S be an instance of $\bar{S}$. Let Q be an SPJ query over $\bar{T}$. The problem of computing $Q^{tuple}(D_S)$ with respect to $\overline{cpM}$ is in PTIME in the size of the mapping and #P-complete in the size of the data.* □

3.6 Other Types of Approximate Schema Mappings

There have been various models proposed to capture uncertainty on mappings between attributes. Gal et al. (2005b) proposes keeping the top-K mappings between two schemas, each with a probability (between 0 and 1) of being true.

Gal et al. (2005a) proposes assigning a probability for matching of every pair of source and target attributes. This notion corresponds to weighted correspondences described in Sect. 3.4.

Magnani and Montesi (2007) have empirically shown that top-k schema mappings can be used to increase the recall of a data integration process, and Gal (2007) described how to generate top-k schema matchings by combining the matching results generated by various matchers. The probabilistic schema mappings we described above are different as they contain all possible schema mappings that conform to the schema-matching results and assigns probabilities to these mappings to reflect the likelihood that each mapping is Nottelmann and Straccia (2007) proposed generating probabilistic schema matchings that capture the uncertainty on each matching step. The probabilistic schema mappings we create not only capture our uncertainty on results of the matching step but also take into consideration various combinations of attribute correspondences and describe a *distribution* of possible schema mappings where the probabilities of all mappings sum up to 1.

There have also been work studying how to use probabilistic models to capture uncertainty on mappings of schema object classes, such as **DatabasePapers** and **AIPapers**. Query answering can take such uncertainty into consideration in computing the coverage percentage of the returned answers and in ordering information sources to maximize the likelihood of obtaining answers early. Specifically, consider two object classes A and B. The goal of the probabilistic models is to capture the uncertainty on whether A maps to B. One method (Florescu et al. 1997) uses probability $P(B|A)$, which is the probability that an instance of A is also an instance of B. Another method (Magnani and Montesi 2007) uses a tuple $< A, B, R, P >$, where R is a set of mutually exclusive relationships between A and B, and P is a probability distribution over R. The possible relationships considered in this model include *equivalent* $=$, *subset-subsumption* $\subset$, *superset-subsumption* $\supset$, *overlapping* $\cap$, *disjointness* $\between$, and *incompatibility* $\not\sim$. In the relational model, an object class is often represented using a relational table; thus, these probabilistic models focus on mapping between tables rather than attributes in the tables.

4 Uncertainty in Mediated Schema

The mediated schema is the set of schema terms (e.g., relations, attribute names) in which queries are posed. They do not necessarily cover all the attributes appearing in any of the sources, but rather the aspects of the domain that are important for the integration application. When domains are broad and there are multiple perspectives on them (e.g., a domain in science that is constantly evolving), there will be uncertainty about which is the correct mediated schema and about the meaning of its terms. Also, when the mediated schema is created automatically by inspecting the sources in a pay-as-you-go system, there will be uncertainty about the mediated schema.

In this section, we first motivate the need for probabilistic mediated schemas (p-med-schemas) with an example (Sect. 4.1). In Sect. 4.2, we formally define p-med-schemas and relate them with p-mappings in terms of expressive power and semantics of query answering. Then, in Sect. 4.3, we describe an algorithm for creating a p-med-schema from a set of data sources. Finally, Sect. 4.4 gives an algorithm for consolidating a p-med-schema into a single schema that is visible to the user in a pay-as-you-go system.

4.1 P-med-Schema Motivating Example

Let us begin with an example motivating p-med-schemas. Consider a setting in which we are trying to automatically infer a mediated schema from a set of data sources, where each of the sources is a single relational table. In this context, the mediated schema can be thought of as a "clustering" of source attributes, with similar attributes being grouped into the same cluster. The quality of query answers critically depends on the quality of this clustering. Because of the heterogeneity of the data sources being integrated, one is typically unsure of the semantics of the source attributes and in turn of the clustering.

Example 9. Consider two source schemas both describing people:

```
S1(name, hPhone, hAddr, oPhone, oAddr)
S2(name, phone, address)
```

In S2, the attribute **phone** can either be a home phone number or be an office phone number. Similarly, **address** can either be a home address or be an office address.

Suppose we cluster the attributes of S1 and S2. There are multiple ways to cluster the attributes, and they correspond to different mediated schemas. Below we list a few of them:

M_1({name}, {phone, hPhone, oPhone}, {address, hAddr, oAddr})
M_2({name}, {phone, hPhone}, {oPhone}, {address, oAddr}, {hAddr})
M_3({name}, {phone, hPhone}, {oPhone}, {address, hAddr}, {oAddr})
M_4({name}, {phone, oPhone}, {hPhone}, {address, oAddr}, {hAddr})
M_5({name}, {phone}, {hPhone}, {oPhone}, {address}, {hAddr}, {oAddr})

None of the listed mediated schemas is perfect. Schema M_1 groups multiple attributes from S1. M_2 seems inconsistent because **phone** is grouped with **hPhone** while **address** is grouped with **oAddress**. Schemas M_3, M_4, and M_5 are partially correct, but none of them captures the fact that **phone** and **address** can be either home phone and home address, or office phone and office address.

Even if we introduce probabilistic schema mappings, none of the listed mediated schemas will return ideal answers. For example, using M_1 prohibits returning correct answers for queries that contain both **hPhone** and **oPhone** because they are taken to be the same attribute. As another example, consider a query that contains phone and address. Using M_3 or M_4 as the mediated schema will unnecessarily favor home address and phone over office address and phone or vice versa. A system with M_2 will incorrectly favor answers that return a person's home address together with office phone number. A system with M_5 will also return a person's home address together with office phone and does not distinguish such answers from answers with correct correlations.

A probabilistic mediated schema will avoid this problem. Consider a probabilistic mediated schema **M** that includes M_3 and M_4, each with probability 0.5. For each of them and each source schema, we generate a probabilistic mapping (Sect. 3). For example, the set of probabilistic mappings **pM** for S_1 is shown in Fig. 4.5a, b.

Now consider an instance of S_1 with a tuple

```
('Alice', '123-4567', '123, A Ave.',
             '765-4321', '456, B Ave.')
```

and a query

Possible Mapping	Probability
{(name, name), (hPhone, hPPhone), (oPhone, oPhone), (hAddr, hAAddr), (oAddr, oAddr)}	0.64
{(name, name), (hPhone, hPPhone), (oPhone, oPhone), (oAddr, hAAddr), (hAddr, oAddr)}	0.16
{(name, name), (oPhone, hPPhone), (hPhone, oPhone), (hAddr, hAAddr), (oAddr, oAddr)}	0.16
{(name, name), (oPhone, hPPhone), (hPhone, oPhone), (oAddr, hAAddr), (hAddr, oAddr)}	0.04

(a)

Possible Mapping	Probability
{(name, name), (oPhone, oPPhone), (hPhone, hPhone), (oAddr, oAAddr), (hAddr, hAddr)}	0.64
{(name, name), (oPhone, oPPhone), (hPhone, hPhone), (hAddr, oAAddr), (oAddr, hAddr)}	0.16
{(name, name), (hPhone, oPPhone), (oPhone, hPhone), (oAddr, oAAddr), (hAddr, hAddr)}	0.16
{(name, name), (hPhone, oPPhone), (oPhone, hPhone), (hAddr, oAAddr), (oAddr, hAddr)}	0.04

(b)

Answer	Probability
('Alice', '123-4567', '123, A Ave.')	0.34
('Alice', '765-4321', '456, B Ave.')	0.34
('Alice', '765-4321', '123, A Ave.')	0.16
('Alice', '123-4567', '456, B Ave.')	0.16

(c)

Fig. 4.5 The motivating example: (**a**) p-mapping for S_1 and M_3, (**b**) p-mapping for S_1 and M_4, and (**c**) query answers w.r.t. **M** and **pM**. Here we denote {phone, hPhone} by hPPhone, {phone, oPhone} by oPPhone, {address, hAddr} by hAAddr, and {address, oAddr} by oAAddr

```
SELECT name, phone, address
FROM People
```

The answer generated by our system with respect to **M** and **pM** is shown in Fig. 4.5c. (As we describe in detail in the following sections, we allow users to compose queries using any attribute in the source.) Compared with using one of M_2 to M_5 as a mediated schema, our method generates better query results in that (1) it treats answers with home address and home phone and answers with office address and office phone equally, and (2) it favors answers with the correct correlation between address and phone number.   □

4.2 Probabilistic Mediated Schema

Consider a set of source schemas $\{S_1, \ldots, S_n\}$. We denote the attributes in schema $S_i, i \in [1, n]$, by $attr(S_i)$, and the set of all source attributes as $\mathscr{A}$, that is, $\mathscr{A} = attr(S_1) \cup \cdots \cup attr(S_n)$. We denote a mediated schema for the set of sources $\{S_1, \ldots, S_n\}$ by $M = \{A_1, \ldots, A_m\}$, where each of the A_i's is called a *mediated attribute*. The mediated attributes are *sets* of attributes from the sources, i.e., $A_i \subseteq \mathscr{A}$; for each $i, j \in [1, m], i \neq j \Rightarrow A_i \cap A_j = \emptyset$.

Note that whereas in a traditional mediated schema an attribute has a name, we do not deal with naming of an attribute in our mediated schema and allow users to use any source attribute in their queries. (In practice, we can use the most frequent source attribute to represent a mediated attribute when exposing the mediated schema to users.) If a query contains an attribute $a \in A_i, i \in [1, m]$, then when answering the query, we replace a everywhere with A_i.

A *probabilistic mediated schema* consists of a set of mediated schemas, each with a probability indicating the likelihood that the schema correctly describes the domain of the sources. We formally define probabilistic mediated schemas as follows.

Definition 11 (Probabilistic Mediated Schema). Let $\{S_1, \ldots, S_n\}$ be a set of schemas. A *probabilistic mediated schema (p-med-schema) for* $\{S_1, \ldots, S_n\}$ is a set

$$\mathbf{M} = \{(M_1, Pr(M_1)), \ldots, (M_l, Pr(M_l))\},$$

where

- For each $i \in [1, l]$, M_i is a mediated schema for $S_1, \ldots, S_n$, and for each $i, j \in [1, l], i \neq j$, M_i and M_j correspond to different clusterings of the source attributes;
- $Pr(M_i) \in (0, 1]$, and $\Sigma_{i=1}^{l} Pr(M_i) = 1$.   □

Semantics of queries: Next, we define the semantics of query answering with respect to a p-med-schema and a set of p-mappings for each mediated schema in the p-med-schema. Answering queries with respect to p-mappings returns a set of answer tuples, each with a probability indicating the likelihood that the tuple occurs as an answer. We consider by-table semantics here. Given a query Q, we compute answers by first answering Q with respect to each possible mapping and then for each answer tuple t by summing up the probabilities of the mappings with respect to which t is generated.

We now extend this notion for query answering that takes p-med-schema into consideration. Intuitively, we compute query answers by first answering the query with respect to each possible mediated schema and then for each answer tuple by taking the sum of its probabilities weighted by the probabilities of the mediated schemas.

Definition 12 (Query Answer). Let S be a source schema and $\mathbf{M} = \{(M_1, Pr(M_1)), \ldots, (M_l, Pr(M_l))\}$ be a p-med-schema. Let $\mathbf{pM} = \{pM(M_1), \ldots, pM(M_l)\}$ be a set of p-mappings where $pM(M_i)$ is the p-mapping between S and M_i. Let D be an instance of S and Q be a query.

Let t be a tuple. Let $Pr(t|M_i), i \in [1, l]$, be the probability of t in the answer of Q with respect to M_i and $pM(M_i)$. Let $p = \Sigma_{i=1}^{l} Pr(t|M_i) * Pr(M_i)$. If $p > 0$, then we say (t, p) is a by-table answer with respect to $\mathbf{M}$ and $\mathbf{pM}$.

We denote all by-table answers by $Q_{\mathbf{M},\mathbf{pM}}(D)$. $\square$

We say that query answers A_1 and A_2 are *equal* (denoted $A_1 = A_2$) if A_1 and A_2 contain exactly the same set of tuples with the same probability assignments.

Expressive power: A natural question to ask at this point is whether probabilistic mediated schemas provide any added expressive power compared to deterministic ones. Theorem 8 shows that if we consider *one-to-many* schema mappings, where one source attribute can be mapped to multiple mediated attributes, then any combination of a p-med-schema and p-mappings can be equivalently represented using a deterministic mediated schema with p-mappings, but may not be represented using a p-med-schema with deterministic schema mappings. Note that we can easily extend the definition of query answers to one-to-many mappings, as one mediated attribute can correspond to no more than one source attribute.

Theorem 8 (Subsumption). *The following two claims hold.*

1. *Given a source schema S, a p-med-schema $\mathbf{M}$, and a set of p-mappings $\mathbf{pM}$ between S and possible mediated schemas in $\mathbf{M}$, there exists a deterministic mediated schema T and a p-mapping pM between S and T, such that $\forall D, Q$: $Q_{\mathbf{M},\mathbf{pM}}(D) = Q_{T,pM}(D)$.*
2. *There exists a source schema S, a mediated schema T, a p-mapping pM between S and T, and an instance D of S, such that for any p-med-schema $\mathbf{M}$ and any set $\mathbf{m}$ of deterministic mappings between S and possible mediated schemas in $\mathbf{M}$, there exists a query Q such that $Q_{\mathbf{M},\mathbf{m}}(D) \neq Q_{T,pM}(D)$.* $\square$

In contrast, Theorem 9 shows that if we restrict our attention to one-to-one mappings, then a probabilistic mediated schema *does* add expressive power.

Theorem 9. *There exists a source schema S, a p-med-schema* **M**, *a set of one-to-one p-mappings* **pM** *between S and possible mediated schemas in* **M**, *and an instance D of S, such that for any deterministic mediated schema T and any one-to-one p-mapping pM between S and T, there exists a query Q such that* $Q_{\mathbf{M},\mathbf{pM}}(D) \neq Q_{T,pM}(D)$.   □

Constructing one-to-many p-mappings in practice is much harder than constructing one-to-one p-mappings. And when we are restricted to one-to-one p-mappings, p-med-schemas grant us more expressive power while keeping the process of mapping generation feasible.

4.3 P-med-Schema Creation

We now show how to create a probabilistic mediated schema **M**. Given source tables $S_1, \ldots, S_n$, we first construct the multiple schemas $M_1, \ldots, M_p$ in **M**, and then assign each of them a probability.

We exploit two pieces of information available in the source tables: (1) pairwise similarity of source attributes, and (2) statistical co-occurrence properties of source attributes. The former is used for creating multiple mediated schemas and the latter for assigning probabilities on each of the mediated schemas.

The first piece of information tells us when two attributes are likely to be similar and is generated by a collection of schema matching modules. This information is typically given by some pairwise attribute similarity measure, say s. The similarity $s(a_i, a_j)$ between two source attributes a_i and a_j depicts how closely the two attributes represent the same real-world concept.

The second piece of information tells us when two attributes are likely to be different. Consider for example, source table schemas

```
S1:  (name,address,email-address)
S2:  (name,home-address)
```

Pairwise string similarity would indicate that attribute address can be similar to both email-address and home-address. However, since the first source table contains address and email-address together, they cannot refer to the same concept. Hence, the first table suggests address is different from email-address, making it more likely that address refers to home-address.

Creating multiple mediated schemas: The creation of the multiple mediated schemas constituting the p-med-schema can be divided conceptually into three steps. First, we remove infrequent attributes from the set of all source attributes, that is, attribute names that do not appear in a large fraction of source tables. This step ensures that our mediated schema contains only information that is relevant and central to the domain. In the second step, we construct a weighted graph whose nodes are the attributes that survived the filter of the first step. An edge in the graph is labeled with the pairwise similarity between the two nodes it connects. Finally, several possible clusterings of nodes in the resulting weighted graph give the various mediated schemas.

Algorithm 1 describes the various steps in detail. The input is the set of source schemas creating $S_1, \ldots, S_n$ and a pairwise similarity function s, and the output is the multiple mediated schemas in **M**. Steps 1–3 of the algorithm find the attributes that occur frequently in the sources. Steps 4 and 5 construct the graph of these high-frequency attributes. We allow an error ϵ on the threshold τ for edge weights. We, thus, have two kinds of edges: *certain edges*, having weight at least $\tau + \epsilon$, and *uncertain edges*, having weight between $\tau - \epsilon$ and $\tau + \epsilon$.

Steps 6–8 describe the process of obtaining multiple mediated schemas. Specifically, a mediated schema in **M** is created for every subset of the uncertain edges. For every subset, we consider the graph resulting from omitting that subset from the graph. The mediated schema includes a mediated attribute for each connected component in the resulting graph. Since, in the worst case, the number of resulting graphs is exponential in the number of uncertain edges, the parameter ϵ needs to be chosen carefully. In addition, Step 6 removes uncertain edges that when omitted will not lead to different mediated schemas. Specifically, we remove edges that connect two nodes already connected by certain edges. Also, we consider only one among a set of uncertain edges that connect a particular node with a set of nodes that are connected by certain edges.

Probability assignment: The next step is to compute probabilities for possible mediated schemas that we have generated. As a basis for the probability assignment, we first define when a mediated schema is *consistent with* a source schema. The probability of a mediated schema in **M** will be the proportion of the number of sources with which it is consistent.

0: **Input**: Source schemas $S_1, \ldots, S_n$.
   Output: A set of possible mediated schemas.
1: Compute $\mathcal{A} = \{a_1, \ldots, a_m\}$, the set of all source attributes;
2: **for each** ($j \in [1, m]$)
   Compute frequency $f(a_j) = \frac{|\{i \in [1,n] | a_j \in S_i\}|}{n}$;
3: Set $\mathcal{A} = \{a_j | j \in [1, m], f(a_j) \geq \theta\}$; //$\theta$ *is a threshold*
4: Construct a weighted graph $G(V, E)$, where (1) $V = \mathcal{A}$, and (2) for each $a_j, a_k \in \mathcal{A}, s(a_j, a_k) \geq \tau - \epsilon$, there is an edge (a_j, a_k) with weight $s(a_j, a_k)$;
5: Mark all edges with weight less than $\tau + \epsilon$ as *uncertain*;
6: **for each** (uncertain edge $e = (a_1, a_2) \in E$)
   Remove e from E if (1) a_1 and a_2 are connected by a path with only certain edges, or (2) there exists $a_3 \in V$, such that a_2 and a_3 are connected by a path with only certain edges and there is an uncertain edge (a_1, a_3);
7: **for each** (subset of uncertain edges)
   Omit the edges in the subset and compute a mediated schema where each connected component in the graph corresponds to an attribute in the schema;
8: **return** distinct mediated schemas.

Algorithm 1: Generate all possible mediated schemas

```
0: Input: Possible mediated schemas M₁,...,Mₗ and source schemas S₁,...,Sₙ.
   Output: Pr(M₁),...,Pr(Mₗ).
1: for each (i ∈ [1,l])
      Count the number of source schemas that are consistent with Mᵢ, denoted as cᵢ;
2: for each (i ∈ [1,l]) Set Pr(Mᵢ) = cᵢ/∑ᵢ₌₁ˡ cᵢ.
```

Algorithm 2: Assign probabilities to possible mediated schemas

```
0: Input: Mediated schemas M₁,...,Mₗ.
   Output: A consolidated single mediated schema T.
1: Set T = M₁.
2: for (i = 2,...,l) modify T as follows:
3:    for each (attribute A' in Mᵢ)
4:       for each (attribute A in T)
5:          Divide A into A ∩ A' and A − A';
6: return T.
```

Algorithm 3: Consolidate a p-med-schema

Definition 13 (Consistency). Let M be a mediated schema for sources $S_1,\ldots,S_n$. We say M is *consistent with* a source schema $S_i, i \in [1,n]$, if there is no pair of attributes in S_i that appears in the same cluster in M.

Intuitively, a mediated schema is consistent with a source only if it does not group distinct attributes in the source (and hence distinct real-world concepts) into a single cluster. Algorithm 2 shows how to use the notion of consistency to assign probabilities on the p-med-schema.

4.4 Consolidation

To complete the fully automatic setup of the data integration system, we consider the problem of consolidating a probabilistic mediated schema into a single mediated schema and creating p-mappings to the consolidated schema. We require that the answers to queries over the consolidated schema be equivalent to the ones over the probabilistic mediated schema.

The main reason to consolidate the probabilistic mediated schema into a single one is that the user expects to see a single schema. In addition, consolidating to a single schema has the advantage of more efficient query answering: queries now need to be rewritten and answered based on only one mediated schema. We note that in some contexts, it may be more appropriate to show the application builder a set of mediated schemas and let her select one of them (possibly improving on it later on).

Consolidating a p-med-schema: Consider a p-med-schema $\mathbf{M} = \{(M_1, Pr(M_1)),\ldots,(M_l, Pr(M_l))\}$. We consolidate $\mathbf{M}$ into a single mediated schema T. Intuitively, our algorithm (see Algorithm 3) generates the "coarsest refinement" of the possible mediated schemas in $\mathbf{M}$ such that every cluster in any of the M_i's

---

0: **Input:** Source S with p-mappings $pM_1, \ldots, pM_l$ for $M_1, \ldots, M_l$.
   Output: Single p-mapping pM between S and T.
1: **For each** $i \in [1, l]$, **modify p-mapping** pM_i: Do the following for every possible mapping m
   in pM_i:

- For every correspondence $(a, A) \in m$ between source attribute a and mediated attribute
  A in M_i, proceed as follows. (1) Find the set of all mediated attributes B in T such that
  $B \subset A$. Call this set $\overline{B}$. (2) Replace (a, A) in m with the set of all (a, B)'s, where $B \in \overline{B}$.

   Call the resulting p-mapping pM_i'.

2: **For each** $i \in [1, l]$, **modify probabilities in** pM_i': Multiply the probability of every schema
   mapping in pM_i' by $Pr(M_i)$, which is the probability of M_i in the p-med-schema. (Note that
   after this step the sum of probabilities of all mappings in pM_i' is not 1.)
3: **Consolidate** pM_i''s: Initialize pM to be an empty p-mapping (i.e., with no mappings). For
   each $i \in [1, l]$, *add pM_i' to pM* as follows:

- For each schema mapping m in pM_i' with probability p: *if m is in pM, with probability*
  p', modify the probability of m in pM to $(p + p')$; *if m is not in pM,* then add m to pM
  with probability p.

4: Return the resulting consolidated p-mapping, pM; the probabilities of all mappings in pM
   add to 1.

Algorithm 4: Consolidating p-mappings

---

is equal to the union of a set of clusters in T. Hence, any two attributes a_i and a_j will be together in a cluster in T if and only if they are together in every mediated schema of **M**. The algorithm initializes T to M_1 and then modifies each cluster of T based on clusters from M_2 to M_l.

Example 10. Consider a p-med-schema $M = \{M_1, M_2\}$, where M_1 contains three attributes $\{a_1, a_2, a_3\}$, $\{a_4\}$, and $\{a_5, a_6\}$, and M_2 contains two attributes $\{a_2, a_3, a_4\}$ and $\{a_1, a_5, a_6\}$. The target schema T would then contain four attributes: $\{a_1\}$, $\{a_2, a_3\}$, $\{a_4\}$, and $\{a_5, a_6\}$.   □

Note that in practice the consolidated mediated schema is the same as the mediated schema that corresponds to the weighted graph with only certain edges. Here, we show the general algorithm for consolidation, which can be applied even if we do not know the specific pairwise similarities between attributes.

Consolidating p-mappings: Next, we consider consolidating p-mappings specified w.r.t. $M_1, \ldots, M_l$ to a p-mapping w.r.t. the consolidated mediated schema T. Consider a source S with p-mappings $pM_1, \ldots, pM_l$ for $M_1, \ldots, M_l$, respectively. We generate a single p-mapping pM between S and T in three steps. First, we modify each p-mapping pM_i, $i \in [1, l]$, between S and M_i to a p-mapping pM_i' between S and T. Second, we modify the probabilities in each pM_i'. Third, we consolidate all possible mappings in pM_i''s to obtain pM. The details are specified in Algorithm 4, as follows.

Note that the second part of Step 1 can map one source attribute to multiple mediated attributes; thus, the mappings in the result pM are one-to-many mappings and so typically different from the p-mapping generated directly on the consolidated schema. The following theorem shows that the consolidated mediated schema and the consolidated p-mapping are equivalent to the original p-med-schema and p-mappings.

Theorem 10 (Merge Equivalence). *For all queries Q, the answers obtained by posing Q over a p-med-schema* $\mathbf{M} = \{M_1, \ldots, M_l\}$ *with p-mappings* $pM_1, \ldots, pM_l$ *is equal to the answers obtained by posing Q over the consolidated mediated schema T with consolidated p-mapping pM.* $\square$

4.5 Other Approaches

He and Chang (2003) considered the problem of generating a mediated schema for a set of Web sources. Their approach was to create a mediated schema that is statistically maximally *consistent* with the source schemas. To do so, they assume that the source schemas are created by a *generative model* applied to some mediated schema, which can be thought of as a probabilistic mediated schema. (Some other works, e.g., (He et al. 2004; He and Chang 2006), have considered correlations for schema matching as well.) The probabilistic mediated schema we described in this chapter has several advantages in capturing heterogeneity and uncertainty in the domain. We can express a wider class of attribute clusterings, and in particular clusterings that capture attribute correlations. Moreover, we are able to combine attribute matching and co-occurrence properties for the creation of the probabilistic mediated schema, allowing for instance two attributes from one source to have a nonzero probability of being grouped together in the mediated schema. Also, the approach for p-med-schema creation described in this chapter is independent of a specific schema-matching technique, whereas the approach in He and Chang (2003) is tuned for constructing generative models and hence must rely on statistical properties of source schemas.

Magnani et al. (2005), proposed generating a set of alternative mediated schemas based on probabilistic relationships between *relations* (such as an Instructor relation intersects with a Teacher relation but is disjoint with a Student relation) obtained by sampling the overlapping of data instances. Here, we focus on matching attributes within relations. In addition, our approach allows exploring various types of evidence to improve matching, and we assign probabilities to the mediated schemas we generate.

Chiticariu et al. (2008), studied the generation of multiple mediated schemas for an existing set of data sources. They consider multitable data sources, not considered in this chapter, but explore interactive techniques that aid humans in arriving at the mediated schemas.

There has been quite a bit of work on automatically creating mediated schemas that focused on the theoretical analysis of the semantics of merging schemas and the choices that need to be made in the process (Batini et al. 1986; Buneman et al. 1992; Hull 1984; Kalinichenko 1990; Miller et al. 1993; Pottinger and Bernstein 2002). The goal of these works was to make as many decisions automatically as possible, but where some ambiguity arises, refer to input from a designer.

4.6   Conclusions

This chapter introduced the notion of a probabilistic mediated schema, and provided algorithms for constructing them automatically by analyzing the source schemas. This allows for automatically establishing a fairly advanced starting point for data integration systems. We believe that the foundation of modeling uncertainty laid out here will also help pinpoint where human feedback can be most effective in improving the semantic integration in the system. In the future, we shall consider such improvement of data integration over time, as well as extensions of our techniques to deal with multiple-table sources.

References

Agrawal S, Chaudhuri S, Das G (2002) DBXplorer: A system for keyword-based search over relational databases. In: ICDE, February 2002. IEEE Computer Society, Washington, DC, p 5

Batini C, Lenzerini M, Navathe SB (1986) A comparative analysis of methodologies for database schema integration. ACM Comput Surv 18(4):323–364

Berlin J, Motro A (2002) Database schema matching using machine learning with feature selection. In: Proceedings of the 14th international conference on advanced information systems engineering (CAiSE02), May 2002. Springer, London, pp 452–466

Buneman P, Davidson S, Kosky A (1992) Theoretical aspects of schema merging. In: Proceedings of EDBT, March 1992. Springer, London, pp 152–167

Chiticariu L, Kolaitis PG, Popa L (2008) Interactive generation of integrated schemas. In: Proceedings of ACM SIGMOD, Vancouver, Canada, June 2008. ACM, NY, pp 833–846

Dhamankar R, Lee Y, Doan A, Halevy AY, Domingos P (2004) iMAP: Discovering complex semantic matches between database schemas. In: Proceedings of ACM SIGMOD, Paris, France, June 2004. ACM, NY, pp 383–394

Do H, Rahm E (2002) COMA – a system for flexible combination of schema matching approaches. In: Proceedings of VLDB, Hong Kong, China, August 2002. VLDB Endowment, pp 610–621

Doan A, Madhavan J, Domingos P, Halevy AY (2002) Learning to map between ontologies on the Semantic Web. In: Proceedings of the international WWW conference, Honolulu, HI, May 2002. ACM, NY, pp 662–673

Dong X, Halevy AY (2005) A platform for personal information management and integration. In: Proceedings of Conference on Innovative Data Research (CIDR), Asilomar, CA

Dong X, Halevy AY, Yu C (2007) Data integration with uncertainty. In: Proceedings of VLDB, Vienna, Austria, September 2007. VLDB Endowment, pp 687–698

Florescu D, Koller D, Levy AY (1997) Using probabilistic information in data integration. In: Proceedings of VLDB, August 1997. Morgan Kaufmann, CA, pp 216–225

Gal A (2007) Why is schema matching tough and what can we do about it? SIGMOD Rec 35(4):2–5

Gal A, Anaby-Tavor A, Trombetta A, Montesi D (2005a) A framework for modeling and evaluating automatic semantic reconciliation. VLDB J 14(1):50–67

Gal A, Modica G, Jamil H, Eyal A (2005b) Automatic ontology matching using application semantics. AI Mag 26(1):21–31

Gal A, Martinez M, Simari G, Subrahmanian V (2009) Aggregate query answering under uncertain schema mappings. In: Proceedings of ICDE, Shanghai, China, March 2009. IEEE Computer Society, Washington, DC, pp 940–951

GoogleBase (2005) GoogleBase. http://base.google.com/

Halevy AY, Ashish N, Bitton D, Carey MJ, Draper D, Pollock J, Rosenthal A, Sikka V (2005) Enterprise information integration: Successes, challenges and controversies. In: SIGMOD, Baltimore, MD, June 2005. ACM, NY, pp 778–787

Halevy AY, Franklin MJ, Maier D (2006a) Principles of dataspace systems. In: PODS, Chicago, IL, June 2006. ACM, NY, pp 1–9

Halevy AY, Rajaraman A, Ordille JJ (2006b) Data integration: The teenage years. In: VLDB, Seoul, Korea, September 2006. VLDB Endowment, pp 9–16

He B, Chang KC (2003) Statistical schema matching across web query interfaces. In: Proceedings of ACM SIGMOD, San Diego, CA, June 2003. ACM, NY, pp 217–228

He B, Chang KCC (2006) Automatic complex schema matching across web query interfaces: A correlation mining approach. TODS 31(1):346–395

He B, Chang KCC, Han J (2004) Discovering complex matchings across web query interfaces: a correlation mining approach. In: KDD

Hristidis V, Papakonstantinou Y (2002) DISCOVER: Keyword search in relational databases. In: Proceedings of VLDB, Seattle, WA, August 2004. ACM, NY, pp 148–157

Hull R (1984) Relative information capacity of simple relational database schemata. In: Proceedings of ACM PODS, Waterloo, ON, April 1984. ACM, NY, pp 97–109

Kalinichenko LA (1990) Methods and tools for equivalent data model mapping construction. In: Proceedings of EDBT, Venice, Italy, March 1990. Springer, NY, pp 92–119

Kang J, Naughton J (2003) On schema matching with opaque column names and data values. In: Proceedings of ACM SIGMOD, San Diego, CA, June 2003. ACM, NY, pp 205–216

Levy A (ed) (2000) Special issue on adaptive query processing. IEEE Data Eng Bull 23(2), IEEE Computer Society, Washington, DC

Madhavan J, Cohen S, Dong X, Halevy A, Jeffery S, Ko D, Yu C (2007) Web-scale data integration: You can afford to pay as you go. In: Proceedings of CIDR, pp 342–350

Magnani M, Montesi D (2007) Uncertainty in data integration: current approaches and open problems. In: VLDB workshop on management of uncertain data, pp 18–32

Magnani M, Rizopoulos N, Brien P, Montesi D (2005) Schema integration based on uncertain semantic mappings. Lecture Notes in Computer Science, vol 3716. Springer, Heidelberg, pp 31–46

Miller RJ, Ioannidis Y, Ramakrishnan R (1993) The use of information capacity in schema integration and translation. In: Proceedings of VLDB, August 1993. Morgan Kaufmann, CA, pp 120–133

Nottelmann H, Straccia U (2007) Information retrieval and machine learning for probabilistic schema matching. Inform Process Manag 43(3):552–576

Pottinger R, Bernstein P (2002) Creating a mediated schema based on initial correspondences. IEEE Data Eng Bull 25:26–31

Rahm E, Bernstein PA (2001) A survey of approaches to automatic schema matching. VLDB J 10(4):334–350

Sarma AD, Dong L, Halevy A (2008) Bootstrapping pay-as-you-go data integration systems. In: Proceedings of ACM SIGMOD, Vancouver, Canada, June 2008. ACM, NY, pp 861–874

Wang J, Wen J, Lochovsky FH, Ma W (2004) Instance-based schema matching for Web databases by domain-specific query probing. In: Proceedings of VLDB, Toronto, Canada, August 2004. VLDB Endowment, pp 408–419

Part II
Quality-Driven Schema Mapping and Evolution

A fundamental problem in information integration is to derive precisely the relationships between elements and structures in heterogeneous schemas. Such process is called *schema mapping* and may utilize the results output by schema matching tools, or simply rely on the correspondences manually provided by the user. In both cases, the correspondences are not by themselves guarantee of good quality and adequacy to the intended semantics. Although there exist several schema mapping tools and techniques, only recently our community is looking at the problem of verification and optimization of the transformations output using those tools and techniques. This part surveys the existing schema mapping algorithms and the most recent developments towards realizing efficient, optimized and correct schema mapping transformations. Along these lines, it also deals with the problem of adapting such mappings when schemas change and evolve, and discusses the impact that schema evolution has on the mapping operators and their composition and inversion. Besides the semantics and the algorithmic issues of schema evolution, this part also analyzes the problems of change specification, evolution transparency, automated generation of evolving mappings, and migration of a predictable instance that minimizes data loss and manual intervention.

Finally, schemas and other related structures often need to be merged. This happens for many reasons such as view integration, data integration or data warehouse creation. This part compares and contrast different approaches for schema merging and schema integration, and mapping creation thereof.

Chapter 5 by Angela Bonifati, Giansalvatore Mecca, Paolo Papotti and Yannis Velegrakis surveys the state of the art of schema mapping approaches. It discusses the advances towards the efficiency of the mapping transformations, their correctness, minimality and optimality. It also underlines the importance of utilizing such mappings in all data transformation stages beyond the specific tool boundaries.

Chapters 6 and 7 deal with mapping-based support for schema evolution. Chapter 6 by Michael Hartung, James Terwilliger and Erhard Rahm introduces the schema evolution problem and the requirements for its effective treatment such as support for a rich set of changes, evolution transparency by providing schema versions and views, and the automated generation of evolution mappings.

Furthermore, it describes how and to what degree recently proposed approaches meet the requirements for a variety of schemas, in particular relational and XML schemas.

Chapter 7 by Ronald Fagin, Phokion G. Kolaitis, Lucian Popa, and Wang-Chiew Tan complements the previous chapter by focusing on the problem of mapping adaptation when schemas evolve. In particular, they survey the recent work on fundamental operators on schema mapping, such as inversion and composition, while discussing the most important developments of their semantics, algorithms and implementation.

Chapter 8 by Rachel Pottinger focuses on the problem of schema merging, mapping creation and schema integration, by surveying their key developments. In particular, generic approaches are considered, along with view integration and data integration techniques that have been important milestones in our field.

Chapter 5
Discovery and Correctness of Schema Mapping Transformations

Angela Bonifati, Giansalvatore Mecca, Paolo Papotti, and Yannis Velegrakis

Abstract Schema mapping is becoming pervasive in all data transformation, exchange, and integration tasks. It brings to the surface the problem of differences and mismatches between heterogeneous formats and models, respectively, used in source and target databases to be mapped one to another. In this chapter, we start by describing the problem of schema mapping, its background, and technical implications. Then, we outline the early schema mapping systems, along with the new generation of schema mapping tools. Moving from the former to the latter entailed a dramatic change in the performance of mapping generation algorithms. Finally, we conclude the chapter by revisiting the query answering techniques allowed by the mappings, and by discussing useful applications and future and current developments of schema mapping tools.

1 Introduction

Currently there are many kinds of scenarios in which heterogeneous systems need to exchange, transform, and integrate data. These include "Extract, Transform and Load" (ETL) applications, object-relational mapping systems, "Enterprise

A. Bonifati (✉)
ICAR-CNR, Italy
e-mail: bonifati@icar.cnr.it

G. Mecca
Università of Basilicata, Potenza, Italy
e-mail: giansalvatore.mecca@unibas.it

P. Papotti
Università Roma Tre, Rome, Italy
e-mail: papotti@dia.uniroma3.it

Y. Velegrakis
Università di Trento, Trento, Italy
e-mail: velgias@disi.unitn.eu

Z. Bellahsene et al. (eds.), *Schema Matching and Mapping*, Data-Centric Systems and Applications, DOI 10.1007/978-3-642-16518-4_5,
© Springer-Verlag Berlin Heidelberg 2011

a

NYSE

name	symbol
Google	GOOG
Yahoo!	YHOO

Public-Company

name	city
Apple	Cup
Adobe	SJ

Public-Grant

company	investigator	amount
Apple	Mike B.	25,000
Adobe	Anne C.	50,000

NSF-Grantee

id	name	symbol
23	Yahoo!	YHOO
25	Adobe	ADBE

NSF-Grant

company	amount
23	18,000
25	50,000

Source Tables

b

Company

id	name	symbol
N1	Google	GOOG
I1	Apple	NULL
23	Yahoo!	YHOO
25	Adobe	ADBE

Grant

amount	company
25,000	I1
18,000	23
50,000	25

Target Tables

Fig. 5.1 Mapping company information

Information Integration" (EII) systems, and "Enterprise Application Integration" (EAI) frameworks.

A common feature of all of these applications is that data is organized according to different descriptions, typically based on a variety of data models and formats. To give one example, consider the scenario in Fig. 5.1.

The inputs to the problem are three data sources about companies, potentially organized according to rather different formats and models: (1) a list of companies from the New York Stock Exchange, *(NYSE)*; (2) a public database concerning companies and grants (*Public-Companies, Public-Grants*); (3) and database of grants from the National Scientific Foundation (*NSF-Grantee, NSF-Grant*). Notice that, for the purpose of this section, we shall assume that source data are relational tables. However, as it will be clear in the following, they might easily be organized according to more complex data models, for example as nested XML documents.

The expected output is an instance of a target database with the following schema: two tables, *Company* and *Grant*, a key constraint on the *Company.name* attribute, and a foreign-key constraint from *Grant.company* to *Company.id*. Assuming the source data are those in Fig. 5.1a, it is natural to expect that the target instance obtained by the translation process is the one in Fig. 5.1b. In fact, informally speaking, such instance has a number of desirable properties: (1) it is a legal instance for the target database; (2) it is "complete," in the sense that it contains all of the information that is in the source tables; (3) at the same time, it is "non-redundant," i.e., no piece of information is reported twice.

It can be seen from this example that computing an output solution requires the definition of some form of *mapping* from the source repository to the target repository. Generally speaking, *mappings*, also called *schema mappings*, are expressions that specify how an instance of the source repository should be translated into an instance of the target repository. To be useful in practical applications, they should have an executable implementation – for example, under the form of SQL queries for relational data, or XQuery scripts for XML.

There are many ways in which such a transformation can be implemented. Often, this is done in a rather procedural fashion, and developers are forced to write quite a lot of code to glue together the various sources. To give an example, in an ETL application a developer would be forced to manually construct a script made of potentially large number of simpler data-transformation steps. In other cases, such as commercial EII systems, transformation steps are often expressed using programming language (such as Java). This procedural style of specifying the mapping has made the problem of exchanging data across different repositories quite a burden, as discussed in Haas (2007).

To alleviate developers from this burden, we can identify two key requirements that a mapping system should have:

- A first key requirement is represented by *ease of use* and productivity. Developers should not be required to manually specify all of the details about the mapping; on the contrary, users would like to specify only a high-level, abstract and declarative representation of the mapping; then, based on this input, the mapping system should be able to generate the actual mappings, by working out the missing details. To support this process, mapping systems usually provide a graphical user interface using which developers may specify the mapping as a set of *value correspondences*, i.e., correspondences among schema elements. In our example, the input provided to the mapping system would be that shown in Fig. 5.2;
- A second essential requirement is concerned with the generation of the target instances, i.e., with the *quality* and efficiency in the generation of solutions.

In this respect, database researchers have identified two main problems: (1) the first one is that of *schema mapping generation*, largely inspired by the seminal Clio papers (Miller et al. 2000; Popa et al. 2002); this is the problem of generating a set of mappings based on the correspondences provided as input by the user; (2) the

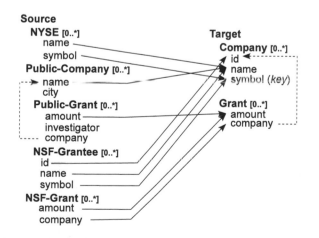

Fig. 5.2 An abstract specification of the mapping as a set of correspondences (*dashed arrows* denote foreign-key constraints)

second one is that of solving the actual *data exchange problem*; originally formalized in Fagin et al. (2005a), this consists in assigning a clear semantics to a given set of mappings, to turn them into executable queries on the source, and updates on the target that generate the desired target instance.

Another important application of schema mappings is query answering (Abiteboul and Duschka 1998). In particular, given a fixed data exchange scenario, target query answering aims at computing the set of answers to a query posed on the target schema. In our example, this amounts to take a query initially expressed on the target tables in Fig. 5.1b, and to reformulate it according to the source tables in Fig. 5.1a.

In recent years, research on schema mappings, data exchange, and query answering have provided quite a lot of building blocks toward this goal. Interestingly, the majority of bulk theoretical ideas for solving the data exchange problem were introduced several years after the first mapping generation techniques had been developed. The main motivation was that of providing a clear theoretical foundation for schema mappings, i.e., a solid formalism that systems could use to reason about mappings and their properties, to optimize them, and to guarantee that data are exchanged in an optimal way.

In the following sections, we provide an overview of these contributions. More specifically:

- Section 2 provides an overview of data exchange theory, and more specifically of the notions of dependencies, mapping scenario, and solution;
- Section 3 introduces the seminal ideas about schema mapping generation, and the early algorithms developed in the framework of the Clio project (Miller et al. 2000; Popa et al. 2002);
- Section 4 describes the recent advancements in terms of schema mapping rewriting techniques that were introduced to improve the quality of solutions;
- Section 5 provides an overview of the complexity results and algorithms developed for query answering over schema mappings;
- Section 6 discusses a number of other interesting developments and applications of schema mapping techniques;
- Finally, Sect. 7 concludes the chapter by discussing the open problems in this area.

2 Preliminaries

To provide a common formalism to be used across the chapter, we first introduce the data model we adopt as a reference. Data exchange was originally formalized for the relation model, so we focus on this data model. Nested sources will be discussed separately in the following sections.

In all of the data exchange theory, databases are considered as collections of relations on two distinct and disjoint domains: a set of *constants*, CONST, a set of *labeled nulls*, NULLS. *Labeled nulls* are used during the generation of solutions to "invent" new values in the target that do not appear in the source database. One way to generate labeled nulls through Skolem functions (Hull and Yoshikawa 1990). A *Skolem function* is an injective function and can be used to produce unique identifiers. It takes one or more arguments and it has the property of producing a unique value for each different set of arguments.

This said, we can formalize the relational model as follows. We fix a set of *labels* $\{A_0, A_1 \ldots\}$, and a set of *relation symbols* $\{R_0, R_1, \ldots\}$. With each relation symbol R, we associate a *relation schema* $R(A_1, \ldots, A_k)$. A *schema* $\mathbf{S} = \{R_1, \ldots, R_n\}$ is a collection of relation schemas. An *instance* of a relation schema $R(A_1, \ldots, A_k)$ is a finite set of tuples of the form $R(A_1 : v_1, \ldots, A_k : v_k)$, where, for each i, v_i is either a constant or a labeled null. An *instance* of a schema $\mathbf{S}$ is a collection of instances, one for each relation schema in $\mathbf{S}$. In the following, we will interchangeably use the positional and nonpositional notation for tuples and facts; also, with an abuse of notation, we will often blur the distinction between a relation symbol and the corresponding instance.

Dependencies and mapping scenarios: Data exchange systems rely on *embedded dependencies* (Beeri and Vardi 1984) to specify mappings. These dependencies are logical formulas of two forms: *tuple-generating dependencies (tgds)* or *equality-generating dependencies (egds)*; each of them has a precise role in the mapping. Informally speaking (the formal definition are reported below):

- *Source-to-target tgds (s-t tgds)*, i.e., tgds that use source relations in the premise, and target relations in the conclusion, are used to specify which tuples should be present in the target based on the tuples that appear in the source; they represent the core of the mapping, since they state how to "move" data from the source to the target;
- *Target tgds*, i.e., tgds the only use target symbols; these are typically used to specify foreign-key constraints on the target;
- *Target egds*, in turn, are typically used to encode key constraints on the target database.

In our example, the desired mapping can be expressed using the following dependencies:

SOURCE-TO-TARGET TGDS
m_1. $\forall s, n: NYSE(s, n) \rightarrow \exists I: Company(I, n, s)$
m_2. $\forall n, c, a, pi: Public\text{-}Company(n, c) \land Public\text{-}Grant(a, pi, n) \rightarrow$
$$\exists I, S: Company(I, n, S) \land Grant(a, I)$$
m_3. $\forall i, n, s: NSF\text{-}Grantee(i, n, s) \rightarrow Company(i, n, s)$
m_4. $\forall a, c: NSF\text{-}Grant(a, c) \rightarrow Grant(a, c)$
TARGET TGDS
t_1. $\forall a, c: Grant(a, c) \rightarrow \exists N, S: Company(c, N, S)$
TARGET EGDS
e_1. $\forall n, n', i, i', s: Company(i, n, s) \land Company(i', n', s) \rightarrow (i = i') \land (n = n')$

Intuitively, each of the s-t tgds specifies how to map the organization of a portion of the source tables to that of a portion of the target tables. In particular, mapping

m_1 copies company names and symbols in the *NYSE* source table to the *Company* table in the target. In doing this, the mapping requires that some value – represented by the I existentially quantified variable – is assigned to the *id* attribute of the *Company* table. The *Public* source contains two relations with companies names and grants that are assigned to them; these information are copied to the target tables by mapping m_2; in this case, a value – again denoted by the I existentially quantified variable – must be "invented" to correlate a tuple in *Grant* with the corresponding tuple in *Company*. Finally, mappings m_3 and m_4 copy data in the *NSF* source tables to the corresponding target tables; note that in this case we do not need to invent any values.

The target tgd encode the foreign key on the target. The target egd simply states that *symbol* is key for *Company*.

To formalize, given two schemas, **S** and **T**, an *embedded dependency* (Beeri and Vardi 1984) is a first-order formula of the form $\forall \overline{x}(\phi(\overline{x}) \rightarrow \exists \overline{y}(\psi(\overline{x}, \overline{y})))$, where $\overline{x}$ and $\overline{y}$ are vectors of variables, $\phi(\overline{x})$ is a conjunction of atomic formulas such that all variables in $\overline{x}$ appear in it, and $\psi(\overline{x}, \overline{y})$ is a conjunction of atomic formulas. $\phi(\overline{x})$ and $\psi(\overline{x}, \overline{y})$ may contain equations of the form $v_i = v_j$, where v_i and v_j are variables.

An embedded dependency is a *tuple-generating dependency* if $\phi(\overline{x})$ and $\psi(\overline{x}, \overline{y})$ only contain relational atoms. It is an *equality generating dependency (egd)* if $\psi(\overline{x}, \overline{y})$ contains only equations. A tgd is called a s-t tgds if $\phi(\overline{x})$ is a formula over **S** and $\psi(\overline{x}, \overline{y})$ over **T**. It is a *target tgd* if both $\phi(\overline{x})$ and $\psi(\overline{x}, \overline{y})$ are formulas over **T**.

A *mapping scenario* (also called a *data exchange scenario* or a *schema mapping*) is a quadruple $\mathcal{M} = (\mathbf{S}, \mathbf{T}, \Sigma_{st}, \Sigma_t)$, where **S** is a source schema, **T** is a target schema, Σ_{st} is a set of s-t tgds, and Σ_t is a set of target dependencies that may contain tgds and egds. If the set of target dependencies Σ_t is empty, we will use the notation $(\mathbf{S}, \mathbf{T}, \Sigma_{st})$.

Solutions. We can now introduce the notion of a *solution* for a mapping scenario. To do this, given two disjoint schemas, **S** and **T**, we shall denote by $\langle \mathbf{S}, \mathbf{T} \rangle$ the schema $\{S_1 \ldots S_n, T_1 \ldots T_m\}$. If I is an instance of **S** and J is an instance of **T**, then the pair $\langle I, J \rangle$ is an instance of $\langle \mathbf{S}, \mathbf{T} \rangle$.

A target instance J is a *solution* of $\mathcal{M}$ and a source instance I (denoted $J \in \mathsf{Sol}(\mathcal{M}, I)$) iff $\langle I, J \rangle \models \Sigma_{st} \cup \Sigma_t$, i.e., I and J together satisfy the dependencies.

Given a mapping scenario $\mathcal{M} = (\mathbf{S}, \mathbf{T}, \Sigma_{st}, \Sigma_t)$, with s-t and target dependencies, we find it useful to define a notion of a *pre-solution* for $\mathcal{M}$ and a source instance I as a solution over I for scenario $\mathcal{M}_{st} = (\mathbf{S}, \mathbf{T}, \Sigma_{st})$, obtained from $\mathcal{M}$ by removing target constraints. In essence, a pre-solution is a solution for the s-t tgds only, and it does not necessarily enforce the target constraints.

Figure 5.3 shows several solutions for our example scenario on the source instance in Fig. 5.1. In particular, solution (a) is a pre-solution, since it satisfies the s-t tgds but it does not comply with the key constraints and therefore it does not satisfy the egds. Solution (b) is a solution for both the s-t tgds and the egds. We want, however, to note that a given scenario may have multiple solutions on a given source instance. This is a consequence of the fact that each tgd only states an

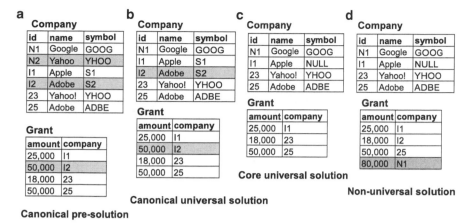

Fig. 5.3 Several solutions for the companies scenario

inclusion constraint, but it does not fully determine the content of the target. To give an example, besides solution (b) in Fig. 5.3, the two target instances (c) and (d) are also solutions for the same source instance.

By looking at these solutions, we notice two things: (1) solution (c) is more compact than solution (b); it can be seen that the grayed tuples in solution (b) are somehow "redundant," since they do not add any information to that contained in solution (c); (2) solution (d) contains a tuple (the one with a gray background) with a ground value (80,000) that does not belong to the source instance. In essence, the space of solutions is quite various: on one side, solutions may have different sizes; intuitively, we prefer those of smaller size; on the other side, some of them may contain some "arbitrary" values that do not really follow from the content of the source instance and from the constraints in $\Sigma_{st} \cup \Sigma_t$.

It is natural to state a couple of quality requirements for solutions to a mapping scenario:

- First, we would like to restrict our attention to those solutions – which we call *universal* – that only contain information that follows from I and $\Sigma_{st} \cup \Sigma_t$;
- Among universal solutions, we would like to select the ones of the smallest size – called the *core universal solutions*.

To formalize these two notions, we introduce the notion of a *homomorphism* among solutions. Given two instances J, J' over a schema $\mathbf{T}$, a *homomorphism* $h : J \rightarrow J'$ is a mapping of the values of $dom(J)$ to the values in $dom(J')$ such that it maps each constant to itself, i.e., for each $c \in const()(J)$, $h(c) = c$, and it maps each tuple in J to a tuple in J', i.e., for each $t = R(A_1 : v_1, \ldots, A_k : v_k)$ in J it is the case that $h(t) = R(A_1 : h(v_1), \ldots, A_k : h(v_k))$ belongs to J'. h is called an *endomorphism* if $J' \subseteq J$; if $J' \subset J$ it is called a *proper endomorphism*.

In essence, a homomorphism is a constant-preserving mapping that can be used to turn one instance into a subset of another. Whenever a homomorphism h turns a tuple t of J into a tuple t' of J', we may be certain that t' contains at least "as much information as" t. Similarly, if h maps J into J', then J' contains at least as much information as J. If, on the contrary, there exists a tuple t in J that contains a constant (like 80,000 in our example) that does not appear in J', i.e., if J contains some "extra" information that is not in J', then there cannot be any homomorphism of t into a tuple of J' and therefore no homomorphism of J itself into J'.

This allows us to formalize the notion of a *universal solution*. A solution J for $\mathcal{M}$ and source instance I is *universal* (Fagin et al. 2005a) (denoted $J \in \mathsf{USol}(\mathcal{M}, I)$) iff for every other solution K for $\mathcal{M}$ and I there is an homomorphism from J to K. In the following, we shall only consider universal solutions.

Among these, we prefer those of minimal size. Given a scenario $\mathcal{M}$, and an instance I, a *core universal solution* (Fagin et al. 2005b) $J \in \mathsf{USol}(\mathcal{M}, I)$, denoted $\mathbf{C} \in \mathsf{Core}(\mathcal{M}, I)$, is a subinstance $\mathbf{C} \subseteq J$ such that there is a homomorphism from J to $\mathbf{C}$, but there is no homomorphism from J to a proper subinstance of $\mathbf{C}$. Cores of universal solutions are themselves universal solutions (Fagin et al. 2005b), and they are all isomorphic to each other. It is therefore possible to speak of *the core solution* as the "optimal" solution, in the sense that it is the universal solution of minimal size (Fagin et al. 2005b).

The chase. A natural question is how it is possible to derive universal solutions for a mapping scenario and a source instance. It turns out that this can be done by resorting to the classical *chase procedure* (Fagin et al. 2005a).

The chase works differently for tgds and egds. Given a vector of variables $\overline{v}$, an *assignment* for $\overline{v}$ is a mapping $a : \overline{v} \to \mathrm{CONST} \cup \mathrm{NULLS}$ that associates with each universal variable a constant in CONST. Given a formula $\phi(\overline{x})$ with free variables $\overline{x}$, and an instance I, we write $I \models \phi(a(\overline{x}))$, whenever I *satisfies* the formula $\phi(a(\overline{x}))$, that is whenever I contains all the atoms in $\phi(a(\overline{x}))$.

Given instances I, J, during the *naive chase* (ten Cate et al. 2009)[1] a tgd $\phi(\overline{x}) \to \exists \overline{y}(\psi(\overline{x}, \overline{y}))$ is fired for all assignments a such that $I \models \phi(a(\overline{x}))$; to fire the tgd, a is extended to $\overline{y}$ by injectively assigning to each $y_i \in \overline{y}$ a fresh null, and then adding the facts in $\psi(a(\overline{x}), a(\overline{y}))$ to J. Consider tgd m_2 in our example:

$$m_2. \ \forall n, c, a, pi, n: Public\text{-}Company(n, c) \wedge Public\text{-}Grant(a, pi, n) \to$$
$$\exists I, S: Company(I, n, S) \wedge Grant(a, I).$$

On source tuples *Public-Company(Adobe, SJ)*, *Public-Grant(Adobe., Anne C., 50,000)* it will generate two target tuples, *Company(N_1, Adobe, N_2)*, and *Grant(50,000, N_1)*, where N_1, N_2 are fresh nulls.

A solution generated by the (naive) chase is called a *canonical solution*. It is possible to prove (Fagin et al. 2005a) that each canonical solution is a universal solution. Chasing the s-t tgds in our example scenario generates the canonical, universal

---

[1] We refer to naive chase rather than to the *standard* chase used in Fagin et al. (2005a), since the naive chase is much simpler and rather straightforward to implement in SQL. Such chase is sometimes calles *oblivious chase*, e.g., in Marnette (2009).

pre-solution in Fig. 5.3a. In Fagin et al. (2005a), the notion of a *weakly-acyclic* set of tgds was introduced to guarantee that the chase terminates and generates a universal solution.

After a canonical pre-solution has been generated by chasing the s-t tgds, to generate an actual universal solution it is necessary to chase the target dependencies. Notice that the chase of target tgds can be defined exactly in the same way, with the variant that it only works for assignments such that $J \models \phi(a(\overline{x}))$. However, in this example, there is no need to chase the target tgd: the pre-solution is also a solution for tgd t_1. In fact, the target tgd states that, whenever a tuple is inserted into the *Grant* table, a corresponding tuple must exist in the the *Company* table, and this is the case in our pre-solution. Generating tgds that have this property is one of the main intuitions behind the Clio algorithms Miller et al. (2000); Popa et al. (2002), which will be discussed in more detail in Sect. 3.

To chase an egd $\phi(\overline{x}) \rightarrow (x_i = x_j)$ over an instance J, for each assignment a such that $J \models \phi(a(\overline{x}))$, if $h(x_i) \neq h(x_j)$, the chase tries to equate the two values. We distinguish two cases: (1) both $h(x_i)$ and $h(x_j)$ are constants; in this case, the chase procedure *fails*, since it attempts to identify two different constants; (2) at least one of $h(x_i)$, $h(x_j)$ is a null – say $h(x_i)$ – in this case chasing the egd generates a new instance J' obtained from J by replacing all occurrences of $h(x_i)$ by $h(x_j)$. To give an example, consider egd e_1:

$$e_1. \ \forall n, n', i, i', s: Company(i, n, s) \wedge Company(i', n', s) \rightarrow (i = i') \wedge (n = n').$$

On the two tuples generated by chasing the tgds, *Company* (23, *Yahoo!, YHOO*), *Company* (N_2, *Yahoo!, YHOO*), chasing the egd equates N_2 to the constant 23, based on the same value for the symbol attribute, *YHOO*. Chasing the egds returns the canonical universal solution in Fig. 5.3b. Notice how the canonical universal solution is not the core universal solution, which in turn is represented in Fig. 5.3c.

Based on these ideas, it is possible to introduce the following procedure to solve a mapping scenario $\mathcal{M}$ given a source instance I:

- First, chase the s-t tgds in Σ_{st} on I to generate a canonical pre-solution, J_{pre};
- Then, chase the target constraints (target tgds and especially egds) on J_{pre} to generate a canonical universal solution, J;
- Minimize J by looking for endomorphic subsets that are still universal solutions to generate the core universal solution, J_0

There currently exist chase engines capable of doing this (Savenkov and Pichler 2008), which we will discuss thoroughly in the remainder of this chapter.

Chasing with SQL. As an alternative, the naive chase of a set of tgds on a given source instance I can be naturally implemented using SQL. Given a tgd $\phi(\overline{x}) \rightarrow \exists \overline{y}(\psi(\overline{x}, \overline{y}))$, to chase it over I we may see $\phi(\overline{x})$ as a first-order query Q_ϕ with free variables $\overline{x}$ over **S**. We may execute $Q_\phi(I)$ using SQL to find all vectors of constants that satisfy the premise.

We now need to insert the appropriate tuples into the target instance to satisfy $\psi(\overline{x}, \overline{y})$. However, to do this, we need to find a way to properly "invent" some fresh nulls for $\overline{y}$. To do this, Skolem functions (Hull and Yoshikawa 1990) are typically used. Given a vector of k universally quantified variables $\overline{x}$, a *Skolem term*[2] over $\overline{x}$ is a term of the form $f(\overline{x})$, where f is a function symbol of arity k. Skolem terms are used to create fresh labeled nulls on the target. Given an assignment of values a for $\overline{x}$, with the Skolem term above we (injectively) associate a labeled null $N_{f(a(\overline{x}))}$.

Based on this, to implement the chase by means of SQL statements, as a preliminary step we replace existential variables in the conclusion by means of Skolem terms. More specifically, for each tgd $m : \phi(\overline{x}) \to \exists\overline{y}(\psi(\overline{x}, \overline{y}))$, we use a different Skolem function f_{m,y_i} for each variable $y_i \in \overline{y}$, and take as argument all universal variables that appear in the conclusion.

To give an example of how the process works, consider tgd m_2 above.

$$m_2. \ \forall n, c, a, pi, n: \textit{Public-Company}(n, c) \wedge \textit{Public-Grant}(a, pi, n) \to$$
$$\exists I, S: \textit{Company}(I, n, S) \wedge \textit{Grant}(a, I).$$

To implement the chase in SQL, the tgd is first rewritten using Skolem terms as follows:

$$m'_2. \ \forall n, c, a, pi, n: \textit{Public-Company}(n, c) \wedge \textit{Public-Grant}(a, pi, n) \to$$
$$\exists I, S: \textit{Company}(f_I(n, a), n, f_S(n, a)) \wedge \textit{Grant}(a, f_I(n, a)).$$

As an example, we show below one of the two SQL statements to which m'_2 is translated (we omit the second on *Grant* for space reasons):

```
INSERT into Company
    SELECT append('fI(',c.name, ',', g.amount, ')'), c.n,
           append('fS(',c.name, ',', g.amount, ')')
    FROM Public-Company c, Public-Grant g
    WHERE c.name = g.company
```

3 Schema Mappings: The Early Years

The design of mappings had for a long time been a manual task. Transformation designers had to express their mappings in complex transformation languages and scripts, and this only after they had obtained a good knowledge and understanding of the semantics of the schemas and of the desired transformation. As schemas started to become larger and more complex, it was soon realized that the manual design of the mappings was at the same time laborious, timeconsuming, and error-prone. While seeking support for mapping designers, mapping tools were created with the intention of raising the level of abstraction and the automated part of the

---

[2] While Skolem terms are usually nested, for the sake of simplicity here we only consider flat terms.

tasks. This section provides an overview of the developments in mapping generation since the very first need of data transformations, until the development of the first schema mapping tools under the form they are widely understood today. Having defined the data exchange problem, this section describes how a mapping scenario can be constructed. The presented algorithm, which is the basis of the Clio (Popa et al. 2002) mapping scenario generation mechanism, has the additional advantage that generates scenarios in which the mappings respect the target schema constraints. In that sense, generating the target instance can be done by taking into consideration only the mappings of the mapping scenario and not the target schema constraints. This kind of mappings are more expressive that other formalisms such as simple correspondence lines (Rahm and Bernstein 2001) or morphisms (Melnik et al. 2005).

3.1   The First Data Translation Systems

Since the beginning of data integration, a major challenge has been the ability to translate data from one format to another. This problem of *data translation* has been studied for many years, in different variants and under different assumptions. One of the first systems was EXPRESS (Shu et al. 1977), a system developed by IBM. A series of similar but more advanced tools have followed EXPRESS. The TXL language (Abu-Hamdeh et al. 1994), initially designed to describe syntactic software transformations, offered a richer set of operations and soon became popular in the data management community. It was based on transformation rules that were fired upon successful parsing of the input data. The problem became more challenging when data had to be transformed across different data models, a situation that was typically met in wrapper construction (Tork-Roth and Schwarz 1997). MDM (Atzeni and Torlone 1997) was a system for this kind of transformations that was based on patterns (Atzeni and Torlone 1995).

   Some later works (Beeri and Milo 1999) proposed a tree-structured data model for describing schemas, and showed that the model was expressive enough to represent relational and XML schemas, paving the way for the later introduction of tree-based transformations. A formal foundation for data translation was created, alongside a declarative framework for data translation (Abiteboul et al. 1997). Based on this work, the TranScm system (Milo and Zohar 1998) used a library of transformation rules and pattern matching techniques to select the most applicable rules between two schemas, in an effort to automate the whole data translation task. Other transformation languages developed in parallel emphasized on the type checking (Cluet et al. 1998) task or on integrity constraint satisfaction (Davidson and Kosky 1997).

3.2 Correspondences

The first step toward the creation of mappings between two schemas was to understand how the elements of the different schemas relate to each other. This relationship had to be expressed in some high level specification. That specification was materialized in the form of correspondences.

A *correspondence* maps atomic elements of a source schema to atomic elements of the target schema. This specification is independent of logical design choices such as the grouping of elements into tables (normalization choices), or the nesting of records or tables (for example, the hierarchical structure of an XML schema). In other words, one need not specify the logical access paths (join or navigation) that define the associations between the elements involved. Therefore, even users that are unfamiliar with the complex structure of the schema can easily specify them. Correspondences can be represented graphically through simple arrows or lines that connect the elements of the two schemas.

The efficacy of using element-to-element correspondences is greatly increased by the fact that they need not be specified by a human user. They could be in fact the result of an automatic component that matches the elements of the two schemas, and then the mapping designer simply verifies the correctness of the results. This task is found in the literature under the name *schema matching* and has received considerable attention, and has led into a variety of methodologies and techniques (Rahm and Bernstein 2001).

A correspondence can be formally described as a tgd with one and only one existentially quantified variable being equal to one of the universally quantified variables, and one term on each side of the dependency (for the case of the relational schemas). The correspondence states that every value of the source schema element represented by the first variable should also exist in the instance values of target schema element represented by the second.

In certain cases, correspondences that involve more than one source schema elements may exist, but there should always be one existentially quantified variable whose value is determined as a function of the universally quantified variables representing the participated source schema elements.

Consider the example of Fig. 5.4a, which is a variation of the example presented previously. Here, the first source consists of only the three relational tables Public-Company, Public-Grant, and Contact, while the target consists of only the table Company. As before, the intra-schema lines represent schema constraints, and in the particular example are foreign key constraints. The red dotted inter-schema lines represent the correspondences. Note that the appearance of an attribute with the same or similar name in both schemas does not necessarily mean that the two attributes represent the same fact. For instance, consider the attributes symbol and id. Although in the companies world these terms may be used interchangingly, in the specific example, the lack of a line among them may be justified by a case in which the attribute id may represent the fiscal number of the company while the attribute symbol may be the symbol with which the company appears in the stock exchange.

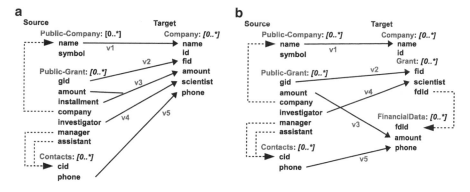

Fig. 5.4 Two schema matching examples

The line v_1 from the attribute **name** of the **Public-Company** table to the attribute **name** of the **Company** table represents a correspondence declaring that the latter has to be populated with values from the former. Its tgd representation is:

$$v_1 : \forall na, sy\ Public-Company(na, sy) \rightarrow$$
$$\exists na2, id, fi, am2, sc, ph2\ Company(na2, id, fi, am2, sc, ph2),\ na2 = na.$$

It can be seen in the above logical expression that among all the existential variables of its right-hand side, only the value of the $na2$ is determined by a source variable, i.e., one of the universally quantified.

A situation that demonstrate the case in which an attribute value in the target schema is created by a combination of attribute values from the source is the one of **amount**. Although the attribute amount appears in both schemas, it may be the case that in the first, amount means the amount of an installment while in the second amount may mean the total figure. In that case, the value of the latter is composed by the value of the former multiplied by the number of installments that is stored in the attribute **installments**. The tgd of the correspondence is:

$$v_3 : \forall gi, um, ln, co, re, ma, as\ Public - Grant(gi, am, in, co, re, ma, as) \rightarrow$$
$$\exists na2, id, fi, am2, sc, ph2\ Company(na2, id, fi, am2, sc, ph2),\ am2 = am * in$$

Note that even in this case, there is only one target schema variable whose value is determined by source variable values.

While easy to create, understand, and manipulate, element correspondences are not expressive enough to describe the full semantics of a transformation. As a consequence, they are inherently ambiguous. There may be many mappings that are consistent with a set of correspondences, and still, not all of them have the same semantics. A mapping generation tool needs to be able to identify what the mapping designer had in mind when he/she provided a given set of correspondences, and generate plausible interpretations to produce a precise and faithful representation of the transformation, i.e., the mappings. For instance, in the schema mapping scenario of Fig. 5.4a, consider only the correspondence v_1. One possible mapping that this correspondence alone describes is that for each Public-Company in the source instance, there should be in the target instance a Company with the same name. Based on a similar reasoning for correspondence v_2, for every Public-Grant with identifier gid in the source instance, it is expected that there should be a Company tuple in the target instance with that grant identifier as attribute fid. By noticing that a Public-Grant is related to a Public-Company through the foreign key on attribute company, one can easily realized that a more natural interpretation of these two correspondences is that every public grant identifier found in a target schema tuple of table Company should have as an associated company name the name of the respective public company that the public grant is associated in the source. Yet, it is not clear, whether public companies with no associated grants should appear in the target table Company with a null fid attribute, or should not appear at all. Furthermore, note that the target schema relation has an attribute phone that is populated from the homonym attribute from the source. This value should not be random but somehow related to the company and the grant. However, note that the Contact table in which the phone is located is related to the grant information through two different join paths, i.e., one on the manager and one on the assistant. The information provided by the correspondence on the phone is not enough to specify whether the target should be populated with the phone of the manager or the phone of the assistant.

The challenging task of interpreting the ambiguous correspondences gave raise to the schema mapping problem as it has been introduced in Sect. 2.

3.3   Schema Mapping as Query Discovery

One of the first mapping tools to systematically study the schema mapping problem was Clio (Miller et al. 2000), a tool developed by IBM. The initial algorithm of the tool considers each target schema relation independently. For each relation R_i, it creates a set V^{R_i} of all the correspondences that are on a target schema element that belongs to the relation R_i. Naturally, all these sets are mutually disjoint. For each such set, a query $Q_{V^{R_i}}$ will be constructed to populate the relation R_i. The latter query is constructed as follows. The set V^{R_i} of correspondences is further divided into maximal subsets such that each such maximal subset $M_k^{V^{R_i}}$ contains at most one correspondence for each attribute of the respective target schema relation. For all the source schema elements used by the correspondences in each such subset, the possible join paths connecting them are discovered, and combined to form the union of join queries. These queries are then combined together through an outer union operator to form the query $Q_{V^{R_i}}$.

3.4   Schema Mapping as Constraint Discovery

The algorithm for managing the schema mapping problem as query discovery failed to handle two important cases. The first, was the complex nesting schema situations, and the second was the management of unspecified attributes, i.e., attributes in the target schema for which there is no correspondence to specify their value, yet, the target schema specification either does not permit a null value, or even if it does, its use will lead to loss of information. Furthermore, it became clear that the schema information in conjunction will the correspondences could not always lead into a full specification of the target instance, but only into a constraint relationship between the source and the target instance. Thus, the notion of a mapping stopped being the actual transformation script and became this notion of inter-schema constraint, expressed as a tgd. This is a more natural view of the mapping problem since with schemas being heterogeneous, it is natural to expect that not all the information represented in the source can also exist in the target, and vice versa. Since a mapping describes only the data that is to be exchanged between the schemas, the information described by the mapping is a subset of the information described by the schemas.

Consider the example of Fig. 5.4b. The situation is more or less the same as the one on its left, with the small difference that the target schema has all the grant information grouped and nested within the company in which the grant belongs. Furthermore, the amount of the grand is not stored within the grand but separately in the FinancialData structure. Note that the Grant structure has an attribute fdid used by no correspondence, thus it could have remained null, if the target schema specification permits it. If not, a random value could have been generated to deal with this restriction. Unfortunately, either of the two actions would break the relationship of the funding information with its amount, since the attribute fdid is actually the foreign key relationship that connects their respective structures.

To discover the intended meaning of the correspondences and generate the mappings, it is important to realize how the elements within a schema relate to each other. This relationship will guide the combination of correspondences into groups and the creation of the expected mappings. The idea for doing so comes from the work on the universal relation (Maier et al. 1984). The universal relation provides a single-relation view of the whole database in a way that the user does not have to specify different tables and join paths. The construction of the universal relation is based on the notion of logical access paths, or *connections*, as they were initially introduced, and are groups of attributes connected either by being in the same table or by following foreign key constraints (Maier et al. 1984).

A generalized notion of a *connection* is that of the *association* (Popa et al. 2002). Intuitively, an *association* represents a set of elements in the same schema alongside their relationships. An association is represented as a logical query whose head consists of a relation with all the attributes mentioned in the body. For simplicity, the head of the association is most of the time omitted. As an example, the following logical query body:

$$A(x, y, z), \ B(u, v, w), \ x = u$$

represents an association that consists of the six attributes of the tables A and B, for which the first is equal to the fourth. Obviously, not all associations are semantically meaningful. In database systems, there are many ways one can specify semantic relationships between schema elements, but three are the most prevalent, the schema structure, the schema constraints, and the user specification, which define three respective kinds of associations.

The structural associations are based on the aggregation of schema elements as it has been specified by the database designer. For instance, the placement of a number of attributes in the same tables means that these attributes are related to each other, most probably by describing different characteristics of the entity that the respective table represents. In a relational schema, there is one structural association for each set of attributes in a table. For a nested schema, there is a structural association for each set element, at any level of nesting. The association is constructed by collecting all the nonset subelements of the set element alongside all the nonset subelements of every set element ancestor. Due to the way structural associations are constructed in nested schemas, they are also known broadly as *primary paths*. The source schema of Fig. 5.4a has the following three primary paths: (1) $Public{-}Company(na, sy)$, (2) $Public{-}Grant(gi, am, in, co, re, ma, as)$, and (3) $Contact(ci, ph)$, while the target schema has only the $Company(na2, id, fi, am, sc, ph2)$.

For the scenario of Fig. 5.4b, the primary paths of the source schema are the same, while those of the target schema are: (1) $Company(na2, id)$, (2) $Company(na2, id, Grant)$, $Grant(fi, sc, fd)$, and (3) $FinancialData(fd2, am2, ph2)$. Note that the structural association that contains the elements of the set element Grant, those of the set element Company are also included since the former is nested within the latter.

Schema formalisms may not always be enough to describe the full semantics of the data. A data administrator may have some knowledge about sets of attributes that are associated that is nowhere recorded. Based on this user knowledge, an association can be constructed. These kinds of associations are known as *user associations* (Velegrakis 2005).

Apart from the schema structure, another way database designers can specify semantic relationships between schema elements is the use of schema constraints. This lead to the form of association called the *logical associations*. A logical association is a maximal set of schema elements that are related either through user specification (user association), or through structural construction (structural association), or through constraints. Since logical associations are based on constraints, they can be used as an alternative for computing different join paths on the schema.

Logical associations, also known in the literature, as logical relations, are computed by using the chase (Maier et al. 1979), a classical method that has been used in query optimization (Popa and Tannen 1999), although originally introduced to test implications of functional dependencies. A chase procedure is a sequence of chase steps. A chase step is an enhancement of an association using a schema constraint. In particular, when the left part of the tgd that expresses a referential constraint is logically implied by the logical representation of the association, then the latter is enhanced with the terms and the conditions of the right-hand side of the tgd of the constraint. This intuitively means that the association is expanded to include the referenced attributes of the constraint. The procedure is repeated until no more schema constraints can be applied, in which case the association has become maximal. This maximal association is a logical association. Maier et al. (Maier et al. 1979) have shown that for the relational model, two different chase sequences with the same set of dependencies, i.e., constraints, generate identical results. Popa (Popa 2000) has shown a similar result for the case of the nested relational model. These two results mean that the the result of the chase of a user or a structural association with a set of constraints is unique. To illustrate how the logical relations are computed, consider again the example on Fig. 5.4b. Let A represent the structural association $Public-Grant(gi, am, co, in, ma, as)$. The tgd expressing the foreign key constraint from the attribute company to name is $Public-Grant(gi, am, co, in, ma, as) \rightarrow Public-Company(na, sy)$, $na = co$. Its left-hand side is the same as A, thus, the question on whether it is logically implied by A is yes, which means that a chase step can be applied on A using the specific constraint. This will enhance A with the contents of the right-hand side of the tgd of the constraint, bringing the association into the form:

$$Public-Grant(gi, am, co, in, ma, as), \ Public-Company(na, sy), \ na = co$$

Further chase steps on the association using the foreign key constraints on the attributes manager and assistant will further expand the association into the form:

$$Public-Grant(gi, am, co, in, ma, as), \ Public-Company(na, sy),$$
$$Contact(cim, phm), \ Contact(cia, pha), \ na = co \land cim = ma \land cia = as .$$

Since no other constraint can be further applied to it A, A in its last form is a logical association.

Associations form the basis for understanding how the correspondences can be combined together to form groups that will produce semantically meaningful mappings. The technique presented here forms the basis of the Clio (Fagin et al. 2009) mapping tool. Given a set of correspondences, Clio generates a mapping scenario with nested tgds. Similar technique has also been adapted by other tools, such as Spicy (Bonifati et al. 2008a) or HePToX (Bonifati et al. 2005). This is done by considering pairs of source and target logical associations. For each such pair, the set of correspondences covered by the pair is discovered. A correspondence is said to be covered by the pair A, B of a source and a target association, if its left and right part (apart from the equality condition) are logically implied by A and B, respectively. A mapping is formed by creating a tgd whose left-hand side consists of association A, and whose right-hand side is the association B enhanced with the conditions of the covered correspondences. Note that the covering of a correspondence is based on the notion of homomorphism. If there are multiple homomorphisms, then there are multiple alternative mappings. Consider, for instance, the source-target logical association pair $Public-Company(na, sy)$ and $Company(na2, id, Grand)$.

Only the correspondence $v1$ is covered by this pair. This leads to the mapping m_1: $Public{-}Company(na, sy) \rightarrow Company(na2, id, Grand), na2 = na$, where the last equation is the one that was on the tgd representation of the correspondence $v1$.

For the source-target logical association pair A and B, where A is

$$Public{-}Grant(gi, am, co, in, ma, as), \; Public{-}Company(na, sy),$$
$$Contact(cim, phm), \; Contact(cia, pha), \; na{=}co \; \wedge \; cim{=}ma \; \wedge \; cia{=}as$$

and B is

$$Company(na2, id, Grand), \; Grant(fi, sc, sd),$$
$$FinancialData(fd2, am2, ph2), \; fd2{=}fd,$$

all the correspondences illustrated in Fig. 5.4 are covered. However, for $v5$ there are two ways that it can be covered, which leads to two different mappings. The first is:

$$Public{-}Grant(gi, am, co, in, ma, as), \; Public{-}Company(na, sy),$$
$$Contact(cim, phm), \; Contact(cia, pha), \; na{=}co \; \wedge \; cim{=}ma \; \wedge \; cia{=}as$$
$$\rightarrow \; Company(na2, id, Grand), \; Grant(fi, sc, sd),$$
$$FinancialData(fd2, am2, ph2), \; fd2{=}fd \; \wedge$$
$$na2{=}na \; \wedge \; fi{=}gi \; \wedge \; am2{=}am \; \wedge \; re{=}sc \; \wedge \; ph2{=}pha.$$

The second mapping is exactly the same with the only difference that the last equality is $ph2{=}phm$ instead of $ph2{=}pha$.

Note that through the right-hand side conditions, the mappings guarantee to generate data that does not violate the constraints of the target schema, which is why finding a solution to a Clio generated scenario does not need to take into consideration the target schema constraints, since they have been taken into consideration in the source-to-target tgd construction.

3.5 Data Exchange and Query Generation

Once the mapping scenario has been constructed, the next step it to find a solution (see Sect. 2). Clio (Popa et al. 2002) was the first tool to consider mappings in a nested relational setting, thus offering not only mappings that were nested tgds, but also an algorithm for generating nested universal solutions.

The algorithm mainly starts by creating a graph of the target schema in which every node corresponds to a schema element, i.e., a table or an attribute in the case of a relational schema. Then, the nodes are annotated with source schema elements from where the values will be derived. These annotations propagate to other nodes based on the nested relationship and on integrity constraint associations. The value for the unspecified elements is the result if a Skolem function that gets as arguments the values of all the source schema elements of the source. The annotations that have been made on the set elements are used to create Skolem functions that drive the right nesting. More details can be found in Fagin et al. (2009).

At this point, the final queries, or transformation scripts in general, can be constructed. First, the variable of every unspecified target schema element in the mapping is replaced by its Skolem function expression. In its simplest brute-force form, the final query is generated by first executing the query described on the left-hand side of the mapping tgd expression for every nesting level, i.e., for every set element of any nesting depth of the target. Then, the Skolem functions that have been computed for the set elements of the target are used to partition the result set of these queries and place them nested under the right elements. The full details of this task can be found in Fagin et al. (2009).

4 Second-Generation Mapping Systems

Inspired by the seminal papers about the first schema mapping system (Miller et al. 2000; Popa et al. 2002), in the following years a rich body of research has proposed algorithms and tools to improve the easiness of use of mapping systems (An et al. 2007; Raffio et al. 2008; Cabibbo 2009; Mecca et al. 2009b) (see Sect. 7 and Chap. 9) and the quality of the solutions they produce. As experimentally shown in Fuxman et al. (2006); Mecca et al. (2009a), different solutions for the same scenario may differ significantly in size and for large source instances the amount of redundancy in the target produced by first generation mapping systems may be very large, thus impairing the efficiency of the exchange and the query answering process. Since the core is the smallest among the solutions that preserve the semantics of the exchange, it is considered a desirable requirement for a schema mapping system to generate executable scripts that materialize core solutions for a mapping scenario.

In this section, we present results related to this latest issue and we show how novel algorithms for mapping generation and rewriting have progressively addressed the challenge of producing the best solution for data exchange.

4.1 Problems with Canonical Solutions

To see how translating data with mapping systems from a given source database may bring to a certain amount of redundancy into the target data, consider again the mapping scenario in Fig. 5.2 and its source instance in Fig. 5.1. To simplify the discussion, in the following we drop the target egd constraints as they are not handled by most mapping systems during the schema mapping generation. Based on the schemas and the correspondences in the scenario, a constraint-driven mapping system such as Clio would rewrite the target tgd constraints into a set of s-t tgds (using the logical associations described in Sect. 3), like the ones below.

m_1. $\forall s, n$: $NYSE(s, n) \rightarrow \exists I$: $Company(I, n, s)$

m_2. $\forall n, c, a, pi$: $Public\text{-}Company(n, c) \wedge Public\text{-}Grant(a, pi, n) \rightarrow$
$$\exists I, S$: Company(I, n, S) \wedge Grant(a, I)$$

m_3. $\forall i, n, s$: $NSF\text{-}Grantee(i, n, s) \rightarrow Company(i, n, s)$

m_4. $\forall a, c$: $NSF\text{-}Grant(a, c) \rightarrow \exists M, S$: $Company(c, M, S) \wedge Grant(a, c)$.

Notice that these expressions are different from those in Sect. 2. In fact, the mapping tool is taking care of the foreign key constraint in m_4 and produces the canonical universal solution in Fig. 5.5a. While this instance satisfies the s-t tgds (and the original target tgd), still it contains many redundant tuples, those with a gray background.

Consider, for example, the tuple $t_1 = $ (N2, Yahoo!, YHOO) in the *Company* table; it can be seen that the tuple is redundant since the target contains another tuple $t_2 = $ (23, Yahoo!, YHOO) for the same company, which in addition to the company name also gives information about its id in the target database (i.e., there is an homomorphism from t_1 to t_2). A similar argument holds for the tuples (I2, Adobe, S2) and (50,000, I2), where I2 and S2 are the values invented by executing tgd m_2, while there are tuples with real id and symbol values for the same company and grant. The core in this example is the solution reported in Fig. 5.5b.

Therefore, a natural requirement for a schema mapping system becomes that of materializing core solutions. We now review the algorithms that have been proposed to compute the core solution in a relational data exchange setting.

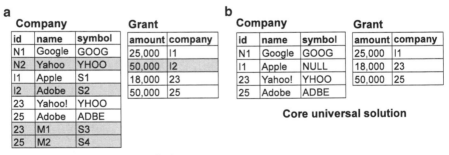

a

Company

id	name	symbol
N1	Google	GOOG
N2	Yahoo	YHOO
I1	Apple	S1
I2	Adobe	S2
23	Yahoo!	YHOO
25	Adobe	ADBE
23	M1	S3
25	M2	S4

Grant

amount	company
25,000	I1
50,000	I2
18,000	23
50,000	25

Canonical universal solution

b

Company

id	name	symbol
N1	Google	GOOG
I1	Apple	NULL
23	Yahoo!	YHOO
25	Adobe	ADBE

Grant

amount	company
25,000	I1
18,000	23
50,000	25

Core universal solution

Fig. 5.5 Canonical and core solutions for the mapping scenario

4.2 Theoretical Results on Core Computation

The first approach that has been studied to generate the core for a relational data exchange problem is to generate the canonical solution, and then to apply a post-processing algorithm for its core identification. It is known that computing the core of an arbitrary relational instance with variables is NP-complete, as many NP-complete problems (e.g., computing the core of a graph (Fagin et al. 2005b; Hell and Nešetřil 1992) or conjunctive query optimization (Chandra and Merlin 1977)) can be reduced to it. In contrast with the case of computing the core of an arbitrary instance, computing the core of a universal solution in data exchange can be done in polynomial time.

In Fagin et al. (2005b), an algorithm is presented that computes the core in polynomial time in a restricted setting, that is, for a data exchange problem whose source-to-target constraints are tgds and whose target constraints consist of arbitrary egds only. More specifically, they proved that the core of a universal solution can be computed in polynomial time in two settings: (1) when the set of target constraints is empty, (2) when the set of target constraints contains egds only. To address these goals, two different methods are provided.

A *greedy* algorithm, given a source instance I, first computes an universal solution J for I, if it exists, and then computes its core by successively removing tuples from J, as long as I and the instance resulting in each step satisfy the s-t tgds and the target constraints. Although the greedy algorithm is conceptually simple, it requires the availability of the source instance I for the execution of the algorithm.

The *blocks* method does not require the availability of the source instance and is based on the relationships among the labeled nulls of a canonical solution J. The *Gaifman graph* of the nulls of J is an undirected graph in which the nodes are the nulls of J and there exists an edge between two labeled nulls whenever there exists some tuple in some relation of J in which both labeled nulls occur. A *block* of nulls is the set of nulls in a connected component of the Gaifman graph of the nulls. Given J as the result of applying the s-t tgds to a ground source instance S, the block method starts from the observation that the Gaifman graph of the labeled nulls of the result instance J consists of connected components whose size is bounded by a constant b. The main step of the algorithm relies on the observation that checking whether there is a homomorphism from any $J \in K$, where K is any set of instances with such bound b, into any arbitrary other instance J_0 is feasible in polynomial time. The algorithm works also for the case where the target constraints consist of egds, which, when applied, can merge blocks by equating variables from different blocks. Thus, after chasing J with egds, the resulting J' can lost the bounded block-size property. However, the authors show an algorithm that looks at the nulls in J and computes its core by successively finding and applying a sequence of small *useful* endomorphisms; where *useful* means that at least one null disappears. More practically, (1) the algorithm starts computing a canonical universal solution J_0, (2) then it recursively generates a sequence of intermediate instances such that, given the intermediate instance J_i, there is a useful endomorphism that is the identity everywhere except for a block from J_i to J_{i+1}; (3) when the algorithm stops, the instance J_i is the core solution. The polynomial-time bound is due to the total number of endomorphisms that the algorithm explores, which is at most n^b for each block of J_0, where b is the maximum number of existentially quantified variables over all the s-t tgds and n is the number of tuples in J_0.

Gottlob and Nash (2008) extended previous results by introducing an algorithm that computes, still in polynomial time, the core solution of a data exchange problem whose target constraints are (weakly-acyclic) tgds and arbitrary egds. The authors introduce novel technical intuitions to compute the core of universal solutions and prove two complexity bounds. Using an exhaustive enumeration algorithm, they get an upper bound of $O(vm|dom(J)|^b)$, where v is the number of variables in the canonical solution J, m is the size of J, and b is the block size of J. There exist cases where a better bound can be achieved by relying on hypertree decomposition techniques. In such cases, the upper bound is $O(vm^{\lceil b/2 \rceil + 2})$, with special benefits if the target constraints of the data exchange scenario are LAV tgds.

The main algorithm in Gottlob and Nash (2008) has been revised in Savenkov and Pichler (2008) (by removing the simulation of egds with full tgds) and in Marnette (2009) (by replacing a key component of the algorithm with a faster one). Also, an implementation of the core-computation algorithm in Gottlob and Nash (2008) has been developed (Savenkov and Pichler 2008): the prototype uses a relational DBMS to chase tgds and egds, and a specialized engine to find endomorphisms and minimize the universal solution.

The algorithms above provide a very general solution to the problem of computing core solutions for a data exchange setting and made significant steps toward the goal of integrating core computations into schema mapping systems. However, experience with these algorithms shows that, although polynomial, they require very high computing times since they look for all possible endomorphisms among tuples in the canonical solution (Savenkov and Pichler 2008; Mecca et al. 2009a). As a consequence, recursive algorithms iterating on intermediate instances hardly scale to large mapping scenarios: the necessity to study more scalable solutions than postprocessing approaches motivated the works that follow.

4.3   Generating Core Solutions with SQL Scripts

The fact that s-t tgds produced by first-generation schema mapping systems may generate redundancy in the target has motivated several practical proposals toward the goal of removing such redundant data. Unfortunately, some of these works are applicable only in some cases and do not represent a general solution to the problem. Only recently, there have been proposals for general rewriting techniques that are able to obtain core solution with executable scripts. As we discuss next, all the mapping systems that attempted to reduce the redundancy in the solutions started from the formalism and the algorithms in Popa et al. (2002).

Early attempts. Nested mappings (Fuxman et al. 2006) are s-t tgds that extend the language of s-t tgds allowing the arbitrary nesting of mapping formulas within other mapping formulas. As an example, the schema mapping from the example in the right-hand side of Fig. 5.4 can be defined by means of nested s-t tgds. We omit the quantifiers for the sake of readability (variables on the right that do not appear on the left are existentially quantified), while the atomic variables are in lowercase and the set variables start with uppercase, as follows:

$$m'_1.\ Public\text{-}Company(sn, ss) \rightarrow [Company(sn, ti, Grant)$$
$$\wedge [Public\text{-}Grant(sg, sa, sn, sr, sm, sa) \wedge Contact(sm, ph) \wedge Contact(sa, ph2) \rightarrow$$
$$Grant(sg, sr, tf) \wedge FinancialData(tf, sa, ph)]].$$

The second mapping is exactly the same with the only difference that the last variable in atom *FinancialData* is $ph2$ instead of ph.

Intuitively, whenever a tgd m_1 writes into a target relation R_1 and a tgd m_2 writes into a relation R_2 nested into R_1, it is possible to "correlate" the two mappings by nesting m_2 into m_1. The correlation among inner and outer mappings can be observed by the variable sn both in *Public-Company* and in *Public-Grant* in the example above. This rewritten mapping reduces the amount of redundant tuples in the target, since the same data is not mapped twice in the generated target instance. The same intuition applies if R_2 contains a foreign key pointing to relation R_1. Nested mappings are correlated in a rewriting step based on a *nestable* property for a given pair of mappings. The property is verified with a syntactical check based on the structures of the schemas involved in the mappings and the correspondences between them. Once the property has been verified for all the mappings composing a scenario, the nesting algorithm constructs a DAG, where a node is a mapping having edges to other mappings for which it is nestable. The DAG represents all the possible ways in which mappings can be nested under other mappings. The algorithm identifies root mappings for the DAG (mappings that are not nestable), for each root mapping traverses the DAG to identify a tree of mappings, and generates a nested mapping for each tree rewriting the variables accordingly to the structure.

As nested mappings factor out common subexpressions, there are many benefits in their use: (1) it is possible to produce more efficient translation queries by reducing the number of passes over the source; (2) the generated data have less redundancy as the same data are not mapped repeatedly by s-t tgds sharing common parts.

Another attempt to reduce the redundancy generated by basic mappings has been proposed by Cabibbo (2009). The work introduced a revision of both the mapping and the query generation algorithms. In the mapping generation phase, the presence of nullable attributes is considered to introduce an extended notion of logical associations, a modified chase procedure to compute them, and novel pruning rules used together with the subsumption and implication rules from Popa et al. (2002). The query generation algorithm is also revised to ensure the satisfaction of target key constraints or to unveil unsatisfiability of such keys. Moreover, when there are key conflicts between groups of logical mappings with the same target relation, an algorithm tries to resolve those conflicts by rewriting conflicting logical mappings in queries with negations. Such interaction between mapping and query generation algorithms allows to have similar benefits to those gained by nested mappings in different relational settings. In particular, those techniques generate target data with less redundancy, as source data involved in the same target key constraints is copied by the generated queries only once.

Unfortunately, the approaches above are applicable only in some specific cases: the above techniques benefits apply only when schemas and correspondences obey to certain structures or require the presence of key constraints to reduce the redundancy in the output. Therefore, those approaches do not represent a general solution to the problem of generating neither core nor compact universal solutions.

SQL core-generation algorithms. The following systems introduce core computation algorithms that, given a set of s-t tgds, enable a more efficient implementation by means of executable scripts that scale well to large databases. This problem has been first approached in Chiticariu (2005), where an algorithm is presented for schema mappings specified by the limited class of s-t tgds with single atomic formulas (without repetition of existential quantified variables) in the conclusions.

The first complete proposal of an algorithm for rewriting s-t tgds to generate core solutions was introduced in Mecca et al. (2009a). This work is based on the exploiting of two key ideas: the notion of *homomorphism among formulas* and the use of *negation* to rewrite tgds.

m_1. $\forall s, n: NYSE(s, n) \rightarrow \exists I: Company(I, n, s)$

m_2. $\forall n, c, a, pi: Public\text{-}Company(n, c) \wedge Public\text{-}Grant(a, pi, n) \rightarrow$
$$\exists I, S: Company(I, n, S) \wedge Grant(a, I)$$

m_3. $\forall i, n, s: NSF\text{-}Grantee(i, n, s) \rightarrow Company(i, n, s)$

m_4. $\forall a, c: NSF\text{-}Grant(a, c) \rightarrow Grant(a, c)$.

The first intuition is that it is possible to analyze the set of formulas to recognize when two tgds may generate redundant tuples in the target. This happens when it is possible to find a homomorphism between the right-hand sides of the two tgds. Consider the right-hand sides of the s-t tgds m_1 and m_3 from the Example in Sect. 2 reported here for convenience; with an abuse of notation, we treat the two formulas as sets of tuples, with existentially quantified variables that correspond to nulls. It can be seen that the conclusion $Company(I, n, s)$ of m_1 can be mapped into the conclusion $Company(i, n, s)$ of m_3 by the following mapping of variables: $I \rightarrow i$, $n \rightarrow n$, $s \rightarrow s$; in this case, they say that m_3 *subsumes* m_1. This gives a condition to intercept possible redundancy that is general (i.e., key constraint on the target is not required to identify causes of redundancy) and necessary, since the actual generation of endomorphisms among facts in the target data depends on values coming from the source. From the complexity viewpoint, checking for the presence of homomorphisms among formulas, i.e., conclusions of tgds, is completely different than doing the same check among instance tuples: since the number of tgds is typically order of magnitudes smaller than the size of an instance, the check among formulas can be carried out very quickly.

Based on these ideas, the algorithm finds all possible homomorphisms among s-t tgd conclusions. More specifically, it looks for variable mappings that transform atoms in the conclusion of one tgd into atoms belonging to the conclusions of other tgds, with the constraint that universal variables are mapped to universal variables. There are two homomorphisms of this form in the running example. The first one is from the right hand side of m_1 to the rhs of m_3, as discussed above. The second one is from the rhs of m_2 to the union of the conclusions of m_3 and m_4 by the following mapping: $I \to i, n \to n, S \to s, a \to a, I \to c$; in this case, the homomorphisms to be valid imply a condition $i = c$ and they say that m_3, m_4 *cover* m_2.

A second intuition is that, whenever two tgds m, m' such that m subsumes m' are identified, it is possible to prevent the generation of redundant tuples in the target instance by executing them according to the following strategy: first, generate the target tuples for m, the "more informative" mapping; then, generate for m' only those tuples that actually add some new content to the target. In the running example, the original s-t tgds can be rewritten as follows:

$$m_3. \ \forall i, n, s: NSF\text{-}Grantee(i, n, s) \to Company(i, n, s)$$
$$m_4. \ \forall a, c: NSF\text{-}Grant(a, c) \to Grant(a, c)$$
$$m'_2. \ \forall n, c, a, pi, s, i: Public\text{-}Company(n, c) \wedge Public\text{-}Grant(a, pi, n) \wedge$$
$$\wedge \neg (NSF\text{-}Grantee(i, n, s) \wedge NSF\text{-}Grant(a, i)) \to$$
$$\exists I, S: Company(I, n, S) \wedge Grant(a, I)$$
$$m'_1. \ \forall s, n, i: NYSE(s, n) \wedge \neg (NSF\text{-}Grantee(i, n, s)) \to \exists I: Company(I, n, s) \, .$$

Once the original tgds have been rewritten in this form, which are called *core schema mappings*, it is easy to generate an executable transformation under the form of relational algebra expressions where negations become difference operators. The algebraic expressions can then be implemented in an executable script, to be run in any database engine. The authors experimentally show that, in the computation of the target instance, with executable scripts there is a gain in efficiency of orders of magnitude with respect to the postprocessing algorithms (Fagin et al. 2005b; Gottlob and Nash 2008; Savenkov and Pichler 2008).

In ten Cate et al. (2009), the authors independently developed an algorithm to rewrite a set of s-t tgds as a *laconic mapping*, that is, a new set of dependencies from which to generate an SQL script that computes core solutions for the original scenario. The algorithm is more general than the one proposed in Mecca et al. (2009a), since it can be applied to dependencies that make use of arbitrary first-order formulas in the premises, and not only conjunctive formulas.

The main algorithm to rewrite schema mappings as laconic is composed of four step. In the first step, it constructs a finite list of potential patterns of tuples in the core. This step is done by an exhaustive analysis of the target right hand side of each s-t tgd in the input mapping. The number of patterns is finite, but exponential in the size of the schema mapping in general. In the running example, the patterns are the right hand sides of the four original mappings. In the second step, the main algorithm computes for each pattern a *precondition*: a first-order formula over the source schema that is able to identify the cases when the core solution will contain the current pattern. This crucial task is done by relying on a procedure called *certain()*, which rewrites the certain answers of a query on the target as a query on the source. Given a source instance I, a schema mapping M, and a query q on the target schema, the set of *certain answers* to q in I with respect to M, is the intersection of the results from the query $q(J_i)$ over all the possible solutions J_i to the mapping. The authors introduce a practical version of the algorithm in which *certain()* relies on a variant of the MiniCon algorithm (Pottinger and Halevy 2001), which works for conjunctive formulas, and they also announce (ten Cate and Kolaitis 2009) a more general algorithm to compute *certain()* on arbitrary FO queries. In the example, the precondition for the pattern $Company(I, n, s)$ is the left hand side of mapping m'_1 above. In the third step, the algorithm generates additional *side-conditions* to handle special cases with self-joins in the conclusion, i.e., s-t tgds in which the same relation symbols occurs more than once in the right-hand side. Side-conditions are Boolean combination of formulas with inequalities. In our example, side-conditions are not generated as there are not self-joins. In the final step, the algorithm put together the laconic schema mapping with preconditions and side-conditions in the left-handside and the respective pattern in the right-handside, thus generating mappings such as m'_1 above.

In terms of dependencies generated by the algorithm, laconic mappings from the algorithm in ten Cate et al. (2009) tend to contain a lower number of dependencies with more complex premises with respect to the core schema mappings from Mecca et al. (2009a), which typically contain more rules. In fact, laconic mappings reason on patterns at a "global" level, while the rewriting algorithm for core schema mappings works at a "local" level, i.e., at the tgd level.

5   Query Answering in Mapping Scenarios

An important application of schema mappings arises in all the scenarios in which queries are formulated against one of the two schemas connected by the mappings and need to be translated against the other schema. In the early years, the semantics of query answering in indefinite databases adopted the notion of "certain answers." This notion has also been adopted in data exchange (Fagin et al. 2005a), while studying the computational complexity of target query answering, i.e., the problem of computing certain answers for a target query q.

As already explained in Sect. 4.3, to represent all possible databases, we must consider the set of all possible target instances J_i consistent with $\mathcal{M}$ and the source instance I. Since there may be several target instances J_i, we must consider the intersection $\bigcap_{J_i} q(J_i)$, the intersection being called the set of the *certain answers* of q.

In Fagin et al. (2005a), the semantics of query answering has been defined by considering the universal solutions. Indeed, it is important to ascertain whether certain answers of a query can be computed by query evaluation on the "good" target instance that has been chosen for materialization. In Sect. 2, we have already introduced universal solutions for a data exchange scenario. Sufficient conditions for the existence of a universal solution have been defined for weakly acyclic tgds (Fagin et al. 2005a). In this special case, polynomial-time algorithms can be defined to determine whether a solution exists and to produce a particular solution, the canonical universal solution (as defined in Sect. 2). By analyzing query answering issues in greater detail, Fagin et al. (2005a) focuses on determining which target queries can be answered using solely the materialized target instance, and studies the computational complexity of computing certain answers for target queries.

Given a fixed data exchange scenario $\mathcal{M} = (\mathbf{S}, \mathbf{T}, \Sigma_{st}, \Sigma_t)$, for each target query q, the problem is to study the computational complexity of the following problem: given a source instance I, find the certain answers of q with respect to I. If q is a union of conjunctive queries, the certain answers of q can be computed on an arbitrary canonical universal solution. Having this solution homomorphisms to all solutions, and being computable in polynomial time, it implies that the certain answers of q as union of conjunctive queries can also be computed in polynomial time. However, if conjunctive queries have inequalities, computing the certain answers becomes a coNP-complete problem (Abiteboul and Duschka 1998). In particular, in Fagin et al. (2005a), it is shown that computing the certain answers of unions of conjunctive queries with at most two equalities per disjunct is a coNP-complete problem. Beyond the intractability result for the case with two or more inequalities, Fagin et al. (2005a) show that there is a polynomial time algorithm for computing certain answers of queries with at most one inequality per disjunct (thus overcoming the result in Abiteboul and Duschka (1998)).

Fagin et al. (2005a) focus on the relational case, whereas Yu and Popa (2004) extend the target query answering to the XML data model, by also covering the presence of target constraints (also called *nested equality-generating dependencies (NEGDS)*. The latter presence further complicates the problem of defining the correct query answering semantics, since merging rules at the target have to be taken into account. In Yu and Popa (2004), a nested extension of the relational chase (Fagin et al. 2005a) is used to accomodate XML target instances. A basic query rewriting algorithm is presented that consists of four phases, precisely rule generation, query translation, query optimization, and query assembly. The basic version ignores the presence of target constraints. Rule generation is done by creating a rule for each root of the target schema, and by taking the mappings into consideration. The goal of this phase is to set of mapping rules that fully specify the target in terms of the sources, and to prepare the target expressions that will be substituted by source expressions in the next phase. Query translation is done by translating the target query into a set of decorrelated source queries, by exploiting the set of mappings. Optimization is then performed to eliminate equal Skolem terms that have been introduced in the previous phase and to guarantee the minimization of the rewriting, as one of the cases in Deutsch et al. (1999). Finally, decorrelated queries get assembled into nested source queries.

The above steps are modified when target constraints are present, since the above query rewriting becomes incomplete. A resolution step needs to be performed before query optimization takes place, to exhaustively explore all possible rewritings and the application of resolution to them. The computation is a tree, whose branching factor corresponds to the multiple ways of applying a resolution step to a query. The resolution step terminates if the set of source constraints obtained by translating the target constraints is acyclic.

However, the query rewriting algorithm may still be incomplete, as it explicitly avoids recursion. The validity of the incomplete results is proved experimentally, by measuring their approximation with respect to the complete set of certain answers. However, it is still an open problem how to bridge the completeness gap in an efficient way.

Target query answering is addressed in HePToX (Bonifati et al. 2010) as backward translation, i.e., translation of a query q over the target schema and against the direction of the mappings. In HePToX, the opposite direction of query translation, namely the forward translation, is also considered, to highlight the importance of having bidirectional mappings, which can be traversed either ways. A key complication in forward translation is that μ, the mapping that transforms instances of **S** to those of **T**, may not be invertible (Fagin 2007). In this direction, the semantics of query answering is still based on certain answers over all possible pre-images I^k for which $J = \mu(I^k)$. This direction is novel and has not been handled in previous work.

To handle this translation, the query q posed against **S** is transformed into a tree pattern (for simplicity, only one tree pattern is considered, although the query translation module can handle joins of tree patterns). The tree pattern is matched against each of the rule bodies in Σ_{st}; this phase is called *expansion*. The tree pattern, possibly augmented with dummy nodes at the end of the expansion, is translated against the rules in Σ_{st}, leading to the *translation* phase. Several translated tree patterns may be merged in the *stitching* phase, and dummy and redundant nodes may be eliminated in the *contraction* phase.

6 Developments and Applications

In this chapter, we discuss the recent developments and applications of schema mapping. Schema mapping is widely known as the "AI-complete" problem of data management, and, as such, exhibits strong theoretical foundations, as it has been highlighted in the previous sections. However, the question we ask ourselves is: what are the real application scenarios in which schema mapping is used? is schema mapping an everyday life problem? All the scenarios that entail the access to multiple heterogenous datasets represent natural applications of schema mapping (Halevy 2010). For instance, executing a Web search leads to dispatch the request to several web sites that are differently structured and have possible overlapping content. Thus, providing a common semantic layer that lets obtain a uniform answer from multiple sites, by means of explicit or implicit correspondences, is the common objective of schema mapping tools. There are several directions on which researchers have focused their attention, and achieved promising results, namely:

(1) extending the expressiveness of schema mappings to cover data-metadata conflicts (Bonifati et al. 2010, 2005; Hernández et al. 2008); (2) extending them to complex data models, such as XML (Arenas and Libkin 2008; Amano et al. 2009) and ontologies (Calì et al. 2009b,a); (3) using mappings in large-scale distributed scenarios (Bonifati et al. 2010, 2005; Ives et al. 2004); (4) normalizing and optimizing schema mappings (Gottlob et al. 2009; Fagin et al. 2008). We underline that all the above achievements correspond to the need of addressing problems that arise in real life applications. Indeed, if we focus on the first direction, we can easily think of heterogeneus data management scenarios in which instances and schemas contain the same content and need to be bridged (Bonifati et al. 2010, 2005; Hernández et al. 2008). As an example, health care environments have typically the information about patients, diseases, and therapy. However, such information is structured quite differently across the various health care databases. Whereas in one database, the diseases are data instances, it may happen that such values become schema components in another database. Such conflicts, known as data-metadata conflicts, may arise in various other situations, such as multimedia databases, data-intensive web sites, heterogeneous parallel, and distributed databases. We illustrate the implications of dealing with data-metadata conflicts, and discuss the schema mapping tools that support data-metadata mappings in Sect. 6.1. Whereas data integration and exchange tasks have been extensively studied for relational schema mappings, only recently a similar theory has been developed for XML schema mappings (Jiang et al. 2007). Such mappings allow navigational queries with joins and tree patterns, thus enlarging the scope of relational queries (Arenas and Libkin 2008; Amano et al. 2009). Along the same line, disparate data sources may be expressed by means of ontological languages, which are more or less expressive fragments of OWL-2 (OWL-Full 2004). Such languages rely on expressive constructs, in which sophisticate semantic relationships are better represented and go far beyond the expressive power of the relational and XML models. Notwithstanding the complexity of handling such languages to express instances, they are becoming more and more important in data modeling, information integration, and development of the Semantic Web. In particular, there has been in the latest years a paradigm shift from decidability issues on ontologies to scalable query answering for suitable fragments, such as Datalog± (Calì et al. 2009a,b). We discuss the issues behind the treatment of both XML and ontological instances and schema mappings tailored to such instances in Sect. 6.2. Third, we focus on the mapping scalability issues that arise in real scenarios exhibiting distributed heterogeneous data. In such cases, not only the semantic of mappings should be correctly interpreted, but also the efficiency of data exchange and query answering should be guaranteed. Examples of such distributed architectures are numerous if we think of Internet-scale applications and novel highly distributed peer-to-peer systems. In Sect. 6.3, we introduce the systems that so far have addressed this problem, discuss their differences, and the future work in this area. Fourth, schema mappings expressed as source-to-target dependencies may be redundant, due to the presence of unnecessary atoms, and unrelated variables. Recent efforts have aimed at simplifying such dependencies, by obtaining a normal form (Gottlob et al. 2009) and by identifying various classes of

equivalences (Fagin et al. 2008). These optimizations are very important in applications, in which mappings are required to be minimal, for efficiency reasons. We discuss the recent approaches (Gottlob et al. 2009; Fagin et al. 2008) in Sect. 6.4.

6.1 Bridging Data and Metadata

HePToX (Bonifati et al. 2010, 2005) has been the first system to introduce data-metadata correspondences that drive the trasformation from the schema components in the source schema to the instance values in the target schema and vice-versa. Such novel correspondences enrich the semantics of the transformation, while at the same time posing new research challenges. HePToX uses a Datalog-based mapping language called TreeLog; being an extension of SchemaLog, it is capable of handling schema and data at par. TreeLog expressions have been inferred from arrows and boxes between elements in the source schema and instances in the target schema that rely on an ad-hoc graphical notation. By virtue of a bidirectional semantics for query answering, correspondences also involving data-metadata conflicts can be traversed by collecting the necessary components to answer the queries. Queries are expressed in XQuery and the underlying data is expressed in XML to maintain the connection with TreeLog expressions, which are intrinsically nested.

Recently, MAD (MetadatA-Data) mappings (Hernández et al. 2008) have been studied as useful extensions in Clio (Popa et al. 2002), which extend the basic mappings expressed as s-t tgds. Contrary to HePToX, such mappings are used for data exchange. To this purpose, output dynamic schemas are defined, since the result of data exchange cannot be determined a priori whenever it depends on the instances. MAD mappings in Clio are also generated from visual specifications, similarly to HePToX and then translated to executable trasformations. The translation algorithm is a two-step algorithm in which the first step "shreds" the source data into views that offer a relational partitioning of the target schema, and the second step restructures the result of the previous step by also taking into account user-defined grouping in target schema with nested sets.

To summarize, Clio derives a set of MAD mappings from a set of lines between a source schema and a target schema. Applying these transformations computes a target instance that adheres to the target schema and to the correspondences. Similarly, HePToX derives a set of TreeLog mapping rules from element correspondences (i.e., boxes and arrows) between two schemas. TreeLog rules are similar in spirit to s-t tgds, although TreeLog has a second-order syntax. However, the problems solved by Clio and HePToX are different. In Clio, the goal is data exchange, while in HePToX turns to be query reformulation in a highly distributed setting, as we will further discuss in Sect. 6.3.

6.2 Extending Schema Mappings to Complex Data Models

We have recently seen research aiming to study the extensions needed to handle the XML data model for schema mapping (Arenas and Libkin 2008; Amano et al. 2009), data transformation (Jiang et al. 2007), and query rewriting (Yu and Popa 2004). The latter (Yu and Popa 2004) starts from proposing novel algorithms to reformulate target queries against the source schemas, based on the mappings and on the target constraints. Given that the data is at the sources, such queries need to be efficiently evaluated and this work considers for the first time both relational and XML schemas. The presence of the target constraints make the problem ways more complicated by the fact that the data transformed according to the mapping needs to be "merged" afterward. A further complication bears from the fact that the target constraints can enable each other in a recursive way and interact with the mappings as well. A canonical target instance is defined that takes into account the presence of target constraints and mappings, and the semantics of query answering is decided upon this target instance. Moreover, a basic query rewriting algorithm focuses on only mappings first, and extends to XML queries and XML mappings the relational techniques for query rewriting using views. The target constraints, namely the NEGDS, covering XML schema key constraints among the others, are then considered in a query resolution algorithm. Schema mapping for XML data has been studied in Jiang et al. (2007), as an extension of the Clio system. In particular, data transformations involving such a complex data model require more complex transformation primitives than previously relational efforts. For instance, a key challenge arises with XML-to-XML data transformation if the target data is generated as a hierarchy with multiple levels of grouping (as in Fig. 5.4b in Sect. 3). In such a case, a deep union operator must be natively implemented in the transformation engine (and this is done in Clio), as XML query languages, such as XQuery, XSLT, and SQL/XML, are not yet suitable for such task of hierarchically merging XML trees. Reasoning about the full structure of XML documents and developing a theory of expressive XML schema mapping has been only recently tackled (Arenas and Libkin 2008; Amano et al. 2009). In particular, Arenas and Libkin (2008) focus on extending the theory of data exchange to XML, and introduced the XML tree patterns as XML schema mappings. Along the same lines, (Amano et al. 2009) present an analog of source-to-target dependencies for XML schema mappings, discuss their properties, including their complexity, and present static analysis techniques for determining the "consistency" between source schemas and target schemas. The problem of consistency was also dealt with in Arenas and Libkin (2008), and in Amano et al. (2009) it is extended to consider all forms of navigational axes and joins for XML query languages.

Recently, database vendors are extending their products to support ontological reasoning capabilities. Following this direction, research on schema mapping and query rewriting (Calì et al. 2009a,b) is focusing on the extension of classical logical formalisms, such as Datalog, to support query answering over ontologies. Datalog$^\pm$ enriches Datalog with existential quantifiers in the rule head, and allows a set of restrictions to guarantee efficient ontology querying. In particular, the tractable fragment of Description Logics, namely *DL-Lite*[15] can be represented with Datalog$^{\pm}$ by filling the gap between databases and the Semantic Web. Suitable fragments of Datalog$^{\pm}$ are embodied by: (1) guarded TGDs (GTGDs); (2) linear TGDs (LTGDs); (3) (1) or (2) with equation-generating dependencies and negative constraints. A tgd σ is guarded iff it contains an atom in its body that has all universally quantified variables of σ. A subset of GTGDs is represented by LTGDs, iff it contains only a singleton body atom. If we look at the s-t tgds illustrated in Sect. 2, then m_1, m_3, and m_4 are LTGDs (and, thus, guarded) and m_2 is a nonguarded TGD. The main result of Calì et al. (2009b) is that query answering with (3) that do not conflict with the tgds is feasible in polynomial time in the data complexity and thus is first-order rewritable.

6.3   Distributing Schema Mappings Across Several Sites

We are currently witnessing a substantial interest in distributed database management systems, called PDMS that are based on highly decentralized P2P infrastructures. Such PDMSs might share heterogeneous data and exchange such data in a seamless fashion.

In Piazza (Ives et al. 2004), each peer stores semantic mappings and storage descriptions. Semantic mappings are equalities or subsumptions between query expressions, provided in XQuery. Storage descriptions are equalities or subsumptions between a query and one or more relations stored on a peer. In Piazza, semantic mappings are first used to do query rewriting using the MiniCon algorithm (Pottinger and Halevy 2001). When semantic mappings cannot be applied further, storage descriptions are used to do query reformulation. The result of this phase is a reformulation of peer relations into stored relations, which can be either in GAV or in LAV style. Query routing in Piazza requires a centralized index that stores all the mappings at a global level.

In HePToX (Bonifati et al. 2005, 2010), the exact mapping rules are derived automatically from correspondences, which are intuitively displayed in a peer-based GUI. In contrast to Piazza, HePToX is totally decentralized and its scalability is less than linear (i.e., logarithmic, as in DHT-based systems). Thus, mappings are locally stored on each peer and used at need when doing query reformulation.

HePToX query rewriting can be done in both directions, along and against the mappings, leading to forward and backward query translations. The semantics of HePToX's forward query translation is similar to answering queries using views (Levy et al. 1995). However, HePToX can leverage Skolem functions and the form of the mapping rules to perform forward translation efficiently. Backward query translation is totally new and was never defined in other systems.

Orchestra (Ives et al. 2008) extends PDMSs for life scientists. It focuses on provenance, trust, and updates. While it can be extended to XML, it uses the relational model. Orchestra's mapping rules translate from tgds to Datalog, rather than HePToX's mapping rules which translate from a visual language to TreeLog. Unlike HePToX, which supports the user in easily creating the mapping between schemas, Orchestra relies on other systems to create the initial mappings. Moreover, the Q system, which is the query module in Orchestra, focuses on keywords queries rather than on XQuery queries.

Calvanese et al. (2004) address data interoperability in P2P systems using expressive schema mappings, also following the GAV/LAV paradigm, and show that the problem is in PTIME only when mapping rules are expressed in epistemic logic.

6.4 Normalizing Schema Mappings

Schema mappings, as high-level specifications describing the relationships between two database schemas, are subject to optimization. Fagin et al. (2008) lay the foundations of schema mapping optimization, by introducing three kinds of equivalence: (1) logical equivalence, stating that two schema mappings $\mathcal{M} = (\mathbf{S}, \mathbf{T}, \Sigma)$ and $\mathcal{M}' = (\mathbf{S}, \mathbf{T}, \Sigma')^3$ are logically equivalent if for every source instance I and target instance J, we have that $(I, J) \models \Sigma$ if and only if $(I, J) \models \Sigma'$; (2) data-exchange equivalence, if for every source instance I, the set of universal solutions for I under $\mathcal{M}$ coincides with the set of universal solutions for I under $\mathcal{M}'$; (3) conjunctive-query equivalence, if for every target conjunctive query Q and for every source instance I, the set of solutions for I under $\mathcal{M}$ is empty if and only if the set of solutions for I under $\mathcal{M}'$ is empty, and, whenever they are not empty, the set of certain answers of Q on I under $\mathcal{M}$ coincides with the set of certain answers of Q on I under $\mathcal{M}'$. Equivalences (2) and (3) coincide with equivalence (1) when $\Sigma = \Sigma_{st}$, but differ on richer classes of equivalences, such as second-order tgds and sets of both Σ_{st} and Σ_t. The assumption of logical equivalence has also been done in Gottlob et al. (2009), which focuses on the normalization of schema mappings with respect to four optimality criteria, precisely cardinality-minimality, antecedent-minimality, conclusion-minimality, and variable-minimality. Following these criteria, given a set of st-tgds in Σ, the total number of st-tgds in this set, the total number of atoms in the antecedent and conclusion of each st-tgd shall be minimal, along with the total number of existentially quantified variables in the conclusion. The presence of egds is not considered in Gottlob et al. (2009) and represents a natural extension. Other than that, much work remains to be done toward defining new heuristics for schema mapping optimization, extending the above criteria to larger classes of rules, and considering the impact of all the equivalences discussed above.

7 Conclusions and Future Work

In this chapter, we have discussed the state of the art of schema mapping algorithms, along with their most recent developments and applications.

We believe that there are quite a lot of open problems in this area, which we attempt to briefly discuss below.

---

[3] We do not distinguish here between Σ_{st} and Σ_t and consider Σ as a set of generic constraints.

First of all, within the data exchange theory the core has been studied only for relational settings, to date there is no formal definition of core solutions for nested scenarios. We believe such a notion is needed in many practical scenarios.

Postprocessing algorithms (Fagin et al. 2005b; Gottlob and Nash 2008; Savenkov and Pichler 2008; Marnette 2009) can handle scenarios with arbitrary target constraints, while by using the rewriting algorithms in Mecca et al. (2009a); ten Cate et al. (2009), the best we can achieve is to generate a solution that does not consider target tgds and edgs. This is especially unsatisfactory for egds, since the obtained solution violates the required key constraints and it is not even a legal instance for the target. As shown in Marnette et al. (2010), this may lead to a high level of redundancy, which can seriously impair both the efficiency of the translation and the quality of answering queries over the target database.

In fact, handling egds is a complicated task. As conjectured in ten Cate et al. (2009), it has recently been shown (Marnette et al. 2010) that it is not possible, in general, to get an universal solution that enforces a set of egds using a first-order language as SQL. For the class of target egds that correspond to functional dependencies, the most common in practical settings Marnette et al. (2010) introduced a best-effort rewriting algorithm that takes as input a scenario with s-t tgds and egds and, whenever this is possible, it rewrites it into a new scenario without egds. Moreover, this algorithm can be combined with existing mapping rewriting algorithms (Mecca et al. 2009a; ten Cate et al. 2009) to obtain SQL scripts that generate core solutions. The paper shows that handling target egds efficiently is possible in many practical cases. This is particularly important in real-world applications of mappings, where key constraints are often present and play an important role.

Another important open problem concerns the expressibility of the GUI of a schema mapping tool. Indeed, many GUIs are limited in the set of primitives they use to specify the mapping scenarios and need to be enriched in several ways. For instance, it would be useful to be able to duplicate sets in the source and in the target and, thus, handle tgds that contain duplicate tables. To a further extent, full control over joins in the two data sources becomes a crucial requirement of schema mapping GUIs, in addition to those corresponding to foreign key constraints; by using this feature, users can specify arbitrary join paths, like self-joins themselves.

This richer set of primitives poses some challenges with respect to the mapping generation and rewriting algorithms as well. In particular, duplications in the target correspond to different ways of contributing tuples to the same set. As we discussed above, this makes the generation of core solutions more delicate, since there exist tgds that write more than one tuple at a time in the same target table, and therefore redundancy can be generated not only across different tgds, but also by firing a single tgd (Mecca et al. 2009a; ten Cate et al. 2009).

Second generation mapping systems have certainly enlarged the class of mappings scenarios that can be handled using a GUI, but a formal characterization of the exact class of mappings that can be expressed with them is still missing. For instance, it is still unclear if every mapping made of conjunctive queries can be expressed by existing GUIs.

Finally, another important problem is the use of mappings in practical user scenarios and applications, thus making them the building blocks of general-purpose data transformation tools. Although previous attempts have been done in this direction (as explained in Sect. 6), more work is still left to fill this gap.

References

Abiteboul S, Duschka OM (1998) Complexity of answering queries using materialized views. In: PODS. ACM, NY, pp 254–263

Abiteboul S, Cluet S, Milo T (1997) Correspondence and translation for heterogeneous data. In: ICDT, Delphi, Greece. Springer, London, pp 351–363

Abu-Hamdeh R, Cordy J, Martin T (1994) Schema translation using structural transformation. In: CASCON. IBM Press, pp 202–215

Amano S, Libkin L, Murlak F (2009) XML schema mappings. In: PODS. ACM, NY, pp 33–42

An Y, Borgida A, Miller R, Mylopoulos J (2007) In: Proceedings of the 23rd International Conference on Data Engineering, ICDE 2007, April 15–20, 2007, The Marmara Hotel, Istanbul, Turkey

Arenas M, Libkin L (2008) XML data exchange: Consistency and query answering. J ACM 55(2):1–72

Atzeni P, Torlone R (1995) Schema translation between heterogeneous data models in a lattice framework. In: Data semantics conference. Chapman & Hall, London, pp 345–364

Atzeni P, Torlone R (1997) MDM: A multiple-data model tool for the management of heterogeneous database schemes. In: SIGMOD. ACM, NY, pp 528–531

Beeri C, Milo T (1999) Schemas for intergration and translation of structured and semi-structured data. In: ICDT. Springer, London, pp 296–313

Beeri C, Vardi M (1984) A proof procedure for data dependencies. J ACM 31(4):718–741

Bonifati A, Chang EQ, Ho T, Lakshmanan L, Pottinger R (2005) HePToX: Marrying XML and heterogeneity in your P2P databases. In: VLDB. VLDB Endowment, pp 1267–1270

Bonifati A, Mecca G, Pappalardo A, Raunich S, Summa G (2008) Schema mapping verification: The spicy way. In: EDBT. ACM, NY, pp 85–96

Bonifati A, Chang EQ, Ho T, Lakshmanan L, Pottinger R, Chung Y (2010) Schema mapping and query translation in heterogeneous P2P XML databases. VLDB J 19(2):231–256

Cabibbo L (2009) On keys, foreign keys and nullable attributes in relational mapping systems. In: EDBT. ACM, NY, pp 263–274

Calì A, Gottlob G, Lukasiewicz T (2009a) Datalog±: A unified approach to ontologies and integrity constraints. In: ICDT. ACM, NY, pp 14–30

Calì A, Gottlob G, Lukasiewicz T (2009b) A general datalog-based framework for tractable query answering over ontologies. In: PODS. ACM, NY, pp 77–86

Calvanese D, De Giacomo G, Lenzerini M, Rosati R (2004) Logical foundations of peer-to-peer data integration. In: ACM PODS. ACM, NY, pp 241–251

Chandra AK, Merlin PM (1977) Optimal implementation of conjunctive queries in relational data bases. In: STOC. ACM, NY, pp 77–90

Chiticariu L (2005) Computing the core in data exchange: Algorithmic issues. MS Project Report, unpublished manuscript

Cluet S, Delobel C, Siméon J, Smaga K (1998) Your mediators need data conversion! In: SIGMOD. ACM, NY, pp 177–188

Davidson S, Kosky A (1997) IEEE Computer Society. In: Proceedings of the Thirteenth International Conference on Data Engineering, April 7–11, 1997 Birmingham UK

Deutsch A, Popa L, Tannen V (1999) Physical data independence, constraints, and optimization with universal plans. In: VLDB. Morgan Kaufmann, CA, pp 459–470

Fagin R (2007) Inverting schema mappings. ACM TODS 32(4)

Fagin R, Kolaitis P, Miller R, Popa L (2005a) Data exchange: Semantics and query answering. TCS 336(1):89–124

Fagin R, Kolaitis P, Popa L (2005b) Data exchange: Getting to the core. ACM TODS 30(1): 174–210

Fagin R, Kolaitis P, Nash A, Popa L (2008) Towards a theory of schema-mapping optimization. In: ACM PODS. ACM, NY, pp 33–42

Fagin R, Haas LM, Hernandez M, Miller RJ, Popa L, Velegrakis Y (2009) Clio: Schema mapping creation and data exchange. In: Borgida A, Chaudhri V, Giorgini P, Yu E (eds) Conceptual modeling: Foundations and applications. Springer, Heidelberg, pp 198–236

Fuxman A, Hernández MA, Howard CT, Miller RJ, Papotti P, Popa L (2006) Nested mappings: Schema mapping reloaded. In: VLDB. VLDB Endowment, pp 67–78

Gottlob G, Nash A (2008) Efficient core computation in data exchange. J ACM 55(2):1–49

Gottlob G, Pichler R, Savenkov V (2009) Normalization and optimization of schema mappings. PVLDB 2(1):1102–1113

Haas LM (2007) Lecture Notes in Computer Science, vol. 4353. In: ICDT, Springer.

Halevy AY (2010) Technical perspective – schema mappings: Rules for mixing data. Commun CACM 53(1):100

Hell P, Nešetřil J (1992) The core of a graph. Discrete Math 109(1–3):117–126

Hernández MA, Papotti P, Tan WC (2008) Data exchange with data-metadata translations. PVLDB 1(1):260–273

Hull R, Yoshikawa M (1990) ILOG: Declarative creation and manipulation of object identifiers. In: VLDB. Morgan Kaufmann, CA, pp 455–468

Ives ZG, Halevy AY, Mork P, Tatarinov I (2004) Piazza: Mediation and integration infrastructure for semantic web data. J Web Sem 1(2):155–175

Ives ZG, Green TJ, Karvounarakis G, Taylor NE, Tannen V, Talukdar PP, Jacob M, Pereira F (2008) The orchestra collaborative data sharing system. SIGMOD Rec 37(3):26–32

Jiang H, Ho H, Popa L, Han W (2007) Mapping-driven XML transformation. In: WWW conference. ACM, NY, pp 1063–1072

Levy AY, Mendelzon A, Sagiv Y, Srivastava D (1995) Proceedings of the fourteenth ACM SIGACT-SIGMOD-SIGART symposium on principles of database systems. ACM Press, San Jose, California, May 22–25, 1995

Maier D, Mendelzon AO, Sagiv Y (1979) Testing implications of data dependencies. ACM TODS 4(4):455–469

Maier D, Ullman JD, Vardi MY (1984) On the foundations of the universal relation model. ACM TODS 9(2):283–308

Marnette B (2009) Generalized schema mappings: From termination to tractability. In: ACM PODS. ACM, NY, pp 13–22

Marnette B, Mecca G, Papotti P (2010) Scalable data exchange with functional dependencies. PVLDB 3(1):106–116

Mecca G, Papotti P, Raunich S (2009a) Core schema mappings. In: SIGMOD. ACM, NY, pp 655–668

Mecca G, Papotti P, Raunich S, Buoncristiano M (2009b) Concise and expressive mappings with +Spicy. PVLDB 2(2):1582–1585

Melnik S, Bernstein P, Halevy A, Rahm E (2005) Supporting executable mappings in model management. In: SIGMOD. ACM, NY, pp 167–178

Miller RJ, Haas LM, Hernandez MA (2000) Schema mapping as query discovery. In: VLDB. Morgan Kaufmann, CA, pp 77–99

Milo T, Zohar S (1998) Using schema matching to simplify heterogeneous data translation. In: VLDB. Morgan Kaufmann, CA, pp 122–133

OWL-Full (2004) OWL web ontology language reference. http://www.w3.org/TR/owl-ref/#OWLFull

Popa L (2000) Object/relational query optimization with chase and backchase. PhD thesis, University of Pennsylvania

Popa L, Tannen V (1999) An equational chase for path-conjunctive queries, constraints, and views. In: ICDT. Springer, London, pp 39–57

Popa L, Velegrakis Y, Miller RJ, Hernandez MA, Fagin R (2002) Translating web data. In: VLDB. VLDB Endowment, pp 598–609

Pottinger R, Halevy A (2001) Minicon: A scalable algorithm for answering queries using views. VLDB J 10(2–3):182–198

Raffio A, Braga D, Ceri S, Papotti P, Hernández MA (2008) Clip: A visual language for explicit schema mappings. In: ICDE. IEEE Computer Society, Washington, DC, pp 30–39

Rahm E, Bernstein PA (2001) A survey of approaches to automatic schema matching. VLDB J 10:334–350

Savenkov V, Pichler R (2008) Towards practical feasibility of core computation in data exchange. In: LPAR. Springer, Heidelberg, pp 62–78

Shu NC, Housel BC, Taylor RW, Ghosh SP, Lum VY (1977) EXPRESS: A data extraction, processing and restructuring system. ACM TODS 2(2):134–174

ten Cate B, Kolaitis PG (2009) Structural characterizations of schema-mapping languages. In: ICDT. ACM, NY, pp 63–72

ten Cate B, Chiticariu L, Kolaitis P, Tan WC (2009) Laconic schema mappings: Computing core universal solutions by means of SQL queries. PVLDB 2(1):1006–1017

Tork-Roth M, Schwarz PM (1997) Don't scrap it, wrap it! A wrapper architecture for legacy data sources. In: VLDB. Morgan Kaufmann, CA, pp 266–275

Velegrakis Y (2005) Managing schema mappings in highly heterogeneous environments. PhD thesis, University of Toronto

Yu C, Popa L (2004) Constraint-based XML query rewriting for data integration. In: SIGMOD conference. ACM, NY, pp 371–382

Chapter 6
Recent Advances in Schema and Ontology Evolution

Michael Hartung, James Terwilliger, and Erhard Rahm

Abstract Schema evolution is the increasingly important ability to adapt deployed schemas to changing requirements. Effective support for schema evolution is challenging since schema changes may have to be propagated, correctly and efficiently, to instance data and dependent schemas, mappings, or applications. We introduce the major requirements for effective schema and ontology evolution, including support for a rich set of change operations, simplicity of change specification, evolution transparency (e.g., by providing and maintaining views or schema versions), automated generation of evolution mappings, and predictable instance migration that minimizes data loss and manual intervention. We then give an overview about the current state of the art and recent research results for the evolution of relational schemas, XML schemas, and ontologies. For numerous approaches, we outline how and to what degree they meet the introduced requirements.

1 Introduction

Schema evolution is the ability to change deployed schemas, i.e., metadata structures formally describing complex artifacts such as databases, messages, application programs, or workflows. Typical schemas thus include relational database schemas, conceptual ER or UML models, ontologies, XML schemas, software interfaces, and workflow specifications. Obviously, the need for schema evolution occurs very often in order to deal with new or changed requirements, to correct deficiencies in the current schemas, to cope with new insights in a domain, or to migrate to a new platform.

M. Hartung (✉) and E. Rahm
University of Leipzig, Ritterstraße 26, 04109 Leipzig, Germany
e-mail: hartung@informatik.uni-leipzig.de, rahm@informatik.uni-leipzig.de

J. Terwilliger
Microsoft Research, Redmond, WA, USA
e-mail: James.Terwilliger@microsoft.com

Z. Bellahsene et al. (eds.), *Schema Matching and Mapping*, Data-Centric Systems and Applications, DOI 10.1007/978-3-642-16518-4_6,
© Springer-Verlag Berlin Heidelberg 2011

Effective support for schema evolution is challenging since schema changes may have to be propagated, correctly and efficiently, to instance data, views, applications, and other dependent system components. Ideally, dealing with these changes should require little manual work and system unavailability. For instance, changes to a database schema S should be propagated to instance data and views defined on S with minimal human intervention. On the other hand, without sufficient support schema evolution is difficult and time-consuming to perform and may break running applications. Therefore, necessary schema changes may be performed too late or not at all resulting in systems that do not adequately meet requirements.

Schema evolution has been an active research area for a long time and it is increasingly supported in commercial systems. The need for powerful schema evolution has been increasing. One reason is that the widespread use of XML, web services, and ontologies has led to new schema types and usage scenarios of schemas for which schema evolution must be supported. The main goals of this survey chapter are as follows:

- To introduce requirements for schema evolution support.
- To provide an overview about the current state of the art and recent research results on schema evolution in three areas: relational database schemas, XML schemas, and ontologies. For each kind of schema, we outline how and to what degree the introduced requirements are served by existing approaches.

While we cover more than 20 recent implementations and proposals, there are many more approaches that can be evaluated in a similar way than we do in this chapter. We refer the reader to the online bibliography on schema evolution under http://se-pubs.dbs.uni-leipzig.de (Rahm and Bernstein 2006) for additional related work. Book chapter 7 (Fagin et al. 2011) complements our paper by focusing on recent work on mapping composition and inversion that support the evolution of schema mappings.

In Sect. 2, we introduce the main requirements for effective schema and ontology evolution. Sections 3 and 4 deal with the evolution of relational database schemas and of XML schemas, respectively. In Sect. 5, we outline proposed approaches for ontology evolution and conclude in Sect. 6.

2 Schema Evolution Requirements

Changes to schemas and ontologies affect the instances described by these metadata structures as well as other dependent system components. Figure 6.1 illustrates some of these dependencies for the evolution of database schemas that are always tightly connected with the instances of the database. So when the schema S of a database with instances D, described by S, is changed to schema S′ the instances must be adapted accordingly, e.g., to reflect changed data types or added and deleted structures in S′. We assume that schema changes from S to S′ are described by a so-called *evolution mapping* (e.g., a set of incremental changes or a higher-level abstraction).

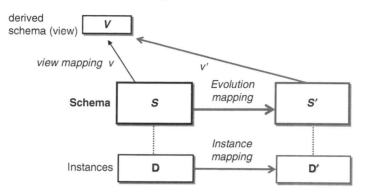

Fig. 6.1 Schema evolution scenario

Similarly, instance changes/migration can be specified by an instance mapping, e.g., a sequence of SQL operations. A main requirement for database schema evolution is thus to propagate the schema changes to the instances, i.e., to derive and execute an instance mapping correctly and efficiently implementing the changes specified in the evolution mapping. Changes to schema S can also affect all other usages of S, in particular the applications using S or other schemas and views related to S. Schema changes may thus have to be propagated to dependent schemas and mappings. To avoid the costly adaptation of applications they should be isolated from schema changes as much as possible, e.g., by the provision of stable schema versions or views. For example, applications using view V remain unaffected by the change from S to S' if the view schema V can be preserved, e.g., by adapting view mapping v to v' (Fig. 6.1). There are similar evolution requirements for XML schemas and ontologies, although they are less tightly connected to instance data and have different usage forms than database schemas as we will see (e.g., XML schemas describing web service interfaces; ontologies may only provide a controlled vocabulary).

In the following sections, we discuss in detail general and more specific desiderata and requirements for effective schema and ontology evolution. These requirements are then used in the subsequent sections to review and compare existing and proposed evolution approaches.

We see the following general desiderata for a powerful schema evolution support:

- *Completeness*: There should be support for a rich set of schema changes and their correct and efficient propagation to instance data and dependent schemas.
- *Minimal user intervention*: To the degree possible, ensure that the schema evolution description is the only input to the system and that other artifacts co-evolve automatically.
- *Transparency*: Schema evolution should result into minimal or no degradation of availability or performance of the changed system. Furthermore, applications and other schema consumers should largely be isolated from the changes, e.g., by support for backward compatibility, versioning, or views.

The general desiderata are hard to meet and imply support for a series of more specific, interrelated features:

- *Rich set of simple and complex changes*: Simple changes refer to the addition, modification, or deletion of individual schema constructs (e.g., tables and attributes of relational databases), while complex changes refer to multiple such constructs (e.g., merging or partitioning tables) and may be equivalent to multiple simple changes. There are two main ways to specify such changes and both should ideally be supported. The straightforward approach is to explicitly specify schema modification statements to incrementally update a schema. Alternatively, one can provide the evolved schema, thereby providing an implicit specification of the changes compared to the old schema. This approach is attractive since it is easy to use and since the updated schema version may contain several changes to apply together.
- *Backward compatibility*: For transparency reasons, schema changes should minimally impact schema consumers and applications. We therefore require support for *backward compatibility* meaning that applications/queries of schema S should continue to work with the changed schema S'. This requires that schema changes do not result in an information loss but preserve or extent the so-called information capacity of schemas (Miller et al. 1994). Changes that are potentially lossy (e.g., deletes) should therefore be either avoided or limited to safe cases, i.e., to schema elements that have not yet been used. As we see, the view concept and schema versioning in combination with schema mappings are main approaches to support backward compatibility.
- *Mapping support*: To automatically propagate schema changes to instances and dependent or related schemas, it is necessary to describe the evolution itself as well as schema dependencies (such as view mappings) by high-level, declarative schema mappings. In the simplest case, the *evolution mapping* between the original schema S and the evolved schema S' consists of the set of incremental changes specified by the schema developer. In case the changes are specified by providing the evolved schema S', the evolution mapping between S and S' still needs to be determined. Ideally, this mapping is (semi-)automatically determined by a so-called *Diff(erence) computation* that can be based on schema matching (Rahm and Bernstein 2001; Rahm 2011) but also has to take into account the (added/deleted) schema elements that exist in only one of the two schemas.

There are different possibilities to represent evolution mappings and other schema mappings. A high flexibility and expressive power is achieved by using different kinds of logical and algebraic mapping expressions that have been the focus of a substantial amount of theoretical research (Cate and Kolaitis 2010). The mapping representation should at least be expressive enough to enable the semi-automatic generation of corresponding instance (data migration) mappings. Further mapping desiderata include the ability to support high-level operations such as composition and inversion of mappings (Bernstein 2003) that support the evolution *(adaptation) of mappings* after schema changes. In the example of Fig. 6.1, such operations can be used to derive the changed view mapping v' by composing the inverse of the evolution mapping with the view mapping v.

- *Automatic instance migration*: Instances of a changed schema or ontology should automatically be migrated to comply with the specified changes. This may be achieved by executing an instance-level mapping (e.g., in SQL or XQuery) derived from the evolution mapping. Database schema evolution also requires the adaptation of affected index structures and storage options (e.g., clustering or partitioning), which should be performed without reducing the availability of the database (online reorganization). There are different options to perform such instance and storage structure updates: either in place or on a copy of the original data. The copy approach is conceptually simpler and keeping the original data simplifies undoing an erroneous evolution. On the other hand, copying is inherently slow for a large amount of data most of which are likely unaffected by the schema change. Furthermore, data migration can be performed eagerly (expensive, but fast availability of changes) or lazily. Instance migration should be undoable if anything goes wrong, which can be achieved by running it under transactional control.
- *Propagation of schema changes to related mappings and schemas*: Schemas are frequently related to other schemas (by mappings) so that schema changes may have to be propagated to these related schemas. This should be performed in a largely automatic manner supporting a maximum of backward compatibility. Important use cases of this general requirement include the maintenance of views, integrated (global) schemas, and conceptual schemas. As discussed view schemas may be kept stable for information-preserving changes by adapting the view mapping according to a schema change; deleted or added schema components on the other hand may also require the adaptation of views. Data integration architectures typically rely on mappings between source schemas and a global target (mediator or warehouse) schema and possibly between source schemas and a shared ontology. Again, some schema changes (e.g., renames) may be covered by only adapting the mappings, while other changes such as the provision of new information in a source schema may have to be propagated to the global schema. Finally, interrelating database schemas with their conceptual abstractions, e.g., in UML or the entity/relationship (ER) model, require evolution support. Changes in the UML or ER model should thus be consistently propagated to the database schema and vice versa (reverse engineering).
- *Versioning support*: Supporting different explicit versions for schemas and ontologies and possibly for their associated instances supports evolution transparency. This is because schema changes are reflected in new versions leaving former versions that are in use in a stable state. Different versioning approaches are feasible, e.g., whether only a sequence of versions is supported or whether one can derive different versions in parallel and merge them later on. For full evolution transparency, it is desirable to not only support backward compatibility (applications/queries of the old schema version S can also use S') but also *forward compatibility* between schema versions S and S', i.e., applications of S' can also use S.

– *Powerful schema evolution infrastructure*: The comprehensive support for sch- ema evolution discussed before requires a set of powerful and easily usable tools, in particular to determine the impact of intended changes, to specify incremen- tal changes, to determine Diff evolution mappings, and to perform the specified changes on the schemas, instances, mappings, and related schemas.

3   Relational Schema Evolution Approaches

By far, the most predominantly used model for storing data is the relational model. One foundation of relations is a coupling between instances and schema, where all instances follow a strict regular pattern; the homogeneous nature of relational instances is a foundational premise of nearly every advantage that relational systems provide, including query optimization and efficient physical design. As a conse- quence, whenever the logical scheme for a table changes, all instances must follow suit. Similarly, whenever the set of constraints on a database changes, the set of instances must be validated against the new set of constraints, and if any violations are found, either the validations must be resolved in some way or, more commonly, the schema change is rejected.

An additional complication is the usually tight coupling between applications and relational databases or at least between the data access tier and the database. Because the SQL query language is statically typed, application queries and business logic applied to query results are tightly coupled to the database schema. Consequently, after a database schema is upgraded to a new version, multiple applications may still attempt access to that database concurrently. The primary built-in support pro- vided by SQL for such schema changes is *external schemas*, known more commonly as views. When a new version of an application has different data requirements, one has several options. First, one can create views to support the new applica- tion version leaving existing structures intact for older versions. Or, one can adapt the existing schema for the new application and maintain existing views to pro- vide backward compatibility for existing applications. In both cases, the views may be virtual, in which case they are subject to the stringent rules governing updatable views, or they may be materialized, in which case the application versions are essen- tially communicating with different database versions. However, the different views have no semantic relationship and no intrinsic notion of schema version, and thus no clean interoperability.

For the rest of this section, we first consider the current state of the art in relational database systems regarding their support for schema evolution. We exam- ine their language, tool, and scenario support. We then consider recent research revelations in support for relational schema evolution. Finally, we use Table 6.1 to summarize the schema evolution support of the considered approaches w.r.t. requirements introduced in Sect. 2.

Table 6.1 Characteristics of systems for relational schema evolution

	Oracle	Microsoft SQL Server	IBM DB2	Panta Rhei, PRISM Curino et al. (2008)	HECATAEUS Papastefanatos et al. (2008, 2010)	DB-MAIN/MeDEA Hick and Hainaut (2006), Domínguez et al. (2008)
Description/focus of work	Commercial relational database system	Commercial relational database system	Commercial relational database system	Evolution mapping language allowing multiple versions of applications to run concurrently	Propagation of evolution primitives between dependent database objects	Conceptual modeling interface, allowing model-driven evolution
Changes						
(1) Richness (simple, complex)	(1) Only simple changes (SQL DDL)	(1) Only simple changes (SQL DDL)	(1) Only simple changes (SQL DDL)	(1) Simple and complex changes (table merging/ partitioning)	(1) Simple changes (SQL DDL). Create statement annotated with propagation policies	(1) Simple changes (add/modify/drop entity type, relationship, attribute, etc.)
(2) Specification (incremental, new schema)	(2) Incremental or new schema (table redefinition)	(2) Incremental	(2) Incremental	(2) Incremental	(2) Incremental	(2) Incremental
Evolution mapping						
(1) Representation	(1) Column mapping between old and new single table or set of incremental changes	(1) Set of incremental changes (SQL DDL)	(1) Set of incremental changes (SQL DDL)	(1) Formal logic and SQL mappings, both forward and backward	(1) None beyond standard DDL execution	(1) Set of incremental changes based on conceptual model

(Continued)

Table 6.1 (Continued)

	Oracle	Microsoft SQL Server	IBM DB2	Panta Rhei, PRISM Curino et al. (2008)	HECATAEUS Papastefanatos et al. (2008, 2010)	DB-MAIN/MeDEA Hick and Hainaut (2006), Domínguez et al. (2008)
(2) DIFF computation	(2) Comparison functionality for two schema versions (diff expressed in SQL DDL)	(2)–	(2)–	(2)–	(2)–	(2)–
Update propagation						
(1) Instances	(1) Non-transactional, instances migrate if no other objects depend on changed table	(1) Transactional DDL, automatic instance translation for objects with no dependents	(1) Transactional DDL, automatic instance translation for objects with no dependents	(1)–	(1)–	(1) Translation of instance data by a extract-transform-load workflow
(2) Dependent schemas	(2)–	(2)–	(2)–	(2) Query rewriting when possible, notification if queries invalid because of lossy evolution	(2) Policies determine how and when to automatically update dependent objects such as views and queries	(2)–

Versioning support	Editions support multiple versions of nonpersistent objects, with triggers, etc., for interacting with tables	Only internal versioning during instance migration	Only internal versioning during instance migration	Generates views to support both forward and backward compatibility, when formally possible	—
Infrastructure/GUI	Oracle change management pack – compares schemas; bundles changes, predicts errors	SSMS creates change scripts from designer changes. DAC packs support schema diff and in-place instance migration for packaged databases	Optim data studio administrator – bundles changes, predicts evolution errors	— Web-based tool for demonstrating query rewriting and view generation	GUI-based tools used to capture user actions while modifying schemas

3.1 Commercial Relational Systems

Relational database systems, both open-source and proprietary, rely on the DDL statements from SQL (CREATE, DROP, and ALTER) to perform schema evolution, though the exact dialect may vary from system to system (Türker 2000). So, to add an integer-valued column C to a table T, one uses the following syntax:

```
ALTER TABLE T ADD COLUMN C int;
```

Other changes are differently specified in commercial DBMS. For instance, renaming a table in Oracle is performed using the following syntax:

```
ALTER TABLE foo RENAME TO bar;
```

SQL Server uses a stored procedure for that particular change:

```
sp_rename 'foo', 'bar', 'TABLE';
```

Schema evolution primitives in the SQL language and in commercial DBMS are atomic in nature. Unless there is a proprietary extension to the language, each statement describes a simple change to a schema. For instance, individual tables may be added or dropped, individual columns may be added or dropped from a table, and individual constraints may be added or dropped. Additionally, individual properties of a single object may be changed; so, one can rename a column, table, or constraint; one can change individual properties of columns, such as their maximum length or precision; and one can change the data type of a column under the condition that the conversion of data from the old type to the new type can be done implicitly.

However, one cannot specify more complex, compound tasks such as horizontal or vertical splitting or merging of tables in commercial DBMS. Such actions may be accomplished as a sequence of atomic actions – a horizontal split, for instance, may be represented as creating each of the destination tables, copying rows to their new tables, and then dropping the old table. Using this piecemeal approach is always possible; however, it loses the original intent that treats the partition action as a single action with its own properties and semantics, including knowing that horizontal merge is its inverse.

The approach that has been taken by and large by commercial vendors is to include at most a few small features in the DBMS itself and then provide robust tooling that operates above the database. One feature that is fairly common across systems is *transactional DDL*; CREATE, ALTER, and DROP statements can be bundled inside transactions and undone via a rollback. A consequence of this feature is that multiple versions of schemas at a time may be maintained for each table and potentially for rows within the table for concurrent access. Even though multiple versions of schema may exist internally within the engine, there is still only a single version available to the application. PostgreSQL, SQL Server, and DB2 all support this feature; in Oracle, DDL statements implicitly mark a transaction boundary and run independently.

Commercial systems automatically perform update propagation for the simple changes they support. Simple actions, such as column addition, deletion, or type changes, can frequently be performed while also migrating existing instance data (provided new columns are allowed to be null). Furthermore, online reorganization is increasingly supported to avoid server downtime for update propagation. So, for instance, DB2 offers a feature where renaming or adjusting the type of a column does not require any downtime to complete, and existing applications can still access data in the table mid-evolution (IBM 2009b). The transactional DDL and internal versioning features also promote high server uptime, as alterations may be made lazily after the transaction has completed while allowing running applications access to existing data.

On the other hand, there is little support to propagate schema changes to dependent schema objects, such as views, foreign keys, and indexes. When one alters a table, either the dependent objects must themselves be manually altered in some way, or the alteration must be aborted. The latter approach takes the majority of the time. For instance, SQL Server aborts any attempt to alter a column if it is part of any index, unless the alteration is within strict limits – namely, the alteration is a widening of a text or binary column. Dropped columns simply cannot participate in any index. DB2 has similar restrictions; Oracle *invalidates* dependent objects like views so that they must be revalidated on next use and fails to execute them if they do not compile against the new schema version.

Commercial DBMS do not support abstract schema mappings but only SQL for specifying view mappings and evolution mappings. There is no support for multiple explicit schema and database versions. Once the DDL statements of an evolution step have been executed, the previous version of the evolved objects is gone. There is no support for applications that were developed against previous versions of the database.

For the rest of this subsection, we will focus on vendor-specific features that go above and beyond the standard DDL capabilities for schema evolution.

Oracle provides a tool called *Change Management Pack* that allows some high-level schema change operations. One can compare two database schemas, batch changes to existing database objects, and determine statically if there will be any possible impacts or errors that may need to be mitigated such as insufficient privileges. The tool then creates scripts comprising SQL DDL statements from the schema difference. This capability is similar to those offered by other commercially available schema difference engines (e.g., Altova DiffDog (Altova 2010)), but does not offer the same level of automatic matching capabilities that can be found in schema-matching research tools.

Since the release of version 9i, Oracle also provides a schema evolution feature called *redefinition* (Oracle Database 10g Release 2 2005). Redefinition is performed on single tables and allows the DBA to specify and execute multiple schema or semantic modifications on a table. Changes such as column addition or deletion, changing partitioning options, or bulk data transformation can be accomplished while the table is still available to applications until the final steps of the update propagation.

Redefinition is a multistep process. It involves creating an *interim* table with the shape and properties that the table is to have post-redefinition and then interlinking the interim table with the original table by a *column mapping* specified as a SQL query. The DBA can periodically synchronize data between the two tables according to the query before finally finishing the redefinition. At the end of the redefinition process, the interim table takes the place of the original table. Only the final step requires the table to go offline.

Finally, Oracle supports a feature called *editions* (Oracle Edition-Based Redefinition 2009). An edition is a logical grouping of database objects such as views and triggers that are provided to applications for accessing a database. Using editions, database objects are partitioned into two sets – those that can be editioned and those that cannot. Any object that has a persistent extent, in particular tables and indexes, cannot be editioned. So, an edition is a collection of primarily views and triggers that provide an encapsulated version of the database.

To illustrate the use of editions, consider a simple scenario of a database that handles data about people (Fig. 6.2). In version 1, the database has a table TPerson with a single column Name. Edition 1 also provides applications with an editioned view 1 over TPerson that includes the name column. Schema evolution is triggered by the need to break apart Name into FirstName and LastName. So, version 2 of the database adds two new columns – FirstName and LastName – to TPerson, but leaves column Name present. Edition 2 of the database includes a new view 2 that leaves out Name but includes FirstName and LastName. A background task, run concurrently with the creation of the edition, copies existing data in Name into the new columns but leaves existing data intact. Furthermore, Edition 2 includes two triggers written by the developer to resolve the differences between the two versions. The forward trigger applies to edition 2 and all future editions and takes the data from FirstName and LastName on inserts and updates and applies the data to Name. The reverse trigger applies to all strictly older editions and translates Name data into FirstName and LastName on insert and update. Note that view 1 is still supported on the changed schema so that its applications continue to work.

The resulting database presents two different external faces to different application versions. Version 1 sees edition 1 with a Name column; and version 2 (and beyond) sees edition 2 with FirstName and LastName columns. Both versions can

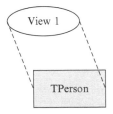

Edition 1, with a view, above the table TPerson

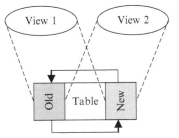

Editions 1 and 2 of the view, with changes to the table and triggers translating between old and new columns TPerson

Fig. 6.2 Editions in Oracle

create and consume data about a person's name, and that data are visible to the other version as well.

While editions solve a significant process problem, it does not solve data semantics problems. For instance, there is no guarantee that the forward and reverse triggers are in any way inverses of one another and are both essentially opaque program codes to the database system.

SQL Server ships with a tool called SQL Server Management Studio (SSMS) that serves as the GUI front end for a database. The tool can present a database diagram for a given database; the developer can then make changes directly to that diagram, such as adding foreign keys or dropping columns, and the changes are then propagated to the database when the diagram is saved. SSMS also has a *generate change script* feature. While editing a table in a designer, SSMS will track the changes that the developer has made on the table. SSMS packages those changes into a script either on demand or whenever the designer is saved or closed.

SQL Server also includes a feature called *Data-Tier Applications* (Microsoft SQL Server 2008 R2 Data-Tier Applications 2010). At the core of the feature is a distributable file called a DAC pack. A DAC pack is essentially a deployable image of a single version of an application database schema. A typical use case is that a developer packages an application with the schema of a database within such a DAC pack. Initially, when a customer installs the DAC pack an empty database is created with the respective table definitions, views, indexes, etc., from the schema. When the developer creates a new version of the application with an evolved version of the database schema, it is again bundled in a DAC (the old schema version is not considered). When the customer installs the new DAC, the existing database is detected and evolved (upgraded) to the new schema version. The current SQL server version does not do any sophisticated schema-matching heuristics, but also does not make any guesses. If a table has the same name in both the before and after versions, and has columns that are named the same, the upgrade will attempt to transfer the data from the old to the new, failing with a rollback if there are errors like incompatible data types. The resulting evolution process is effectively able to add or drop any objects – tables, columns, indexes, constraints, etc. – but unable to perform any action that requires user intent to capture semantics, such as object renaming (which to an automated process appears like a drop followed by an add). What the approach thus supports are common evolution scenarios of schema element adds and drops for which instance data can be migrated without either developer or user intervention.

IBM DB2 includes a tool called Optim Data Studio Administrator, which is a workbench tool for displaying, creating, and editing database objects with a live connection to a database (IBM 2009a). The interface has a largely hierarchical layout, with databases at the top of the hierarchy moving down to tables and displayed column properties. One can use the tool to manually edit schema objects and commit them to the database. Data Studio Administrator can batch changes together into a script that can subsequently be deployed independently. The script can be statically checked to determine whether the operation can be performed without error. For instance, when changing a column's data type, the default operation is to unload the data from the column's table, make the change to the type, and then reload the data.

If the type changes in such a way that will cause data type conflicts, Data Studio Administrator will alert the user that an error exists and offer the potential solution of casting the column's data on reload.

3.2 Research Approaches

PRISM (Curino et al. 2008) is a tool that is part of a larger project called *Panta Rhei*, a joint project between UCLA, UC San Diego, and Politecnico di Milano investigating schema evolution tools. The PRISM tool is one product of that joint venture that focuses on relational evolution with two primary goals: allow the user to specify schema evolution with more semantic clarity and data preservation and grant multiple versions of the same application concurrent access to the same data.

One contribution of the work on PRISM is a language of schema modification operators (SMOs). The SMO language closely resembles the DDL language in the SQL standard in that it is a textual, declarative language. The two languages also share some constructs, including "CREATE TABLE" and "ADD COLUMN." However, the two languages have two fundamental distinctions.

First, for every statement expressed using the SMO language, there are formal semantics associated with it that describe forward and reverse translation of schemas. The reverse translation defines, for each statement, the "inverse" action that effectively undoes the translation. The only SMO statements that lack these forward and reverse translations are the CREATE TABLE and DROP TABLE operations; logical formalism for these statements is impossible, since one is effectively stating that a tuple satisfies a predicate in the before or after state, but that the predicate itself does not exist in the other state. The work on PRISM describes "quasi-inverses" of such operations; for instance, if one had copied the table before dropping it, one could recover the dropped information from other sources. PRISM offers some support for allowing a user to manually specify such inverses.

Second, SMO and SQL DDL have a different philosophy for what constitutes an atomic change. SQL DDL has a closure property – one can alter any schema S into another schema S' using a sequence of statements in the language. The statements may be lossy to data, but such a sequence will always be possible. The SMO statements have a different motivation, namely, each statement represents a common database restructuring action that requires data migration. Rather than set the unit of change to be individual changes to individual database elements, the unit of change in PRISM more closely matches high-level refactoring constructs such as vertical or horizontal partitioning. For instance, consider the following statements:

```
MERGE TABLE R, S INTO T
PARTITION TABLE T INTO S WITH T.X < 10, T
COPY TABLE R INTO T
```

These three statements merge two tables, partition a table into two based on a predicate, and copy a table, respectively. Each statement and its inverse can be represented as a logical formula in predicate calculus as well as SQL statements that describe the alteration of schema and movement of data. For instance, the merge statement above may be represented in SQL as follows:

```
CREATE TABLE T (the columns from either R or S)
INSERT INTO T
  SELECT * FROM R
  UNION
  SELECT * FROM S
DROP TABLE R
DROP TABLE S
```

The second major contribution of PRISM is support for database versioning with backward and forward compatibility. When starting with version N of a database, if one uses SMOs to create version N + 1 of the database, PRISM will provide at least one of the following services to applications whenever the SMOs are deemed to be invertible or the user provides a manual workaround:

- Automatic query rewriting of queries specified against version N into semantically equivalent queries against schema N + 1, and vice versa.
- Views that expose version N of the schema using version N + 1 as a base.

The authors examine the entire schema edit history of the database behind Wikipedia and create a classification of high-level restructuring that covers the vast majority of changes that have occurred in the history of that data repository.

HECATAEUS (Papastefanatos et al. 2010) focuses on the dependencies between schema components and artifacts such as views and queries. Recall that commercial systems have tight restrictions on schema evolution when dependencies exist; one cannot drop a column from a table if a view has been created that references that table. Using HECATAEUS, the developer is given fine-grained control over when to propagate schema changes to an object to the queries, statements, and views that depend on it.

A central construct in HECATAEUS is an *evolution policy* (Papastefanatos et al. 2008). Policies may be specified on creation of tables, views, constraints, or queries. One specifies an evolution policy using a syntactic extension to SQL. For instance, consider the following table definition:

```
CREATE TABLE Person (
  Id INT PRIMARY KEY,
  Name VARCHAR(50),
  DateOfBirth DATE,
  Address VARCHAR(100),
  ON ADD Attribute TO Person THEN Propagate)
```

This DDL statement constructs a table with a policy that states that any added attribute should be automatically added as well to any dependent object. For instance, consider the following view:

```
CREATE VIEW BobPeople AS
SELECT Id, DateOfBirth, Address FROM Person
WHERE Name = 'Bob'
```

If one were to subsequently add a new column "City" to the Person table, the BobPeople view definition would be automatically updated with an additional column Person as well.

Policies are specified on the object to be updated, not the dependent objects. Each policy has three enforcement options: propagate (automatically propagate the change to all dependents), block (which prevents the change from being propagated to dependents), or prompt (meaning the user is asked for each change which action to take). For both propagate and block options, queries are rewritten to either take the new schema semantics into account or preserve the original semantics. The available policies depend on the object being created; for instance, tables may have policies added for adding, dropping, or renaming attributes; drop or rename the relation; or add, drop, or modify constraint.

DB-MAIN is a conceptual modeling platform that offers services that connect models and databases. For instance, one can reverse engineer from a database a conceptual model in an entity–relationship model with inheritance, or one can forward engineer a database to match a given model. The relationship between such models and databases is generally straightforward – constructs like inheritance that exist in the model that have no direct analog in the relational space map to certain patterns like foreign keys in predictable ways (and detectable, in the case of reverse engineering a model from a database).

Research over the last decade from DB-MAIN includes work on ensuring that edits to one of those artifacts can be propagated to the other (Hick and Hainaut 2006). So, for instance, changes to a model should propagate to the database in a way that evolves the database and maintains the data in its instance rather than dropping the database and regenerating a fresh instance. The changes are made in a nonversioning fashion in that, like vanilla DDL statements, the changes are intended to bring the database to its next version and support applications accessing the new version without any guarantee of backward compatibility.

Because DB-MAIN is a tool, it can maintain the history of operations made to the graphical representation of a model. Graphical edits include operations like adding or dropping elements (entity types, relationships, attributes, etc.) as well as "semantics-preserving" operations like translating an inheritance relationship into a standard relationship or reifying a many-to-many relationship into an entity type. Each model transformation is stored in a history buffer and replayed when it is time to deploy the changes to a database instance. A model transformation is coupled with a designated relational transformation as well as a script for translating instance data – in essence, a small extract-transform-load workflow. The set of available translations is specified against the conceptual model rather than the relational model, so while it is not a relational schema evolution language by definition, it has the effect of evolving relational schemas and databases by proxy.

MeDEA (Domínguez et al. 2008) is a tool that, like DB-MAIN, exposes relational databases as conceptual models and then allows edits to the conceptual model to be propagated back to schema changes on the relational database. A key distinction between MeDEA and DB-MAIN is that MeDEA has neither a fixed modeling language nor a fixed mapping to the database. For instance, the conceptual model for a database may be constructed in UML or an extended ER diagram.

As a result, the relationship between model and database is fluid as well in MeDEA. Given a particular object in the conceptual model, there may be multiple ways to represent that object as schema in the database. Consequently, when one adds a new object to an existing model (or an empty one), the developer has potentially many valid options for persistence. A key concept in MeDEA is the encapsulation of those evolution choices in *rules*. For each incremental model change, the developer chooses an appropriate rule that describes the characteristics of the database change. For instance, consider adding to an ER model a new entity type that inherits from an existing entity type. The developer in that situation may choose as follows:

– To add a new relational table with the primary key of the hierarchy and the new attributes of the type as column, plus a foreign key to the parent type's table (the "table-per-type" mapping strategy).
– To add a new relational table with columns corresponding to all attributes of the new type including inherited attributes (the "table-per-concrete class" mapping strategy).
– To add columns to the table of the parent type, along with a discriminator or a repurposing of an existing discriminator column (the "table-per-hierarchy" mapping strategy).

Each of these strategies may be represented as a rule that may be applied when adding a new type.

Impact Analysis (Maule et al. 2008) is an approach that attempts to bridge the loose coupling of application and schema when the database schema changes. The rough idea is to inform the application developer of potential effects of a schema change at application design time. A complicating factor is that the SQL that is actually passed from application to database may not be as simple as a static string; rather, the application may build such queries or statements dynamically. The work uses dataflow analysis techniques to estimate what statements are being generated by the application, as well as the state of the application at the time of execution so as to understand how the application uses the statement's results.

The database schema evolution language is assumed to be SQL in this work. Schema changes are categorized by their potential impact according to existing literature on database refactoring (Ambler and Sadalage 2006). For instance, dropping a column will cause statements that refer to that column to throw errors when executed, and as such is an error-level impact. Impact analysis attempts to recognize these situations at design time and register an error rather than rely on the application throwing an error at runtime. On the other hand, adding a default value to a column will trigger a warning-level impact notice for any statement referring to that column because the semantics of that column's data has now changed – the default value may now be used in place of null – but existing queries and statements will still compile without incident. DB-MAIN and MeDea focus on propagating changes between relational schemas and conceptual models.

A significant amount of research has recently been dedicated to automatic *mapping adaptation* (Yu and Popa 2005) to support schema evolution and is surveyed in chapter 7 (Fagin et al. 2011). This work mostly assumed relational or nested relational schemas and different kinds of logical schema mappings. For these settings, the definition and implementation of two key operators, composition and inversion of mapping, have been studied. These operators are among those proposed in the context of model management, a general framework to manipulate schemas and mappings using high-level operators to simplify schema management tasks such as schema evolution (Bernstein 2003; Bernstein and Melnik 2007). A main advantage of composition and inversion is that they permit the reuse of existing mappings and their adaptation after a schema evolves. The proposed approaches for mapping adaptation still have practical limitations with respect to a uniform mapping language, mapping functionality, and performance so that more research is needed before their broader usability.

3.3 Summary

Table 6.1 shows a side-by-side comparison of most of the approaches described in this section for key requirements of Sect. 2. With the exception of the Panta Rhei project, all solutions focus on the simple (table) changes of SQL DDL. Oracle is the only system that also allows the specification of changes by providing a new version of a table to be changed as well as a column mapping. Commercial GUIs exist that can support simple diffing and change bundling, but eventually output simple SQL DDL without version mappings or other versioning support. Oracle's edition concept makes versioning less painful to emulate, though underlying physical structures are still not versioned. Overall, commercial DBMS support only simple schema changes and incur a high manual effort to adapt dependent schemas and to ensure backward compatibility. PRISM adds value by enabling versioning through interversion mappings, forward and backward compatibility, and formal guarantees of information preservation when applicable. HECATAEUS improves flexibility by specifying how to update dependent schema objects in a system when underlying objects evolve.

4 XML Schema Evolution

XML as a data model is vastly different than the relational model. Relations are highly structured, where schema is an intrinsic component of the model and an integral component in storage. On the other hand, XML is regarded as a *semistructured* model. Instances of XML need not conform to any schema, and must only conform to certain well-formed-ness properties, such as each start element having an end tag, attributes having locally distinct names, etc. Individual elements may contain structured content, wholly unstructured content, or a combination of both. In addition, the initial purpose and still dominant usage of XML is as a document structure and communication medium and not a storage model, and as such, notions of schema for XML are not nearly as intrinsic to the model as with relations. However, a notion of schema for XML is important for application interoperability to establish common communication protocols.

Given that the very notion of XML schemas is relatively new, the notion of schema evolution in XML is equally new. While there have been many proposed schema languages for XML, two have emerged as dominant – Document type definitions (DTDs) and XML Schema, with XML Schema now being the W3C recommendation. Each schema language has different capabilities and expressive power and as such has different ramifications on schema evolution strategies. None of the proposed XML schema languages, including DTDs and XML Schema, have an analogous notion of an "ALTER" statement from SQL allowing incremental evolution. Also unlike the relational model, XML does have a candidate language for referring to schema elements called *component designators* (W3C 2010); however, while the language has been used in research for other purposes, it has to date not been used in the context of schema evolution. Currently, XML schema evolution frameworks either use a proprietary textual or graphical language to express incremental schema changes or require the developer to provide the entire new schema.

The W3C – the official owners of the XML and XML Schema recommendations – have a document describing a base set of use cases for evolution of XML Schemas (W3C 2006). The document does not provide any language or framework for mitigating such evolutions, but instead prescribes what the semantics and behavior should be for certain kinds of incremental schema evolution and how applications should behave when faced with the potential for data from multiple schema versions. For instance, Sect. 2.3 lists use cases where the same element in different versions of a schema contains different elements. Applications are instructed to "ignore what they don't expect" and be able to "add extra elements without breaking the application."

All of the use cases emphasize application interoperability above all other concerns, and in addition that each application be allowed to have a local understanding of schema. Each application should be able to both produce and consume data according to the local schema. This perspective places the onus on the database or middle tier to handle inconsistencies, in sharp contrast to the static, structured nature of the relational model, which generally assumes a single working database schema with homogeneous instances that must be translated with every schema change. Thus, commercial and research systems have taken both approaches from the outset; some systems (e.g., Oracle) assume uniform instances like a relational system, while other systems (e.g., DB2) allow flexibility and versioning within a single collection of documents.

A key characteristic of a schema language such as DTDs and XML Schemas is that it determines what elements may be present in instance documents and in what order and multiplicity. Proprietary schema alteration languages thus tend to have analogous primitive statements, e.g., change an element's multiplicity, reorder elements, rename an element, insert or remove elements from the sequence, etc. Researchers have created a taxonomy of possible incremental changes to an XML schema (Moto et al. 2007) that is useful for evaluating evolution support in existing systems:

1. Add a new optional or required element to a type.
2. Delete an element from a type.
3. Add new top-level constructs like complex types.
4. Remove top-level constructs.
5. Change the semantics of an element without changing its syntax – for instance, if the new version of an application treats the implicit units of a column to be in metric where previous versions did not.
6. Refactor a schema in a way that does not affect instance validation – for instance, factoring out common local type definitions into a single global type definition.
7. Nest a collection of elements inside another element.
8. Flatten an element by replacing it by its children.
9. Rename an element or change its namespace.
10. Change an element's maximum or minimum multiplicity.
11. Modify an element's type, either by changing it from one named type to another or adding or changing a restriction or extension.
12. Change an element's default value.
13. Reorder elements in a type.

For each class of change, Moto et al. (2007) describe under what conditions a change in that class will preserve forward and backward compatibility. For instance, if in version 2 of a schema one adds optional element X to a type from version 1, any application running against version 1 will be able to successfully run against version 2 and vice versa so long as version 2 applications do not generate documents with element X. If element X is required rather than optional, the two versions are no longer interoperable under this scheme. The same logic can be applied to instances: an instance of schema version 1 will validate against version 2 if X is optional and will not if X is required.

For the rest of this section, we will describe the current state of the art in XML schema evolution as present in commercially available systems and research works. For each solution, in addition to comparing the solution against the requirements outlined in Sect. 2, we describe the classes of incremental changes that the solution supports and in what way it mitigates changes that must be made to either applications or instances. Table 6.2 shows the characteristics of the main approaches considered, which are discussed at the end of this section.

Table 6.2 Characteristics of XML schema evolution systems

	Oracle	Microsoft SQL Server	IBM DB2	Altova Diff Dog	XEM Kramer (2001), Su et al. (2001)	Model-based approaches (X-Evolution, CoDEX, UML)	Temporal XML schema
Description/focus of work	Commercial relational system with XML support	Commercial relational system with XML support	Commercial relational system with XML support	Commercial tool for XML schema diffing	DTD-based incremental changes to schema	View XML schema in a conceptual model	Allow time-varying instances to validate against time-varying schema
Change types							
(1) Richness (simple, complex)	(1) Simple, e.g., addition of an optional element or attribute	(1)–	(1)–	(1) Simple changes like rename, element reordering (additions and multiplicity changes unclear)	(1) Changes determined by DTD data model, e.g., add element or attribute	(1) Changes determined by conceptual model, e.g., rename_type or change_cardinality	(1)–
(2) Specification (incremental, new schema)	(2) Incremental using diffXML language or specification of new schema	(2) Addition of new schemas to existing schema sets	(2) New schema versions are specified as new schemas	(2) Supply of old/new schema	(2) Incremental	(2) Incremental	(2) New versions are added to running temporal schema

(Continued)

Table 6.2 (Continued)

	Oracle	Microsoft SQL Server	IBM DB2	Altova Diff Dog	XEM Kramer (2001), Su et al. (2001)	Model-based approaches (X-Evolution, CoDEX, UML)	Temporal XML schema
Evolution mapping							
(1) Representation	(1) Set of changes based on diffXML update language	(1)–	(1)–	(1) Set of element-element correspondences	(1) Set of incremental changes	(1) Set of incremental changes	(1)–
(2) DIFF computation	(2) Manually specified or XMLdiff function	(2)–	(2)–	(2) Semi-automatically derived (manual correction via GUI possible)	(2)–	(2)–	(2)–
Update propagation							
(1) Instances	(1) Specified in XSLT (copyEvolve procedure)	(1) None – documents must validate against new and old schemas	(1) None – documents must validate against the new version that exists at insertion	(1) Generation of XSLT to transform documents	(1) Each schema change is coupled with a series of XML data changes such as addDataEl or destroyDataEl	(1) Each schema change is coupled with a series of XML data changes using XQuery Update or proprietary update languages	(1) No need – documents validate against the version of the document at a given time slice

(2) Dependent schemas	(2)–	(2)–	(2)–	(2)–	(2)–	(2)–
Versioning support	–	All documents validate against their original schema version	–	–	–	Documents and schemas are both allowed to be versioned
Infrastructure/GUI	Libraries exist to diff two schemas at an XML document level	–	GUI to perform diff and to manually correct match results	–	Tool-based generation of changes, capture user actions	–

4.1 Commercial DBMS Systems

All three of the leading commercial database systems at the time of publication – Oracle, Microsoft SQL Server, and IBM DB2 – provide support for storage of XML data validated against an XML schema. Both of the major open-source relational database offerings – PostgreSql and MySql – have support for storing XML, but do not yet support schema validation in their standard configurations. We now briefly describe how each of the three major vendors supports XML schemas in general as well as how each vendor handles changes to those schemas. Furthermore, we discuss evolution support in the native XML database system Tamino.

Oracle offers two very different ways to evolve an XML schema (Oracle XML Schema Evolution 2008). The first is a *copy-based* mechanism that allows a great deal of flexibility. Data from an XML document collection are copied to a temporary location, then transformed according to a specification, and finally replaced in its original location. The second is an *in-place* evolution that does not require any data copying but only supports a limited set of possible schema changes.

Oracle has supported XML in tables and columns since version 9i (9.0.1) as part of XML DB, which comes packaged with Oracle since version 9.2. One can specify a column to have type XMLType, in which case each row of the table will have a field that is an XML document, or one can specify a table itself to have type XMLType, where each row is itself an XML document. In both cases, one can specify a single schema for the entire collection of documents. For instance, one can specify an XML column to have a specified given schema as follows:

```
CREATE TABLE table_with_xml_column
   (id NUMBER, xml_document XMLType)
   XMLTYPE COLUMN xml_document
   ELEMENT "http://tempuri.com/temp.xsd#Global1";
```

Note that when specifying a schema for an XML column or document, one must also specify a single global element that must serve as the document root for each document instance. In the example above, schema temp.xsd has a global element Global1 against which all document roots must validate.

The copy-based version of schema evolution is performed using the DBMS_XMLSCHEMA.copyEvolve stored procedure. The procedure takes as input three arrays: a list of schema URLs representing the schemas to evolve, a list of XML schema documents describing the new state of each schema in the first list, and a list of transformations expressed in XSLT. Each transformation corresponds to a schema based on its position in the list; so, the first transformation on the list is used to translate all instances of the first schema to conform to the first new schema definition, and so on.

There are a few restrictions on the usage of copyEvolve. For instance, the list of input schemas must include all dependent schemas of anything in the list, even if those schemas have not changed. There are also some additional steps that must be performed whenever global element names change. However, from an expressiveness perspective, one can use the procedure to migrate any schema to any other schema. There is no correctness validation that the specified transformations actually provide correct instance translation, so in the event that translated documents do not actually conform to the new schema, an error is thrown mid-translation.

The second in-place method of evolution is performed using a different procedure called DBMS_XMLSCHEMA.inPlaceEvolve. Because the evolution is performed in place, the procedure does not have any parameters guiding physical migration, given that there is none. The in-place evolution procedure has much less expressive power than the copy version – for this procedure, there is a full reverse-compatibility restriction in place. It is not just the case that all existing instances of the old schema must also conform to the new schema without alteration; it must be the case that all *possible* instances of the old schema must conform to the new one as well. Therefore, the restriction can be statically determined from the schemas and is not a property of the documents currently residing in the database. So, for instance, schema elements cannot be reordered, and elements that are currently singletons cannot be changed to collections and vice versa. The restriction guarantees that the relational representation of the schema does not change, which ensures that the in-place migration does not impose relational disk layout changes.

The kinds of changes that in-place migration does support include as follows:

- Add a new optional element or attribute (a subset of change class 1 from earlier in the section).
- Add a new domain value to an enumeration (subset of change class 11).
- Add a new global element, attribute, or type (change class 3).
- Change the type of an element from a simple type to a complex type with simple content (change class 6).
- Delete a global type, if it does not leave elements orphaned (subset of change class 4).
- Decrease the minOccurs for an instance, or increase the maxOccurs (subset of change class 10).

This list is not comprehensive, but is representative. It is clear from these changes that any valid instance of the old schema will still be valid after any of these changes. To specify these incremental changes, Oracle has a proprietary XML difference language called *diffXML* that is not specific to schemas but rather describe a diffgram between two XML document instances (and XML schemas are, of course, XML documents themselves). Expressions in diffXML loosely resemble expressions in XML update facility in that they have primitives that append, delete, or insert nodes in an XML document. However, diffXML expressions are XML documents rather than XQuery expressions. For instance, one can change the MaxLength restriction facet to 28 in a type using the following sequence of nodes:

```
<xd:delete-node xpath="/schema/complexType
  [@name'Foo']//maxLength/>
<xd:append-node
  parent-xpath = "/schema
    /complexType[@name='Foo']//restriction"
```

```
node-type = "element">
<xd:content>
  <xs:maxLength value = "28"/>
</xd:content>
< /xd:append-node>
```

Note that the expression language used to navigate an XML schema is vanilla XPath. The xd namespace is the namespace for the diffXML language, and xd:content nodes contain fragments of XML schema using the xs namespace.

One can specify a diffXML document manually, or one can generate it from the XMLDiff function, available both in Oracle's SQL dialect and Java. As mentioned earlier, XMLDiff operates on any XML documents, not just XML schemas, so the in-place evolution is essentially migrating schema by incrementally modifying the schema documents as instances under a guarantee that there will be no cascading effects of the migration.

Microsoft SQL Server, like Oracle, supports storing a collection of homogeneous XML documents in a relation column (Pal et al. 2006). Whereas instances in an XML-typed column or table in Oracle must conform to a specific schema with a specific global element as root, an XML-typed column in SQL Server validates against any schema in a collection of schemas and allows any global element as root. One specifies an XML Schema Collection in SQL server using a DDL statement:

```
CREATE XML SCHEMA COLLECTION [<relational_schema>.]
   sql_identifier AS Expression
```

Once a schema collection has been created, it can be assigned to be the schema for any column whose type is XML. Also, once the collection is created, there are only two operations that can be done on it – drop it or alter it by adding new constructs. The ALTER statement is the only form of schema evolution that SQL Server allows without manually dropping the schema, manually translating instances, and reestablishing the schema. The ALTER statement has only one form:

```
ALTER XML SCHEMA COLLECTION [relational_schema.]
   sql_identifier ADD Expression
```

For both the CREATE and ALTER statements, the expression must be a forest of valid XML schema documents. The ALTER statement can add schema elements to namespaces that already exist in the collection or to new namespaces.

The monotonic nature of alterations to a schema collection X means that, for the most part, documents that conform to collection X will continue to validate against the collection after alteration (maintaining the same reverse-compatibility restriction of the in-place evolution in Oracle). The one exception is if the collection contains a lax validation wildcard or any element whose type is xs:anyType. In such a case, the addition of new global elements to the schema collection could cause documents to fail validation. So, if any existing schema elements include such a construct, revalidation of existing documents will happen any time new global elements are added, and if the revalidation fails, the action is aborted.

IBM DB2 takes a different approach to XML schema validation, one that embraces the XML notion of interoperability rather than instance homogeneity (Beyer et al. 2005). Rather than apply a single schema or schema set against an entire collection of documents in a table or column, DB2 schema validation occurs on a per-document basis. XML documents may be validated against a schema at the time of insertion; however, the schema against which to validate the document is not determined by the schema associated with the column, since there by definition is no such schema. Rather, the schema is determined by attributes within the document to be inserted, or by manually specifying a schema as an argument to the XMLValidate function. Once a document has been validated, the document is adorned with metadata that verifies that the document was validated as well as information to help optimize query processing.

Like Oracle's schema registration service and SQL Server's schema collections, DB2 requires one to register XML schemas in the system prior to use:

```
register xmlSchema 'foo://tempuri.com/schema.xsd'
        from 'schema-v1.xsd' as schemaV1 complete
```

DB2 has no support for schema evolution per se, as different versions of the same schema appear in the database repository as unconnected documents. One also does not update document instances from one version of a schema to another, similar to SQL Server. Researchers from IBM have described how to support schema versioning using a complete scenario (Beyer et al. 2005); the scenario involves a relational table that correlates the currently registered schemas (and thus schema versions) with the applications currently using them. All of the mitigation of schema versioning is handled by the tables and protocols set up in the scenario rather than inside the engine.

Since the engine does not enforce document homogeneity, it allows documents from multiple schemas and thus multiple schema versions to coexist in a single corpus with full fidelity. Rather than automatically evolve instances, the documents exist in their original form, associated with its original schema.

Native XML databases, unlike relational systems, are built from the ground up to support XML storage. Relatively few of these systems support XML schemas or schema evolution. One notable exception is *Tamino* (Software AG 2006).

Like Oracle, Tamino can store XML data in a fashion that is XML schema dependent, i.e., the physical structures may be optimized, possibly by mapping to relations, knowing that the XML data is regularly structured in some way. Also similarly to Oracle, Tamino allows schemas to evolve under the same restrictions as Oracle's in-place migration mechanism. One specifies a new schema version wholesale – no mapping or incremental changes are possible – providing the entire schema document, and passing it to the same _define command to define an initial version.

Where Tamino differs from Oracle is that Tamino allows the stored data to determine reverse compatibility rather than the schema document versions themselves. One can pass a parameter to the _define command to attempt to do some static validation first – determining just from the documents themselves whether it is possible for reverse compatibility to be guaranteed – but eventually all documents are validated against the new schema at evolution time and, if any fail validation, the change is rejected.

4.2 Mapping Tools

Altova (Altova 2010) does specialize in XML-specific tools for document and data management. Altova provides a tool called DiffDog that can perform XML schema matching and diffing. The tool takes as input two XML schema instances and performs element-to-element matching. The tool's result can be manually modified to accommodate renames that the automatic algorithm does not immediately catch. From a diff result, the tool generates an XSLT script that translates valid documents of one schema into valid documents of the other schema. The tool can thus handle renaming and reordering of elements in a fairly straightforward manner. It is unclear from documentation whether the tool can handle addition of required elements or changes in multiplicity; such changes would not be straightforward in the user interface of the tool. There is also no mechanism to incrementally alter schemas – schemas are diffed wholesale. A related tool Altova MapForce is used to generate XSLT mappings between different XML schemas that are not in an evolution relationship but may differ to a larger extent. The initial schema matching is therefore to be provided by a human user.

Research on schema matching and mapping has also resulted in several tools to semi-automatically determine executable mappings such as Clio, e.g., for instance migration after schema evolution (Jiang et al. 2007; Bonifati et al. 2011). The tools do not provide for incremental evolutions per se, but map between the old and the evolved schema. None of the existing mapping-based tools provide full support for all of the features of XML Schema; for instance, Clio supports a significant subset of XML Schema but not element order, choice particles, or element multiplicity restrictions other than zero, one, or unbounded.

4.3 Research Approaches

As of the year 2000, the DTD was the predominant method for schematizing XML documents. As the decade progressed, XML Schema became the dominant schematizing technology for XML. That same trend has been mirrored in research; schema evolution techniques introduced earlier in the decade focused more on changes to a DTD, while more recent publications cover the far more expressive XML Schema recommendation.

XEM (Kramer 2001; Su et al. 2001) – XML Evolution Management – is a framework introduced by Worcester Polytechnic Institute in 2001 describing evolution management in DTDs. The approach predates schema evolution in any of the commercial systems introduced in the previous section. The work provides a sound and complete set of change operations. The set is sound in that each evolution primitive is guaranteed to maintain all validity and integrity properties; post-evolution, all documents will still be well-formed XML and will still validate against the DTD. The set is complete in that one can start with any DTD and arrive at any other valid DTD using only changes from the set. The set of schema changes is as follows:

- Create a DTD element type (change class 3).
- Delete a DTD element type (change class 4).
- Insert DTD element or attribute into an existing element type (change class 1).
- Remove an element or attribute from an existing element type (change class 2).
- Change the quantifier on an element in a type (change class 10, limited to the kinds that DTD is capable of).
- Nest a set of adjacent elements in a type beneath a new element (change class 7).
- Flatten a nested element (change class 8).

Each individual change to a DTD induces a change on all valid documents to maintain document validity. For instance, if one adds a new required element or changes the quantifier on an element so that it becomes required, XEM will automatically add a default element to all instances that lack the element. Note that this evolution scheme takes a relational approach to evolution in the sense that all instances must evolve to match the new schema rather than allowing documents to belong to multiple versions simultaneously.

DTD-Diff (Leonardi et al. 2007) is an algorithm and tool for detecting changes between versions of a DTD. The algorithm takes as input two DTD instances and returns a list of changes from the following categories:

- Adding or deleting element, attribute, or entity declarations (change classes 3 and 4).
- Change the content of an element type by adding, removing, or reordering nodes (change classes 1, 2, 11, and 13).
- Change element cardinality (change class 10, limited to DTD support).
- Update attribute or entity facets such as changing a default value of an attribute or updating the replacement text of an entity declaration (change classes 5 and 12).

The set of supported changes explicitly does not include construct renaming, due to the fully automated nature of the difference engine – one could imagine adding support for allowing the result of a matching graph as additional input to handle such renaming, though. The authors claim that applying existing XML document change detection algorithms to instances of XML Schema (which are themselves XML documents) does not necessarily yield semantically correct or optimal changes.

Diagram-based evolution (Domínguez et al. 2005) is a way to bypass the absence of a standard evolution language by allowing the developer to express evolution intent using a tool. One such effort uses UML diagrams as a front end for an XML schema; in turn, changes to a diagram translate to changes on the associated schema. In that framework, a UML diagram is used as a conceptual model for an XML schema and its corresponding documents. The UML diagrams supported by the framework do not have the same expressive power as the full XML schema language, and so the work focuses on the subset of XML Schema to which the UML language maps cleanly. Changes to the UML diagrams within a tool then induce changes to the underlying schema and instances in the form of deployable XSLT documents.

The set of changes that the UML framework supports is thus heavily influenced by the tooling support. For instance, the change that is described in depth in Domínguez et al. (2005) is a refactoring operation that translates an attribute in a UML class into its own class:

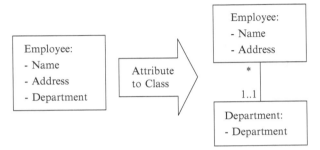

In general, each class corresponds to a type in an XML schema with an element and a key. Attributes correspond to nested elements, while associations map to key references. The refactoring operation above therefore results in removing the nested element from the Employee type, creating a new type and element with a key for Department, and a key reference between the two types. An XSLT stylesheet is also generated to migrate data to ensure Department data is not lost.

A similar and more recent approach is *CoDEX* (Klettke 2007), which uses a conceptual model that is closely aligned with XML Schema rather than using UML. Again, incremental changes made to the conceptual model result in changes to the associated schema and valid documents. The work on CoDEX also describes an algebra that does preprocessing on incremental changes. As the user edits the model, a log of actions is recorded, which can subsequently be optimized using reduction rules. For instance, adding a new element then renaming it is equivalent to simply adding the element with the new name to begin with.

X-Evolution (Guerrini and Mesiti 2009; Mesiti et al. 2006) is another framework that defines incremental schema evolution in terms of a tool, in this case a graph representation of the schema. Like CoDEX and the UML tools, X-Evolution supports a set of evolution primitives; the list is too long to mention in-line, but covers change classes except 7, 8, and 13 from our running list (and the algorithm in X-Evolution could be altered in a fairly straightforward way to accommodate them). X-Evolution is also able to handle a kind of change not listed in the change taxonomy at all – specifically, changing a content particle's type, say, from ALL to SEQUENCE or CHOICE. A subset of the list of incremental evolutions is classified as having no effect on validation, such as the removal of a global type that has no current element instances. With any such evolution, no document revalidation is necessary – this list of validation-less changes tracks with the research done in Moto et al. (2007).

A key contribution of the work on X-Evolution is *incremental repudiation and revalidation*. Given an incremental change to a schema, X-Evolution runs one of two algorithms at the user's request – one that tests valid documents to see if they are still valid post-validation and one that alters valid documents to make them valid with respect to the new schema. Both algorithms are incremental, as the documents are not re-validated en masse. Instead, only the parts of the document that correspond to the altered part of the document are re-validated (or altered).

Temporal XML Schema (Currim et al. 2009) – also referred to as *τXSchema* – is a way to formalize the temporal nature of schema and document versioning. The framework is assembled by the same research group that helped develop the temporal extensions to SQL. In all other frameworks discussed to date, the relationship between versions of schemas and documents are informal if they exist at all; two versions of the same schema version are considered to be two separate schemas, related to each other only by whatever point-in-time script was used to perform the migration. τXSchema makes evolution over time a first-class concept, modeling different versions of the same conventional XML schema in the same document.

τXSchema enforces the standard constraints of an XML schema. Assuming that a temporal document is valid with respect to a temporal schema, restricting the document to a single point in time produces a document that is valid with respect to its XML schema at that same point in time. Any conventional schema constraint must be valid at all points in time as well, such as keys, key references, and data type restrictions. In addition, temporal documents and schemas are still valid XML documents with additional elements and attributes added to reflect temporal characteristics; τXSchema provides extensions to existing XML tools that perform the additional temporal validation of documents.

4.4 Summary

Table 6.2 shows a comparison of most of the previously mentioned approaches to XML evolution relative to the characteristics laid out in Sect. 2. In general, commercial options support evolution where instances may need to be revalidated but need not be updated. The exception is Oracle, where one can specify XSLT scripts to migrate instances. There is no commonly supported evolution language to specify incremental updates, a shortcoming that research approaches circumvent by inventing proprietary solutions. XEM and model-based solutions attempt to couple incremental schema changes with incremental data changes, which often results in empty or default element generation to fill gaps where a document no longer validates. None of the solutions explicitly support versioning unless they support multiple versions appearing side by side physically in persistent storage, as IBM and temporal XSchema do. Altova presents a dedicated diffing tool with noncomplete capabilities, and model-driven approaches offer a GUI-based method to specify incremental changes. Mapping tools such as Clio also support diff computation and instance migration for XML-like schemas. Currently, there is not yet any support for adapting dependent mappings/schemas for XML schema evolution.

5 Ontology Evolution

Gruber (1993) characterizes an ontology as the explicit specification of a conceptualization of domain. While there are different kinds of ontologies, they typically provide a shared/controlled vocabulary that is used to model a domain of interest using concepts with properties and relationships between concepts. In the recent past, such ontologies have been increasingly used in different domains to semantically describe objects and to support data integration applications. For example, there are a growing number of life science ontologies, e.g., the ontologies managed in the open biomedical ontologies (OBO) Foundry (Smith et al. 2007). The existing ontologies are not static but are frequently evolved to incorporate the newest knowledge of a domain or to adapt to changing application requirements.

There are several differences between ontologies and relational schemas that influence their evolution:

- Ontologies are conceptually more abstract models than database schemas and come in different variations ranging from controlled vocabularies and thesauri over is-a hierarchies/taxonomies and directed a-cyclic graphs (DAG) to frame-based and formal representations (Lassila and McGuinness 2001). For instance, ontology languages such as RDF or OWL allow the specification of concept hierarchies with multiple inheritance, cardinality constraints, inverse or transitive properties, and disjoint classes. The kind and expressiveness of ontologies determine the kind of changes that should be supported for ontology evolution. For instance, Noy and Klein (2004) propose a set of 22 simple and complex ontology change operations such as concept creation, reclassification of a concept, or merge/split of concepts.
- The role of instances differs between ontologies and relational schemas. For example, many ontologies include instances but do not clearly separate them from other parts of the ontologies such as concepts and relationships. In other cases, instances are described by ontologies but are maintained outside the ontology within separate data sources. These differences impact update propagation of ontology changes since the separately maintained instances may not be under the control of the ontology editors.
- In contrast to database schemas, the development and evolution of ontologies is often a collaborative and decentralized process. Furthermore, new ontologies often reuse existing ones, i.e., an ontology engineer uses a common ontology as the basis for domain-specific extensions. These aspects lead to new synchronization requirements for ontology changes. Furthermore, ontologies serving a whole domain likely introduce many usage dependencies, although ontology providers usually do not know which applications/users utilize their ontology. Supporting different ontology versions is a main approach to provide stability for ontology applications. For example, there are daily new versions for the popular Gene Ontology.

Despite these differences, it is easy to see that the schema evolution requirements introduced in Sect. 2 also apply to ontology evolution, in particular support for a rich set of changes, expressive mappings, update propagation to instances and dependent schemas/ontologies, versioning, and user-friendly tools.

For the rest of this section, we will describe representative approaches on ontology evolution and how they meet the introduced requirements. Table 6.3 comparatively shows selected approaches that are discussed at the end of the section.

5.1 Research Approaches

The *Protégé* system supports different kinds of collaborative ontology evolution meeting varying functional requirements (Noy et al. 2006). First, ontologies can be modified synchronously or asynchronously. Synchronous editing is performed on a centrally stored ontology that can be modified concurrently by several developers. For asynchronous editing collaborators check out the latest ontology version, change it offline, and merge their changes into a common version later on. Second, ontologies may internally be versioned or not. Ontologies may so periodically be archived with the possibility to roll back to a former version. Alternatively, all changes are continuously directed to a single (the most recent) ontology version. Third, ontology changes may be subject to the approval of designated curators to resolve potential problems and maintain a high quality. Usually, such a curation is performed before releasing a new version of an ontology. Finally, ontology changes may be monitored (logged) or not.

The ontology evolution framework supports a rich set of simple and complex changes that can be annotated (Noy et al. 2006). These changes are classified within a change and annotation ontology (CHAO). Annotation includes the type of ontology change, the class/property/instance that was changed, the user and date/time when the change was performed. The two main approaches to specify changes are supported: specification (and logging) of incremental change operations and the provision of a new ontology version. In the latter case, the Diff evolution mapping is semi-automatically determined.

Protégé uses the PROMPTDIFF algorithm (Noy and Musen 2002) to determine an evolution mapping between two input ontology versions. The two versions V1 and V2 are compared using an iterative algorithm combining different heuristic matchers (e.g., single unmatched sibling, unmatched inverse slots, or same type/name) until no more changes are found. The found changes are presented in a so-called difference table containing a set of tuples that interrelate elements of V1 with elements of V2. Each tuple specifies a change operation (add, delete, split, merge, and map) and its parameters.

The different kinds of ontology evolution are implemented in the Protégé ontology editor within two plugins: Change-management plugin and the PROMPT plugin. The Change-management plugin can be used to access a list of changes, allows users to add annotations, and enables to study the history of concepts, i.e., users can examine what modifications happened on a particular concept in the history. The PROMPT plugin implements the PROMPTDIFF algorithm and provides

Table 6.3 Characteristics of selected ontology evolution systems

	Protégé Noy et al. (2004, 2006), Noy and Musen (2002)	KAON Stojanovic et al. (2002)	OntoView Klein et al. (2002)	OnEX Hartung et al. (2008, 2009, 2010), Kirsten et al. (2009)
Description/focus of work	Flexible framework for ontology management and evolution	Process for consistent ontology evolution	Version management and comparison for RDF-based ontologies	Quantitative evolution analysis for life science ontologies and mappings
Supported ontology formats	RDF/OWL, further formats via import plugins	RDF/OWL	RDF	OBO, RDF, CSV; further formats via adaptable import
Change types				
(1) Richness (simple, complex)	(1) Simple and complex (siblings_move, …)	(1) Simple and complex (merge, copy, …)	(1) Simple	(1) Simple and complex (merge, split, …)
(2) Specification (incremental, new schema)	(2) Incremental or specification of new ontology version	(2) Incremental	(2) Integration of new versions	(2) Integration of new versions
Evolution mapping				
(1) Representation	(1) Incremental changes or difference table for two versions	(1) Incremental changes	(1) Set of changes interrelating two versions	(1) Set of changes interrelating two versions
(2) DIFF computation	(2) PROMPTDIFF algorithm	(2)–	(2) Rule-based diff computation	(2) Matching and rule-based diff computation

Update propagation				
(1) Instances	(1)–	(1) Migration of instances managed with the ontology	(1)–	(1) Adaptation of annotations affected by ontology change
(2) Dependent schemas	(2)–	(2) Recursive application of evolution process on dependent ontologies	(2)–	(2)–
Versioning support	Sequential versioning	–	Sequential versioning based on CVS	Supports existing sequential ontology versions
Infrastructure/GUI	Protégé ontology editor with PROMPT and change management plugin	GUI-based editor in KAON infrastructure	Web-based application to access, compare, and version ontologies	Web-based application to explore changes in life science ontologies

facilities to accept/reject performed changes for curators. Besides these two plugins, the Protégé environment provides functionality for editing in a client–server mode as well as transaction and undo support.

The *KAON* prototype (Karlsruhe Ontology and Semantic Web Tool Suite) providing a graphical user interface for incrementally editing ontologies within a process of six phases (Stojanovic et al. 2002). For each change, the following sequential phases are needed: (1) Change Capturing, (2) Change Representation, (3) Semantics of Change, (4) Change Implementation, (5) Change Propagation, and (6) Change Validation. The evolution process can be cyclic, i.e., after the last phase, the process can be re-executed for further ontology changes.

In the first phase (Change Capturing), the ontology engineer decides about the necessary ontology changes, e.g., to delete a concept. In phase 2 (Change Representation), such change requests are translated into a formal change representation. The approach distinguishes between elementary (simple) as well as composite (complex) changes that can be expressed by a series of elementary ones. In total, 16 elementary changes (additions/deletions/modifications of concepts, properties, axioms, and subclass relationships) and 12 composite changes (merging and moving of concepts, concept duplication/extraction, etc.) are distinguished.

Phase 3 uses the formal change representation to identify potential problems (inconsistencies) that the intended changes can introduce within the ontology. For example, the deletion of a concept C impacts its children and instances. Different evolution strategies can be specified to deal with such situations, e.g., one can delete the children as well or move the children to be subconcepts of C's parent concept. To reduce the manual effort for such decisions, different default evolution strategies can be specified. Furthermore, the evolution strategies to resolve inconsistencies may be automatically determined controlled by general goals such as minimizing the number of ontology changes or keeping the ontologies flat.

The resulting changes are presented to the user for confirmation and are then implemented in phase 4. All performed changes are logged in a version log; an explicit versioning does not take place. The following phase 5 (Propagation) is responsible to propagate the ontology changes to dependent applications or other ontologies that extend the modified ontology. This approach assumes that the consumers of the ontology are known and that the ontology evolution process can be recursively applied on the dependent ontologies. The final Validation phase gives ontology engineers the possibility to review the performed changes with the option of undoing changes. Moreover, she can initiate further change requests by starting another evolution cycle.

The *OntoView* system (Klein et al. 2002) focuses on versioning support for RDF-based ontologies. The system is inspired by the concurrent versioning system (CVS), which is used in collaborative software development. One of its core functions is to structurally compare ontology versions to determine different types of changes (representing a Diff evolution mapping). Nonlogical changes denote changes in the label or comment of a concept. Logical definition changes may affect the formal semantics of a concept, e.g., modifications on subClassOf, domain/range of properties, or property restrictions. Further change types include identifier changes and the addition/deletion of definitions. More complex changes such as merges or splits of concepts are not supported.

The detection algorithm is inspired by the UNIX diff operation but uses the ontology graph structure and RDF triples <subject, predicate, object> as the basis for the version comparison. Change detection between two graphs is based on IF–THEN rules that specify conditions on triples in the old/new ontology and produce resulting changes if the conditions are fulfilled. The authors argue that they can specify and detect almost every change type using this mechanism except identifier changes.

Ontology evolution explorer (OnEX) is a web-based system for exploring changes in numerous life science ontologies (Hartung et al. 2009). It uses existing ontology versions and identifies the differences between succeeding versions of an ontology. The differences are represented by evolution mappings consisting of simple changes (adds, deletes, updates of concepts/relationships, and attributes) that are identified by comparing the unambiguous accession numbers of elements available in life science ontologies (Hartung et al. 2008). OnEX can be used to determine the stability and specific change history of ontologies and selected concepts of interest. Furthermore, one can determine whether given annotations referring to an ontology version have been invalidated, e.g., due to deletes. Such annotations can then be semi-automatically migrated to be consistent with the newest version of the respective ontology.

OnEX uses a tailored storage model to efficiently store all ontology versions in its repository by utilizing that succeeding ontology version differ only to a small degree (Kirsten et al. 2009). Currently, OnEX provides access to about 700 versions of 16 life science ontologies.

The ontology diff algorithm proposed in Hartung et al. (2010) determines an evolution mapping between two ontology versions. The evolution mapping consists of a set of simple as well as complex ontology changes (e.g., merging or splitting of concepts). The approach is based on an initial matching of the ontology version and applies so-called Change Operation Generating Rules (COG rules) for deriving the change operations of the evolution mapping. For instance, the rule for determining a merge of multiple concepts looks as follows:

$$\exists mapC(a, c) \land \exists mapC(b, c) \land \neg \exists mapC(a, d) \land \neg \exists mapC(b, e)$$
$$\land a \neq b \land c \neq d \land c \neq e \quad \rightarrow \textbf{create}[merge(\{a\}, c)], \textbf{create}[merge(\{b\}, c)]$$

The rule derives that concepts a and b are merged into concept c if there are two match correspondences $mapC(a,c)$ and $mapC(b,c)$ and if a and b are not connected to any other concept. The approach could be validated for different kinds of ontologies.

Change detection using a version log: Plessers and De Troyer (2005) builds upon the KAON ontology evolution process (Stojanovic et al. 2002). The proposed evolution process consists of five phases: (1) Change Request, (2) Change Implementation, (3) Change Detection, (4) Change Recovery, and (5) Change Propagation. The main difference is in the Change Detection phase where additional implicit changes are detected based on the history (log) of previous changes as well as the so-called version log containing the different versions of ontology concepts during their lifetime.

Changes are either basic (simple) or composite and defined declaratively using the change definition language (CDL), which is based on RDF/OWL. Both kinds of changes are determined by evaluating the old and new ontology versions w.r.t. rule-based change definitions. For example, the change definition

$$\forall \ p \in P, A \in C : addDomain(p, A) \leftarrow \neg hasDomain(p, A, v_{i-1})$$
$$\wedge \ hasDomain(p, A, v_i)$$

specifies that the basic change $addDomain(p, A)$ to add A as the domain of property p has occurred when this domain has not been in the old version v_{i-1} but in the changed version v_i. Composite changes are more difficult to determine since they involve several ontology elements that may be subject to changes themselves that may have to be taken into account. The correct identification of such changes is important to correctly adapt instances of the ontology. For instance, we may have two basic changes to move property p from class $C1$ to class $C2$ followed by a subclass addition between $C1$ and $C2$. Treating these changes independently would first delete all properties p in instances of $C1$. However, the following addition of a subclass relationship between $C1$ and $C2$ would require the addition of property p to the $C1$ instances. By finding out that the two basic changes realize the composite change of moving up p in the class hierarchy, the unnecessary deletions of p values can be avoided.

Detection of high-level changes in RDF/S ontologies: Papavassiliou et al. (2009) focuses on the detection of high-level changes (diff) between two RDF/S-based ontology versions. Their framework uses a formal language to define changes and distinguishes between basic, composite, and heuristic changes. Heuristic changes refer to changes that are detected by matchers employing heuristic techniques to determine that classes have been renamed, merged, or split. The proposed algorithm focuses on the detection of basic and composite changes and utilizes the so-called low-level delta containing the RDF triples that have been added and deleted between two versions V1 and V2 of a RDF/S knowledge base. Changes are described by triples consisting of (1) required added RDF triples, (2) required deleted RDF triples, and (3) a set of conditions that need to be fulfilled. For instance, the change *Delete_Superclass(x,y)*, which removes the is-a relationship between x and y, can be described as follows: (1) no added triple exists, (2) the deletion of a triple $(x, subClassOf, y)$ exists, and (3) x is a class in V1. The detection algorithm first uses the low-level delta and the change descriptions to find potential changes between V1 and V2. The second step then iteratively selects changes that meet the conditions and reduces the set of changes in the low-level delta. The algorithm first identifies composite changes and then basic ones.

5.2   Summary

Table 6.3 shows a comparison of most systems that are discussed. While the first two systems Protégé and KAON support complete processes for ontology evolution, OntoView and OnEX focus on the management of existing ontology versions developed elsewhere. Supported ontology formats are primarily RDF and OWL; Protégé and OnEX can integrate further formats (e.g., OBO). With the exception of OntoView, all systems support both simple and complex changes. The representation and determination of an evolution mapping between two ontology versions differs among the systems. Protégé is most flexible for specifying ontology changes by supporting both incremental changes and the provision of a new ontology version; the other systems follow only one of the two possibilities. A Diff computation is supported by all systems except KAON. The update propagation to instances and related data is partially supported in KAON and OnEX. KAON uses evolution strategies to adapt instances managed together with the ontology. OnEX supports the identification and migration of annotations affected by ontology changes. With the exception of KAON, all systems support sequential versioning. Graphical user interfaces are provided by all systems: Protégé and KAON are editor-like applications, while OntoView and OnEX are web-based.

6   Conclusions

Effective schema evolution is a long-standing problem that is difficult to address since schema changes impact existing instances, index and storage structures as well as applications, and other schema consumers. We introduced the main requirements for effective schema evolution and provided an overview about the current state of the art on the evolution of relational schemas, XML schemas, and ontologies. More than 20 approaches have been analyzed against the introduced requirements and we used several tables to compare most of these approaches side by side. The introduced methodology should be similarly applicable to evaluate further schema or ontology evolution approaches. We summarize some of our observations as follows

Commercial DBMS currently restrict their support for evolving relational schemas to simple incremental changes and instance migration, while there is not yet support to semi-automatically propagate changes to dependent schemas, mappings, and applications. Filling this gap requires support for the determination and processing of expressive schema mappings that have been studied in recent research approaches such as Pantha Rei/Prism and in model management research (Bernstein and Melnik 2007).

The evolution of XML schemas is easier than for relational schemas since the schemas can be extended by optional components that do not invalidate existing instances. Due to the absence of a standard schema modification language, schema changes are usually specified by providing a new version of the schema. In research approaches, schema matching and mapping techniques are being used to semi-automatically derive the evolution mapping between two schema versions and to derive a corresponding instance-level mapping for instance migration. Support for propagating changes of XML schemas to dependent schemas or applications have not yet been studied sufficiently.

Research on ontology evolution considers both the adoption of incremental changes and the provision of new schema versions to specify several changes at once. Several approaches have been proposed to semi-automatically determine Diff evolution mappings by comparing two ontology versions. These mappings are usually represented by sets of simple or complex changes. While instance migration has been considered to some extent, the propagation of ontology changes to dependent ontologies/schemas, or applications have not yet found sufficient attention.

Despite recent progress, we therefore see a need for substantially more research on schema evolution, also in areas not discussed in this chapter. For example, distributed architectures with many schemas and mappings need powerful mapping and evolution support, e.g., to propagate changes of a data source schema to merged (global) schemas. New challenges are also posed by dynamic settings such as *stream systems* where the data to be analyzed may change its schema, e.g., by providing new or changed attributes. A first approach in this area is Fernández-Moctezuma et al. (2009). They propose certain extensions for schema consumers such as query operators to deal with changed schemas.

References

Altova DiffDog (2010) http://www.altova.com/diffdog

Ambler SW, Sadalage PJ (2006) Refactoring databases: Evolutionary database design. Addison Wesley, MA

Bernstein PA (2003) Applying model management to classical meta data problems. In: Proceedings of Conference on Innovative Database Research (CIDR) 2003. ACM, NY, pp 209–220

Bernstein PA, Melnik S (2007) Model management 2.0: manipulating richer mappings. In: Proceedings of ACM SIGMOD conference. ACM, NY, pp 1–12

Beyer K, Oezcan F, Saiprasad S, Van der Linden B (2005) DB2/XML: Designing for evolution. In: Proceedings of ACM SIGMOD conference. ACM, NY, pp 948–952

Bonifati A, Mecca G, Papotti P, Velegrakis Y (2011) Discovery and correctness of schema mapping transformations. In: Bellahsene Z, Bonifati A, Rahm E (eds) Schema matching and mapping, Data-Centric Systems and Applications Series. Springer, Heidelberg

Cate BT, Kolaitis PG (2010) Structural characterizations of schema-mapping languages. Comm ACM 53(1):101–110

Curino CA, Moon HJ, Zaniolo C (2008) Graceful database schema evolution: The PRISM workbench. In: Proceedings of VLDB conference. VLDB Endowment. pp 761–772

Currim F, Currim S, Dyreson CE, Joshi S, Snodgrass RT, Thomas SW, Roeder E (2009) tXSchema: Support for data-and schema-versioned XML documents. TimeCenter Technical Report TR-91, Aalborg University, Denmark

Domínguez E, Lloret J, Rubio AL, Zapata, MA (2005) Evolving XML schemas and documents using UML class diagrams. In: Proceedings of DEXA conference. Springer, Heidelberg

Domínguez E, Lloret J, Rubio AL, Zapata MA (2008) MeDEA: A database evolution architecture with traceability. Data Knowl Eng 65(3):419–441

Fagin R, Kolaitis PG, Popa L, Tan W (2011) Schema mapping evolution through composition and inversion. In: Bellahsene Z, Bonifati A, Rahm E (eds) Schema matching and mapping, Data-Centric Systems and Applications Series. Springer, Heidelberg

Fernández-Moctezuma R, Terwilliger JF, Delcambre LML, Maier D (2009) Toward formal semantics for data and schema evolution in data stream management systems. In: Proceedings of ER workshops. Springer, Heidelberg, pp 85–94

Gruber TR (1993) A translation approach to portable ontology specifications. In: Knowledge acquisition, vol 5(2). Academic, London, pp 199–220

Guerrini G, Mesiti M (2009) XML schema evolution and versioning: current approaches and future trends. In: Open and novel Issues in XML database applications. Future directions and advanced technologies. IDEA Group, pp 66–87

Hartung M, Kirsten T, Rahm E (2008) Analyzing the evolution of life science ontologies and mappings. In: Proceedings of 5th international workshop data integration in the life sciences (DILS). LNCS, vol 5109. Springer, Heidelberg

Hartung M, Kirsten T, Gross A, Rahm E (2009) OnEX – Exploring changes in life science ontologies. BMC Bioinformatics 10:250

Hartung M, Gross A, Rahm E (2010) Rule-based determination of Diff evolution mappings between ontology versions. Technical report, University of Leipzig

Hick JM, Hainaut JL (2006) Database application evolution: a transformational approach. Data Knowl Eng 59(3):534–558

IBM (2009a) Database version control with IBM Optim Database Administrator V2.2. http://www.ibm.com/developerworks/data/library/techarticle/dm-0704henry/index.html

IBM (2009b) DB2 9.7: Online schema change. http://www.ibm.com/developerworks/data/library/techarticle/dm-0907db2outages/index.html

Jiang H, Ho H, Popa L, Han WS (2007) Mapping-driven XML transformation. In: Proceedings of WWW conference. ACM, NY, pp 1063–1072

Kirsten T, Hartung M, Gross A, Rahm E (2009) Efficient management of biomedical ontology versions. In: Proceedings on the move to meaningful internet systems (OTM) workshops. Springer, Heidelberg, pp 574–583

Klein M, Fensel D, Kiryakov A, Ognyanov D (2002) Ontology versioning and change detection on the web. In: Proceedings of 13th international conference on knowledge engineering and knowledge management. Ontologies and the semantic web. Springer, Heidelberg

Klettke M (2007) Conceptual XML schema evolution – the CoDEX approach for design and redesign. In: Proceedings of BTW workshops, pp 53–63

Kramer D (2001) XEM: XML evolution management. Master's Thesis, Worcester Polytechnic Institute

Lassila O, McGuinness, D (2001) The role of frame-based representation on the semantic web. Knowledge Systems Laboratory Report KSL-01-02, Stanford University

Leonardi E, Hoaia TT, Bhowmicka SS, Madria S (2007) DTD-Diff: A change detection algorithm for DTDs. Data Knowl Eng 61(2):384–402

Maule A, Emmerich W, Rosenblum DS (2008) Impact analysis of database schema changes. In: Proceedings of international conference on software engineering (ICSE). ACM, NY, pp 451–460

Mesiti M, Celle R, Sorrenti, MA, Guerrini G (2006) X-Evolution: A system for XML schema evolution and document adaptation. In: Proceedings of EDBT, 2006. Springer, Heidelberg

Microsoft SQL Server 2008 R2 Data-Tier Applications (2010) http://msdn.microsoft.com/en-us/library/ee240739(SQL.105).aspx

Miller R, Ioannidis YE, Ramakrishnan R (1994) Schema equivalence in heterogeneous systems: Bridging theory and practice. Inform Syst 19(1):3–31

Moto MM, Malaika S, Lim L (2007) Preserving XML queries during schema evolution. In: Proceedings of WWW conference. ACM, NY, pp 1341–1342

Noy NF, Klein M (2004) Ontology evolution: Not the same as schema evolution. Knowl Inform Syst 6(4):428–440

Noy NF, Musen MA (2002) PromptDiff: A fixed-point algorithm for comparing ontology versions. In: Proceedings of the national conference on artificial intelligence. American Association for Artificial Intelligence, CA, pp 744–750

Noy NF, Kunnatur S, Klein M, Musen, MA (2004) Tracking changes during ontology evolution. In: Proceedings of international semantic web conference (ISWC). Springer, Heidelberg, pp 259–273

Noy NF, Chugh A, Liu W, Musen, MA (2006) A framework for ontology evolution in collaborative environments. In: Proceedings of international semantic web conference (ISWC). Springer, Heidelberg, pp 544–558

Oracle Database 10g Release 2 (2005) Online data reorganization & redefinition, white paper. May 2005

Oracle Edition-Based Redefinition (2009) Whitepaper. Available at http://www.oracle.com/technology/deploy/availability/pdf/edition_based_redefinition.pdf

Oracle XML Schema Evolution (2008) Chapter 9 of Oracle XML DB, Developer's Guide, 11g Release, May 2008

Pal S, Tomic D, Berg B, Xavier J (2006) Managing collections of XML schemas in Microsoft SQL Server 2005. In: Proceedings of EDBT conference. Springer, Heidelberg, pp 1102–1105

Papastefanatos G, Vassiliadis P, Simitsis A, Aggistalis K, Pechlivani F, Vassiliou Y (2008) Language extensions for the automation of database schema evolution. In: Proceedings of the 10th international conference on enterprise information systems (ICEIS). INSTICC, pp 74–81

Papastefanatos G, Vassiliadis P, Simitsis A, Vassiliou Y (2010) HECATAEUS: Regulating schema evolution. In: Proceedings of ICDE, pp 1181–1184

Papavassiliou V, Flouris G, Fundulaki I, Kotzinos D, Christophides V (2009) On detecting high-level changes in RDF/S KBs. In: Proceedings of 8th international semantic web conference (ISWC). Springer, Heidelberg, pp 473–488

Plessers P, De Troyer O (2005) Ontology change detection using a version log. In: Proceedings of 4th international semantic web conference (ISWC). Springer, Heidelberg, pp 578–592

Rahm E (2011) Towards large-scale schema and ontology matching. In: Bellahsene Z, Bonifati A, Rahm E (eds) Schema matching and mapping, Data-Centric Systems and Applications Series. Springer, Heidelberg

Rahm E, Bernstein PA (2001) A survey of approaches to automatic schema matching. VLDB J 10(4):334–350

Rahm E, Bernstein PA (2006) An online bibliography on schema evolution. SIGMOD Rec 35(4):30–31

Smith B, Ashburner M, Rosse C et al (2007) The OBO Foundry: coordinated evolution of ontologies to support biomedical data integration. Nat Biotechnol 25(11):1251–1255

Software AG (2006) Tamino XML schema user guide 4.4.1. http://documentation.softwareag.com/crossvision/ins441_j/print/tsl.pdf

Stojanovic L, Maedche A, Motik B, Stojanovic N (2002) User-driven ontology evolution management. In: Proceedings of 13th international conference on knowledge engineering and knowledge management. Springer, London, pp 285–300

Su H, Rundensteiner E, Kramer D, Chen L, Claypool K (2001) XEM: Managing the evolution of XML documents. In: Proceedings international workshop on research issues in data engineering (RIDE). IEEE Computer Society, Washington, DC

Türker C (2000) Schema evolution in SQL-99 and commercial (object-) relational DBMS. Database schema evolution and meta-modeling. LNCS, vol 2065. Springer, Heidelberg, pp 1–32

W3C (2006) XML schema versioning use cases. Framework for discussion of versioning, 2006. http://www.w3.org/XML/2005/xsd-versioning-use-cases

W3C (2010) XML component designators, 2010 http://www.w3.org/TR/xmlschema-ref/

Yu C, Popa L (2005) Semantic adaptation of schema mappings when schemas evolve. In: Proceedings VLDB conference. VLDB Endowment, pp 1006–1017

Chapter 7
Schema Mapping Evolution Through Composition and Inversion

Ronald Fagin, Phokion G. Kolaitis, Lucian Popa, and Wang-Chiew Tan

Abstract Mappings between different representations of data are the essential building blocks for many information integration tasks. A schema mapping is a high-level specification of the relationship between two schemas, and represents a useful abstraction that specifies how the data from a source format can be transformed into a target format. The development of schema mappings is laborious and time consuming, even in the presence of tools that facilitate this development. At the same time, schema evolution inevitably causes the invalidation of the existing schema mappings (since their schemas change). Providing tools and methods that can facilitate the adaptation and reuse of the existing schema mappings in the context of the new schemas is an important research problem.

In this chapter, we show how two fundamental operators on schema mappings, namely composition and inversion, can be used to address the mapping adaptation problem in the context of schema evolution. We illustrate the applicability of the two operators in various concrete schema evolution scenarios, and we survey the most important developments on the semantics, algorithms, and implementation of composition and inversion. We also discuss the main research questions that still remain to be addressed.

1 Introduction

Schemas and schema mappings are two fundamental metadata components that are at the core of heterogeneous data management. Schemas describe the structure of the various databases, while schema mappings describe the relationships between

R. Fagin (✉) and L. Popa
IBM Almaden Research Center, San Jose, CA, USA
e-mail: fagin@almaden.ibm.com, lucian@almaden.ibm.com

P.G. Kolaitis and W.-C. Tan
IBM Almaden Research Center, San Jose, CA, USA
and
UC Santa Cruz, Santa Cruz, CA 95064, USA
e-mail: kolaitis@cs.ucsc.edu, wctan@cs.ucsc.edu

Z. Bellahsene et al. (eds.), *Schema Matching and Mapping*, Data-Centric Systems and Applications, DOI 10.1007/978-3-642-16518-4_7,
© Springer-Verlag Berlin Heidelberg 2011

them. Schema mappings can be used either to transform data between two different schemas (a process typically called *data exchange* [Fagin et al., 2005a] or *data translation* [Shu et al., 1977]) or to support processing of queries formulated over one schema when the data is physically stored under some other schemas (a process typically encountered in *data integration* [Lenzerini, 2002] and also in *schema evolution* [Curino et al., 2008]).

A schema mapping is typically formalized as a triple $(\mathbf{S}, \mathbf{T}, \Sigma)$, where $\mathbf{S}$ is a source schema, $\mathbf{T}$ is a target schema, and Σ is a set of dependencies (or constraints) that specify the relationship between the source schema and the target schema. Schema mappings are necessarily dependent on the schemas they relate. Once schemas change (and this inevitably happens over time), the mappings become invalid. A typical solution is to regenerate the mappings; however, this process can be expensive in terms of human effort and expertise, especially for complex schemas. Moreover, there is no guarantee that the regenerated mappings will reflect the original semantics of the mappings. A better solution is to provide principled solutions that reuse the original mappings and *adapt* them to the new schemas, while still incorporating the original semantics. This general process was first described in Velegrakis et al. [2003], which called it *mapping adaptation* and also provided a solution that applied when schemas evolve in small, incremental changes. In this paper, we describe a more general formalization of the mapping adaptation problem, where schema evolution can be specified by an arbitrary schema mapping. Under this formalization, which is in the spirit of model management [Bernstein, 2003], the new, adapted mapping is obtained from the original mapping through the use of schema mapping operators.

The two operators on schema mappings that we need to consider are *composition* [Bernstein et al., 2008, Fagin et al., 2005b, Madhavan and Halevy, 2003, Nash et al., 2005] and *inversion* [Arenas et al., 2008, Fagin, 2007, Fagin et al., 2008b, 2009b]. These operators turn out to be quite fundamental, with many applications in metadata management [Bernstein, 2003] and for schema evolution. In particular, the two operators of composition and inversion provide a principled way to solving the problem of adapting a schema mapping when schemas evolve. We will use Fig. 7.1 to describe, at a high-level, the operators of composition and inversion, and their application in the context of schema evolution. First, assume that we are given a schema mapping $\mathcal{M}$ (the "original" schema mapping) that describes a relationship or a transformation from a source schema $\mathbf{S}$ to a target schema $\mathbf{T}$. To "reuse" the original schema mapping $\mathcal{M}$ when schemas evolve, we need to handle changes in either the target schema or the source schema.

Target schema evolution. Assume that the target schema evolves to a new target schema $\mathbf{T}'$, and that we model this evolution as a schema mapping $\mathcal{M}'$ from $\mathbf{T}$ to $\mathbf{T}'$. Intuitively, $\mathcal{M}'$ is a new data transformation that converts instances of $\mathbf{T}$ to instances of $\mathbf{T}'$. Note that generating such $\mathcal{M}'$ is an instance of the general schema mapping creation problem and can be done manually or with the help of tools such as Clio, described elsewhere [Fagin et al., 2009a]. Based on $\mathcal{M}$ and $\mathcal{M}'$, we can then obtain a new mapping from $\mathbf{S}$ to $\mathbf{T}'$ by applying the composition operator. Composition operates, in general, on two *consecutive* schema mappings $\mathcal{M}$ and

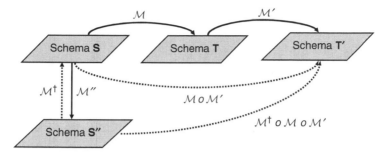

Fig. 7.1 Application of composition and inversion in schema evolution

M', where the target schema of M is the source schema of M'. The result is a schema mapping $M \circ M'$ that has the same effect as applying first M and then M'. For our schema evolution context, $M \circ M'$ combines the original transformation M with the evolution mapping M'.

Source schema evolution. Assume now that the source schema evolves to a new source schema S'', and that we model this evolution as a schema mapping M'' from S to S''. Intuitively, M'' represents a data transformation that converts instances of S to instances of S''. We need to obtain a new schema mapping that reflects the original schema mapping M (or rather $M \circ M'$ after target schema evolution) but uses S'' as the source schema. Note that in this case we cannot directly combine M'' with $M \circ M'$ via composition, since M'' and $M \circ M'$ are not consecutive. To be able to apply composition, we need first to apply the inversion operator and obtain a schema mapping $M^\dagger$ that "undoes" the effect of M''. Once we obtain a suitable $M^\dagger$, we can then apply the composition operator to produce $M^\dagger \circ M \circ M'$. The resulting schema mapping, which is now from S'' to T', is an adaptation of the original schema mapping M that works on the evolved schemas.

While the composition of two schema mappings (under a fairly natural semantics [Fagin et al., 2004, Melnik, 2004]) always exists and it is "only" a matter of expressing the composition in a suitable language for schema mappings, the situation is worse for inversion. In general, a schema mapping may lose information and, as a result, it may not be possible to revert the transformation in a way that recovers the original data. Hence, an exact inverse [Fagin, 2007] may not exist, and one needs to look beyond such exact inverses. As a result, there are several notions of "approximations" of inverses that have recently been developed: quasi-inverses [Fagin et al., 2008b], maximum recoveries [Arenas et al., 2008], maximum extended recoveries [Fagin et al., 2009b]. In this paper, motivated by the applications to schema evolution, we take a more pragmatic approach for the treatment of the various notions of inverse and emphasize the *operational* aspect behind them. In particular, we focus on two types of inverses, which were first introduced in Fagin et al. [2009b] and which have a clear operational semantics based on the notion of chase that makes them attractive from a practical point of view. The first type of such operational inverses, which are called *chase-inverses*, can be used to recover the original data (without loss) via the chase. In general, this recovery is up to homomorphic equivalence due to the presence of nulls; in the ideal case when the original source instance is recovered exactly, we call the chase-inverse an *exact* chase-inverse. The second type of operational inverses, which we call *relaxed chase-inverses*,[1] are relaxations of chase-inverses that work in situations where there is information loss and, hence, chase-inverses do not exist. Intuitively, a relaxed chase-inverse recovers the original source data as well.

In this chapter, we use various concrete examples of schema evolution to illustrate the main developments and challenges behind composition and inversion and their applications to schema evolution. We note that we are focused here on composition and inversion; a companion book chapter [Hartung et al., 2011] will give a separate overview of the schema evolution area in general. In our survey, we illustrate the concept of composition, and then discuss the two flavors of operational inverses mentioned above. At the same time, we discuss the languages in which such composition and inversion can be expressed. In the context of the schema evolution scenarios that we consider, these languages vary in complexity from GAV schema mappings to LAV and GLAV schema mappings (the latter are also known as source-to-target tuple-generating dependencies, or s-t tgds [Fagin et al., 2005a]) and then to mappings specified by second-order (SO) tgds [Fagin et al., 2005b]. During the exposition, we will proceed from simpler, easier scenarios of schema evolution to more challenging scenarios, and illustrate how composition and inversion techniques can be put together into a framework that deals with schema evolution problems.

In a separate section, we examine in detail two systems that implement one or both of the above schema mapping operators to deal with aspects of schema evolution. The first one is an implementation of mapping composition [Yu and Popa, 2005] that is part of the Clio system is based on the SO tgds introduced in Fagin et al. [2005b] and is specifically targeted at the problem of mapping adaptation in the context of schema evolution. The second system is the PRISM workbench [Curino et al., 2008] for query migration in the presence of schema evolution. This system is based on query rewriting under constraints and in particular on the chase and backchase framework [Deutsch et al., 1999]. However, before it can apply such query rewriting, the PRISM system needs to implement both mapping composition and inversion. The notion chosen here for inversion is based on quasi-inverses [Fagin et al., 2008b].

We end the paper with a discussion of the main open research questions that still remain to be solved. Perhaps the most important open issue here is to find a unifying schema-mapping language that is closed under both composition and the various flavors of inverses, and, additionally, has good algorithmic properties.

---

[1] These were introduced in Fagin et al. [2009b] under a different name: *universal-faithful inverses*. However, the term *relaxed chase-inverses*, which we use in this paper, is a more suggestive term that also reflects the relationship with the chase-inverses.

2 Preliminaries

A *schema* **R** is a finite sequence $\langle R_1, \ldots, R_k \rangle$ of relation symbols, where each R_i has a fixed arity. An *instance* I over **R** is a sequence $(R_1^I, \ldots, R_k^I)$, where each R_i^I is a finite relation of the same arity as R_i. We shall often use R_i to denote both the relation symbol and the relation R_i^I that instantiates it. We assume that we have a countably infinite set Const of *constants* and a countably infinite set Var of *labeled nulls* that is disjoint from Const. A *fact* of an instance I (over **R**) is an expression $R_i^I(v_1, \ldots, v_m)$ (or simply $R_i(v_1, \ldots, v_m)$), where R_i is a relation symbol of **R** and $v_1, \ldots, v_m$ are constants or labeled nulls such that $(v_1, \ldots, v_m) \in R_i^I$. The expression $(v_1, \ldots, v_m)$ is also sometimes referred to as a *tuple* of R_i. An instance is often identified with its set of facts.

A *ground* instance over some schema is an instance such that all values occurring in its relations are constants. In general, however, instances over a schema may have individual values from Const ∪ Var; thus, some of the values in the instances may be nulls representing unknown information. Such (non-ground) instances naturally arise in data integration, data exchange and also schema evolution. We will see examples of instances with nulls all throughout this paper.

Next, we define the concepts of *homomorphism* and *homomorphic equivalence*, which we use frequently throughout this paper. Let I_1 and I_2 be instances over a schema **R**. A function h from Const ∪ Var to Const ∪ Var is a *homomorphism* from I_1 to I_2 if for every c in Const, we have that $h(c) = c$, and for every relation symbol R in **R** and every tuple $(a_1, \ldots, a_n) \in R^{I_1}$, we have that $(h(a_1), \ldots, h(a_n)) \in R^{I_2}$. We use the notation $I_1 \to I_2$ to denote that there is a homomorphism from I_1 to I_2. We say that I_1 is *homomorphically equivalent* to I_2 if $I_1 \to I_2$ and $I_2 \to I_1$, and we write this as $I_1 \leftrightarrow I_2$.

Schema mappings: A *schema mapping* is a triple $\mathcal{M} = (\mathbf{S}, \mathbf{T}, \Sigma)$, where **S** is a source schema, **T** is a target schema, and Σ is a set of constraints (typically, formulas in some logic) that describe the relationship between **S** and **T**. We say that $\mathcal{M}$ is syntactically *specified by*, or, *expressed by* Σ. Furthermore, $\mathcal{M}$ is semantically identified with the binary relation:

$$\text{Inst}(\mathcal{M}) = \{(I, J) \mid I \text{ is an } \mathbf{S}\text{-instance}, J \text{ is a } \mathbf{T}\text{-instance}, (I, J) \models \Sigma\}.$$

We will use the notation $(I, J) \in \mathcal{M}$ to denote that the ordered pair (I, J) satisfies the constraints of $\mathcal{M}$; furthermore, we will sometimes define schema mappings by simply defining the set of ordered pairs (I, J) that constitute $\mathcal{M}$ (instead of giving a set of constraints that specify $\mathcal{M}$). If $(I, J) \in \mathcal{M}$, we say that J is a *solution* of I (with respect to $\mathcal{M}$).

In general, the constraints in Σ are formulas in some logical formalism. In this chapter, we will focus on schema mappings specified by source-to-target tuple-generating dependencies.

An *atom* is an expression of the form $R(x_1, \ldots, x_n)$, where R is a relation symbol and $x_1, \ldots, x_n$ are variables that are not necessarily distinct. A source-to-target tuple-generating dependency (s-t tgd) is a first-order sentence φ of the form

$$\forall \mathbf{x}(\varphi(\mathbf{x}) \rightarrow \exists \mathbf{y} \psi(\mathbf{x}, \mathbf{y})),$$

where $\varphi(\mathbf{x})$ is a conjunction of atoms over $\mathbf{S}$, each variable in $\mathbf{x}$ occurs in at least one atom in $\varphi(\mathbf{x})$, and $\psi(\mathbf{x}, \mathbf{y})$ is a conjunction of atoms over $\mathbf{T}$ with variables in $\mathbf{x}$ and $\mathbf{y}$. For simplicity, we will often suppress writing the universal quantifiers $\forall \mathbf{x}$ in the above formula. Another name for s-t tgds is global-and-local-as-view (GLAV) constraints (see Lenzerini 2002). They contain GAV and LAV constraints, which we now define, as important special cases.

A global-as-view (GAV) constraint is an s-t tgd in which the right-hand side is a single atom with no existentially quantified variables, that is, it is of the form

$$\forall \mathbf{x}(\varphi(\mathbf{x}) \rightarrow P(\mathbf{x})),$$

where $P(\mathbf{x})$ is an atom over the target schema. A *local-as-view* (LAV) constraint is an s-t tgd in which the left-hand side is a single atom, that is, it is of the form

$$\forall \mathbf{x}(Q(\mathbf{x}) \rightarrow \exists \mathbf{y} \psi(\mathbf{x}, \mathbf{y})),$$

where $Q(\mathbf{x})$ is a atom over the source schema.[2]

We often write a *LAV schema mapping* to mean a schema mapping specified entirely by LAV s-t tgds. A strict LAV schema mapping is a LAV schema mapping where it is specified entirely by strict LAV s-t tgds. Similarly, a GAV schema mapping (respectively, GLAV schema mapping) is a schema mapping specified entirely by GAV s-t tgds (respectively, GLAV s-t tgds).

Chase. The *chase procedure* has been used in a number of settings over the years. Close to our area of interest, the chase procedure has been used in Fagin et al. [2005a] to give a natural, operational semantics for data exchange. Specifically, in data exchange, if $\mathcal{M}$ is a fixed schema mapping specified by s-t tgds, then the chase procedure can be used to compute, given a source instance I, a target instance $chase_{\mathcal{M}}(I)$ for I that has a number of desirable properties. First, $chase_{\mathcal{M}}(I)$ is a *universal solution* [Fagin et al., 2005a] of I with respect to the schema mapping $\mathcal{M}$. Universal solutions are the most general solutions that one can obtain for a given source instance I with respect to $\mathcal{M}$ in the sense that a universal solution has homomorphisms into every solution of I with respect to $\mathcal{M}$. Second, $chase_{\mathcal{M}}(I)$ is computed in time bounded by a polynomial in the size of I.

There are several variants of the chase procedure. Here, we will consider the variant of chase described in Fagin et al. [2005a]. The chase on I with a schema mapping $\mathcal{M}$ produces a target instance, denoted as $chase_{\mathcal{M}}(I)$, as follows: For

---

[2] A stricter version of LAV s-t tgds, where no repeated variables in the left-hand side $Q(\mathbf{x})$ are allowed and all variables in $\mathbf{x}$ appear in the right-hand side, is also used in literature. We refer to this type of LAV s-t tgds as *strict* LAV s-t tgds.

every s-t tgd

$$\forall \mathbf{x}(\varphi(\mathbf{x}) \rightarrow \exists \mathbf{y}\psi(\mathbf{x}, \mathbf{y}))$$

in Σ and for every tuple $\mathbf{a}$ of constants from the active domain of I, such that $I \models$ $\varphi(\mathbf{a})$, if there does not exist a tuple $\mathbf{b}$ of constants or labeled nulls, such that $\psi(\mathbf{a}, \mathbf{b})$ exists in $chase_{\mathcal{M}}(I)$, then we add to $chase_{\mathcal{M}}(I)$ all facts in $\psi(\mathbf{a}, \mathbf{N})$, where $\mathbf{N}$ is a tuple of new, distinct labeled nulls interpreting the existential quantified variables $\mathbf{y}$. We sometimes say that $\mathcal{M}$ *has been applied to I to produce* $chase_{\mathcal{M}}(I)$ to mean that I has been chased with $\mathcal{M}$ to produce $chase_{\mathcal{M}}(I)$.

We end this section by giving two examples of the chase in action. Variations of the schemas and the mappings used in these examples will appear throughout the paper. First, let $\mathcal{M}_1$ be a LAV schema mapping specified by:

$$\texttt{Takes}\,(n,m,co) \rightarrow \exists s(\texttt{Student}\,(s,n,m) \wedge \texttt{Enrolled}\,(s,co))$$

Here, we assume that the source schema has a ternary relation symbol $\texttt{Takes}$ and the target schema has two binary relation symbols, $\texttt{Student}$ and $\texttt{Enrolled}$. The mapping takes input tuples of the form (n,m,co) in $\texttt{Takes}$, where n represents a student name, m represents a major for the student, and co represents a course that the student takes. For each such input tuple, the mapping asserts the existence of two target tuples: a tuple (s,n,m) in $\texttt{Student}$, and a tuple (s,co) in $\texttt{Enrolled}$. These tuples are related by the fact that the same student id s occurs in both.

Let I be the source instance consisting of the following two facts:

$$\texttt{Takes}\,\textit{(John, CS, CS101)},$$
$$\texttt{Takes}\,\textit{(Ann, Math, MATH203)}.$$

The chase of I with $\mathcal{M}_1$ will then produce a target instance J that consists of the following four facts:

$$\texttt{Student}\,(N_1, \textit{John, CS}), \texttt{Enrolled}\,(N_1, \textit{CS101}),$$
$$\texttt{Student}\,(N_2, \textit{Ann, Math}), \texttt{Enrolled}\,(N_2, \textit{MATH203}).$$

In the above instance, N_1 and N_2 are nulls (representing student ids for *John* and *Ann*, respectively). The chase of I with $\mathcal{M}_1$ works by exhaustively determining facts in the source instance that can "trigger" the s-t tgd in $\mathcal{M}_1$ to generate new target facts. The first fact in I, namely, $\texttt{Takes}(\textit{John, CS, CS}101)$, triggers the s-t tgd in $\mathcal{M}_1$, resulting in the addition of two target facts: $\texttt{Student}(N_1, \textit{John, CS})$ and $\texttt{Enrolled}(N_1, \textit{CS}101)$. Observe that this *chase step* instantiates the existentially quantified variable s in the tgd with the null N_1, which effectively associates the newly created $\texttt{Student}$ and $\texttt{Enrolled}$ facts together. Similarly, the second source fact also triggers the s-t tgd in $\mathcal{M}_1$ to generate two target facts: $\texttt{Student}(N_2, \textit{Ann, Math})$ and $\texttt{Enrolled}(N_2, \textit{MATH203})$. After this, no other source facts could trigger the s-t tgd in $\mathcal{M}_1$ to generate new target facts. Hence, the chase terminates with the target instance that consists of the above four facts.

As another example, let $\mathcal{M}_2$ be a GAV schema mapping specified by:

$$\texttt{Student}\,(s,n,m) \wedge \texttt{Enrolled}\,(s,co) \rightarrow \texttt{Takes}'\,(s,n,co)$$

This schema mapping combines information in Student and Enrolled into the Takes′ relation. Observe that Takes′ contains information about student ids, name, and courses (as opposed to name, major, and course in Takes). Suppose I consists of the following facts:

$$\text{Student } (111, John, CS), \text{Enrolled } (111, CS101),$$
$$\text{Student } (111, John, Math), \text{Enrolled } (111, MATH101).$$

The chase of I with $\mathcal{M}_2$ will produce the following target instance:

$$\text{Takes}' (111, John, CS101),$$
$$\text{Takes}' (111, John, MATH101).$$

The source facts Student$(111, John, CS)$ and Enrolled$(111, CS101)$ together trigger the s-t tgd in $\mathcal{M}_2$ to produce Takes′$(111, John, CS101)$. In addition, the source facts Student$(111, John, Math)$ and Enrolled$(111, MATH101)$ trigger the s-t tgd in $\mathcal{M}_2$ to produce Takes′$(111, John, MATH101)$ in the target. After this, even though the source facts Student$(111, John, CS)$ and Enrolled $(111, MATH101)$ also trigger the s-t tgd in $\mathcal{M}_2$, this chase step is not taken since the target fact Takes $(111, John, MATH101)$ already exists in the target instance. It is easy to observe that no other source facts would trigger the s-t tgd in $\mathcal{M}_2$, and hence J is the result of the chase. Also note that, as opposed to the previous example, there is no need to generate nulls in the target, since $\mathcal{M}_2$ has no existentially quantified variables (i.e., it is a GAV mapping).

3 An Ideal Scenario of Evolution

We start our exposition of the application of composition and inversion to schema evolution, by considering first a relatively "simple" example of schema evolution. For this section, we will refer to the schema evolution scenario that is graphically illustrated in Fig. 7.2.

We first assume the existence of a schema mapping $\mathcal{M}$ from a source schema **S**, consisting of one relation Takes, to a target schema **T**, consisting of two relations Student and Enrolled. The Takes relation contains tuples relating student ids

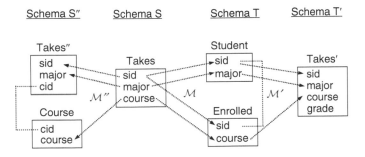

Fig. 7.2 Our first scenario of schema evolution

with their majors and the courses they take. According to the mapping $\mathcal{M}$, each tuple of Takes is split into two tuples, one in Student and the other in Enrolled, that share the same sid value. Formally, the schema mapping is given by the following two assertions:

$$\mathcal{M}: \text{ Takes } (s, m, co) \rightarrow \text{Student } (s, m)$$
$$\text{Takes } (s, m, co) \rightarrow \text{Enrolled } (s, co)$$

Note that $\mathcal{M}$ is an example of both a GAV mapping and an (strict) LAV mapping. Also note that in this example we have a variation of the earlier $\mathcal{M}_1$ (in Sect. 2); in this variation, the sid value in the target is not existentially quantified, but instead it is copied directly from the source relation Takes.

We next address the issues of schema evolution, starting with the target schema first.

3.1 Target Evolution: GAV–GLAV Composition

Let us assume that the target schema evolves to a new schema $\mathbf{T}'$ consisting of one relation Takes' that combines all the attributes in $\mathbf{T}$ (i.e., sid, major, course) and further includes an extra grade attribute. Moreover, assume that the evolution mapping from $\mathbf{T}$ to $\mathbf{T}'$ is:

$$\mathcal{M}': \text{Student } (s, m) \wedge \text{Enrolled } (s, co) \rightarrow \exists G \text{ Takes}' (s, m, co, G)$$

In contrast to the original mapping $\mathcal{M}$, the above $\mathcal{M}'$ is an example of a more general GLAV mapping: it is neither LAV (since there is more than one atom on the left-hand side) nor GAV (since there is an existential quantifier on the right-hand side).

Before we can show how to adapt the mapping $\mathcal{M}$ to the new target schema, we formally state what composition means.

Definition 1. (Composition of Schema Mappings [Fagin et al., 2005b]) Let $\mathcal{M}_{12} = (\mathbf{S}_1, \mathbf{S}_2, \Sigma_{12})$ and $\mathcal{M}_{23} = (\mathbf{S}_2, \mathbf{S}_3, \Sigma_{23})$ be schema mappings such that the schemas $\mathbf{S}_1$, $\mathbf{S}_2$, and $\mathbf{S}_3$ have no relation symbol in common pairwise. A schema mapping $\mathcal{M}_{13} = (\mathbf{S}_1, \mathbf{S}_3, \Sigma_{13})$ is a *composition* of $\mathcal{M}_{12}$ and $\mathcal{M}_{23}$ (written $\mathcal{M}_{13} = \mathcal{M}_{12} \circ \mathcal{M}_{23}$) if $M_{13} = \{(I_1, I_3) \mid \text{there exists } I_2 \text{ such that } (I_1, I_2) \in \mathcal{M}_{12} \text{ and } (I_2, I_3) \in \mathcal{M}_{23}\}$.

The important computational problem associated with mapping composition is the following: Given two schema mappings $\mathcal{M}_{12}$ and $\mathcal{M}_{23}$ how do we compute, and in what language can we express, a set Σ_{13} of constraints that specifies the composition $\mathcal{M}_{13}$ of $\mathcal{M}_{12}$ and $\mathcal{M}_{23}$? The answer to the above question very much depends on the language in which the input schema mappings are specified.

For our running example, to adapt the above mapping $\mathcal{M}$ to the new target schema, we must compose $\mathcal{M}$ with the evolution mapping $\mathcal{M}'$. As it turns out, we are in an "easy" case where we can express the result of this composition as a GLAV mapping. This is essentially due to the fact that the first mapping is GAV. (The second mapping $\mathcal{M}'$ is a GLAV mapping.) We shall see that in cases where $\mathcal{M}$ is LAV or GLAV the composition need not be first-order and we need a more powerful language to express the composition. For the scenario in this section, the fact that the composition is a GLAV mapping follows from the next theorem.

Theorem 1 (Fagin et al. 2005b). *Let $\mathcal{M}_1$ and $\mathcal{M}_2$ be two consecutive schema mappings. The following hold:*

1. *If $\mathcal{M}_1$ and $\mathcal{M}_2$ are GAV mappings, then $\mathcal{M}_1 \circ \mathcal{M}_2$ can be expressed as a GAV mapping.*
2. *If $\mathcal{M}_1$ is a GAV mapping and $\mathcal{M}_2$ is a GLAV mapping then $\mathcal{M}_1 \circ \mathcal{M}_2$ can be expressed as a GLAV mapping.*

As a more general result, we obtain the following corollary that applies to a chain of GAV mappings followed by a GLAV mapping.

Corollary 1. *Let $\mathcal{M}_1, \ldots, \mathcal{M}_{k+1}, \mathcal{M}_k$ be consecutive schema mappings. If $\mathcal{M}_1$, $\ldots$, $\mathcal{M}_k$ are GAV mappings and M_{k+1} is a GLAV mapping, then the composition $\mathcal{M}_1 \circ \ldots \circ M_k \circ \mathcal{M}_{k+1}$ can be expressed as a GLAV mapping.*

Concretely, for our scenario, it can be verified that the following GLAV mapping is the composition of $\mathcal{M}$ and $\mathcal{M}'$:

$$\mathcal{M} \circ \mathcal{M}' : \text{Takes}\,(s,m,co) \wedge \text{Takes}\,(s,m',co') \to \exists G\ \text{Takes}'\,(s,m,co',G)$$

Observe that the self-join on Takes in the above composition is needed. This can be traced to the fact that students can have multiple majors, in general. At the same time, the Takes relation need not list all combinations of major and course for a given sid. However, the evolution mapping $\mathcal{M}'$ requires all such combinations. The composition $\mathcal{M} \circ \mathcal{M}'$ correctly accounts for all these subtle semantic aspects.

To see a concrete example, consider the following instance of Takes:

$$\text{Takes}\,(007, Math, MA201)$$
$$\text{Takes}\,(007, CS, CS101)$$

In the above instance, 007 identifies a student (say, Ann) who has a double major (in $Math$ and CS) and takes two courses. Given the above instance, the composition $\mathcal{M} \circ \mathcal{M}'$ requires the existence of the following four Takes' facts, to account for all the combinations between Ann's majors and the courses that Ann took.

$$\text{Takes}'\,(007, Math, MA201, G_1)$$
$$\text{Takes}'\,(007, Math, CS101, G_2)$$
$$\text{Takes}'\,(007, CS, MA201, G_3)$$
$$\text{Takes}'\,(007, CS, CS101, G_4)$$

In practice, we would also have an additional target constraint (a functional dependency) on Takes' specifying that sid together with course functionally determines grade. This functional dependency would then force the equality of G_1 and G_3, and also the equality of G_2 and G_4 in the above instance.

Composition Algorithm. Next, we explain on our example how the composition algorithm of Fagin et al. [2005b] arrives at the formula that specifies $\mathcal{M} \circ \mathcal{M}'$. We give an intuitive explanation of the algorithm rather than a complete and formal one. Recall that $\mathcal{M}$ is specified by the following GAV s-t tgds

$$\mathcal{M}: \text{ Takes } (s, m, co) \rightarrow \text{Student } (s, m)$$
$$\text{Takes } (s, m, co) \rightarrow \text{Enrolled } (s, co)$$

and that $\mathcal{M}'$ is specified by the following GLAV s-t tgd

$$\mathcal{M}': \text{Student } (s, m) \wedge \text{Enrolled } (s, co) \rightarrow \exists G \text{ Takes}' (s, m, co, G).$$

Intuitively, the composition algorithm will replace each relation symbol from **T** in $\mathcal{M}'$ by relation symbols from **S** using the GAV s-t tgds of $\mathcal{M}$. In this case, the fact Student(s, m) that occurs on the left-hand side of $\mathcal{M}'$ can be replaced by a Takes fact, according to the first GAV s-t tgd of $\mathcal{M}$. Hence, we arrive at an intermediate tgd shown below:

$$\text{Takes } (s, m, co') \wedge \text{Enrolled } (s, co) \rightarrow \exists G \text{ Takes}' (s, m, co, G).$$

Observe that a new variable co' in Takes is used instead of co. This avoids an otherwise unintended join with Enrolled, which also contains the variable co. (This is accomplished in the algorithm by a variable renaming step.)

Next, the composition algorithm will replace Enrolled(s, co) with a Takes fact, based on the second GAV s-t tgd of $\mathcal{M}$. We then obtain the following GLAV s-t tgd from the source schema **S** to the new target schema **T**'. This tgd[3] specifies the composition $\mathcal{M} \circ \mathcal{M}'$.

$$\text{Takes } (s, m, co') \wedge \text{Takes } (s, m', co) \rightarrow \exists G \text{ Takes}' (s, m, co, G).$$

3.2 Source Evolution: The Case of a Lossless Mapping

Let us now assume that the source schema evolves to a new schema S'' consisting of the two relations Takes$''$ and Course shown in Fig. 7.2. Thus, in the new schema, courses are stored in a separate relation and are assigned ids (cid). The relation Takes$''$ is similar to Takes except that course is replaced by cid. Let us assume that the source evolution is described by the following LAV mapping:

---

[3] Note that it is logically equivalent to the earlier way we expressed $\mathcal{M} \circ \mathcal{M}'$, and where the roles of co and co' were switched.

$\mathcal{M}''$: Takes $(s,m,co) \rightarrow \exists C$ (Takes$''$ $(s,m,C) \wedge$ Course (C,co)).

Note first that in the figure the direction of $\mathcal{M}''$ is the reverse of the direction of the original mapping $\mathcal{M}$. Intuitively, the assertions of $\mathcal{M}''$ imply a data flow from the schema **S** to the schema **S**$''$, where facts over **S**$''$ are required to exist based on facts over **S**. To enable the application of the same composition techniques as we used for target evolution, we first need to invert the mapping $\mathcal{M}''$. After inversion, we can then combine the result, via composition, with the previously obtained $\mathcal{M} \circ \mathcal{M}'$.

From a practical point of view, the important (and ideal) requirement that we need from an inverse is to be able to recover the original source instance. Concretely, if we apply the mapping $\mathcal{M}''$ on some source instance I and then we apply the candidate inverse on the result of $\mathcal{M}''$, we would like to obtain the original source instance I. Here, applying a schema mapping $\mathcal{M}$ to an instance I means generating the instance $chase_\mathcal{M}(I)$. The next definition captures the requirements of such an inverse.

Definition 2 (Exact chase-inverse). Let $\mathcal{M}$ be a GLAV schema mapping from a schema S_1 to a schema S_2. We say that $\mathcal{M}^*$ is an *exact chase-inverse* of $\mathcal{M}$ if $\mathcal{M}^*$ is a GLAV schema mapping from S_2 to S_1 with the following property: for every instance I over S_1, we have that $I = chase_{\mathcal{M}^*}(chase_\mathcal{M}(I))$.

For our example, consider the following candidate inverse of $\mathcal{M}''$:

$\mathcal{M}^\dagger$: Takes$''$ $(s,m,c) \wedge$ Course $(c,co) \rightarrow$ Takes (s,m,co)

As it turns out, this candidate inverse satisfies the above requirement of being able to recover, exactly, the source instance. Indeed, it can be immediately verified that for every source instance I over **S**, we have that $chase_{\mathcal{M}^\dagger}(chase_{\mathcal{M}''}(I))$ equals I. Thus, $\mathcal{M}^\dagger$ is an exact chase-inverse of $\mathcal{M}''$.

Since $\mathcal{M}^\dagger$ is a GAV mapping, we can now apply Corollary 1 and compose $\mathcal{M}^\dagger$ with $\mathcal{M} \circ \mathcal{M}'$ to obtain a schema mapping from **S**$''$ to **T**$'$. The result of this composition is the following (GLAV) schema mapping:

$$\mathcal{M}^\dagger \circ \mathcal{M} \circ \mathcal{M}' : \text{ Takes}'' (s,m,c) \wedge \text{Course} (c,co) \wedge$$
$$\text{Takes}'' (s,m',c') \wedge \text{Course} (c',co')$$
$$\rightarrow \exists G \text{ Takes}' (s,m',co,G)$$

3.3 A More General Notion of Chase-Inverses

The schema mapping $\mathcal{M}^\dagger$ used in Sect. 3.2 is an exact chase-inverse in the sense that it can recover the original source instance I exactly. In general, however, equality with I is too strong of a requirement, and all we need is a more relaxed form of equivalence of instances, where intuitively the equivalence is modulo nulls. In this section, we start with a concrete example to show the need for such relaxation. We then give the general definition of a chase-inverse [Fagin et al., 2009b] and discuss its properties and its application in the context of schema evolution.

We observe that the schema mapping $\mathcal{M}''$ in Sect. 3.2 is similar to the following general pattern:

$$P(x, y) \rightarrow \exists z \, (Q(x, z) \wedge Q'(z, y)).$$

Here, for simplicity, we focus on schema mappings on binary relations. (In particular, $\mathcal{M}''$ can be forced into this pattern if we ignore the major field in the two relations Takes and Takes''.) The important point about this type of mappings is that they always have an exact chase-inverse. Consider now a variation on the above pattern, where Q' is the same as Q. Thus, let $\mathcal{M}$ be the following schema mapping:

$$\mathcal{M}: \quad P(x, y) \rightarrow \exists z \, (Q(x, z) \wedge Q(z, y)).$$

The following schema mapping $\mathcal{M}^*$ is a natural candidate inverse of $\mathcal{M}$:

$$\mathcal{M}^*: \quad Q(x, z) \wedge Q(z, y) \rightarrow P(x, y).$$

Consider now the source instance $I = \{P(1, 2), P(2, 3)\}$. Then the result of applying $\mathcal{M}$ to I is

$$chase_{\mathcal{M}}(I) = \{Q(1, n_1), Q(n_1, 2), Q(2, n_2), Q(n_2, 3)\},$$

where n_1 and n_2 are two nulls introduced by the chase (for the existentially quantified variable z). Furthermore, the result of applying $\mathcal{M}^*$ to the previous instance is

$$chase_{\mathcal{M}^*}(chase_{\mathcal{M}}(I)) = \{P(1, 2), P(2, 3), P(n_1, n_2)\}.$$

Thus, we recovered the two original facts of I but also the additional fact $P(n_1, n_2)$ (via joining $Q(n_1, 2)$ and $Q(2, n_2)$). Therefore, $\mathcal{M}^*$ is not an exact chase-inverse of $\mathcal{M}$. Nevertheless, since n_1 and n_2 are nulls, the extra fact $P(n_1, n_2)$ does not add any new information that is not subsumed by the other two facts. Intuitively, the last instance is equivalent (although not equal) to the original source instance I.

The above type of equivalence between instances with nulls is captured, in general, by the notion of *homomorphic equivalence*. Recall that two instances I_1 and I_2 are homomorphically equivalent, with notation $I_1 \leftrightarrow I_2$, if there exist homomorphisms in both directions between I_1 and I_2.

We are now ready for the main definition in this section.

Definition 3 (Chase-inverse). Let $\mathcal{M}$ be a GLAV schema mapping from a schema $\mathbf{S_1}$ to a schema $\mathbf{S_2}$. We say that $\mathcal{M}^*$ is a *chase-inverse* of $\mathcal{M}$ if $\mathcal{M}^*$ is a GLAV schema mapping from $\mathbf{S_2}$ to $\mathbf{S_1}$ with the following property: for every instance I over S_1, we have that $I \leftrightarrow chase_{\mathcal{M}^*}(chase_{\mathcal{M}}(I))$.

Intuitively, the above definition uses homomorphic equivalence as a replacement for the usual equality between instances. This is consistent with the fact that, in the presence of nulls, the notion of homomorphism itself becomes a replacement for the usual containment between instances. Note that when I_1 and I_2 are ground, $I_1 \to I_2$ is the same as $I_1 \subseteq I_2$. However, when I_1 has nulls, these nulls are allowed to be homomorphically mapped to other values (constants or nulls) inside I_2. This reflects the fact that nulls represent unknown information.

The existence of a chase-inverse for $\mathcal{M}$ implies that $\mathcal{M}$ has no information loss, since we can recover an instance that is the same modulo homomorphic equivalence as the original source instance. At the same time, a chase-inverse is a relaxation of the notion of an exact chase-inverse; hence, it may exist even when an exact chase-inverse does not exist.

Both examples of chase-inverses that we have given, namely $\mathcal{M}^\dagger$ in Sect. 3.2 and $\mathcal{M}^*$ in this section, are GAV mappings. This is not by accident. As the following theorem shows, we do not need the full power of GLAV mappings to express a chase-inverse: whenever there is a chase-inverse, there is a GAV chase-inverse. The main benefit of this theorem is that it may keep composition simpler. In particular, we may still be able to apply Corollary 1 as opposed to the more complex composition techniques of Sect. 4.

Theorem 2 (Fagin et al. 2010). *Let $\mathcal{M}$ be a GLAV schema mapping. If $\mathcal{M}$ has a chase-inverse, then $\mathcal{M}$ has a GAV chase-inverse.*

We remark that other, more general notions of inverses exist that are not based on the chase. The first notion of an "exact" inverse, capturing the case of no loss of information, was introduced by Fagin [Fagin, 2007]. An exact inverse $\mathcal{M}^*$ of $\mathcal{M}$ is a schema mapping $\mathcal{M}^*$ satisfying the equation $\mathcal{M} \circ \mathcal{M}^* = \mathrm{Id}$ where Id is the "identity" GLAV schema mapping that maps each relation in a schema to a copy of it. Subsequently, extended inverses [Fagin et al., 2009b] were introduced as an extension of exact inverses that is able to handle instances with nulls (i.e., non-ground instances). Without giving the exact definition of extended inverses here, we point out that chase-inverses coincide with the extended inverses that are specified by GLAV constraints. Thus, from a practical point of view, chase-inverses are important special cases of extended inverses, with good algorithmic properties.

We conclude this section with a corollary that summarizes the applications of chase-inverses together with the earlier Corollary 1 to our schema evolution context.

Corollary 2. *Let $\mathcal{M}$, $\mathcal{M}'$, and $\mathcal{M}''$ be schema mappings as in Fig. 7.1 such that $\mathcal{M}$ is a GAV mapping and $\mathcal{M}'$ and $\mathcal{M}''$ are GLAV mappings. Assume that $\mathcal{M}''$ has a chase-inverse, and let $\mathcal{M}^\dagger$ be a GAV chase-inverse of $\mathcal{M}''$. Then the mapping $\mathcal{M}^\dagger \circ \mathcal{M} \circ \mathcal{M}'$ can be expressed as a GLAV mapping.*

We note that a chase-inverse may not exist in general, since a schema mapping may lose information and hence it may not be possible to find a chase-inverse. The above corollary depends on the fact that the schema mapping $\mathcal{M}''$ has a chase-inverse. In Sect. 5, we shall address the more general case where $\mathcal{M}''$ has no chase-inverse.

The other important restriction in the above corollary is that the original schema mapping $\mathcal{M}$ must be GAV and not GLAV. We shall lift this restriction in the next section.

4 Composition: The Need for Second-Order TGDs

In this section, we discuss a more general schema mapping language as well as a more general composition result that enables us, in particular, to handle the general case of composing GLAV mappings. In particular, in our schema evolution context, we show how to handle the case where $\mathcal{M}$ is a GLAV mapping instead of a GAV mapping. We start by showing first that the composition $\mathcal{M} \circ \mathcal{M}'$ becomes challenging in such a case. We then illustrate the necessity of SO tgds [Fagin et al., 2005b] as a more powerful language needed to express such a composition.

For this section, we shall consider a very simple scenario [Fagin et al., 2005b] that is graphically illustrated in Fig. 7.3. In this scenario, the source schema **S** consists of one relation Emp with a single attribute for employee id (eid). The target schema **T** consists of one relation Reports that associates each employee with his/her manager. In the target relation, mgr is itself an employee id (the employee id of the manager). Assume that we have the following schema mapping that describes the relationship between a database over **S** and a database over **T**:

$$\mathcal{M} : \mathtt{Emp}(e) \to \exists M\ \mathtt{Reports}(s, M)$$

Note that the above mapping is a very simple example of a LAV mapping that is not a GAV mapping.

Let us assume that the target schema evolves to a new schema **T′** consisting of the two relations Manager and SelfMgr shown in Fig. 7.3. Moreover, assume that the evolution mapping from **T** to **T′** is given by:

$$\mathcal{M}' : \mathtt{Reports}(e, m) \to \mathtt{Manager}(e, m)$$
$$\mathtt{Reports}(e, e) \to \mathtt{SelfMgr}(e)$$

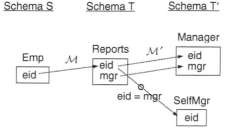

Fig. 7.3 A target evolution scenario that needs SO tgds

Thus, in the new schema, the relation `Manager` of $\mathbf{T}'$ is intended to be a copy of the relation `Reports` of $\mathbf{T}$, while the relation `SelfMgr` is intended to contain all employees who are their own managers, that is, employees for which the `eid` field equals the `mgr` field in the relation `Reports` of $\mathbf{T}$. Note that the evolution mapping $\mathcal{M}'$ is a GAV mapping.

To express the composition $\mathcal{M} \circ \mathcal{M}'$ for this example, it turns out that we cannot use GLAV constraints. It is shown in Fagin et al. [2005b] that there is no (finite or infinite) set of GLAV constraints that specifies $\mathcal{M} \circ \mathcal{M}'$. However, the following SO tgd specifies the composition $\mathcal{M} \circ \mathcal{M}'$:

$$\exists f(\; \forall e(\texttt{Emp}(e) \rightarrow \texttt{Manager}(e, f(e)))$$
$$\wedge \; \forall e(\texttt{Emp}(e) \wedge (e = f(e)) \rightarrow \texttt{SelfMgr}(e))).$$

We will formally define SO tgds shortly. For now, we note that SO tgds strictly include GLAV constraints and make essential use of function symbols. In particular, the above SO tgd uses a function symbol f and an equality $e = f(e)$. The use of both equalities and function symbols is, in general, necessary. As it can be seen, the above SO tgd consists of two inner implications, $\forall e(\texttt{Emp}(e) \rightarrow \texttt{Manager}(e, f(e)))$ and $\forall e(\texttt{Emp}(e) \wedge (e = f(e)) \rightarrow \texttt{SelfMgr}(e))$, which share a universally quantified unary function symbol f. Intuitively, the first part of the SO tgd states that every employee in `Emp` has a manager who is given by the value $f(e)$. The second part of the SO tgd states that if an employee e in `Emp` has a manager equal to itself (i.e., $e = f(e)$), then this employee must appear in the `SelfMgr` relation in the target.

Next, we provide the precise definition of an SO tgd and give an informal description of the composition algorithm of Fagin et al. [2005b] that derives SO tgds such as the above one. The definition of an SO tgd makes use of the concept of a *term*, which we define first.

Given a collection $\mathbf{x}$ of variables and a collection $\mathbf{f}$ of function symbols, a *term* *(based on $\mathbf{x}$ and $\mathbf{f}$)* is defined inductively as follows:

1. Every variable in $\mathbf{x}$ is a term.
2. If f is a k-ary function symbol in $\mathbf{f}$ and $t_1, \ldots, t_k$ are terms, then $f(t_1, \ldots, t_k)$ is a term.

Definition 4. (Second-order tuple generating dependencies [Fagin et al., 2005b]) Let $\mathbf{S}$ be a source schema and $\mathbf{T}$ a target schema. A second-order tuple-generating dependency (SO tgd) is a formula of the form:

$$\exists \mathbf{f}((\forall \mathbf{x}_1(\phi_1 \rightarrow \psi_1) \wedge \ldots \wedge \forall \mathbf{x}_n(\phi_n \rightarrow \psi_n))),$$

where

1. Each member of $\mathbf{f}$ is a function symbol.
2. Each ϕ_i is a conjunction of

   - Atomic formulas of the form $S(y_1, \ldots, y_k)$, where S is a k-ary relation symbol of schema $\mathbf{S}$ and $y_1, \ldots, y_k$ are variables in $\mathbf{x}_i$, not necessarily distinct, and
   - Equalities of the form $t = t'$, where t and t' are terms based on $\mathbf{x}_i$ and $\mathbf{f}$.

3. Each ψ_i is a conjunction of atomic formulas $T(t_1, ..., t_l)$, where T is an l-ary relation symbol of schema $\mathbf{T}$ and $t_1, ..., t_l$ are terms based on $\mathbf{x}_i$ and $\mathbf{f}$.
4. Each variable in $\mathbf{x}_i$ appears in some atomic formula of ϕ_i.

Composition algorithm for SO tgds. We now illustrate the steps of the composition algorithm using the schema mappings $\mathcal{M}$ and $\mathcal{M}'$ in this section. For the complete details of the algorithm, we refer the reader to Fagin et al. [2005b]. The first step of the algorithm is to transform $\mathcal{M}$ and $\mathcal{M}'$ into schema mappings that are specified by SO tgds (if they are not already given as SO tgds). Each GLAV constraint can be transformed into an SO tgd by skolemization, that is, by replacing each existentially quantified variable by a Skolem term. For our example, we transform $\mathcal{M}$ into a schema mapping specified by the following SO tgd:

$$\exists f(\forall e(\texttt{Emp}(e) \rightarrow \texttt{Reports}(e, f(e)))).$$

Here, f is an existentially quantified function and the term $f(e)$ replaces the earlier existentially quantified variable M. The second mapping $\mathcal{M}'$ needs no skolemization since there are no existentially quantified variables. The corresponding SO tgd for $\mathcal{M}'$ is simply one with no existentially quantified functions and consisting of the conjunction of the two constraints that specify $\mathcal{M}'$.

After this, we initialize two sets, S and S', to consist of all the implications of the SO tgds in $\mathcal{M}$ and, respectively, $\mathcal{M}'$.

S : $\texttt{Emp}(e_0) \rightarrow \texttt{Reports}(e_0, f(e_0))$
S' : $\texttt{Reports}(e, m) \rightarrow \texttt{Manager}(e, m)$, $\texttt{Reports}(e, e) \rightarrow \texttt{SelfMgr}(e)$

Observe that the existential quantifiers of function symbols as well as the universal quantifiers in front of the implications are omitted, for convenience. Additionally, we have renamed the variables in S so that they are disjoint from the variables used in S'.

Next, for each implication in S', we consider each relational atom on the left-hand side of the implication and replace that atom based on all the implications in S whose right-hand side have an atom with the same relation symbol. For our example, we will replace $\texttt{Reports}(e, m)$ of the first implication in S' using the sole implication in S, whose right-hand side also has a $\texttt{Reports}$ atom. Replacement proceeds by equating the terms in corresponding positions of $\texttt{Reports}(e_0, f(e_0))$ and $\texttt{Reports}(e, m)$, and then adding the left-hand side of the implication in S. In this case, we obtain the equalities $e_0 = e$ and $f(e_0) = m$ and we add the relational atom $\texttt{Emp}(e_0)$. Hence, the first implication of S' becomes:

$$\chi_1 : \texttt{Emp}(e_0) \wedge (e_0 = e) \wedge (f(e_0) = m) \rightarrow \texttt{Manager}(e, m).$$

Similarly, the second implication of S_{23} becomes:

$$\chi_2 : \texttt{Emp}(e_0) \wedge (e_0 = e) \wedge (f(e_0) = e) \rightarrow \texttt{SelfMgr}(e).$$

The implications χ_1 and χ_2 can be simplified by replacing every occurrence of e_0 with e (according to the equality $e_0 = e$). In addition, χ_1 can be further simplified by replacing m with $f(e)$. We obtain:

$$\chi_1: \text{Emp}(e) \to \text{Manager}(e, f(e))$$
$$\chi_2: \text{Emp}(e) \wedge (f(e) = e) \to \text{SelfMgr}(e).$$

At this point, the resulting implications describe a relationship between relation symbols of **S** and relation symbols of **T'**. The final SO tgd that describes the composition $\mathcal{M} \circ \mathcal{M}'$ is obtained by adding all the needed universal quantifiers in front of each implication and then by adding in all the existentially quantified functions (at the beginning of the formula). For our example, we obtain:

$$\exists f (\forall e \, \chi_1 \wedge \forall e \, \chi_2).$$

The following theorem states that SO tgds suffice for composition of GLAV mappings. Moreover, SO tgds are closed under composition. Thus, we do not need to go beyond SO tgds for purposes of composition.

Theorem 3 (Fagin et al. 2005b). *Let $\mathcal{M}$ and $\mathcal{M}'$ be two consecutive schema mappings.*

1. *If $\mathcal{M}$ and $\mathcal{M}'$ are GLAV, then $\mathcal{M} \circ \mathcal{M}'$ can be expressed by an SO tgd.*
2. *If $\mathcal{M}$ and $\mathcal{M}'$ are SO tgds, then $\mathcal{M} \circ \mathcal{M}'$ can be expressed by an SO tgd.*

Moreover, it is shown in Fagin et al. [2005b] that SO tgds form a minimal language for the composition of GLAV mappings, in the sense that every schema mapping specified by an SO tgd is the composition of a finite number of GLAV schema mappings.

The above theorem has an immediate consequence in the context of target schema evolution. As long as the original schema mapping $\mathcal{M}$ is GLAV or given by an SO tgd, and as long as we represent the target evolution $\mathcal{M}'$ by a similar type of mapping, the new adapted mapping can be obtained by composition and can be expressed as an SO tgd.

Additionally, the above theorem also applies in the context of source schema evolution, provided that the source evolution mapping $\mathcal{M}''$ has a chase-inverse. We summarize the applicability of Theorem 3 to the context of schema evolution as follows.

Corollary 3. *Let $\mathcal{M}$, $\mathcal{M}'$, and $\mathcal{M}''$ be schema mappings as in Fig. 7.1 such that $\mathcal{M}$ and $\mathcal{M}'$ are SO tgds (or, in particular GLAV mappings) and $\mathcal{M}''$ is a GLAV mapping. If $\mathcal{M}''$ has a chase-inverse $\mathcal{M}^\dagger$, then the mapping $\mathcal{M}^\dagger \circ \mathcal{M} \circ \mathcal{M}'$ can be expressed as an SO tgd.*

The important remaining restriction in the above corollary is that the source evolution mapping $\mathcal{M}''$ must have a chase-inverse and, in particular, that $\mathcal{M}''$ is a lossless mapping. We address next the case where $\mathcal{M}''$ is lossy and, hence, a chase-inverse does not exist.

5 The Case of Lossy Mappings

We have seen earlier that *chase-inverses*, when they exist, can be used to recover the original source data either *exactly*, in the case of exact chase-inverses, or *modulo homomorphic equivalence*, in general. However, chase-inverses do not always exist. Intuitively, a schema mapping may drop some of the source information, by either projecting or filtering the data, and hence it is not possible to recover the same amount of information. In this section, we look at relaxations of chase-inverses, which we call *relaxed chase-inverses* [Fagin et al., 2009b], and which are intended for situations where there is information loss. Intuitively, a relaxed chase-inverse recovers the original source data as well as possible.

5.1 Relaxed Chase-Inverses

We consider a variation of the scenario described in Fig. 7.2. In this variation, the evolved source schema $\mathbf{S}''$ is changed so that it no longer contains the major field. The new source evolution scenario is illustrated graphically in Fig. 7.4a. The source evolution mapping $\mathcal{M}''$ is now given as:

$$\mathcal{M}'' : \text{Takes}(s, m, co) \rightarrow \exists C \ (\text{Takes}''(s, C) \land \text{Course}(C, co)).$$

The natural "inverse" that one would expect here is the following mapping:

$$\mathcal{M}^\dagger : \text{Takes}''(s, c) \land \text{Course}(c, co) \rightarrow \exists M \ \text{Takes}(s, M, co).$$

First of all, it can be verified that $\mathcal{M}^\dagger$ is not a chase-inverse for $\mathcal{M}''$. In particular, if we start with a source instance I for Takes where the source tuples contain some constant values for the major field, and then apply the chase with $\mathcal{M}''$ and then the reverse chase with $\mathcal{M}^\dagger$, we obtain another source instance U for Takes where the

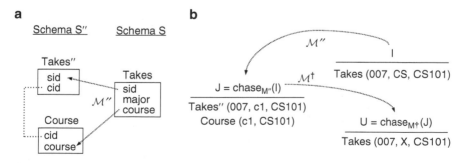

Fig. 7.4 (a) A case where $\mathcal{M}''$ is a lossy mapping. (b) Recovery of an instance U such that $U \leftrightarrow_{\mathcal{M}''} I$

tuples have nulls in the `major` position. Consequently, the resulting source instance U cannot be homomorphically equivalent to the original source instance I. To give a concrete example, consider the source instance I over the schema $\mathbf{S}$ that is shown in Fig. 7.4b. If we apply the chase with $\mathcal{M}''$ on I, we obtain the instance J shown in the same figure. Here, c_1 is a null that is assigned as the course id for $CS101$. If we now apply $\mathcal{M}^\dagger$ to J, we obtain another source instance U, where a null X is used in place of a major.

As it can be seen, the recovered source instance U is not homomorphically equivalent to the original source instance: there is a homomorphism from U to I, but no homomorphism can map the constant CS in I to the null X in U. Intuitively, there is information loss in the evolution mapping $\mathcal{M}''$, which does not export the `major` field. Later on, in Sect. 5.2, we will show that in fact $\mathcal{M}''$ has no chase-inverse; thus, we cannot recover a homomorphically equivalent source instance.

At the same time, it can be argued, intuitively, that the source instance U that is recovered by $\mathcal{M}^\dagger$ in this example is the "best" source instance that can be recovered, given the circumstances. We will make this notion precise in the next paragraphs, leading to the definition of a relaxed chase-inverse. In particular, we will show that $\mathcal{M}^\dagger$ is a relaxed chase-inverse.

Data exchange equivalence. First, we observe that the source instance U that is recovered by $\mathcal{M}^\dagger$ contains all the information that has been present in the original source instance I *and* has been exported by $\mathcal{M}''$. Indeed, if we now apply the mapping $\mathcal{M}''$ on U, we obtain via the chase an instance that is the same as J modulo null renaming (i.e., the chase may generate a different null c_2 instead of c_1). Thus, the following holds:

$$chase_{\mathcal{M}''}(U) \leftrightarrow chase_{\mathcal{M}''}(I),$$

where recall that $\leftrightarrow$ denotes homomorphic equivalence of instances. Intuitively, the above equivalence says that U is as good as I from the point of view of the data they export via $\mathcal{M}''$. Thus, intuitively, U and I are also equivalent, although in a weaker sense. This weaker notion of equivalence is captured by the following definition, which was first given in Fagin et al. [2008b].

Definition 5. Let $\mathcal{M}$ be a GLAV schema mapping from $\mathbf{S}_1$ to $\mathbf{S}_2$. Let I and I' be two instances over $\mathbf{S}_1$. We say that I and I' are *data exchange equivalent with respect to* $\mathcal{M}$ if $chase_{\mathcal{M}}(I) \leftrightarrow chase_{\mathcal{M}}(I')$. We also write in such case that $I \leftrightarrow_{\mathcal{M}} I'$.

For our example, we have that $U \leftrightarrow_{\mathcal{M}''} I$. At this point, we could take such a condition (i.e., the recovery of an instance U that is data exchange equivalent to I) to be the requirement for a relaxation of a chase-inverse. Such relaxation would be consistent with the earlier notion of chase-inverse and lead into a natural hierarchy of inverses. More precisely, if $\mathcal{M}$ is a GLAV schema mapping, then we could have three types of chase-based inverses $\mathcal{M}^*$, which increasingly relax the equivalence requirement between I and $chase_{\mathcal{M}^*}(chase_{\mathcal{M}}(I))$:

1. $I = chase_{\mathcal{M}^*}(chase_{\mathcal{M}}(I))$ (exact chase-inverse)
2. $I \leftrightarrow chase_{\mathcal{M}^*}(chase_{\mathcal{M}}(I))$ (chase-inverse)
3. $I \leftrightarrow_{\mathcal{M}} chase_{\mathcal{M}^*}(chase_{\mathcal{M}}(I))$.

Somewhat surprisingly, having just the third condition is too loose of a requirement for a good notion of a relaxation of a chase-inverse. As we show next, we need to add an additional requirement of homomorphic containment.

Relaxed chase-inverse: Stronger requirement. We illustrate the need for the extra condition by using our example. Refer again to the schema mapping $\mathcal{M}''$ in Fig. 7.4a and the natural candidate inverse $\mathcal{M}^\dagger$ introduced earlier. As shown in Fig. 7.4b, given the source instance I, the mapping $\mathcal{M}^\dagger$ recovers an instance U such that U and I are data exchange equivalent with respect to $\mathcal{M}''$. However, there can be many other instances that are data exchange equivalent to I but intuitively are incorrect. Consider, for example, the following instance:

$$U' = \{\texttt{Takes}(007, 007, CS101)\}$$

Like U, the instance U' is data exchange equivalent to I with respect to $\mathcal{M}''$. (The only difference from U is in the *major* field, which is not used by the chase with $\mathcal{M}''$.) Furthermore, such instance U' would be obtained if we use the following "inverse" instead of $\mathcal{M}^\dagger$:

$$\mathcal{M}_1^\dagger : \texttt{Takes}''(s, c) \wedge \texttt{Course}(c, co) \rightarrow \texttt{Takes}(s, s, co).$$

Intuitively, the instance U' and the mapping $\mathcal{M}_1^\dagger$ are not what we would expect from a natural inverse. In the instance U', the $\texttt{sid}$ value 007 is artificially copied into the $\texttt{major}$ field, and the resulting $\texttt{Takes}$ fact represents *extra* information that did not appear in the original source instance I. We can rule out bad "inverses" such as $\mathcal{M}_1^\dagger$ by requiring any recovered instance to also have a homomorphism into I. Intuitively, this is a soundness condition saying that the recovered instance does not have extra facts that were not present in I. Note that the earlier instance U does have a homomorphism into I.

Putting it all together, we now formally capture the two desiderata discussed above (data exchange equivalence and homomorphic containment) into the following definition of a *relaxed chase-inverse*.

Definition 6 (Relaxed chase-inverse). Let $\mathcal{M}$ be a GLAV schema mapping from a schema S_1 to a schema S_2. We say that $\mathcal{M}^*$ is a *relaxed chase-inverse* of $\mathcal{M}$ if $\mathcal{M}^*$ is a GLAV schema mapping from S_2 to S_1 such that, for every instance I over S_1, the following properties hold for the instance $U = chase_{\mathcal{M}^*}(chase_{\mathcal{M}}(I))$:

(a) $U \leftrightarrow_{\mathcal{M}} I$ (data exchange equivalence w.r.t. $\mathcal{M}$),
(b) $U \rightarrow I$ (homomorphic containment).

The notion of relaxed chase-inverse originated in Fagin et al. [2009b], under the name of *universal-faithful inverse*. The definition given in Fagin et al. [2009b] had, however, a third condition called *universality*, which turned out to be redundant (and equivalent to homomorphic containment). Thus, the formulation given here for a relaxed chase-inverse is simpler.

Coming back to our example, it can be verified that the above $\mathcal{M}^\dagger$ satisfies the conditions of being a relaxed chase-inverse of $\mathcal{M}''$, thus reflecting the intuition that $\mathcal{M}^\dagger$ is a good "approximation" of an inverse in our scenario.

Since $\mathcal{M}^\dagger$ is a GLAV mapping, we can now apply the composition of $\mathcal{M}^\dagger$ with $\mathcal{M} \circ \mathcal{M}'$ to obtain an SO tgd that specifies $\mathcal{M}^\dagger \circ \mathcal{M} \circ \mathcal{M}'$. This SO tgd is the result of adapting the original schema mapping $\mathcal{M}$ to the new schemas $\mathbf{S}''$ and $\mathbf{T}'$. We leave the full details to the reader.

5.2 More on Relaxed Chase-Inverses

It is fairly straightforward to see that every chase-inverse is also a relaxed chase-inverse. This follows from a well-known property of the chase that implies that whenever $U \leftrightarrow I$ we also have that $U \leftrightarrow_{\mathcal{M}} I$. Thus, the notion of relaxed chase-inverse is a generalization of the notion of chase-inverse; in fact, it is a strict generalization, since the schema mapping $\mathcal{M}^\dagger$ in Sect. 5.1 is a relaxed chase-inverse of $\mathcal{M}''$ but not a chase-inverse of $\mathcal{M}''$. However, for schema mappings that have a chase-inverse, the notions of a chase-inverse and of a relaxed chase-inverse coincide, as stated in the following theorem, which can be derived from results in Fagin et al. [2009b].

Theorem 4. *Let $\mathcal{M}$ be a GLAV schema mapping from a schema $\mathbf{S}_1$ to a schema $\mathbf{S}_2$ that has a chase-inverse. Then the following statements are equivalent for every GLAV schema mapping $\mathcal{M}^*$ from $\mathbf{S}_2$ to $\mathbf{S}_1$:*

(i) $\mathcal{M}^*$ is a chase-inverse of $\mathcal{M}$.
(ii) $\mathcal{M}^*$ is a relaxed chase-inverse of $\mathcal{M}$.

As an immediate application of the preceding theorem, we conclude that the schema mapping $\mathcal{M}''$ in Sect. 5.1 has no chase-inverse, because $\mathcal{M}^\dagger$ is a relaxed chase-inverse of $\mathcal{M}''$ but not a chase-inverse of $\mathcal{M}''$.

In Sect. 3.3, we pointed out that chase-inverses coincide with the extended inverses that are specified by GLAV constraints. For schema mappings that have no extended inverses, a further relaxation of the concept of an extended inverse has been considered, namely, the concept of a *maximum extended recovery* [Fagin et al., 2009b]. It follows from results established in Fagin et al. [2009b] that relaxed chase-inverses coincide with the maximum extended recoveries that are specified by GLAV constraints.

6 Implementations and Systems

In this section, we examine systems that implement composition and inversion and apply them to the context of schema evolution. We do not attempt to give here a complete survey of all the existing systems and implementations but rather focus on two systems that are directly related to the concepts described earlier and also targeted at schema evolution.

The first system that we will discuss is an implementation of mapping composition that is reported in Yu and Popa [2005] and is targeted at the mapping adaptation problem in the context of schema evolution. This implementation is part of the Clio system [Fagin et al., 2009a] and builds on the schema mapping framework of Clio. In particular, it is focused on schema mappings that are expressed as SO tgds [Fagin et al., 2005b]. A different implementation of mapping composition that is worth noting, but which we do not discuss in detail in here, is the one reported in Bernstein et al. [2008]. This system allows a schema mapping to contain not only source-to-target constraints, but also target constraints, source constraints, and target-to-source constraints. Furthermore, the focus is on expressing the composition as a first-order formula (when possible). In this approach, a significant effort is spent on eliminating second-order features (via deskolemization). As a result, the composition algorithm is inherently complex and may not always succeed in finding a first-order formula, even when one exists.

The second system that we will discuss in this section is a more recent one, reported in Curino et al. [2008], and includes both composition and inversion as part of a framework for schema evolution. This system is focused on the query migration (or adaptation) problem in the context of schema evolution.

6.1 Mapping Composition and Evolution in Clio

The system described in Yu and Popa [2005] is part of the larger Clio system [Fagin et al., 2009a] and is the first reported implementation of mapping composition in the context of schema evolution. In this system, both source schema evolution and target schema evolution are described through mappings, which are given in the same language as the original schema mapping (that is to be adapted). However, differently from the earlier diagram shown in Fig. 7.1, the source evolution is required to be given as a schema mapping from S'' to S, and not from S to S''. (The latter would, intuitively, be a more natural way to describe an evolution of S into S''.) The main reason for this requirement is that the system described in Yu and Popa [2005] preceded the work on mapping inversion. Thus, the only way to apply mapping composition techniques was to require that all mappings form a chain, as seen in Fig. 7.5.

In the system implemented in Yu and Popa [2005], the schema mapping language that is used to specify the input mappings (i.e., the original mapping $\mathcal{M}$ and the evolution mappings $\mathcal{M}'$ and $\mathcal{M}''$) are based on SO tgds [Fagin et al., 2005b]. One reason for this choice is that, as discussed earlier, GLAV mappings are not closed under composition, while SO tgds form a more expressive language that includes GLAV mappings and, moreover, is closed under composition. Another reason is that SO tgds, independently of mapping composition, include features that are desirable for any schema mapping language. In particular, the Skolem terms that can be used

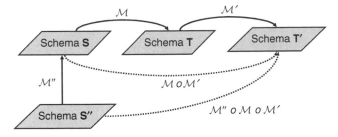

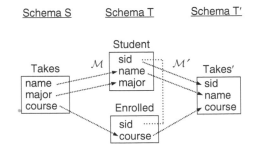

Fig. 7.5 Using composition (only) in schema evolution

Fig. 7.6 Example to illustrate SO tgd-based composition and minimization

in SO tgds enable a much finer control over the creation of new data values (e.g., ids) in the process of data exchange. We shall give such example shortly. A related point is that the language used in Yu and Popa [2005] (and also in the larger Clio system) is actually a nested relational extension of SO tgds that can handle XML schemas and can be compiled into XQuery and XSLT. We will not elaborate on the XML aspect here and refer the interested readers to either Haas et al. [2005] or Yu and Popa [2005].

Another main ingredient of the system described in Yu and Popa [2005] is the use of an operational semantics of mapping composition that is based on the chase. Under this semantics, the composition algorithm needs to find an expression that is chase-equivalent only, rather than logically equivalent, to the composition of the two input mappings. (We define shortly what chase-equivalence means.) In turn, the use of this chase-based semantics of composition enables *syntactic minimization* of the outcome of mapping composition. For schema evolution, such minimization is shown to be essential in making the outcome of mapping adaptation intuitive (and presentable) from a user point of view. This is especially true for the larger schemas that arise in practice, where the outcome of mapping composition (under the general semantics) is complex, contains many self-joins, and it is generally hard to understand.

To make the above ideas more concrete, consider the following schema evolution scenario depicted in Fig. 7.6. This scenario is a variation on the earlier schema evolution scenario described in Fig. 7.2. In the new scenario, we focus on the target schema evolution alone. Furthermore, there are several changes in the schemas as well as the mappings. We assume that the source schema **S** consists of one relation Takes where instead of a student id (sid) we are given a student name (name). However, the target schema **T**, consisting of the two relations Student and Enrolled, still requires a student id that must relate the two relations. The schema mapping that relates the two schemas is now given as the following SO tgd:

$$\mathcal{M}: \exists f(\ \text{Takes}(n,m,co) \rightarrow \text{Student}(f(n),n,m)$$
$$\wedge\ \text{Takes}(n,m,co) \rightarrow \text{Enrolled}(f(n),co)\ )$$

In the above SO tgd, f is an existentially quantified Skolem function and, for each student name n, the Skolem term $f(n)$ represents the associated student id that is used to populate both Student and Enrolled tuples. The use of such Skolem terms offer fine control over the creation of target values. By changing the parameters given to the Skolem function, one can change how the target values are populated. For example, if we know that a student name does not uniquely identify a student, but the student name together with the major does, then we can change $f(n)$ to $f(n,m)$ to reflect such dependency.

Assume now that the target schema evolves to a new schema **T'** that consists of a single relation Takes' that keeps the association between sid, name, and course, while dropping the major. The target evolution can be described by the following mapping:

$$\mathcal{M}': \ \text{Student}(s,n,m) \wedge \text{Enrolled}(s,co) \rightarrow \text{Takes}'(s,n,co).$$

It can be verified that the composition of $\mathcal{M}$ and $\mathcal{M}'$ is expressed by the following SO tgd:

$$\sigma: \ \exists f(\ \text{Takes}(n,m,co) \wedge \text{Takes}(n',m',co') \wedge (f(n) = f(n'))$$
$$\rightarrow \text{Takes}'(f(n'),n',co)\ )$$

This mapping is surprisingly complex, but still correct (i.e., σ expresses $\mathcal{M} \circ \mathcal{M}'$). It accounts for the fact that, given a source instance I over **S** and a target instance J over **T**, two different student names n and n' occurring in different tuples of I may relate to the same sid in J. In other words, the function f that is existentially quantified by the original mapping $\mathcal{M}$ may have the property that $f(n) = f(n')$ for some distinct names n and n'. To account for such possibility, the composition σ includes a self-join on Takes and the test $f(n) = f(n')$.

Minimization of SO tgds under chase-equivalence. If we now take the operational view behind schema mappings, the above σ can be drastically simplified. Under the operational view, a mapping $\mathcal{M}$ does not describe an arbitrary relationship between instances I and J over two schemas but rather a transformation which, given a source instance I, *generates* the target instance $J = chase_{\mathcal{M}}(I)$. We refer the reader to Fagin et al. [2005b] for the definition of the chase with SO tgds. Here, we point out that an important property of this chase is that it always generates different values (nulls) for different arguments to the Skolem functions. Hence, for our example, the equality $f(n) = f(n')$ can happen only if $n = n'$. As a result, the above σ reduces to the following SO tgd:

$$\sigma_0 : \quad \exists f(\; \text{Takes}(n,m,co) \rightarrow \text{Takes}'(f(n),n,co) \;).$$

The above SO tgd is much simpler and more intuitive than the earlier σ. Just by looking at the diagram in Fig. 7.6, one would expect the overall adapted mapping from $\mathbf{S}$ to $\mathbf{T}'$ to be as close as possible to an identity schema mapping. The SO tgd σ_0 accomplishes this desideratum while still incorporating the id generation behavior via $f(n)$ that is given in the original mapping $\mathcal{M}$.

The reduction algorithm implemented in Yu and Popa [2005] systematically replaces every equality between two Skolem terms with the same function symbol by the equalities of their arguments, until all equalities that involve such Skolem terms are eliminated. The algorithm also eliminates every implication where the left-hand side contains an equality between two Skolem terms that use different Skolem functions. Intuitively, such equalities cannot be satisfied during the chase; hence, the implications that contain them can be dropped. Finally, the algorithm uses conjunctive-query minimization [Chandra and Merlin, 1977] type of techniques to eliminate any redundant relational atoms in the resulting mappings. For example, in the above σ, once we replace $f(n) = f(n')$ with $n = n'$, the second Takes atom becomes $\text{Takes}(n, m', co')$; it can then be eliminated, since it is subsumed by the first Takes atom, and neither m' nor co' is used in the right-hand side of the implication.

The main observation behind this reduction algorithm is that its output SO tgd (e.g., σ_0) is *chase-equivalent* to the input SO tgd (e.g., σ).

Definition 7. Let $\mathcal{M}_1$ and $\mathcal{M}_2$ be two schema mappings from $\mathbf{S}$ to $\mathbf{T}$ that are specified by SO tgds (or in particular by GLAV mappings). We say that $\mathcal{M}_1$ and $\mathcal{M}_2$ are *chase-equivalent* if, for every source instance I, we have that $chase_{\mathcal{M}_1}(I) \leftrightarrow chase_{\mathcal{M}_2}(I)$.

Theorem 5 (Yu and Popa 2005). *Every SO tgd σ is chase-equivalent to its reduced form σ_0.*

We note that the above σ_0 is not logically equivalent to the input σ. In general, the notion of chase-equivalence is a relaxation of the concept of logical equivalence. A systematic study of relaxed notions of equivalence of schema mappings appeared later in Fagin et al. [2008a]. For schema mappings specified by GLAV mappings or, more generally, by SO tgds, the above notion of chase-equivalence turns out to be the same as the notion of *CQ-equivalence* of schema mappings studied in Fagin et al. [2008a]. There, two schema mappings $\mathcal{M}_1$ and $\mathcal{M}_2$ are CQ-equivalent if for every source instance I, the *certain answers* of a conjunctive query q are the same under both $\mathcal{M}_1$ and $\mathcal{M}_2$. For our example, the CQ-equivalence of σ_0 and σ is another argument of why we can use σ_0 instead of σ.

We also note that σ_0 represents a relaxation of the composition $\mathcal{M} \circ \mathcal{M}'$ (since σ_0 is chase-equivalent but not logically equivalent to σ, which expresses $\mathcal{M} \circ \mathcal{M}'$). Such relaxation of composition appears early in the work of Madhavan and Halevy [Madhavan and Halevy, 2003].[4] The concept used there is based, implicitly, on CQ-equivalence; however, their results are limited to GLAV mappings, which, in general, are not powerful enough to express composition (even under the relaxed form) [Fagin et al., 2005b].

Since schemas can be quite large in practice, mapping composition as well as mapping reduction can be expensive. Therefore, a great deal of the work in Yu and Popa [2005] is spent on developing pruning techniques that identify the parts of a schema mapping that are not affected by the changes in the schemas, and hence do not need to be involved in the process of composition and reduction. We refer the interested reader to Yu and Popa [2005] for more details on this.

6.2   The PRISM Workbench: Query Adaptation

The PRISM project, described in Curino et al. [2008], has the overall goal of automating as much as possible the database administration work that is needed when schemas evolve. Under this general umbrella, one of the main concrete goals in PRISM is to support migration (or adaptation) of queries from old (legacy) schemas to the new evolved schemas. Similar to the Clio-based schema evolution system in Yu and Popa [2005], PRISM also uses schema mappings (although in a restricted form) to describe the evolution of schemas. However, differently from the Clio-based system, the focus in PRISM is not on mapping adaptation but on query adaptation. More concretely, in the Clio-based system, we are given a schema mapping from $\mathbf{S}$ to $\mathbf{T}$ and the goal is to adapt it when either $\mathbf{S}$ or $\mathbf{T}$ changes, while in PRISM we are given a query q over a schema $\mathbf{S}$ and the goal is to adapt it when $\mathbf{S}$ changes. Because it is targeted at queries, PRISM makes prominent use of query rewriting. In particular, it applies the chase and backchase algorithm introduced in Deutsch et al. [1999] for query rewriting under constraints. Additionally, PRISM also makes use of the schema mapping operations that we described earlier (i.e., composition and inversion) to enable the application of the query rewriting algorithm and to optimize its application.

We use Fig. 7.7 to illustrate the type of functionality that PRISM aims to achieve. There, schema $\mathbf{S}$ represents an initial (legacy) schema that goes through several steps of change, forming a schema evolution chain: from $\mathbf{S}$ to $\mathbf{S}_1$, then to S_2, and so on. Each of the evolution steps can be described by a mapping. However, these mappings are not arbitrary and must correspond to a set of predefined schema modification operations (SMOs) that allow only for certain type of schema modifications. Examples of such modifications are: copying of a table, renaming of a table or of a column, taking the union of two tables into one, decomposing a table into two,

---

[4] In fact, that is how Madhavan and Halevy defined composition of schema mappings.

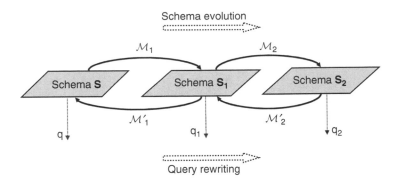

Fig. 7.7 Schema evolution and query rewriting in PRISM

and others. These operations are chosen carefully so that they represent the most common forms of schema evolution that arise in practice, but also to allow for invertibility. More precisely, each of the evolution mappings that are allowed in PRISM is guaranteed to have a quasi-inverse [Fagin et al., 2008b]. Thus, in Fig. 7.7, $\mathcal{M}'_1$ is a quasi-inverse of $\mathcal{M}_1$, and $\mathcal{M}'_2$ is a quasi-inverse of $\mathcal{M}_2$. The main reason for why each evolution mapping must have a reverse mapping is that the presence of mappings in both directions (i.e., from $\mathbf{S}$ to $\mathbf{S}_1$, and from $\mathbf{S}_1$ to $\mathbf{S}$) is essential for the application of query reformulation algorithms, as we explain next.

More concretely, query reformulation in PRISM can be phrased as follows. We are given a query q over the original schema $\mathbf{S}$. We assume one step of evolution, with mapping $\mathcal{M}_1$ from $\mathbf{S}$ to $\mathbf{S}_1$ and reverse mapping $\mathcal{M}'_1$ from $\mathbf{S}_1$ to $\mathbf{S}$. The problem is to find a query q_1 over the schema $\mathbf{S}_1$ such that q_1 is equivalent to q, where equivalence is interpreted over the union $\mathbf{S} \cup \mathbf{S}_1$ of the two schemas and where $\mathcal{M}_1$ and $\mathcal{M}'_1$ form constraints on the larger schema. In other words, we are looking for a query q_1 to satisfy $q(K) = q_1(K)$, for every instance K over $\mathbf{S} \cup \mathbf{S}_1$ such that K satisfies the union of the constraints in $\mathcal{M}_1$ and $\mathcal{M}'_1$. In turn, this is an instance of the general problem of query reformulation under constraints [Deutsch et al., 2006], which can be solved by the chase and backchase method [Deutsch et al., 1999]. The application of the chase and backchase method in this context consists of, first, applying the chase on q with the constraints in $\mathcal{M}_1$, and then on applying the (back) chase with the reverse constraints in $\mathcal{M}'_1$ to find equivalent rewritings of q.

Before we concretely illustrate on an example the application of the chase and backchase in the PRISM context, we need to point out that for multiple evolution steps, the query reformulation problem needs to take into account all the direct and reverse mappings along the chain (e.g., $\mathcal{M}_1$, $\mathcal{M}_2$, $\mathcal{M}'_1$, and $\mathcal{M}'_2$ for two evolution steps). Thus, as the evolution chain becomes longer, the number of constraints involved in query reformulation becomes larger. To reduce the number of constraints needed for rewriting, PRISM makes repeated use of composition to replace two consecutive schema mappings by one schema mapping. Since PRISM restricts mappings such as $\mathcal{M}_1$ and $\mathcal{M}_2$ to always be GAV schema mappings, the composition $\mathcal{M}_1 \circ \mathcal{M}_2$ can also be expressed as a GAV mapping (see our earlier Theorem 1,

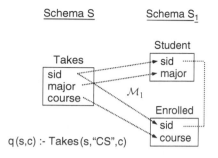

Fig. 7.8 Example of schema evolution with a query to be rewritten

part 1). The same cannot be done for the reverse schema mappings (e.g., $\mathcal{M}'_1$ and $\mathcal{M}'_2$), which are quasi-inverses of the direct mappings, and require in general a more complex language that includes disjunction (see Fagin et al. 2008b). The exact language in which to express composition of such schema mappings (i.e., with disjunction) is an open research problem.

To make the above ideas more concrete, consider the following schema evolution example shown in Fig. 7.8. This example is based on two of our earlier schemas (see **S** and **T** in Fig. 7.2). Here, the schema **S** represents the "old" schema, which then evolves into a "new" schema $\mathbf{S}_1$. The evolution step from **S** to $\mathbf{S}_1$ can be described by one of the SMOs that the PRISM workbench allows. In particular, this evolution step is an application of the Decompose operator where the table Takes is split into two tables Student and Enrolled that share the common attribute sid. The application of the Decompose operator in this case can be represented by the following GAV mapping (this is the same as the earlier $\mathcal{M}$ in Sect. 3):

$$\mathcal{M}_1 : \quad \texttt{Takes}(s, m, co) \rightarrow \texttt{Student}(s, m)$$
$$\texttt{Takes}(s, m, co) \rightarrow \texttt{Enrolled}(s, co).$$

Assume now that we have a legacy query q that is formulated in terms of the old schema. This query, shown in Fig. 7.8, retrieves all pairs of student id and course, where the major is "CS." The goal is to adapt, via query rewriting, the query q into a new query q_1 that is formulated in terms of the new schema $\mathbf{S}_1$ and is equivalent to q.

The first step is to retrieve a quasi-inverse $\mathcal{M}'_1$ of $\mathcal{M}_1$. As mentioned earlier, each evolution step in PRISM is an instance of one of the predetermined SMOs. Thus, a quasi-inverse always exists and can be chosen by the system or by the user. In this case, the following is a quasi-inverse of $\mathcal{M}_1$:

$$\mathcal{M}'_1 : \texttt{Student}(s, m) \wedge \texttt{Enrolled}(s, co) \rightarrow \texttt{Takes}(s, m, co).$$

The next step is to apply the chase and backchase algorithm to find rewritings of q that are equivalent given the union of the constraints in $\mathcal{M}_1$ and $\mathcal{M}'_1$. The following query over schema $\mathbf{S}_1$ is such an equivalent rewriting and will be returned by the chase and backchase algorithm.

$$q_1(s,c) \;:-\; \texttt{Student}(s, \text{``}CS\text{''}) \wedge \texttt{Enrolled}(s,c).$$

The above quasi-inverse $\mathcal{M}'_1$ also happens to be a chase-inverse of $\mathcal{M}_1$. In general, however, quasi-inverses differ from chase-inverses (or relaxed chase-inverses), and one may find quasi-inverses with nonintuitive behavior (e.g., a quasi-inverse that is not a chase-inverse, even when a chase-inverse exists). We note that the PRISM development preceded the development of chase-inverses or relaxed chase-inverses.

We also remark that the language needed to express quasi-inverses requires disjunction. As a result, PRISM uses an extension of the chase and backchase algorithm that is able to handle disjunctive dependencies; this extension was developed as part of MARS [Deutsch and Tannen, 2003]. Finally, we note that we may not always succeed in finding equivalent reformulations, depending on the input query, the evolution mappings and also on the quasi-inverses that are chosen. Hence, PRISM must still rely on a human DBA to solve exceptions.

7 Other Related Work

We have emphasized in this paper the operational view of schema evolution, where a schema mapping $\mathcal{M}$ is viewed as a transformation, which given an instance I produces $chase_{\mathcal{M}}(I)$. Under this view, we have emphasized two types of operational inverses: the chase-inverse (with its exact variation), which corresponds to the absence of information loss, and the relaxed chase-inverse, which is designed for the case of information loss. However, there is quite a lot of additional (and related) work on mapping inversion that studies more general, nonoperational notions of inverses. These notions can be categorized into three main notions: inverses [Fagin, 2007], quasi-inverses [Fagin et al., 2008b], and maximum recoveries [Arenas et al., 2008].

Most of the technical development on inverses, quasi-inverses, and maximum recoveries was originally focused on the case when the source instances were assumed to contain no nulls, that is, they were assumed to be ground. However, in practice, such an assumption is not realistic, since an instance with nulls can easily arise as the result of another schema mapping. This is especially true in schema evolution scenarios, where we can have chains of mappings describing the various evolution steps. To uniformly deal with the case where instances can have nulls, the notions of inverses and of maximum recoveries were extended in Fagin et al. [2009b] by systematically making use of the notion of homomorphism between instances with nulls as a replacement for the more standard containment of instances. In addition to their benefit in dealing with nonground instances, it turns out that the two extended notions, namely extended inverses and maximum extended recoveries, have the operational counterpart that we want. More concretely, when $\mathcal{M}$ is a GLAV mapping, we have that: (1) extended inverses that are also expressed as GLAV mappings coincide with chase-inverses, and (2) maximum extended recoveries that are also expressed as GLAV mappings coincide with relaxed chase-inverses (Note that extended inverses and maximum extended recoveries, or any of the other semantic notions of inverses, need not be expressible as GLAV mappings, in general). This correspondence between two very general semantic notions, on the one hand, and two procedural and practical notions of inverses, on the other, is interesting in itself.

Finally, we note that there are certain limitations to what composition and inversion can achieve in the context of schema evolution. For example, if we refer back to Fig. 7.1, it is conceivable that the composition $\mathcal{M} \circ \mathcal{M}'$ does not always give the "complete" mapping from $\mathbf{S}$ to $\mathbf{T}'$. Instead, the "complete" mapping from $\mathbf{S}$ to $\mathbf{T}'$ may require *merging* the schema mapping $\mathcal{M} \circ \mathcal{M}'$ with an additional mapping that relates directly $\mathbf{S}$ to $\mathbf{T}'$. Such additional mapping may be defined separately by a user to account for, say, a schema element that occurs in both $\mathbf{S}$ and $\mathbf{T}'$ but does not occur in $\mathbf{T}$. The operation of merging two schema mappings appears in the model management framework [Melnik et al., 2005] under the term *Confluence*; a more refined version of merge, together with an algorithm for it, appears in Alexe et al. [2010].

8 Concluding Remarks

In this chapter, we illustrated how the composition operator and the inverse operator on schema mappings can be applied to schema evolution. The techniques presented here rely on the existence of chase-inverses or relaxed chase-inverses, which, in particular, are required to be specified by GLAV constraints. Much more remains to be done in the study of schema mappings for which no relaxed chase-inverse exists. In this direction, research issues include: (1) What is the exact language for expressing maximum extended recoveries? (2) How does this language compose with SO tgds? (3) What do inverses of SO tgds look like? More broadly, is there a unifying schema-mapping language that is closed under both composition and the various flavors of inverses, and, additionally, has good algorithmic properties?

Acknowledgements The authors thank Erhard Rahm for reading an earlier version of this chapter and providing valuable feedback. The research of Kolaitis and Tan is supported by NSF grant IIS-0430994 and NSF grant IIS-0905276. Tan is also supported by NSF CAREER award IIS-0347065.

References

Alexe B, Hernández MA, Popa L, Tan WC (2010) MapMerge: Correlating independent schema mappings. In: PVLDB, vol 3(1), pp 81–92

Arenas M, Pérez J, Riveros C (2008) The recovery of a schema mapping: Bringing exchanged data back. In: PODS. ACM, NY, pp 13–22

Bernstein PA (2003) Applying model management to classical meta-data problems. In: Conference on innovative data systems research (CIDR), Asilomar, CA, pp 209–220

Bernstein PA, Green TJ, Melnik S, Nash A (2008) Implementing mapping composition. VLDB J 17(2):333–353

222 R. Fagin et al.

Chandra AK, Merlin PM (1977) Optimal implementation of conjunctive queries in relational data bases. In: ACM symposium on theory of computing (STOC). ACM, NY, pp 77–90

Curino C, Moon HJ, Zaniolo C (2008) Graceful database schema evolution: The PRISM workbench. PVLDB 1(1):761–772

Deutsch A, Tannen V (2003) MARS: A system for publishing XML from mixed and redundant storage. In: International conference on very large data bases (VLDB). VLDB Endowment, pp 201–212

Deutsch A, Popa L, Tannen V (1999) Physical data independence, constraints and optimization with universal plans. In: International conference on very large data bases (VLDB). Morgan Kaufmann, CA, pp 459–470

Deutsch A, Popa L, Tannen V (2006) Query reformulation with constraints. SIGMOD Rec 35(1):65–73

Fagin R (2007) Inverting schema mappings. ACM Trans Database Syst (TODS) 32(4), Article No. 11

Fagin R, Kolaitis PG, Popa L, Tan WC (2004) Composing schema mappings: Second-order dependencies to the rescue. In: ACM symposium on principles of database systems (PODS). ACM, NY, pp 83–94

Fagin R, Kolaitis PG, Miller RJ, Popa L (2005a) Data exchange: Semantics and query answering. Theor Comput Sci (TCS) 336(1):89–124

Fagin R, Kolaitis PG, Popa L, Tan WC (2005b) Composing schema mappings: Second-order dependencies to the rescue. ACM Trans Database Syst (TODS) 30(4):994–1055

Fagin R, Kolaitis PG, Nash A, Popa L (2008a) Towards a theory of schema-mapping optimization. In: ACM symposium on principles of database systems (PODS). ACM, NY, pp 33–42

Fagin R, Kolaitis PG, Popa L, Tan WC (2008b) Quasi-inverses of schema mappings. ACM Trans Database Syst (TODS) 33(2), Article No. 11

Fagin R, Haas LM, Hernández MA, Miller RJ, Popa L, Velegrakis Y (2009a) Clio: Schema mapping creation and data exchange. In: Conceptual modeling: Foundations and applications, Essays in Honor of John Mylopoulos. Springer, Heidelberg, pp 198–236

Fagin R, Kolaitis PG, Popa L, Tan WC (2009b) Reverse data exchange: Coping with nulls. In: ACM symposium on principles of database systems (PODS). ACM, NY, pp 23–32

Fagin R, Kolaitis PG, Popa L, Tan WC (2010) Reverse data exchange: Coping with nulls. In: ACM symposium on principles of database systems (PODS). ACM, NY, pp 23–32

Haas LM, Hernández MA, Ho H, Popa L, Roth M (2005) Clio grows up: From research prototype to industrial tool. In: SIGMOD. ACM, NY, pp 805–810

Hartung M, Terwilliger J, Rahm E (2011) Recent advances in schema and ontology evolution. In: Bellahsene Z, Bonifati A, Rahm E (eds) Schema matching and mapping. Data-Centric Systems and Applications Series. Springer, Heidelberg

Lenzerini M (2002) Data integration: A theoretical perspective. In: ACM symposium on principles of database systems (PODS). ACM, NY, pp 233–246

Madhavan J, Halevy AY (2003) Composing mappings among data sources. In: International conference on very large data bases (VLDB). VLDB Endowment, pp 572–583

Melnik S (2004) Generic model management: Concepts and algorithms. Lecture Notes in Computer Science, vol 2967. Springer, Heidelberg

Melnik S, Bernstein PA, Halevy A, Rahm E (2005) Applying model management to executable mappings. In: SIGMOD, ACM, NY, pp 167–178

Nash A, Bernstein PA, Melnik S (2005) Composition of mappings given by embedded dependencies. In: ACM symposium on principles of database systems (PODS). ACM, NY, pp 172–183

Shu NC, Housel BC, Taylor RW, Ghosh SP, Lum VY (1977) EXPRESS: A data extraction, processing, amd restructuring system. ACM Trans Database Syst (TODS) 2(2):134–174

Velegrakis Y, Miller RJ, Popa L (2003) Mapping adaptation under evolving schemas. In: International conference on very large data bases (VLDB). VLDB Endowment, pp 584–595

Yu C, Popa L (2005) Semantic adaptation of schema mappings when schemas evolve. In: VLDB. VLDB Endowment, pp 1006–1017

Chapter 8
Mapping-Based Merging of Schemas

Rachel Pottinger

Abstract Merging schemas or other structured data occur in many different data models and applications, including merging ontologies, view integration, data integration, and computer supported collaborative work. This paper describes some of the key works in merging schemas and discusses some of the commonalities and differences.

1 Introduction

Schemas, ontologies and other related structures commonly need to be merged in a number of different applications. This happens for a number of reasons. For example:

View integration: Different users have their own aspects of a common application that they are interested in. For example, in creating a database for a university, the registrar has a different view from a professor, and both have different views from a student. In view integration, each user group creates its own "view" of what should be in the schema and then these different views are combined to create one global schema in which the data is stored.

Data integration: Users may want to query over multiple databases. For example, a BioMedical researcher may want to query both HUGO and OMIM for information on genes, and then use the gene information to query SwissProt for which proteins those genes encode. Because the researcher does not want to learn each of the schemas, and yet creating a warehouse of the entire set of databases is infeasible because of size and access restrictions, the user would like to just query one schema once and have the system figure out how to translate the queries over the sources. Such a system is called a data integration system.

R. Pottinger
University of British Columbia, 201-2366 Main Mall, Vancouver, BC, Canada V6T 1Z4
e-mail: rap@cs.ubc.ca

Z. Bellahsene et al. (eds.), *Schema Matching and Mapping*, Data-Centric Systems and Applications, DOI 10.1007/978-3-642-16518-4_8,

Merging ontologies: An ontology describes the concepts in a domain and the relationships between those concepts [Fikes, 1996]. Ontologies are a commonplace in varied domains such as anatomy and civil engineering. Often a domain has more than one "standard" ontology for the same general concepts. For example, the foundational model of anatomy (FMA) [Rosse et al., 1998] is designed to model anatomy in great detail, whereas the Galen Common Reference Model [Rector et al., 1994] is designed to model anatomy for clinical applications. Because these two ontologies serve different communities, they have different concepts even though the domain is roughly the same. Merging the two ontologies would allow users to understand how all the concepts are related.

All of these applications have the same problem: given the two or more structured representations of data – which we often refer to as *models* [Bernstein et al., 2000] – combine the models to form one unified representation. These applications may also seek to create the mappings between the unified version and the input smaller schemas/ontologies. Many different works have looked at these different problems, both alone and in consort. This paper surveys some of the works in this area. In particular, Sect. 2 begins by describing a number of theoretical works that are relevant for multiple merging situations. Section 3 looks at works on view integration. Section 4 looks at work on data integration. Section 5 looks at work on merging ontologies. Section 6 looks at generic approaches for merging structured data representations. Section 7 surveys work on a variation of the problem: the data to be merged has been modified from a common ancestor and now the changes must be incorporated together. This variation is common both in file systems and in computer supportive collaborative work. Section 8 discusses commonalities and differences. Finally, Sect. 9 concludes.

Throughout this paper, we assume that the relationships between the schemas have already been created; this is beyond the scope of the paper. Interested readers in creating mappings are referred to existing surveys [Rahm and Bernstein, 2001, Doan and Halevy, 2004].

2 Theoretical Underpinnings

2.1 Information Capacity

The key notion of information capacity [Hull, 1984] is that when comparing two schemas E and G, one can consider how much of the data in E can be accessed using G and vice versa.

Miller et al. [1993] study which properties of information capacity are required for both data integration and view integration. The key to understanding the requirements is the definitions of equivalence and dominance:

To be information capacity preserving, a mapping I(S1) → I(S2) must be defined on every element in S1 and functional in both directions. If so, then S2 *dominates*

S1, denoted S1 $\leq$ S2. If S1 $\leq$ S2 and S2 $\leq$ S1, then S1 and S2 are equivalent, denoted S2 $\equiv$ S1, and I is an *equivalence preserving mapping*. Informally, this means that if S1 dominates S2, then it is possible to retrieve all the information from S2 by accessing S1; if the two are equivalent, one can get all the information from S2 by querying S1 and one can get all the information from S1 by querying S2.

Miller et al. show that in data integration, querying the source schemas from the integrated views requires that the integrated schema dominates the union of local schemas. In view integration, querying the integrated schema through the user views requires that the union of user views dominates the integrated schema. This notion of completeness in creating a merged or mediated schema is common, not just for information capacity but in other generic merging algorithms such as the specification by Buneman et al. [1992].

Ontology merging algorithms often use notions of completeness as well. However, ontology merging algorithms do not use information capacity as a basis for comparison since ontologies often lack data. Instead, they check to ensure that all concepts from the input ontologies appear in the merged ontology.

2.2   Instance-Level Constraints and Schema Merging

One natural question when examining work on merging schemas is how to deal with instance-level constraints such as key constraints and foreign keys. Unfortunately, as shown in Convent [1986] merging schemas is undecidable as soon as instance-level constraints are considered, even with a very simple representation of schemas. While Convent [1986] specifically considers relational view integration where the integrity constraints are keys and foreign keys, it generalizes to other schema merging areas as well.

Convent [1986] concentrates primarily on what it means to have incompatible constraints. Informally, this means that if users are trying to integrate views, then for each user's view, it should be possible to access those instances from the global schema – note that this is very similar to the information capacity requirement laid out in Sect. 2.1 by Miller et al. [1993]. Unfortunately, Convent [1986] shows that having incompatible constraints is undecidable even in this very basic case. Because of this early undecidability result, schema merging works typically do not consider instance-level constraints.

3   View Integration

As mentioned in Sect. 1, view integration is the problem of integrating the views/ requirements that different users have of a schema, and then creating one global schema. Typically, this global schema is one in which the data is actually stored. Some systems may also allow the existing user views to persist, and then mappings may be created from the user views to the global schema where the data is stored. This problem has been studied for quite some time, and is the subject of an early survey [Batini et al., 1986]. Batini et al. [1986] categorizes view integration work as taking one or more of the following steps:

Preintegration: Deciding which schemas to be integrated, in which order the integration should occur, and various preferences (e.g., if one of the schemas is "preferred" over the other).

Comparison of the schemas: Determining the correspondences and detecting the possible conflicts. In this context, a conflict is when a concept is represented differently in the input schemas. For example, a simple conflict might be that there is an attribute "Last Name" in one schema that is represented by an attribute "LName" in another schema.

Conforming the schemas: resolving the conflicts between the schemas; the authors note that automatic resolution is not typically possible in schema conformation.

Merging and restructuring: Now that the schemas are ready to be superimposed, how should they be combined? Batini et al. [1986] offers the following qualitative criteria to decide on the "correctness" of the merged schema:

- Completeness and correctness
- Minimality
- Understandability

These criteria are seen again and again in a number of different guises throughout the schema merging literature. As far as schema merging is concerned, this categorization is the main contribution of Batini, Lenzerini, and Navathe's paper; the bulk of the remainder is concentrated on matching. Again, matching (i.e., determining what concepts in one schema are related to the concepts in another schema) is outside the scope of this paper and is surveyed in existing surveys (e.g., Rahm and Bernstein 2001, Doan and Halevy 2004, Rahm 2011) (see also Chap. 2). Our work focuses on the "merging and restructuring."

The view integration problem was subsequently studied in many areas, including ER diagrams [Song et al., 1996, Lee and Ling, 2003], XML [Beeri and Milo, 1999, Tufte and Maier, 2001, Yang et al., 2003], semi-structured data [Bergamaschi et al., 1999], relational and object-oriented databases [Larson et al., 1989, Shu et al., 1975, Biskup and Convent, 1986, Navathe and Gadgil, 1982, Shoval and Zohn, 1991], and others. The remainder of this section details a few of the schema merging algorithms in the context of view integration.

3.1 Biskup and Convent

Biskup and Convent [1986] define a formal language for view integration and then proceed to integrate based on that language. This fairly early work provides a list of details need to be provided to create a view integration system:

- The data model.
- A language specifying the constraints of how the schemas are related. In this case, the authors use a variation on relational algebra. The precise constraints that are considered are described below.
- A formalization of conflicts. As in Batini, Lenzerini, and Navathe's work, a conflict is when a concept is represented differently in the input schemas (e.g., two corresponding attributes being called "Last Name" and "Lname").
- Some explanation of when the global schema will provide all the information that the users require (i.e., is it complete).
- A formal definition based on the concepts above.

After taking these items as input, the authors produce a global schema that meets those requirements, along with mappings that relate the global schema to the source schemas. The mappings between the views and the global schema are essentially the same as the language used to represent the constraints between the views for most of the constraints given. However, while the algorithm details what the global schema should be, and an example shows what the view to global schema mapping would look like, there is no algorithm given for creating the view to global schema mapping.

A key facet of their approach is that their constraints can only exist between single relationships. They also assume that each attribute can be related to a single other attribute. The set of constraints that they consider is entirely instancebased. These three restrictions combine to result in a fairly straightforward merge. Despite these limitations, the paper is a large step forward, largely to the overall framework. Informally, the constraints that they consider are:

- Identity constraints – the key of one relation is the same as the key of another relation, and their instances are the same.
- Selection constraints – the key of one relation is the same as the key of another relation. The instances of the key of one relation can be expressed as a selection of the instances of the key on the other relation.
- Disjoint constraints – the key of one relation is the same as the key of another relation. The instances of the keys are disjoint.
- Containment constraint – the key of one relation is the same as the key of another relation. The instance of one key is a subset of the instances of another relation. This relationship is like the selection constraint, but not easily quantifiable.

Unsurprisingly, given that one of the authors is also an author of the work on the undecidability of constraints in Sect. 2.2, they do not consider the case of conflicting constraints.

The desired result is a global schema, G, that fits two criteria, both based on Atzeni et al. [1982] notion of "weakly included." In particular, it must be that:

- G can be queried using only relational algebra and exactly the same view definitions will be retrieved.
- G is minimal – nothing that exists outside of the initial views is stored in G.

The first of these is similar to Hull's notion of maintaining information capacity [Hull, 1984]; the second is one of the requirements in Batini et al. [1986].

Based on these requirements, the outcome of the merge is a set of relations, where each of the relations of the first three types of constraints (i.e., all but containment constraints) mean that the relations are combined, with all of their attributes present in the global schema. For containment constraints, the two relations are left separate, since there can be no way of determining what relational algebra operator to use.

3.2 Casanova and Vidal

Casanova and Vidal [1983] describe a method for performing view integration. In particular, they break the problem into two parts: combination and optimization.

The combination phase consists of gathering all of the views, as well as determining the dependencies between schemas. The optimization phase concentrates on both minimizing the schema and reducing redundancy. They concentrate on the optimization phase, which is akin to the problem considered in semantic merge.

The kinds of dependencies that they consider are, as in Biskup and Convent [1986], instance based. They consider the following dependency types:

- Functional dependencies
- An inclusion dependency says that one relation contains a subset of the tuples in another
- An exclusion dependency says that the instances of a relation are disjoint.
- A union functional dependency essentially allows functional dependencies to be declared valid across different schemas

The authors show that in general trying to optimize an integration with the above dependencies is intractable, so they concentrate on a limited subset of schemas. Essentially, these restrictions limit where the different kinds of dependencies can be applied, as well as assuming that the schemas are already in Boyce Codd Normal Form (BCNF).

Their goal is to create an optimization that is minimal in size, and also removes redundancy. They also want to ensure that any consistent state of the initial schema can be mapped into a consistent state of the transformed schema and vice versa – a notion very similar to the idea of completeness. To achieve these goals, their transformation removes many inclusion dependencies or union functional dependencies (since they may be a source of redundancy), as well as vacuous exclusion dependencies.

They provide an algorithm that will perform the optimization for the limited cases. Note that their algorithm creates the unified schema, but does not create the mapping from the unified schema to the initial views.

There are a number of other schema merging works in the view integration domain around this period, including Shoval and Zohn [1991] and Navathe and Gadgil [1982]. Generally, these works build on approximately the same foundation: define what it means to merge and what it means for there to be a conflict. Most of these works assume that conflict resolution will be fully automatic. Additionally, most of these works assume that there is no *structural* conflict (e.g., that a merged column should belong to two different tables). This kind of more complex conflict resolution is explored more fully in the next section.

3.3 Spaccapietra and Parent

Spaccapietra and Parent [1994] work in the context of ERC+ [Spaccapietra et al., 1992], which extends an early version of entity relationship diagrams [Chen, 1976]. In ERC+, there are three basic types of objects: attributes, entities, and relationships. While there are differences between ERC+ and Chen's original ER diagram, for the purposes of this paper, the primary difference is that ERC+ allows complex attributes (i.e., attributes can have subattributes) (Fig. 8.1).

Spaccapietra and Parent assume that the matching or aligning work has already been completed by the database administrator or some view integration tool. Their method for merging the data once these mappings (based on Superviews [Motro, 1987]) have been created is fully automatic. However, this is at least partially possible because the authors do not consider constraints or ordering of any type, thus avoiding the undecidability result of Sect. 2.2.

Spaccapietra and Parent [1994] concentrates on rules for view integration, and the merging algorithm that uses them. They have two overriding principles: (1) integration rules should apply to both objects and the links between them, and (2) if there is a choice to be made, they choose the least restrictive option. According to these principles, they have created 6 integration rules that can be combined for their merging algorithm. The rules, as named by Spaccapietra and Parent, are:

1. *Elements integration rule:* For any two matching elements that are not of the same type, the resulting element is an entity type. If the two matching types are

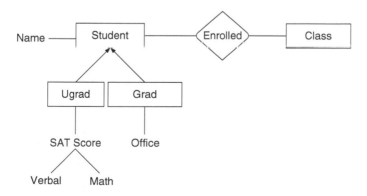

Fig. 8.1 An example ERC+ diagram. The entities are represented by *rectangles*, the relationships are represented by *diamonds*, and attributes are represented by plain text

not attributes and are of the same type, then the resulting element is of the original type.

2. *Links integration rule:* For any pair of elements that are matched to each other, if the elements are of the same type, then the links between them are of the same type.

3. *Paths integration rule:* If there is a direct path between two nonattribute elements in one model and an equivalent indirect path in the other model, choose the indirect path. The reason for this is that the indirect path contains more information, and the direct path can always be inferred from the indirect path.

4. *Integration of attributes of corresponding elements:* For elements that are already integrated, if each attribute pair in the original diagrams match, add the attributes to the resulting schema.

5. *Attributes with path integration rule:* If there is a direct path between an element and an attribute in one model and an indirect path between the corresponding pair in the other model, choose the indirect path.

6. *Add rule for elements and links without correspondent:* Add all elements that exist in one model and not in the other.

At a high level, their algorithm first merges the nonattribute elements, then merges the paths, and finally merges the attributes. The full algorithm is described in Spaccapietra and Parent [1994].

This work is notable because it marks a departure of focus from the existing literature: it concentrates on the fact that type information may conflict (rules 1 and 2) as well as the fact that some relationships that exist *explicitly* in the input schemas can be represented *implicitly* in the resulting schema (rules 3 and 5). This use of implicit relationships is featured prominently in later work, particularly in generic schema merging (Sect. 6). It is probably not a coincidence that this work, like the generic work, is not based in the relational model: the more direct representation of relationships between schema elements allows the authors to deal with complex relationships without running into the undecidability result in Convent [1986].

3.4 Rosenthal and Reiner

A contemporary work with Spaccapietra and Parent [1994] is The Database Design and Evaluation Workbench [Rosenthal and Reiner, 1994]. The workbench allows users to manipulate schemas, including combining multiple views into one schema. Their ER-based system largely focuses on "rearrangements," which transform the input but leave the content "equivalent" to the input. The primary transformations that they considered were:

- Duplicating the attributes of an entity to propagate to related entities, or alternately removing duplication if necessary.
- Simplifying relationships by decomposing them into two simpler relationships.

- Inferring constraints from existing constraints, or alternately removing duplicate constraints.
- Creating keys.

The definition of equivalent, while different in a few details, is very similar to the notion of information capacity in Sect. 2.1. One scenario that they tackle is that of view integration. The authors state that their goals are much more pragmatic than some of the existing work; as previously discussed [Batini et al., 1986, Biskup and Convent, 1986, Casanova and Vidal, 1983], take a more theoretical approach. As such, Rosenthal and Reiner concentrate on a usable tool: they only detect homonyms and synonyms, and such conflicts are presented to the user for resolution. They then perform a duplicate removing union between the two schemas. No mappings are created between the schemas.

These works represent the type of focus on schema merging present in the more recent view integration literature. After this point, more of the database research in schema merging came from data integration (Sect. 4) and generic schema management (Sect. 6).

4 Data Integration

As motivated in the introduction, in data integration, there exists a set of heterogeneous, independent sources that contain related data. To have these sources be queried efficiently, a mediated schema can be created. Because these sources are independent, heterogeneous, and often change rapidly, it is not possible to then import all of the data into the mediated schema. Instead, the users query the mediated schema, and then the system translates the queries over the mediated schema into queries over the sources.

While much of the time this mediated schema is created manually, there exist a number of works that discuss creating the mediated schema based on the sources.

4.1 Data Warehousing

DWQ is a system for creating a data warehouse from the sources [Calvanese et al., 1999]. Calvanese et al. [2001] focuses on the data integration aspects of DWQ. This paper describes their system on how to use data integration in data warehousing. One issue with building a data warehouse is that it often has to be highly tuned for the specific queries; e.g., one might want to have a star schema (i.e., a base "fact" table from which various dimensions measuring things such as time and location radiate) for the data warehouse instead of whatever format just happens to be the merged result of the sources.

Their solution is to create a conceptual model, which "corresponds roughly to the notion of integrated conceptual schema in the traditional approaches to schema integration."

They consider that both the data warehouse and the source schema are views over the conceptual schema (i.e., local-as-view (LAV) [Vijayaraman et al., 1996]). As mappings they use "adorned queries," where the adornment is an annotation on the variables in the query; these are referred to as Reconciliation Correspondences. In particular, they consider three types of Reconciliation Correspondences: Conversion, Matching, and Merging Correspondences. Conversion Correspondences make data level transformations between the same real world objects. For example, one might use a Conversion Correspondence to translate between income defined monthly and income defined yearly. Matching Correspondences specify the matching. The Merging Correspondences show how to merge the data based on the existing Conversion and Matching Correspondences; they consist largely of calls to the Conversion and Matching Correspondences.

4.2   Pottinger and Bernstein

The authors of Pottinger and Bernstein [2008] take as input a pair of relational source schemas and a mapping between them, and then create a relational mediated schema and the mappings from the mediated schema to the source. They also show how this can be extended to a larger set of schemas. The mappings that they expect between the sources is a set of conjunctive mappings similar to the ones in Madhavan and Halevy [2003] – i.e., a set of select-project-join queries.

For example, assume that there are two travel websites: TravelOn and GoTravel. Assume that TravelOn has the relations TravelOnGuide(Name, ID) and TravelOn-Bio(ID, Bio) for tour guides and their bios, respectively. GoTravel may, in contrast, have the single relation GoTravel-Guide(Name, Bio) to represent both those concepts. One possible mapping between these sources is the following:

Guide(Name, Bio) :- TravelOn-Guide(Name, ID), TravelOn-Bio(ID, Bio)
Guide(Name, Bio) :- GoTravel-Guide(Name, Bio).

This mapping holds the standard Datalog semantics: Guides can be found either by taking the join of TravelOn-Guide and TravelOn-Bio on ID, or by looking at GoTravel-Guide. Hence, it shows that the two concepts are mapped to each other since instances of the same concept can be found by either conjunctive query. The question is: what should be in the mediated schema?

Informally, Pottinger and Bernstein [2008] requires completeness, accessibility to both all of the input relation (i.e., it preserves information capacity (see Sect. 2.1)), makes the concepts that are mentioned in the mappings accessible, does not combine relations unless they are related by the mappings, and finally is minimal.

In the case of our guide relation, this means that the mediated schema should contain the relation Guide(Name, ID, Bio). Additionally, there also needs to be mappings between the source schemas and the mediated schema. This is done through two sets of views. First, a set of views define an intermediate schema in terms of the mediated schema. These are called LAV views after the data integration architecture, where local sources are defined as views over the mediated schema [Vijayaraman et al., 1996]. Continuing with our travel example, the LAV views are:

I-TravelOn-Guide(Name, ID, Bio) :- Guide(Name, ID, Bio)
I-GoTravel-Guide(Name, Bio):- Guide(Name, ID, Bio).

A separate set of views defines the intermediate schema in terms of the sources. These are called global-as-view (or GAV) mappings after the data integration architecture, where the global sources are defined as views over the mediated schema (see [Lenzerini, 2002] for a discussion of GAV as well as how it relates to LAV). Our final set of views for our travel example is thus the GAV views:

I-TravelOnGuide(Name, ID, Bio):- TravelOn-Guide(Name, ID),
                              TravelOn-Bio(ID, Bio)
I-GoTravel-Guide(Name, Bio) :- GoTravel-Guide(Name, Bio).

An interesting result of this paper is that the mappings that are created between the mediated schema and the sources are a very limited form of global-local-as-view (GLAV) mappings [Friedman et al., 1999] (i.e., mappings where either the local or the global schema can be defined as the head of a view); in particular, the LAV views each only have one subgoal in them. This is important because the LAV views require using answering queries using views (see [Halevy, 2001] for a survey), and having only one subgoal in the LAV view means that answering queries is very fast. This is particularly of note since the local sources will be related to each other in this fashion – regardless of how the mediated schema is created – so this result shows what we should expect even if the mediated schema is created in some other fashion.

4.3 BAV

Both-as-view (BAV) [Pidduck et al., 2002, McBrien and Poulovassilis, 2003] is a framework to support schema transformation and integration. Similar to GLAV mappings [Friedman et al., 1999], BAV allows the definition of views between the mediated schema and the local sources in both direction – it treats both the global and the local schemas as sources. A key focus of their work is the transformations that make this possible – how can the mediated schema be related to the source schemas. They additionally provide a method to update a mediated schema based on the integration of new source schemas. To do so, they create a mapping that directly calls for the addition, deletion, and renaming of attributes and relations in the mediated schema.

5 Ontology Merging

An ontology specifies a domain-specific vocabulary of objects and a set of relationships between the objects in the vocabulary [Fikes, 1996] (see also Chap. 2).
In general, an ontology can be viewed as a graph of hierarchical objects that have
specific attributes and constraints on those attributes and objects. The hierarchies
in an ontology can be more than simple is-a generalizations and specializations –
ontologies can also have notions of "containment" or "type of" or "part of." For the
purposes of this paper, the different kinds of relationships do not matter; the fact
that there are different kinds of relationships is the only part that is relevant. The
objects in an ontology may have various structures; for the purpose of this paper, we
can think of them as either being classes with various attributes or instances. While
constraints may exist on attributes, classes, or instances, in general these constraints
are not treated in the ontology merging literature.

Two sample ontologies are shown in Fig. 8.2. The classes are shown as ovals. The
attributes are represented by text. A solid line represents inheritance. A dashed line
indicates that an attribute is a member of that class. An example constraint might
state that "SAT score" is at most 1,600.

5.1 SMART and Prompt

One representative work on merging ontologies began with an algorithm called
SMART [Noy and Musen, 1999a,b] and was later renamed Prompt [Noy and Musen,
2000].

SMART tackles the problems of both merging and aligning ontologies. *Alignment* is the problem of taking two related ontologies and establishing links between
them to indicate where they match (much as in the database literature). *Merging* is

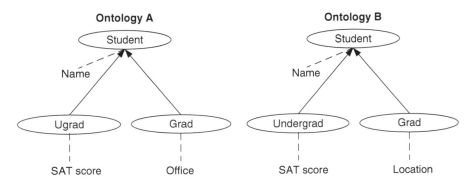

Fig. 8.2 Two sample ontologies. The classes are shown as *ovals*. The attributes are represented by
text. A *solid line* represents inheritance. A *dashed line* represents that an attribute is a member of
that class

the problem of taking two ontologies and combining them to form a third ontology. So, for example, alignment of the ontologies in Fig. 8.2 might tell us that element pairs with the same name are aligned with each other, that "Ugrad" matches with "Undergrad," and that "Office" matches with "Location." Merging the two ontologies would result in a single ontology with the same structure as both ontologies A and B since the two are structurally identical, but there would be some resolution of the naming differences (e.g., a decision would have to be made as to what to call the node that describes undergraduates).

SMART is used for both merging and alignment. The algorithm is not completely automatic for either operation; there are stages that must be performed by the user, even after the initial setup has occurred.

SMART keeps track of its state with two data structures: the *Conflicts list* and the *ToDo list*. The Conflicts list details the inconsistencies in the current state of the process that must be resolved before the resulting ontology can be in a "logically consistent state." The ToDo list keeps track of operations which should be done but are not required in order for the resulting ontology to be in a logically consistent state (e.g., if an action results in two attributes in the same classes with a similar name, SMART might add to the ToDo list a suggestion that one of them be removed). Since determining the source of a problem may enable the user to optimize the problem's resolution, each item in the ToDo and Conflicts list contains a reference back to the operation that triggered it. More details of SMART and Prompt, particularly on the matching and alignment aspects, can be found in Falconer and Noy [2011].

An outline of the SMART algorithm for merging is shown below. Note that the merging process requires also performing an alignment, so steps for both appear in the algorithm:

1. The user performs setup by loading the ontologies, A and B and specifying some options such as specifying if there is a preferred ontology. The result, the ontology C, is initialized to be a new ontology with a new root and A and B as that root's children.
2. SMART generates an initial list of suggestions of what should be aligned/merged. In this stage, SMART relies largely on content or syntactic information. The names of the objects are examined, but structural information (i.e., the position of the classes or their participation in specific relations) is not used.

   - For each pair of classes $a \in A$ and $b \in B$ with identical names SMART either merges the a and b in C or removes either a or b from C.
   - For each pair of classes $a \in A$ and $b \in B$ with linguistically similar names a link is created between them in C. This means that both a and b are still in C, but SMART suggests that they may need to be merged by adding them to the ToDo list.

3. The user selects and performs an operation such as merging a class or resolving an item on the ToDo or Conflict lists.
4. SMART performs any automatic updates that it can and create new suggestions. It has the ability to:

a. Execute any changes automatically determined as necessary by SMART.
b. Add any conflicts caused by the user's actions in step 3 to the Conflicts list.
c. Add to the ToDo list any other suggested operations or make new suggestions based on linguistic or structural similarity.

5. Steps 3 and 4 are repeated until the ontologies are completely merged or aligned.

5.2 Chimæra

The Ontolingua Server [Farquhar et al., 1996] is designed to make all parts of dealing with ontologies easier; they have a large collection of tools to allow users to create, view, manipulate, publish, and share ontologies. One of the tools is Chimæra[McGuinness et al., 2000], an environment for merging and testing ontologies.

Their system, like SMART, is designed to help users merge their ontologies. The difference is that where SMART concentrates on actually merging ontologies (e.g., automatically merging two classes with the same name), and Chimæra only points out the areas where merging is likely to be required. Their goal was to build a tool that "focuses the attention of the editor on particular portions of the ontology that are semantically interconnected and in need of repair or further merging." [McGuinness et al., 2000]

The authors identify a number of key features that a merging tool must support [McGuinness et al., 2000]. They propose that a merging tool have support for:

- Searching for names across multiple ontologies,
- Renaming in a systematic fashion,
- Merging multiple terms into a single term,
- Focusing the user's attention on term merging based on term names,
- Browsing classes and attributes,
- Modifying subsumption relationships in classes and attributes, and
- Recognizing logical inconsistencies introduced by merges and edits.

5.3 FCA Merge

FCA Merge [Nebel, 2001] from Stumme and Maedche merges ontologies based on a lattice approach; they perform a match (in database terms) or an alignment (ontology terms) automatically. The lattice describes both the structure of the merged document and which elements in the ontology match according to the classes' semantic content. The created lattice may contain both nodes that are labeled with more than one class (indicating that merging may be required) and nodes with no corresponding class in the original ontology (suggesting that the user may want to insert a new class). Interestingly, the lattices are found automatically [Bouzeghoub et al., 2000], but the merging is largely manual. To determine how to merge a node in the lattice, they distinguish four cases:

- *There is one class at the node:* In this case, the answer is found automatically; there are no conflicts and the class at that node is added to the resulting merged ontology.
- *There are two or more classes at the node:* In this case, the user is asked what should be done.
- *There are no classes at a nonroot node:* Here, the user must decide whether to add a class or not.
- *There are no classes at a root node:* In this final case, the user must decide whether to add a new top level class to the resulting ontology.

As seen from the description, FCA Merge makes no attempt to resolve any conflicts.

5.4   Ontology Merging Analysis

Each of the three systems, SMART, Chimæra, and FCA Merge, takes a very different approach to merging ontologies. Unlike database research (i.e., view integration and data integration), all three systems view the problem of merge to intrinsically require user intervention. SMART takes the most automatic approach of the three by merging some concepts from different ontologies without requiring any user intervention, but even this is limited: the user still must guide the system whenever the names of the classes that match are too different. Even if the names are linguistically similar, there is little that SMART can do automatically other than point the user at any potential conflicts unless the choice is clear from the preferred ontology. Chimæra provides very little automatic support; it focuses the user's attention on possibly related classes but has no conflict resolution support. FCA Merge provides amazing support for automatically matching the classes in the ontologies including doing some very sophisticated linguistic checks, but provides very little support for automatically merging classes in the ontology if any sort of conflict exists.

Together, these solutions define an overall compendium of interesting and useful features for ontology merging. SMART provides the notion of a preferred ontology that can help the system to work automatically. They also suggest the process of maintaining a list for the user of both where the user *must* perform an action and where the user *should* perform an action with the Conflict and ToDo lists. The Chimæra system offers good guidelines on what interactions must be available to merge ontologies. Finally, FCA Merge introduces the notion of additional nodes that are not present in either original ontology but may make the structure of the resulting ontology more sensible.

6 Generic Schema Merging

6.1 Buneman, Davidson, and Kosky

Buneman et al. [1992] delve into some of the theory of schema merging. In particular, they start once again with the assumption that elements are matched by name – i.e., they have avoided the matching problem entirely. The goal is to think of this from a lattice perspective (much like the one later used by FCA Merge) and describe two different theoretical perspectives: either the least upper bound (i.e., take everything that is available in either schema, which is rather like taking the union) or the greatest lower bound (i.e., take everything that is available in both schemas, which is rather like taking the intersection).

They, like most works here, focus on the least upper bound. Once having decided that the least upper bound is the correct semantics, the question is what kind of conflicts should be resolved. They use a very basic meta-model to allow them to concentrate on some very fundamental conflicts. In particular, their meta-model allows for elements which have only names as attributes. Their meta-model allows for two types of edges: is-a and has-a. They represent the fact that an element r Has-a element x of type y by an arrow from r to y with the label x. They do not consider constraints on the instances. Given these limited types of edges, they can focus on what would happen if two elements are combined resulting in the merged element having two types. For example, Fig. 8.3a says that element R has a Q of type P and S. Naturally, this does not make sense. Hence, their solution is to say that there should be a new type, and that both of the original types inherit from this type, as shown in Fig. 8.3b.

This kind of work shows the fundamental issues that have to be explored to merge schemas regardless of application or data model.

6.2 Model Management

Pottinger and Bernstein [2003] and Rondo [Melnik et al., 2003] both describe merge operators for Model Management [Bernstein et al., 2000]. The goal of Model

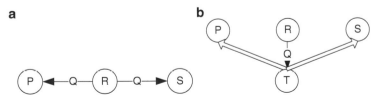

Fig. 8.3 Buneman et al. [1992] show that one conflict that occurs during the merging of schemas is that if there are two elements in the resulting merge that have different types (**a**), then a new type can be created which inherits from both original types (**b**)

Management is to allow structured representations of data – referred to as *models* – to be manipulated in bulk by using a set of generic and reusable operators. Because these works concentrate on the schema level rather than the data level, they do not consider instance level constraints.

Rondo [Melnik et al., 2003] is a Model Management system prototype. As such, it fully explores all Model Management operators (e.g., Merge, Match, Compose, Diff) and includes a Merge definition based entirely on equality mappings. Two elements can be declared to be equal, and each 1–1 mapping relationship can specify a preference for one element over another. Like Buneman et al. [1992], Rondo essentially creates the duplicate-free union of the elements and relationships involved. As with the view integration work in Sect. 3, both works consider schema-level conflicts, where elements in one schema are represented differently from elements in another schema (e.g., "Last Name" and "Lname"). Some conflicts require removing elements or relationships from the merged model (e.g., if an SQL column belongs to two tables in a merge result, it must be deleted from one of them). As in Pottinger and Bernstein [2003], Rondo's Merge resolves such meta-model conflicts later in a separate operator.

Pottinger and Bernstein [2003] concentrates on fully describing a Merge operator for Model Management. One if its contributions is defining three types of conflicts that have to be resolved in combining two schemas:

- *Representation conflicts:* Representation conflicts occur when there are two representations of the same real world concept. For example, the elements representing the concept of "name" may have different names. This corresponds to "comparison of the schemas" in Batini et al. [1986], and is resolved outside of Merge (since it may occur in other operators as well).
- *Meta-model conflicts:* Meta-model conflicts occur when the resulting Merge violates the constraints of a specific model, but not the constraints mandatory for *all* models. This is just like how in Rondo [Melnik et al., 2003] an SQL column can belong to only one table: there is nothing inherent in having structured data that says that a child must belong to only one parent. Similarly to Rondo, these conflicts must be resolved elsewhere.
- *Fundamental conflicts:* Fundamental conflicts are conflicts that occur during a Merge and must be resolved for the resulting model to be valid in *any* model. This notion of what must be true for any model is called the "meta-meta model" – for example, a relational schema is a model, the relational model is the meta-model, and the meta-meta model restricts what must be true in any meta-model.

Unlike many existing works, the Merge in Pottinger and Bernstein [2003] (hereafter Vanilla Merge after its meta-meta model, which is named Vanilla) allows complex mappings between elements in the model and many different types of relationships between elements; in particular, the mapping is also a first-class model. The mapping resolves conflicts by first taking values from the mapping, then from the (optional) preferred model, then from any model. For example, Fig. 8.4 shows two models (Model A and Model B) and a mapping (Map_{AB}) between them. This example extends an example in Pottinger and Bernstein [2003]. Figure 8.5 shows the

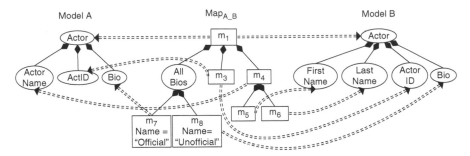

Fig. 8.4 An example mapping for the merge in Pottinger and Bernstein [2003]

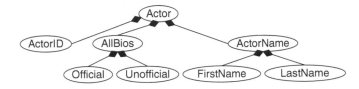

Fig. 8.5 The result of performing the merge in Pottinger and Bernstein [2003] on the models and mappings in Fig. 8.4

result of performing the merge in Fig. 8.4. The diamond-headed intra-model edges indicate a containment relationship. The double arrowed inter-model relationships indicate equality between elements. Looking carefully at Map$_{AB}$ reveals that there is an element **All Bios**, which is not mapped to by any element, but contains the Bios from models **A** and **B**, both of which have been renamed.

This complex mapping allows users to generically yet accurately represent the way that the elements are related to each other. As with other mappings, creating this style of mapping is beyond the scope of this paper; [Wang and Pottinger, 2008] studies how to create these mappings.

Vanilla Merge defines what the output should be based on the principles laid out in many other papers referenced here, including the least upper bound notion from Buneman et al. [1992].

While Vanilla Merge defines that there may be other fundamental conflicts, the fundamental conflicts in the Vanilla meta-meta conflict are the one type conflict (an adjustment of the conflict discussed in Buneman et al. [1992] for the Vanilla meta-meta-model) and acyclicity.

6.3 Providing Choices to Users

Chiticariu et al. [2008] concentrate more on how the *user* interacts with the system. In particular, the authors assume that they are trying to merge a set of schemas. They model these schemas as graphs containing elements related by has-a relationships.

Like the model management work, they assume that they are given a set of input mappings that relate the two schemas. Unlike previous work on graph-based models, such as the ontology merging work in Sect. 5, the authors assume that if two elements are marked as being a match, that this is a *possible* place that they should be merged in the result. The goal of their system is to help users understand the space of possibilities that arise when a pair of elements are combined – what is the impact on the rest of the schema?

Radwan et al. [2009] build upon Chiticariu et al. [2008] by helping to automate the process of choosing how the schemas should be merged and presenting this result to the user. They use some of the schema matcher's internal information to help chose which possible elements to merge. A key feature of their system is that like Pottinger and Bernstein [2003] they create more complex edges than simple equalities. In particular, if two concepts are deemed similar, then they are either (1) merged, or (2) related through a "has" edge – they make this choice if the similarity between two elements is quite high in one direction but low in the other.

Both works provide a valuable complement to the more theory-based papers that make up the bulk of the papers cited here, and also dovetail nicely with some of the work on user preference in ontology merging systems, e.g., SMART (see Sect. 5.1).

7 Three-Way Merge

A final version of the merge problem is when the user is trying to merge two objects that are derivatives of a common ancestor. This problem occurs in both computer supported collaborative work (CSCW) [Munson and Dewan, 1994, Berlage and Genau, 1993, Berger et al., 1998] and file merging [Balasubramaniam and Pierce, 1998]. In these contexts, there is a common ancestor and the two later models must be merged together based on the relationship between them and their common ancestor. With the added information from the common ancestor, the initial matching is much simpler, but the merging can be much more difficult.

For example, if there is a change that occurs only in one model, then the system will probably want to give preference to the changed model. This would seem to make the problem easier, but there are likely to be other constraints (e.g., the other model is preferred because it was modeled by an expert), which actually make the problem more difficult. Another example of this is that if both models diverge from the original, then it may be impossible to guess what the user wants. The presence of this information means that there are additional semantic constraints that must be satisfied, but the incompleteness of the information and the possibility of contradicting other information means that these additional constraints must be satisfied with no guarantee of a clear resolution to any of the constraints.

The work in this area that is the most flexible and automatic is that by Munson and Dewan [Munson and Dewan, 1994]. They propose a system that, depending on the parameters that are specified, can be either manual, semiautomatic, or fully automatic. Users who choose a more automatic system are likely to receive a merged result that does not correspond to exactly what they want, but they will not have to manually guide the system. The model that they look at, while applicable to files, considers the general case of objects by encapsulating the differences in the object types as described below.

They investigate two different types of merges, *consolidation merges* and *reconciliation merges*. In a consolidation merge, the assumption is that the changes made in both models should be integrated; most changes will not conflict with one another too much, and that changes from both models should be incorporated into their system. In a reconciliation merge, the assumption is that the merge is being performed to resolve conflicts. The two different types of merges call for very different outcomes.

Their system operates using a number of merge matrices. A merge matrix for two models to be merged, say A and B, has the rows represent edits made to achieve model A and the columns represent the edits needed to achieve model B. The matrix entries dictate how to merge the result of each (row, column) pair of edits. For example, a merge matrix for an object that is a sequence of elements may look like the one below (from Munson and Dewan 1994):

Sequence	Insert element	Delete element	Change element	No change
Insert element	Both			Row
Delete element		Row	User	Row
Change element		User	Merge edits	Row
No change	Column	Column	Column	

The blank entries represent situations that are either impossible (e.g., deleting an entry in one model and adding it in another) or where no change is required (e.g., if the element stays the same in both models). The entries that specify "row" mean that the version of the element from the model represented in the row should be taken, and similarly "column" indicates that the column's version should be taken. So, for example, if a sequence were unchanged in model A and deleted in model B, the action would be dictated by the entry at (no change, delete element), which, in this case is to delete the sequence since that is the action performed in model B, the one represented by the column.

The specification of these elements in the merge matrix is what allows for the algorithm to move on the scale from manual to automatic merging; if there are no entries that require manual intervention, then the algorithm is fully automatic.

In addition to the algorithm, they also list the characteristics that a merge tool should have. They state that a merge tool should support:

- Automatic merging,
- Interactive merging,
- Merging of both text files and more structured objects,
- Use of the semantics of the objects to drive the merging (rather than just a requirement that all objects merge in the same way), and
- Specification of preferred policies by the user.

8 Discussion

These diverse areas differ greatly in terms of goal, context, data model and more, but there are a number of similarities. We now discuss some of the similarities and differences across these different research areas. Because evaluating the quality of automatic merging algorithms is an open problem, we do not compare the approaches based on quality.

8.1 Separation of Match and Merge

Ontology merging, view integration, and CSCW all separate matching and merging. Ontology merging calls the difference alignment and merging [Noy and Musen, 2000], but despite defining them as separate problems, the techniques that they use still force the system to perform both actions at the same time. The work on view integration also requires a matching step to occur before the merging process can begin. However, as it processes the matched elements, it may discover more matches that can be made to help with the merging process [Spaccapietra and Parent, 1994]. CSCW and Model Management make a complete separation between matching and merging. A question is thus how much less efficient does it become to completely divorce the merging from the matching. In some cases, interleaving the matching with the merging (e.g., as in view integration) can cut down on the initial matching that needs to be done. However, there has been substantial work on schema matching as an independent problem (see [Rahm and Bernstein, 2001, Doan and Halevy, 2004] for some surveys). This increases the likelihood that future works on merging schemas will use the results of these matching algorithms as input and thus schema merging and matching will become more, rather than less, distinct over time.

The work in Radwan et al. [2009] represents a pull in the other direction, as it exploits information about the potential matches to suggest merge results. It would be interesting to see how the work in Radwan et al. [2009] can extend the work of various schema matchers.

8.2 Treating Models Asymmetrically

One idea that occurs repeatedly in all of these works is that the models are treated asymmetrically, allowing for the algorithms to function more automatically in the presence of conflicting choices. This may be because one model is more general or stable than the other and thus assumed to be the "preferred" model [Noy and Musen, 1999a]. This allows merging operations to proceed much more automatically by giving it a clear indicator which element to prefer in the case of a conflict.

8.3 Data Model Differences

The different problems examined used very different data models (ontologies, ERC+ diagrams, etc), but for the most part the subset of the data models that were used were very similar. The authors largely ignored the parts of the data models that contained significant differences, (e.g., constraints in databases or ontologies).

All of the models that were considered were very simple; they essentially contained objects with subelements and these objects needed to be mapped; whether the subelement was a class or an attribute made very little difference.

The main difference that occurred was that in the merging of the ERC+ diagrams, the "relationship" elements had no real corresponding member in any of the other works. However, the relationships were treated in a fashion almost identical to those as entities, and when there was a choice to be made, the result was to revert to an entity.

The similarity of the approaches emphasizes the underlying common structure of the many diverse approaches.

8.4 Structure vs. Content

Another issue addressed by each system was how much the merge is driven by the structure vs. the content. Structure refers to the way that the objects relate to one another (e.g., class x is the parent of class y). Content refers to the data values for a given object (e.g., the name of the class is "Bob"). In most cases, the authors concentrated on the structure of models at least as much as the content, but both were necessary. An interesting point to note is that content is more likely to be needed in performing a match than in performing a merge, and thus systems that match and merge at the same time rely more on content than systems that make a cleaner separation between the two.

Of the ontology merging systems, SMART, on the one hand, concentrates mainly on resolving conflicts that arise by similar names, but it also looks to make sure that the children are merged. Chimæra, on the other hand, concentrates on structure over content. Two of its three modes of exploration rely entirely on structural searching and leave the content checking to the user. The third, however, relies completely on content. Both of these systems perform alignment at the same time as merging, however, so their dependence on content is not surprising.

In the third ontology merging system, FCA Merge, alignment is performed before the merge, and the merging pays very little attention to the content. In view integration, the problem is almost entirely structural if one considers paths to be entirely structural rather than content. The names are ignored almost completely as one would expect given that matching has already occurred.

8.5 Binary Merge vs. N-ary Merge

Many different situations, such as view integration, solve the problem of merging more than two models at the same time. However, in almost every case this is broken down into a series of two way merges. Break down of an n-ary merge follows either a ladder strategy, wherein a new component schema is integrated with an existing intermediate result at each step, or a balanced binary strategy wherein the models are divided into pairs at the start and are integrated in a symmetric pattern [Batini et al., 1986]. Thus even in situations where n-ary merge would be appropriate, the problem can be, and often is, broken down into a number of binary merges.

8.6 Can Merge be Fully Automatic?

One natural question is whether merge can be fully automatic. Based on these systems, it would appear that it cannot. Even with the limited problems that the above systems address, most of them require user intervention or error handling even though most do not consider either constraints or ordering.

However, with enough parameters set to allow the system to resolve any conflicts that arise, it is possible to have a largely if not entirely automatic version of merge. In addition to setting parameters to allow for the merge to be tailored to the above semantic differences, some of the parameters that should be considered are:

- Is there a preferred model and if so which one?
- If there are two matched objects and one has a more restrictive type than the other (e.g., an integer vs. a double), which would the user prefer? Both have their utilities; if there is an application built on top of the databases, it may be an advantage to require the more restrictive type. However, the less restrictive type allows more expressiveness.

A fully automatic system would not allow the different semantics and user desires to be fully taken into account. A system that required too many knobs would be annoying and frustrating for the user. Thus, any merge system must strike a balance. The most solution is to allow the setting of a number of parameters but to provide default settings to make the common case perform correctly.

8.7 User Interaction Requirements

Both the Chimæra ontology merger [McGuinness et al., 2000] and Munson and Dewan's work in CSCW [Munson and Dewan, 1994] describe interactions that the user should be able to have with the tool when performing a merge. Combined, they list a great number of the goals that any merge operator for Model Management should provide. The combined list yields that a generic merge operator should support:

- Renaming in a systematic fashion
- Merging multiple elements into a single element
- Modifying subsumption relationships in objects
- Automatic merging
- Interactive merging
- Merging many different types of objects
- The semantics of the objects to drive the merging rather than just requiring that all objects merge in the same way
- The users to specify what policies they prefer

Allowing all of these interactions will give the users the control that they need over the merging process.

9 Conclusions

This paper surveyed what it means to merge complex structures, such as relational schemas or ontologies, through a variety of applications, including view integration, data integration, and computer supported collaborative work. The work has a long history. Advances in other areas such as schema matching are likely to mean that work on merging continues to be a fruitful and interesting subject for the foreseeable future.

Acknowledgements Thanks are given to Phil Bernstein and Alon Halevy for their previous work and discussion with the author on the subject and to Jamila Salari, Steve Wolfman, and the editors for reading earlier drafts of this paper.

References

Atzeni P, Ausiello G, Batini C, Moscarini M (1982) Inclusion and equivalence between relational database schemata. Theor Comp Sci 19:267–285

Balasubramaniam S, Pierce BC (1998) What is a file synchronizer? In: ACM/IEEE international conference on mobile computing and networking (MOBICOM). pp 98–108

Batini C, Lenzerini M, Navathe S (1986) A comparative analysis of methodologies for database schema integration. ACM Comput Surveys 18(4):323–364

Beeri C, Milo T (1999) Schemas for integration and translation of structured and semi-structured data. In: International conference on database theory (ICDT). Springer, Heidelberg, pp 296–313

Bergamaschi S, Castano S, Vincini M (1999) Semantic integration of semistructured and structured data sources. SIGMOD Rec 28(1):54–59

Berger M, Schill A, Vöksen G (1998) Coordination technology for collaborative applications: Organizations, processes, and agents. Springer, London

Berlage T, Genau A (1993) A framework of shared applications with a replicated architecture. In: ACM symposium on user interface software and technology. ACM, NY, pp 249–257

Bernstein PA, Halevy AY, Pottinger R (2000) A vision of management of complex models. SIGMOD Rec 29(4):55–63

Biskup J, Convent B (1986) A formal view integration method. In: ACM SIGMOD international conference on management of data (SIGMOD). ACM, NY, pp 398–407

Bouzeghoub M, Klusch M, Nutt W, Sattler U (eds) (2000) Proceedings of the 7th international workshop on knowledge representation meets databases (KRDB 2000). CEUR Workshop Proceedings, vol. 29. CEUR-WS.org, Berlin, Germany, August 21, 2000

Buneman P, Davidson SB, Kosky A (1992) Theoretical aspects of schema merging. In: International conference on extending database technology (EDBT). Springer, London, pp 152–167

Calvanese D, Giacomo GD, Lenzerini M, Nardi D, Rosati R (1999) Data integration and reconciliation in data warehousing: Conceptual modeling and reasoning support. Network Inform Syst 2:413–432

Calvanese D, de Giomo G, Lenzerini M, Nardi D, Rosati R (2001) Data integration in data warehousing. Int J Cooper Inform Syst 10:237–271

Casanova M, Vidal V (1983) Towards a sound view integration methodology. In: PODS. ACM, NY, pp 36–47

Chen PP (1976) Entity relation model – toward a unified view of the data. ACM Trans Database Syst 1(1):9–36

Chiticariu L, Kolaitis P, Popa L (2008) Interactive generation of integrated schemas. In: SIGMOD. ACM, NY, pp 833–846

Convent B (1986) Unsolvable problems related to the view integration approach. In: ICDT. Springer, NY, pp 141–156

Doan A, Halevy AY (2004) Semantic integration research in the database community: A brief survey. AI Mag 25(1):109–112

Falconer SM, Noy N (2011) Interactive techniques to support ontology matching. In: Bellahsene Z, Bonifati A, Rahm E (eds) Schema matching and mapping. Data-Centric Systems and Applications. Springer, Heidelberg

Farquhar A, Fikes R, Rice J (1996) The ontolingua server: A tool for collaborative ontology construction. Technical Report KSL-96-26 KSL-96-26, Stanford University Knowledge Systems Laboratory

Fikes R (1996) Ontologies: What are they, and where's the research? In: Principles of knowledge representation and reasoning (KR), pp 652–653

Friedman M, Levy A, Millstein T (1999) Navigational plans for data integration. In: Proceedings of the national conference on artificial intelligence (AAAI). American Association for Artificial Intelligence, CA, pp 67–73

Halevy AY (2001) Answering queries using views: A survey. VLDB J 10(4):270–294

Hull R (1984) Relative information capacity of simple relational database schemata. In: Symposium on principles of database systems (PODS). ACM, NY, pp 97–109

Larson JA, Navathe SB, Elmasri R (1989) A theory of attribute equivalence in databases with application to schema integration. Trans Software Eng 15(4):449–463

Lee ML, Ling TW (2003) A methodology for structural conflict resolution in the integration of entity-relationship schemas. Knowl Inform Syst 5(2):225–247

Lenzerini M (2002) Data integration: A theoretical perspective. In: Symposium on principles of database systems (PODS). ACM, NY, pp 233–246

Madhavan J, Halevy AY (2003) Composing mappings among data sources. In: Very large data bases conference (VLDB). VLDB Endowment, pp 572–583

McBrien P, Poulovassilis A (2002) Schema evolution in heterogenous database architectures, a schema transformation approach. In: International conference on advanced information systems engineering (CAiSE), pp 484–499

McBrien P, Poulovassilis A (2003) Data integration by bi-directional schema transformation rules. In: International conference on data engineering (ICDE). Springer, London, pp 227–238

McGuinness DL, Fikes R, Rice J, Wilder S (2000) An environment for merging and testing large ontologies. In: Principles of knowledge representation and reasoning (KR), pp 483–493

Melnik S, Rahm E, Bernstein PA (2003) Rondo: A programming platform for generic model management. In: ACM SIGMOD international conference on management of data (SIGMOD). ACM, NY, pp 193–204

Miller RJ, Ioannidis YE, Ramakrishnan R (1993) The use of information capacity in schema integration and translation. In: Very large data bases conference (VLDB). Morgan Kaufmann, CA, pp 120–133

Motro A (1987) Superviews: Virtual integration of multiple databases. Trans Software Eng SE-13(7):785–798

Munson JP, Dewan P (1994) A flexible object merging framework. In: Conference on computer supported cooperative work (CSCW). ACM, NY, pp 231–242

Navathe SB, Gadgil SG (1982) A methodology for view integration in logical database design. In: VLDB. Morgan Kaufmann, CA, pp 142–164

Nebel B (ed) (2001) Proceedings of the seventeenth international joint conference on artificial intelligence, IJCAI 2001. Morgan Kaufmann, Seattle, Washington, USA, August 4–10, 2001

Noy NF, Musen MA (1999a) An algorithm for merging and aligning ontologies: automation and tool support. In: Proceedings of the Workshop on ontology management at sixteenth national conference on artificial intelligence (AAAI-99), Orlando, FL. Available as SMI technical report SMI-1999-0799

Noy NF, Musen MA (1999b) SMART: Automated support for ontology merging and alignment. In: Proceedings of the twelfth workshop on knowledge acquisition, modeling and management, Banff, Canada. Available as SMI technical report SMI-1999-0813

Noy NF, Musen MA (2000) Proceedings of the seventeenth national conference on artificial intelligence and twelfth conference on innovative applications of artificial intelligence. AAAI Press/The MIT Press, Austin, Texas, USA, July 30 – August 3, 2000

Pidduck AB, Mylopoulos J, Woo CC, Özsu MT (eds) (2002) Advanced information systems engineering, 14th international conference, CAiSE 2002, Toronto, Canada, May 27–31, 2002, Proceedings, Lecture Notes in Computer Science, vol. 2348, Springer, Heidelberg

Pottinger R, Bernstein PA (2008) Schema merging and mapping creation for relational sources. In: EDBT. ACM, NY, pp 73–84

Pottinger RA, Bernstein PA (2003) Merging models based on given correspondences. In: Very large data bases conference (VLDB). VLDB Endowment, pp 862–873

Radwan A, Popa L, Stanoi IR, Younis A (2009) Top k generation of integrated schemas based on directed and weighted correspondences. In: SIGMOD. ACM, NY, pp 641–654

Rahm E (2011) Schema matching and mapping. Bellahsene Z, Bonifati A, Rahm E (eds) Towards large-scale schema and ontology matching. Data-Centric Systems and Applications. Springer, Heidelberg

Rahm E, Bernstein PA (2001) A survey of approaches to automatic schema matching. VLDB J 10(4):334–350

Rector AL, Gangemi A, Galeazzi E, Glowinski AJ, Rossi-Mori A (1994) The GALEN CORE model schemata for anatomy: towards a re-usable application-independent model of medical concepts. In: Twelfth international congress of the European Federation for Medical Informatics, MIE-94, Lisbon, Portugal, pp. 229–233

Rosenthal A, Reiner D (1994) Tools and transformations – rigorous and otherwise – for practical database design. ACM Trans Database Syst 19(2):167–211

Rosse C, Shapiro LG, Brinkley JF (1998) The digital anatomist foundational model: principles for defining and structuring its concept domain. Proc AMIA Symp 1998:820–824

Shoval P, Zohn S (1991) Binary-relationship integration methodology. Data Knowl Eng 6:225–250

Shu NC, Housel BC, Lum VY (1975) Convert: A high level translation definition language for data conversion. Commun ACM 18(10):557–567

Song WW, Johannesson P, Bubenko J Janis A (1996) Semantic similarity relations in schema integration. Data Knowl Eng 19(1):65–97

Spaccapietra S, Parent C (1994) View integration: A step forward in solving structural conflicts. IEEE Trans Data Knowl Data Eng (TKDE) 6(2):258–274

Spaccapietra S, Parent C, Dupont Y (1992) Model independent assertions for integration of heterogeneous schemas. VLDB J 1(1):81–126

Tufte K, Maier D (2001) Aggregation and accumulation of xml data. IEEE Data Eng Bull 24:34–39

Vijayaraman TM, Buchmann AP, Mohan C, Sarda NL (eds) (1996) VLDB'96, Proceedings of 22th international conference on very large data bases. Morgan Kaufmann, Mumbai, September 3–6, 1996

Wang T, Pottinger R (2008) Semap: A generic mapping construction system. In: EDBT. ACM, NY, pp 97–108

Yang X, Lee ML, Ling TW (2003) Resolving structural conflicts in the integration of XML schemas: A semantic approach. In: ER. Springer, Heidelberg, pp 520–533

Part III
Evaluating and Tuning of Matching Tasks

The increasing demand of matching and mapping tasks in modern integration scenarios has led to a plethora of tools for facilitating these tasks. While the plethora made these tools available to a broader audience, it led to some form of confusion regarding the exact nature, goals, core functionalities expected features and basic capabilities of these tools. This great diversity makes comparative performance evaluations a difficult task. Thus, the development of comparison standards that will allow the evaluation of the tools becomes necessary.

These standards are particularly important for mapping and matching system users since they allow them to evaluate the relative merits of the systems and take the right business decisions. They are also important for mapping system developers, since they offer a way of comparing the system against competitors, and motivating improvements and further development. Finally, they are important to researchers since they serve as illustrations of the existing system limitations, triggering further research in the area.

Tuning schema matching tools is another important means to improve the quality of mappings and performance time. Most matching tools are semi-automatic meaning that to perform well, an expert must tune some (matcher-specific) parameters (i.e., thresholds, weights, etc.). Often this tuning can be a difficult task as the meaning of these parameters and their effect on matching quality can only be seen through trial and error. Indeed, studies have shown how important and difficult tuning is, and that without tuning most matchers perform poorly.

Part III of this book includes two chapters, which are devoted to evaluation and tuning techniques of schema matching and mapping systems.

Chapter 9 written by Yannis Velegrakis et al. provides a generic overview of the existing efforts on benchmarking schema matching and mapping tools. It offers a comprehensive description of the problem, lists the basic comparison criteria and techniques and provides a description of the main functionalities and characteristics of existing tools.

Chapter 10 written by Zohra Bellahsene et al. is devoted to tuning aspect of schema matching tools. After describing the principles of the main tuning techniques, this chapter covers the latest approaches and tools that have been designed for tuning purpose and discusses their capabilities in terms of flexibility and extensibility.

Chapter 9
On Evaluating Schema Matching and Mapping

Zohra Bellahsene, Angela Bonifati, Fabien Duchateau, and Yannis Velegrakis

Abstract The increasing demand of matching and mapping tasks in modern integration scenarios has led to a plethora of tools for facilitating these tasks. While the plethora made these tools available to a broader audience, it led to some form of confusion regarding the exact nature, goals, core functionalities, expected features, and basic capabilities of these tools. Above all, it made performance measurements of these systems and their distinction a difficult task. The need for design and development of comparison standards that will allow the evaluation of these tools is becoming apparent. These standards are particularly important to mapping and matching system users, since they allow them to evaluate the relative merits of the systems and take the right business decisions. They are also important to mapping system developers, since they offer a way of comparing the system against competitors, and motivating improvements and further development. Finally, they are important to researchers as they serve as illustrations of the existing system limitations, triggering further research in the area. In this work, we provide a generic overview of the existing efforts on benchmarking schema matching and mapping tasks. We offer a comprehensive description of the problem, list the basic comparison criteria and techniques, and provide a description of the main functionalities and characteristics of existing systems.

Z. Bellahsene
University of Montpellier II, 34000 Montpellier, France
e-mail: bella@lirmm.fr

A. Bonifati (✉)
ICAR-CNR, Italy
e-mail: bonifati@icar.cnr.it

F. Duchateau
CWI, Amsterdam, The Netherlands
e-mail: fabien@cwi.nl

Y. Velegrakis
University of Trento, Trento, Italy
e-mail: velgias@disi.unitn.eu

Z. Bellahsene et al. (eds.), *Schema Matching and Mapping*, Data-Centric Systems
and Applications, DOI 10.1007/978-3-642-16518-4_9,
© Springer-Verlag Berlin Heidelberg 2011

1 Introduction

The Web has become the world's largest database. Daily, thousands of organizations and individuals are making their repositories available online. To exploit the full potential of these sources, modern information systems and Web applications must be able to retrieve, integrate, and exchange data. Unfortunately, the repositories and applications are developed by different people, at different times, with varying requirements in mind. Thus, the underlying data is inherently highly heterogeneous. To cope with the heterogeneity and achieve interoperability, a fundamental requirement is the ability to match and map data across different formats. These two tasks are found in the literature under the names *matching* [Rahm and Bernstein, 2001] and *mapping* [Miller et al., 2000], respectively. A match is an association between individual structures in different data sources. Matches are the required components for every mapping task. The mappings are the products of the latter. A mapping, in particular, is an expression that describes how the data of some specific format is related to data of another. The relationship forms the basis for translating the data in the first format into data in the second.

Mappings can be found in almost every aspect of data management. In information integration systems [Lenzerini, 2002], mappings are used to specify the relationships between every local and the global schema. In schema integration, mappings specify how an integrated schema is constructed from the individual input schemas [Batini et al., 1986]. In data exchange [Fagin et al., 2005] and P2P settings [Halevy et al., 2003, Bernstein et al., 2002], mappings are used to describe how data in one source are to be translated into data conforming to the schema of another. A similar use is found in schema evolution [Lerner, 2000] where mappings describe the relationship between the old and new version of an evolved schema.

Mapping generation had been for a long time a manual task, performed mainly by data professionals with good understanding of the semantics of the different schemas and with expertise in the transformation language. But as schemas have started to become larger and more complicated, the process has become laborious, time-consuming and error-prone. On top of that, the modern mashup technologies [Wun, 2009] have given to regular Internet users the ability to build their own integration applications, systems, and services. In this process, these users have to strive with the complexities of the schemas, the peculiarities of the transformation language, and the many other technical details of the data transformation specification. The need for designing and developing tools to support the mapping designer in the mapping specification task has been apparent. Those tools are known as mapping tools, and they offer support in different styles and flavors. Certain tools raise the abstraction level by providing sophisticated graphical interfaces [Altova, 2008] or high-level mapping languages [Bernstein and Melnik, 2007]. Others offer advanced algorithms performing part of the reasoning the mapping designer has to make [Popa et al., 2002, Do and Rahm, 2002, Mecca et al., 2009, Madhavan et al., 2001], while some offer designer guidance [Alexe et al., 2008a]. Today, there exists a plethora of such systems, including the Altova Mapforce [Altova, 2008], IBM Rational Data Architect [IBM, 2006], Microsoft BizTalk

Mapper, which is embedded in Microsoft Visual Studio [Microsoft, 2005], Stylus Studio[Stylus Studio, 2005], BEA AquaLogic [Carey, 2006], and the research prototypes Rondo [Do and Rahm, 2002], COMA++ [Aumueller et al., 2005], Harmony [Mork et al., 2008], S-Match [Giunchiglia et al., 2005], Cupid [Madhavan et al., 2001], Clio [Popa et al., 2002], Tupelo [Fletcher and Wyss, 2006], Spicy [Bonifati et al., 2008a], and HePToX [Bonifati et al., 2010].

Despite the availability of the many mapping tools, no generally accepted benchmark has been developed for comparing and evaluating them. As it is the case with other benchmarks, such a development is of major importance for assessing the relative merits of the tools. This can help customers in making the right investment decisions and selecting among the many alternatives the tools that better fit their business needs. A benchmark can also help the mapping tool developers as it offers them a common metric to compare their own achievements against those of the competitors. Such comparisons can boost competition and drive the development toward systems of higher quality. A benchmark is also offering the developers a generally accepted language for talking to customers and describing the advantages of their tools through well-known features that determine performance, effectiveness, and usability. Furthermore, the benchmark can highlight limitations of the mapping tools or unsupported features that may not have been realized by the developers. Finally, a benchmark is also needed in research community [Bertinoro, 2007]. Apart from a common platform for comparison, a benchmark allows researchers to evaluate their achievements not only in terms of performance but also in terms of applicability in real-world situations.

In this work, we summarize and present in a systematic way existing efforts toward the characterization and evaluation of mapping tools, and the establishment of a benchmark. After a quick introduction of the architecture and main functionality of matching and mapping tools in Sect. 2, we describe the challenges of building a matching/mapping system benchmark in Sect. 3. Section 4 presents existing efforts in collecting real-world test cases with the intention of using them in evaluating the matching and mapping systems. Section 5 addresses the issue of creating synthetic test cases that are targeting the evaluation of specific features of the mapping systems. Finally, Sects. 6 and 7 present different metrics that have been proposed in the literature for measuring the efficiency and effectiveness of matching/mapping systems, respectively.

2 The Matching and Mapping Problem

Matching is the process that takes as input two schemas, referred to as the *source* and the *target*, and produces a number of matches, aka *correspondences*, between the elements of these two schemas [Rahm and Bernstein, 2001]. The term schema is used with the broader sense and includes database schemas [Madhavan et al., 2001], ontologies [Giunchiglia et al., 2009], or generic models [Atzeni and Torlone, 1995]. A match is defined as a triple $\langle S_s, E_t, e \rangle$, where S_s is a set of elements from the source, E_t is an element of the target schema, and e is a matching expression that specifies a relationship between the element E_t and the elements in S_s. Note that the expression e does not specify how the elements in S_s relate to each other. Most of the time, a match is as simple as an equality or a set-inclusion relationship between an element of the source and an element of the target. There are, however, cases in which the relationship can be more complex, e.g., a concatenation function, some arithmetic operation, a relationship over scalars like $=$ or $\leq$, a conceptual model relationship such as the part-of, or some set-oriented relationships, such as overlaps or contains. Schema matching tools employ a number of different techniques to discover this kind of relationships. They can range from structural [Madhavan et al., 2001] and name similarities to semantic closeness [Giunchiglia et al., 2004] and data value analysis [Doan et al., 2001, 2004]. A schema matching tool accepts as input the two schemas and generates the set of matches. Since any schema matching process is based on semantics, its final output needs to be verified by a human expert. The matching process can be roughly divided into three phases: the prematch, the match, and the postmatch phase. During the first phase, the matcher performs some computations and processes the data. Typically, this involves the training of the classifiers in the case of machine learning-based matchers, the configuration of the various parameters like thresholds and weight values used by the matching algorithm, and the specification of auxiliary information, such as domain synonyms and constraints [Giunchiglia et al., 2009]. During the second phase, the actual discovery of the matches takes place. At the end, the matcher outputs the matches between elements of these data sources. During the postmatch phase, the users may check and modify the displayed matches if needed.

Given a source and a target schema, a *mapping* is a relationship, i.e., a constraint, that must hold between their respective instances. For the mappings to be generated, a fundamental requirement are the matches between the elements of the schemas. These matches can be either generated automatically through a matching process or can be manually provided by an expert user. In contrast to matches, which specify how instance values of individual source and target schema elements relate to each other, a mapping additionally specifies how the values within the same instance relate to each other. For example, a match may specify that the dollar price of a product in the target corresponds to the multiplication of the price of the product in the source (expressed in some foreign currency) multiplied by the exchange rate. The mapping is the one that specifies that the exchange rate with which the product price in the source is multiplied is the exchange rate of the currency in which the price of the product is expressed. The mapping does so by specifying the right join path between the price and the exchange rate attributes.

Mappings can be used in many different ways. In the case in which the target schema is a virtual, i.e., not materialized, database as in virtual information integration systems, in P2P applications, or in data repositories that publish an interface schema, the mappings can be used for query answering by driving the translation of queries on the target schema to queries on the source [Lenzerini, 2002]. Another major application of mappings is data exchange [Fagin et al., 2003] in which given a source instance, the mappings are used to drive the materialization of a target

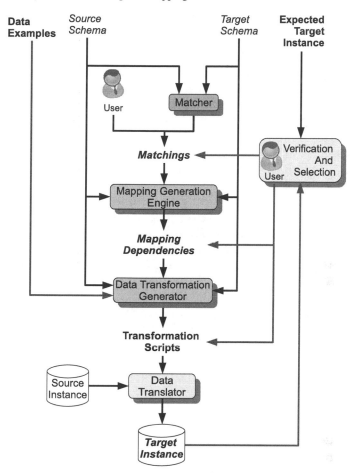

Fig. 9.1   Overview of the matching, mapping, and data exchange tasks

instance. Since mappings are interschema constraints, they may not be enough to fully specify the target instance. In other words, given a source instance and a set of mappings between a source and a target schema, there may be multiple target instances that satisfy the mappings. Finding the best target instance is known in the literature as the data exchange problem [Fagin et al., 2005]. Once the right target instance is decided, the mappings can be converted into a transformation script that translates an instance of the source schema into some target schema representation. This transformation script is typically expressed in some executable language such as XQuery, XSLT, or SQL.

A mapping tool is a tool that assists the mapping designer in generating the mappings using less effort, in less time and with fewer mistakes. Mapping tools can be classified into two large categories based on what they consider as a mapping. The first category is the one that makes a clear distinction between mapping generation, i.e., the generation of the interschema constraints, and the data exchange, i.e., the generation of the transformation script. Tools in this category include the research prototypes Clio [Popa et al., 2002] and Spicy++ [Mecca et al., 2009]. Their main goal is the generation of the mappings in the form of constraints, which can then be used either for information integration or for data exchange. To facilitate the latter case, the tools may be equipped with a data exchange module that converts the generated mappings into some transformation script that can be executed on the source instance to produce the target. The generated mappings are typically expressed through some declarative specification in a logic formalism. The most widely used such formalism is the *tuple generating dependency*, or *tgd* in short [Abiteboul et al., 1995]. The second large class of mapping tools are those that make no distinction between mapping generation and data exchange. For these tools, the notion of mapping generation is actually the creation in some native language of the final transformation script that provides a full specification of the target instance in terms of a source instance. Characteristic representatives in this category are the commercial tools Altova MapForce [Altova, 2008] and Stylus Studio [Stylus Studio, 2005].

In what follows, we use the term mapping tool to describe a tool in either category, and the term mapping to describe the output of such a tool, no matter whether it is an interschema constraint or a transformation script. In case we want to emphasize that a mapping is not a transformation script, we use the term *mapping dependency*.

The design of existing mapping tools is based on the idea of providing the mapping designer with a graphical representation of the two schemas and a set of graphical constructs representing high-level transformation abstractions. Using these graphical constructs, the mapping designer provides a specification of the desired mappings. The level of abstraction of the graphical objects may vary from direct correspondences [Popa et al., 2002, Mecca et al., 2009], i.e., matches, to graphical representations of primitive operations of the transformation script language [Altova, 2008, Stylus Studio, 2005]. The high-level graphical constructs provided by the mapping designer are easy to use, but they are inherently ambiguous. The mapping tool will have to interpret them and make an educated guess of a transformation that the mapping designer had in mind to create [Velegrakis, 2005]. An a posteriori verification is then necessary to ensure that the generated mappings are indeed those intended by the designer. Clearly, the simpler the graphical constructs are, the easier the task is for the designer, but at the same time, the more the intelligence required by the tool to interpret these constructs and infer the desired mappings.

A number of mapping tools are equipped with a matching module, which can be used by the mapping designer to suggest possible matches. One such tool is Clio [Popa et al., 2002] whose matching component is based on attribute feature analysis [Naumann et al., 2002]. It generates matches in the form of *attribute correspondences*, i.e., interschema lines connecting atomic type schema elements, annotated with some value transformation functions. Other tools [Bernstein and Melnik, 2007] have the matching task not as an add-on component, but as a fully integrated and indistinguishable part of the tool. Spicy [Bonifati et al., 2008a] is between these two alternatives. It has a matching module similar to the one in Clio but is used as an integral part of the tool, allowing it to accept as input only the pair of source and target schema, if needed.

Since matching and mapping tools try to guess the intentions of the designer based on the provided input, it is natural to assume that their output is not always the one anticipated by the designer. As already mentioned, an a posteriori verification is necessary. Nevertheless, there is a significant number of tools that allow the active participation of the designer in the matching/mapping generation phase to guide the whole process and arrive faster at the desired result. For example, once some matchings/mappings have been generated, the designer can verify their correctness. If she feels unsatisfied by the result, she can go back and modify some intermediate steps, for instance, she can tune the matcher, select a fraction of the set of the generated matches, enhance the matches by introducing new matches not automatically generated by the matcher, tune the mapping generation process by accepting only a fraction of the generated mappings, or even edit directly the mappings. User participation is highly active in Tupelo [Fletcher and Wyss, 2006] where mapping generation is studied as a search problem driven by input data examples. Domain knowledge, that is usually an input to the matcher, is also used as input to the mapping discovery module. User feedback can be used to improve the effectiveness of the discovered semantic functions, i.e., the matches, and of the structural relationships, i.e., the mapping dependencies, that in turn can be entrusted to a data mapping module for generating the final transformation query.

Many mapping tools are used as schema integration tools. Schema integration is the process of merging multiple source schemas into one integrated schema, aka the global or mediated schema. The integrated schema serves as a uniform interface for querying the data sources. Nowadays, construction of integrated schemas has become a laborious task mainly due to the number, size, and complexity of the schemas. On the other hand, decision makers need to understand, combine, and exploit in a very short time all the information that is available to them before acting [Smith et al., 2009]. This reality requires the rapid construction of large prototypes and the flexible evolution of existing integrated schemas from users with limited technical expertise. Matching and mapping tools facilitate that goal. A mapping designer may be presented with a number of source schemas and an empty target. Through a graphical interface, source schema elements can be selected and "dropped" into the target. When the elements are dropped into the target, the mappings specifying how the target elements are related to those in the sources are automatically or semiautomatically generated. This functionality is graphically depicted in Fig. 9.2. Note that schema integration involves additional tasks; however, here we concentrate only on the part related to matching and mapping.

A special case of mapping tools are the ETL systems. An ETL system is a tool designed to perform large-scale extract–transform–load operations. The transformation performed by an ETL system is typically described by a graph flowchart in which each node represents a specific primitive transformation and the edges between the nodes represent flow of data produced as a result of a primitive operator and fed as input in another. Figure 9.3 illustrates such a data flowchart. The

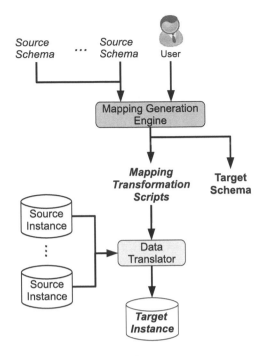

Fig. 9.2 Overview of the schema integration task

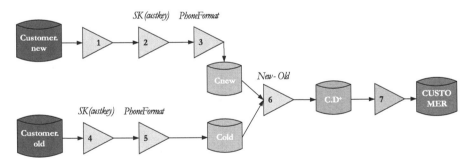

Fig. 9.3 An ETL data flowchart

triangles represent transformation operators, and the cylinders represent data stored in some media. Although ETL systems are typically not considered mapping tools, they share many similarities with them. First, their main goal is also to facilitate the designer in describing a data transformation from one format to another. Second, they often provide a graphical interface, and they produce as a final output transformation scripts. Finally, there are mapping tools currently in the market [Stylus Studio, 2005] that operate very close to the ETL model. Their graphical interface provides a set of primitive transformations that the designer can combine together to provide a full specification of the transformation that needs to be applied on the data. Their output looks like an ETL flowchart. ETL systems require no large intelligent capabilities, since the input provided by the designer is so detailed that only a limited form of reasoning is necessary. Similar to ETL systems are mashup editors [Heinzl et al., 2009] that try to facilitate the mashup designer. The operational goals of mashup editors are similar to those of ETL systems, so we do not consider them as a separate category.

We use the term matching or mapping *scenario* to refer to a particular instance of the matching or mapping problem, respectively. A scenario is represented by the input provided to the matching or mapping tool. More specifically, a matching scenario is a pair of source and target schema. A mapping scenario is a pair of source and target schema alongside a specification of the intented mappings. A *solution* to a scenario is a set of matches, respectively mappings, that satisfy the specifications set by the scenario.

3 Challenges in Matching and Mapping System Evaluation

A fundamental requirement for providing universal evaluation of matching and mapping tools is the existence of benchmarks. A benchmark for a computer application or tool is based on the idea of *evaluation scenarios*, i.e., a standardized set of problems or tests serving as a basis for comparison.[1] An evaluation scenario for a matching/mapping tool is a scenario alongside the expected output of the tool, i.e., the expected solution. Unfortunately, and unlike benchmarks for relational database management tools, such as, TPC-H [Transaction Processing Performance Council, 2001], or for XML query engines, such as, XMach [Bohme and Rahm, 2001], X007 [Bressan et al., 2001], MBench [Runapongsa et al., 2002], XMark [Schmidt et al., 2002], and XBench [Yao et al., 2004], the design of a benchmark for matching/mapping tools is fundamentally different and significantly more challenging [Okawara et al., 2006], mainly due to the different nature, goals, and operational principles of the tool.

One of the differences is the fact that given a source and a target schema, there is not always one "correct" set of matches or mappings. In query engines [Transaction Processing Performance Council, 2001, Bohme and Rahm, 2001], the correct answer to a given query is uniquely specified by the semantics of the query language. In matching/mapping tools, on the other hand, the expected answer depends not only on the semantics of the schemas, which by nature may be ambiguous, but also on the transformation that the mapping designer was intending to make. The situation reminisces the case of Web search engines, where there are many documents returned as an answer to a given keyword query, others more and others less related to the query, but which document is actually the correct answer can only be

---

[1] Source: Merriam Webster dictionary.

decided by the user that posed the keyword query. For that reason, many evaluations of matching or mapping tools are performed by human experts.

Another difficulty faced during the design of evaluation techniques for mapping tools is the lack of a clear specification of the input language, i.e., a standardized formalism with well-defined semantics. In contrast to benchmarks for relational [Transaction Processing Performance Council, 2001] and XML systems [Bohme and Rahm, 2001] that could leverage from the respective SQL and XQuery standard query languages, it is still not clear how to describe a scenario. Formally describing the schemas is not an issue, but describing the intended transformation, i.e., the input that the designer needs to provide, is. The best way to unambiguously specify the intended transformation is through a transformation language script, or a mapping in some formalism, but there are two main issues with this option. First, there are no guarantees that the mapping tool will be able to accept the specific formalism as input, or at least that there will be an unambiguous translation of the input from the formalism into the input language supported by the mapping tool. The second issue is that such an approach beats the purpose of a mapping tool, which is intended to shield the mapping designer from the complexity and the peculiarities of the transformation language. It is actually for that reason that mapping tool developers have opted for simpler, higher-level specification languages, such as visual objects, direct lines between schema elements, or the output of the matching process in general. Unfortunately, such specification is by nature ambiguous. Consider one of the already identified [Alexe et al., 2008c] ambiguous situations, described in Fig. 9.4. It is a simple scenario in which the mapping designer needs to copy the *company* data from the source into *organizations* data in the target. To specify this, the designer draws the two interschema lines illustrated in Fig. 9.4. When these are fed to a popular commercial mapping tool, the tool generates a transformation script, which generates the target instance illustrated in Fig. 9.5a when executed on the instance of Fig. 9.4. A different tool, for the same input, produces a transformation script that generates the instance illustrated in Fig. 9.5b. A third one produces a script that generates the instance of Fig. 9.5c, which is most likely the one the mapping designer had in mind to create. These differences are not an error from the side of the tools, rather a consequence of the fact that in the absence of a global agreement on the semantics of the matches, or the input language in general, different tools may interpret them differently and may require different inputs for generating the same mappings. In the above example, the tool that generated the instance in Fig. 9.5a could have also produced the instance of Fig. 9.5c, if the designer had provided one more match from the element *Company* to the element *Organization*. This match (which is between nonleaf elements) is not allowed at all in the tool that created the instance of Fig. 9.5c. The issue is also highly related to the level of intelligence and reasoning capabilities that the tools are offering. Some tools may require a minimum input from the user, and through advanced reasoning they may be able to generate the intended mappings [Bonifati et al., 2008b, Fagin et al., 2009a]. Others may require the designer to be more explicit when describing the transformation she has in mind to create [Altova, 2008, Stylus Studio, 2005]. Even by considering only

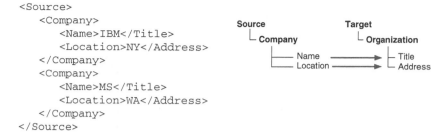

```
<Source>
    <Company>
        <Name>IBM</Title>
        <Location>NY</Address>
    </Company>
    <Company>
        <Name>MS</Title>
        <Location>WA</Address>
    </Company>
</Source>
```

Fig. 9.4 A simple mapping scenario and the source schema instance

```
<Target>                    <Target>                    <Target>
  <Organization>              <Organization>              <Organization>
    <Title>IBM</Title>          <Title>IBM</Title>          <Title>IBM</Title>
    <Title>MS</Title>           <Address>NY</Address>       <Address>NY</Address>
    <Address>NY</Address>     </Organization>             </Organization>
    <Address>WA</Address>    </Target>                    <Organization>
  </Organization>                                           <Title>IBM</Title>
</Target>                                                    <Address>NY</Address>
                                                          </Organization>
                                                        </Target>

         (a)                        (b)                        (c)
```

Fig. 9.5 Three different target instances generated by different tools

matches, there is a large variety of specification options as a recent classification of mapping tools illustrates [Legler and Naumann, 2007].

The input problem goes even further. Some mapping tools allow the designer to edit the generated mappings or transformation scripts to correct or enhance them. In that way, the generated output is restricted only by the expressive power of the mapping language or of the transformation script. Under such circumstances, a scenario should be extended to include, apart from the two schemas and the intended mapping specification, the modifications/corrections that the designer does on the generated output. However, allowing the designer to edit the output makes unfair any comparison to mapping tools that operate under the principle that the designer can only use the high-level graphical input language [Altova, 2008].

Another issue of inconsistency across different matching and mapping tools is the lack of a standardized output. Some matching tools generate only 1–1 identity function matches, i.e., simple interschema correspondences, while others generate more complex relationships. Furthermore, some mapping tools generate mappings as interschema dependencies only, while others produce also the transformation scripts. The problem is becoming more crucial due to the fact that there is no unique way of generating a target instance. Two different mapping tools may produce completely different transformation scripts and yet generate the same target instance.

Deciding the metrics with which success is measured is another challenging task. Since a general goal of a mapping tool is to reduce the required programming effort, measuring the effort spent for a matching or a mapping task using a tool can serve as an indication of the success of the tool. Unfortunately, such metrics are not broadly accepted, since they highly depend on the user interface. An advanced user interface will lead to good evaluation results, which means that the evaluation of a mapping tool is actually a graphical interface evaluation. Furthermore, the fact that there is no global agreement on the expressive power of the interface poses limits on the evaluation scenarios that can be run. A mapping tool with a simple interface may require less designer effort but may also be limited on the kind of mappings or transformations it can generate. This has led a number of researchers and practitioners into considering as an alternative metric the expressive power of the mappings that the tool can generate, while others talked about the quality of the mappings themselves [Bonifati et al., 2008b] or the quality of the integrated schema, for the case in which the mapping tool is used for schema integration. The quality of the integrated schema is important for improving query execution time, successful data exchange, and accurate concept sharing. Unfortunately, there is no broadly accepted agreement on how mapping quality is measured; thus, to provide meaningful comparisons, an evaluation method should consider a number of different metrics for that purpose.

Developing evaluation techniques for mapping tools is also limited by the non deterministic output of the scenarios. In contrast to query engines, different mapping tools may generate different results for the same input, without any of the results being necessarily wrong. In particular, for a given high-level mapping specification, there may be different interpretation alternatives, and each tool may choose one over another. The ability to effectively communicate to the mapping designer the semantics of the generated output is of major importance to allow the designer to effectively guide the tool toward the generation of the desired mappings. One way to do so is to present the designer with the target instance that the generated mappings can produce. This is not always convenient, practical, or even feasible, especially for large complicated instances. Presenting the mapping to the designer seems preferable [Velegrakis, 2005], yet it is not always convenient, since the designer may not be familiar with the language in which the mappings are expressed. An attractive alternative [Alexe et al., 2008a] is to provide carefully selected representative samples of the target instance or synthetic examples that effectively illustrate the transformation modeled by the generated mappings. This option is becoming particularly appealing nowadays that more and more systems are moving away from exact query semantics toward supporting keyword [Bergamaschi et al., 2010] and approximate queries, or queries that embrace uncertainty in the very heart of the system [Ioannou et al., 2010].

4 Real-World Evaluation Scenarios

A close look at popular benchmarks can reveal a common design pattern. The benchmark provides a number of predefined test cases that the tool under evaluation is called to successfully execute. The tool is then evaluated based on the number of these cases that were indeed implemented successfully. The TPC-H benchmark [Transaction Processing Performance Council, 2001], for instance, consists of a set of predefined queries on a given database, with each of these queries testing a specific feature of the query language that the query engine is expected to support. For each such query, the benchmark provides the expected correct answer against which the results of the query execution on the under evaluation engine can be compared. Accordingly, a mapping tool benchmark should provide a set of evaluation scenarios, i.e., scenarios alongside the expected result.

There has been a number of efforts toward building collections of evaluation scenarios. There is an unquestionable value to these collections. The ability of a mapping method or tool to successfully execute the evaluation scenarios is a clear indication of its practical value. By successful execution, we mean that the tool is able to generate the expected output as described by the evaluation scenario. Although these collections are built based on criteria such as popularity, community acceptance, or by contributions of interested parties and by the user base, they often lack systematic categorization of the cases they test. For instance, they may have multiple evaluation scenarios testing the same feature of the tool, or they may provide no generalized test patterns. For that reason, this kind of collections are typically termed as *testbeds* or *standardized tests*.

A complete and generic benchmark should go beyond a simple set of test cases. It should offer a systematic organization of tests that is *consistent*, *complete*, and *minimal*. Consistent means that the existence of every test case should be justified by some specific feature upon which the tool or technique is evaluated through the test case. Complete means that for every important feature of the mapping tool under evaluation there is a test case. Minimal means that there are no redundant test cases, i.e., more than one test case for the same feature.

To evaluate a matching tool on a given evaluation scenario, the scenario is provided to the tool that produces a solution. That generated solution, which in the case of a matching tool is a set of matches, is then compared against the expected set of matches that the evaluation scenario contains. If the two sets are the same, then the tool is said to be successful for this scenario. The evaluation scenarios are typically designed to check a specific matching situation. Success or failure to a specific scenario translates into the ability or inability of the matching tool under evaluation to handle the specific matching situation. This kind of evaluation is the one for which testbeds are designed for. The Ontology Alignment Evaluation Initiative [Euzenat et al., 2006], OAEI in short, is a coordinated international initiative that every year organizes a matching competition for ontologies. Ontologies can be seen as semantic schemas; thus, ontology matching is considered part of the general matching problem. The initiative provides the contesters with a set of matching test scenarios with which the contesters test their tools. Throughout the year, individuals may also submit to the initiative various scenarios they meet in practice. As a result, the collected scenarios of the initiative constitute a good representation of the reality. In some recent evaluation of a number of matching tools [Kopcke and Rahm, 2010], the number of real-world test problems that the matching tool could handle featured as one of the main comparison criteria. The OAEI scenarios may be further enhanced with datasets. In a recent effort [Giunchiglia et al., 2009], an extension was proposed that contains 4,500 matches between three different Web directories and has three important features, namely, it is error-free, has a low complexity, and has a high discriminative capability, a notion that is explained later. Unfortunately, despite the fact that there is a strong need for comparing matchers using identical evaluation scenarios,[2] there has been no broadly accepted agreement until today on what these evaluation scenarios should be.

The XBenchMatch [Duchateau et al., 2007] is a benchmark for matching tools. It defines a set of criteria for testing and evaluating matching tools. It may focus mostly on the assessment of the matching tools in terms of matching quality and time performance but provides a testbed involving ten datasets that can be used to quickly benchmark new matching algorithms [Duchateau, 2009]. These matching scenarios have been classified according to the tasks they reflect, either at the data level, e.g., the structure or the degree of heterogeneity, or at the matching process level, e.g., the scale. Although collaborative work can help providing new datasets with their correct set of matches, the creation of such a large and complete set still remains a challenge.

It is important to add here that one of the challenges during the creation of test scenarios is deciding what the correct matches will be. As mentioned in the previous section, for a given matching scenario, there may be multiple correct answers. Opting for one of them may not be fair for the others. For this reason, in cases like OAEI, the test scenarios designers perform a careful selection so that the scenarios have no multiple alternatives, or in the case that they have, the one that is considered as the correct answer to the chosen scenario is the one that is most obvious or the one that the exclusive majority of matching users would have considered as correct.

One of the first benchmarks for mapping tools is the STBenchmark [Alexe et al., 2008c]. It contains a list of basic test scenarios, each consisting of a source schema, a target schema, and a transformation query expressed in XQuery. The choice of describing the mapping specification in XQuery was made to avoid any misinterpretation of the mapping that needs to be achieved. This, of course, does not mean that the mappings that the mapping tool will generate will have to be necessarily in XQuery, but they have to describe an equivalent mapping. Furthermore, the selection of XQuery as a mapping specification language causes no major issues to the mapping tool evaluators, since such users are in general more experienced than regular mapping designers. They can easily understand the full details of the expected transformation, and by using the mapping tool interface, they can try to materialize it. For mapping tools that accept matches as input, conversion from XQuery to matches is a straightforward task.

Each STBenchmark mapping scenario is carefully designed to test the ability of the mapping tool to create transformations of a specific kind. The evaluator is expected to understand first the desired transformation by studying the transformation script, and then try to implement it through the interface provided by

---

[2] Netrics HD blog, April 2010: http://www.netrics.com/blog/a-data-matching-benchmark.

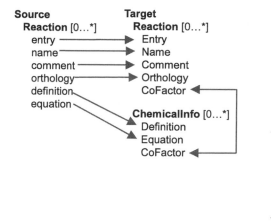

Source
Reaction [0…*]
  entry
  name
  comment
  orthology
  definition
  equation

Target
Reaction [0…*]
  Entry
  Name
  Comment
  Orthology
  CoFactor

ChemicalInfo [0…*]
  Definition
  Equation
  CoFactor

```
<Target>
for $x0 in / Source / Reaction
let $id = genID ($x0)
return
  <Reaction>
    <Entry> $x0/name/text()
    <Name> $x0/name/text()
    <Comment> $x0/comment/text()
    <Orthology> $x0/orthology/text()
    <CoFactor> $id </CoFactor>
  </Reaction>
for $x0 in /Source/Reaction
let $id = genID($x0)
return
  <ChemicalInfo>
    <Definition> $x0/definition/text()
    <Equation> $x0/equation/text()
    <CoFactor> $id
  </ChemicalInfo>
</Target>
```

Fig. 9.6 A mapping scenario for vertical partition

the mapping tool that wants to be evaluated. Some of the scenarios provided by STBenchmark are related to copying structures, constant value generation, horizontal and vertical partitioning, key generation, nesting and unnesting of structures, different join path selection, aggregation, value combination, and many others. Figure 9.6 illustrates an example of one of these scenarios. The list of scenarios has been collected by a study of the related information integration literature and many practical applications. Definitely, one cannot build an exhaustive set of testing scenarios. There will always be cases that remain untested. This is the case even with query engine benchmarks. However, what is important for a benchmark is to cover the majority of the cases that are met in practice [Alexe et al., 2008b].

An important issue that must be brought here is that general-purpose evaluation tools should contain examples from the domains the tool is intended to be used [Kopcke and Rahm, 2010]. It is a known fact that certain matching or mapping tools perform well on data with certain characteristics. Thus, such tools should be evaluated using scenarios from that area. General-purpose benchmarks should provide scenarios from different domains. Each STBenchmark test scenario, for instance, is accompanied by a source instance with data extracted from the DBLP bibliographic server,[3] the BioWarehouse[4] collection, and other similar real sources.

The approach of using predefined evaluation scenarios is also followed by Thalia [Hammer et al., 2005], a benchmark for evaluating integration tools. Recall that in the schema integration task, the input to the tool is a set of source schemas for which the mapping designer is called to generate the integrated schema and the mappings that populate it from source data. Thalia provides a rich set of test data for integration problems exhibiting a wide variety of syntactic and semantic

---

[3] http://www.informatik.uni-trier.de/ ley/db/.
[4] biowarehouse.ai.sri.com.

heterogeneities. It also provides twelve test queries, each requiring the resolution of a particular type of heterogeneity.

5 Synthetic Evaluation Scenarios

An important issue for a benchmark is to have not only fixed evaluation scenarios but also scenarios representing generic patterns. In a world where the data is becoming increasingly complicated, it is crucial to stress-test the tools for data and schemas of different sizes. This means that matching and mapping benchmarks should support dynamic generation of evaluation scenarios of different sizes with which one can test how the tool under evaluation scale up.

Unfortunately, such a pluralism may be hard to find in real-world applications, mainly due to privacy reasons, or because they typically originate from a single domain that restricts their pluralism and makes them unsuitable for general-purpose evaluations. Thus, a benchmark should be able to create synthetic test cases in a systematic way that stress-test the mapping tools and allow the evaluation of their performance under different situations.

In the case of a matching tool, generation of a synthetic test scenario involves the creation of a source and a target schema, alongside the expected matches. The construction of the two schemas should be done in parallel so that for every part of the source schema, the part of the target schema with which it matches is known. For the case of a mapping tool, the situation is similar, but instead of the expected matches, the synthetic test scenario should have the expected transformation. The construction of the latter should also be orchestrated with the construction of the two schemas. For mapping tools in schema integration, a test scenario consists of a set of source schemas, the expected integrated schema, and the specification on how the expected integrated schema is related to the individual source schemas.

Generation of synthetic scenarios has in general followed two main approaches: the *top-down* and the *bottom-up* approach. The former starts with some large scenario and by removing parts of it generates other smaller scenarios. The latter constructs each scenario from scratch. Both approaches can be applied in the case of synthetic scenario generation for matching and mapping tools.

The top-down approach starts with an existing large source and target schema, and systematically removes components to generate smaller scenarios satisfying specific properties. The properties depend on the features of the matching or mapping task that needs to be evaluated. An example of an ontology matching evaluation dataset that has been built using the top-down approach is TaxME2 [Giunchiglia et al., 2009]. In TaxME2, a set of original ontologies are initially constructed out of the Google, Yahoo, and Looksmart Web directories. In the sequel, matches across these ontologies are also defined and characterized. For every pair of ontologies, portions are cut out alongside matches using elements from these portions. The remaining parts of the two ontologies are used as the source and the target, and the remaining matches form the expected correct matches. The process is repeated multiple times, each time using a different portion that leads to the creation of a new matching evaluation scenario. The selection of the portions was done in a way that preserved five main properties: (1) the complexity of the matching operators, (2) the incrementality, i.e., the ability to reveal weaknesses of the matching tool under evaluation, (3) the ability to distinguish among the different matching solutions, (4) the quality preservation, meaning that any matching quality measure calculated on the subset of the schemas did not differ substantially from the measure calculated on the whole dataset, and (5) the correctness, meaning that any matches considered were correct.

A top-down approach has also been proposed for data exchange systems [Okawara et al., 2006] and is the model upon which the THALIA [Hammer et al., 2005] integration benchmark is based. In particular, Thalia provides a large dataset and the filters that can select portions of this dataset in terms of values and schemas.

eTuner [Lee et al., 2007] is a tool for automatically tuning matchers that utilizes the instance data in conjunction with the schema information and can also be used to create synthetic scenarios in the top-down fashion. It starts with an initial schema, and splits it into two, each keeping the same structure but half of the instance data. The correct matches between the schemas generated by the split are known, and the idea is to apply transformations to one of the two schemas to create a new schema. The transformations are based on rules at three levels: (1) modifications on the structure of the schema, (2) changes of the schema element names, and (3) perturbations of the data. The matchings between schema elements are traced through the whole process so that they are known at the end and are used for evaluating the matchers. A limitation of eTuner is that the user needs to create or find a reference ontology. Furthermore, the set of modifications that can be performed on the data is limited, making the perturbated data look less similar to natural real-world data.

In the bottom-up approach of synthetic scenario generation, some small scenario is used as a seed for the construction of more complex scenarios. STBenchmark [Alexe et al., 2008b] is based on this idea to provide synthetic mapping test scenarios, i.e., a synthetic source schema, a target schema, an expected mapping between the source and the target schema, and an instance of the source schema. The seeds it uses are its basic scenarios that were mentioned in the previous section. Given a basic scenario, STBenchmark constructs an expanded version of it. The expanded version is an image of the original scenario but on a larger scale. The scale is determined by dimensions specified through configuration parameters representing characteristics of the schemas and the mappings. For instance, in a *copy* basic scenario, the configuration parameters are the average nesting depth of the schemas and the average number of attributes of each element. In the *vertical partition* scenario (ref. Fig. 9.6), on the other hand, the configuration parameters include additionally the length of join paths, the type of the joins, and the number of attributes involved in each such join. Expanded scenarios can then be concatenated to produce even larger mapping scenarios. Figure 9.7a illustrates an expanded *unnest* basic mapping scenario, and Fig. 9.7b illustrates how a large synthetic scenario is created by concatenating smaller scenarios. STBenchmark[5] has also the ability to

---

[5] www.stbenchmark.org.

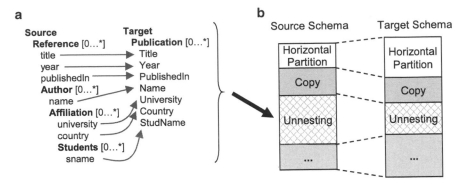

Fig. 9.7 Basic scenario expansion and synthetic scenario generation

create synthetic mapping scenarios that involve complex transformations coming from a combination of transformations that the basic mapping scenarios describe. For the generation of the instance of the source schema, STBenchmark generates a ToXGene [Barbosa et al., 2002] configuration template with which one can invoke ToXGene to produce the data of the source instance.

In the area of schema matching, the ISLab Instance Matching Benchmark [Ferrara et al., 2008] is also following a bottom-up approach. It uses several algorithms to create different data sets. It initially requires the creation of a reference ontology for a specific domain. Then, this ontology is populated with instances by querying Web sites. For example, *IMDB* enables the population of a *movie* ontology. Subsequently, a number of modifications on the data takes place, with three goals in mind: (1) to introduce variations in the data values, e.g., typographical errors, (2) to introduce structural heterogeneity, e.g., properties represented by different structural levels, aggregations, and others, and (3) to introduce local heterogeneity, which mainly includes semantic variations that requires ontological reasoning to cope with. Once the modifications have been performed, the benchmark users are provided with the initial reference ontology and the modified one, against which they evaluate matching tools.

6 Measuring Efficiency

6.1 Matching/Mapping Generation Time

Since one of the goals of mapping tools is to assist the matching/mapping designer in performing the time-consuming matching and mapping tasks faster, time plays a major role in measuring the performance of matching/mapping tools. Nevertheless, mapping tools like Spicy [Bonifati et al., 2008b], HePToX [Bonifati et al., 2005], or Clio [Popa et al., 2002], in their evaluation experiments, make only a small reference to mapping generation time, and evaluation techniques proposed by Spicy [Bonifati et al., 2008a] or STBenchmark [Alexe et al., 2008c] do not elaborate extensively on the issue. This is not an omission on their behalf. It reflects the fact that it is hard to measure time when human participation, in our specific case for the verification and guidance of the mapping tool, is part of the process. The time required by humans to understand the mappings generated by the tool and provide feedback is orders of magnitude higher than the one the tool requires for computing the mappings.

The situation is slightly different in matching tools where there is limited human intervention. Although computation time is still a central factor, it is not as important as the quality of the generated matches. A recent evaluation on a number of matching tools [Yatskevich, 2003] has extended previous evaluations [Do et al., 2003] by adding time measures for matching tasks on real-world matching scenarios. Unfortunately, these metrics have yet to be materialized in an a benchmark. In a more recent comparison [Kopcke and Rahm, 2010] of state-of-the-art matching tools, generation time has been one of the main comparison criteria and is also one of the metrics used by matching evaluation tools like XBenchMatch [Duchateau et al., 2007] and the ISLab Instance Matching Benchmark [Ferrara et al., 2008].

6.2 Data Translation Performance

It has already been mentioned that one of the popular uses of mappings is to translate data from one source to another, i.e., the data exchange task. This translation is done by materializing the target or integrated instance from the data of one or more source instances according to the mappings. Data sources typically contain a large number of records. This means that if the mappings are numerous and describe complex transformations, then the time required to materialize the target instance may be significant. Based on this observation, it is clear that one of the factors to characterize the quality of a mapping tool is by the performance of the execution of the transformations described by the generated mappings. Metrics that can be used to measure such performance are the overall execution time and the degree of parallelization.

[Time] The most general-purpose metric is the time required to perform the overall transformation time. Although this parameter is not explicitly stated in any matching or mapping evaluation effort, certain extensive experiments found in the literature [Alexe et al., 2008c] illustrate its importance. The generation of good transformation scripts is actually a way to characterize good mapping tools. Note that to avoid falling into the trap of evaluating the query execution engine instead of the mapping tool, when measuring the performance of the generated transformation scripts, all the comparison and evaluation experiments should be performed on the same transformation engine.

There has been an increasing interest toward efficient methods for generating the right target instance given a mapping scenario, and more specifically in generating the *core*. The core [Fagin et al., 2003] is a minimum universal solution [Fagin et al., 2005]. Core identification has been shown to be a co-NP hard problem [Fagin et al., 2005] for certain mapping dependencies. Despite these complexity results, there have been successful developments of efficient techniques that given two schemas and a set of mapping dependencies between them, in the form of tuple generating dependencies, produce a set of transformation scripts, e.g., in XSLT or SQL, whose execution efficiently generates a core target instance [Mecca et al., 2009, ten Cate et al., 2009].

Time performance is becoming particularly critical in ETL tools that typically deal with large volumes of data. Recent ETL benchmarks [Simitsis et al., 2009] consider it as one of the major factors of every ETL tool evaluation. Other similar factors that are also mentioned in ETL benchmarks are the workflow execution throughput, the average latency per tuple, and the workflow execution throughput under failures. The notion of time performance in ETL tools extends beyond the end of the ETL workflow construction by considering, apart from the data translation time, the time required to answer business-level queries on the transformed data.

[Parallelization] One way to improve the data transformation time is to increase parallelization by generating mappings with minimum interdependencies. There are in general two broad categories of parallel processing: pipelining and partitioning. In pipelining, different parts of the transformation are executed in parallel in a system with more than one processor, and the data generated by one component are consumed immediately by another component without the need of waiting for the first component to fully complete its task. Pipelining works well for transformations that do not involve extremely large amounts of data. If this is not the case, a different parallelization mechanism called partitioning is preferable. In partitioning, the data is first divided into different parts, and then, the transformation described by the mappings is applied on each partition independently of the others [Simitsis et al., 2009].

6.3 Human Effort

Since the goal of a matching or mapping tool is to alleviate the designer from the laborious task of matching and mapping specification, it is natural to consider as one of the evaluation metrics of such a tool the effort required by the mapping designer.

In a schema matching task, the input consists of only the two schemas. Since the task involves semantics, the designer must go through all the produced matches and verify their correctness. Consequently, the effort the designer needs to spend during a matching task can be naively quantified by the number of matches produced by the matcher and by their complexity.

A matcher may produce not only false positives but also false negatives, which the matching designer will have to add manually to the result of the matcher, or will have to tune the tool to generate them. Two metrics have been proposed in the literature for quantifying this effort. One is the *overall*, which is also found under the name *accuracy* [Melnik et al., 2002] and is defined by the formula that follows:

$$Overall = Recall \times \left(2 - \frac{1}{Precision}\right) \tag{9.1}$$

Recall and precision are metrics that are presented later and evaluate the accuracy of the generated matches intuitively. The *overall* metric evaluates the amount of work an expert must provide to remove irrelevant matches (false positives) and to add those relevant that were not discovered (false negatives) [Do et al., 2003]. The metric returns a value between $-\infty$ and 1. The greater the overall value is, the less effort the designer has to provide. It is a general belief [Do et al., 2003] that a precision below 50% implies that more effort is required from the designer to remove the false matches and add those missing than to manually do the matching. This is why such situations have a negative *overall* value. A limitation of the *overall* metric is that it assumes equal effort for removing an irrelevant match and for adding a missing one, which is rarely the case in the real world.

Another metric to measure the human effort is the human-spared resources (HSR) [Duchateau, 2009]. It counts the number of designer interactions required to correct both precision and recall, i.e., to manually obtain a 100% f-measure, a quality metric that is discussed later. In other words, HSR takes into account not only the effort to validate or invalidate the discovered matches but also the effort to discover those missing. HSR is sufficiently generic, can be expresse in the range of [0, 1] or in time units (e.g., seconds), and does not require any input other than the one for computing precision, recall, f-measure, or overall. The only limitation is that it does not take into account the fact that some matching tools may return the top-K matches instead of all of them.

In the schema mapping process, if the mapping specification is provided by the designer and is not taken from the output of an automatic matching task, the situation is different. The designer is required to provide input to the mapping tool through its interface, not only at the beginning but also throughout the mapping generation process, since the designer will have to continuously verify the tool-generated mappings and provide the respective modifications. Thus, the effort of the mapping designer can be measured by the number of inputs the designer provides to the tool.

This evaluation criterion is essentially an evaluation of the graphical interface of the tool. It is true that the more intelligence a tool incorporates in interpreting the mapping designer input, the less input effort is required by the designer. However, certain interfaces may be so well designed that even if there are many tasks the mapping designer needs to do, the human effort is kept to the minimum.

STBenchmark introduces a simple usability (SU) model, intended to provide a first-cut measure on the amount of effort required for a mapping scenario. It is based on a rough counting of the mouse clicks and keystrokes to quantify effort. This is important even if the time required for the mapping specification is much smaller in comparison to the time needed by the generated mappings to become transformation scripts and be executed. The click log information describing a mapping design for STBenchmark looks like this: *Right mouse click to pull up menu, left mouse click to select a schema element, typing a function into a box*, etc. Since different actions may require more effort than others [MacKenzie et al., 1991], for example, a point-and-click is much easier than dragging or typing, weights can be assigned to each type of action to build a cost model for quantifying the total required effort.

One of the limitations of the above model is that it does not distinguish between clicks leading to the final mapping design and corrective actions, such as, undo or delete operations. It assumes that the mapping designer is familiar with the mapping tool and makes no mistakes. Another limitation is that the model does not capture the time the designer spends on thinking. A mapping tool that requires the designer think for long time before designing the mapping with only few clicks should not be considered more efficient than others that require less thinking by the designer but a few more clicks. A final limitation of this idea is that the model does not consider features such as presentation layout, visual aids, access to frequently used tasks, etc.

In the area of schema integration, the Thalia benchmark [Hammer et al., 2005] can be used for objectively evaluating the capabilities of integration technology by taking into account, besides the correctness of the solution, the amount of pro-grammatic effort (i.e., the complexity of external functions) needed to resolve any heterogeneity. For a fair comparison, any measurement of the needed effort must be done on the implementation of the twelve queries that Thalia provides. However, Thalia, does not provide any specifications on how this "effort" is to be measured.

7 Measuring Effectiveness

Measuring the effectiveness of a mapping or matching tool means measuring whether (or how much) the tool can fulfill its expectations for a given task. In the case of matching, an expert user typically knows what the correct matches are, and the matching tool is expected to find them. Thus, evaluating its effectiveness boils down to a comparison between the expected set of matchings and the set of match-ings that the tool generated. The situation is slightly different for the case of mapping systems. Since the expected output of a mapping system is a set of mappings that is used to generate the target (or global) instance, evaluating whether the mapping system has fulfilled its expectations can be done by checking whether the generated mappings can produce the expected target instance, or how close to the expected instance is the one that the generated mappings produce. This comparison can be done either extensionally, by comparing instances, or intensionally, by comparing the generated transformation expressions, i.e., the mappings. In this section, we pro-vide an overview of metrics that have been used in the literature for measuring such effectiveness.

7.1 Supported Scenarios

One way to evaluate a matching or mapping tool is by counting the percentage of scenarios it can successfully implement from a provided list of scenarios. A basic assumption is that there is an oracle providing the ground truth for each of these scenarios, i.e., the set of expected matches/mappings. This oracle is typically an expert user. A match/mapping generated by a tool is characterized as correct if it is part of the ground truth, or incorrect, otherwise. The successful implementation of a scenario by a tool is the generation of the expected matches/mappings.

Provided with a rich set of mapping scenarios, one can test different aspects of a mapping tool. The effectiveness of the tool is the percentage of these scenarios that the tool could successfully implement. This approach is the one followed by STBenchmark [Alexe et al., 2008b]. The scenarios the benchmark provides have been collected from the related scientific literature and real-world applications.

The characterization of the effectiveness of a tool based on the notion of the successful or unsuccessful implementation of scenarios may not be the optimal approach especially in the case of systems. Very often, a mapping tool may not be able to produce exactly the expected mappings, yet it may be able to generate a pretty good approximation of them, or mappings that produce a target instance very close to the expected one. Under the above model, such a tool will be unfairly penalized as unsuccessful, even though the final result is very close to the one expected. For this reason, a metric measuring proximity of the produced results to the expected is becoming an increasingly popular alternative.

7.2 Quality of the Generated Matchings/Mappings

Four metrics that have been used extensively in the area of matching tool evaluation are the *precision, recall, f-measure,* and the *fallout* [Euzenat and Shvaiko, 2007]. They are all intended to quantify the proximity of the results generated by a matching tool to those expected. They are based on the notions of *true positives, false positives, true negatives,* and *false negatives.* Given two schemas S and T, let $\mathcal{M}$ represent the set of all possible matches that can exist between their respective elements. Assume that an oracle provides the list of expected matches. These matches are referred to as *relevant*, and all the other matches in $\mathcal{M}$ as *irrelevant*. The matching tool provides a list of matches that it considers true. These are the *tool relevant matches*, while the remaining matches in $\mathcal{M}$ are the *tool irrelevant matches*. A match in $\mathcal{M}$ is characterized as true positive, false positive, true negative, or false negative, depending on which of the above sets it belongs. The respective definitions are illustrated in Table 9.1.

The precision, recall, and f-measure [Van-Risbergen, 1979] are well known from the information retrieval domain. They return a real value between 0 and 1 and have been used in many matching evaluation efforts [Duchateau et al., 2007, Do et al., 2002]. Figure 9.8 depicts a matching example. It illustrates two schemas

Table 9.1 Contingency table forming the base of evaluation measures

	Relevant matches	Irrelevant matches
Tool relevant matches	TP (true positive)	FP (false positive)
Tool irrelevant matches	FN (false negative)	TN (true negative)

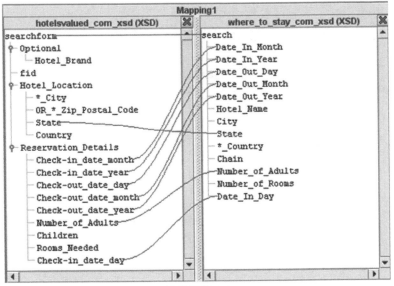

(a) COMA++

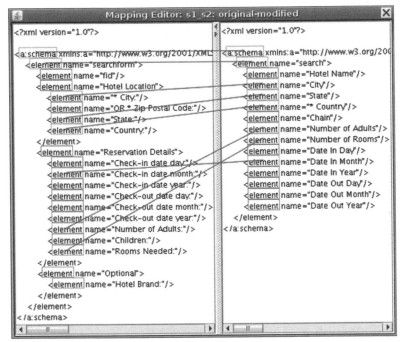

(b) Similarity Flooding

Fig. 9.8 Correspondences discovered by two schema matchers

related to hotel reservations and the relevant matches (illustrated by the interschema lines) generated by two matching tools, COMA++ [Aumueller et al., 2005] and Similarity Flooding [Melnik et al., 2002], denoted as SF in short. COMA++ has discovered 9 matches, while SF has discovered 7. Note that for SF, the matches between the root elements of the schemas are not considered.

[Precision] The *precision* calculates the proportion of relevant matches discovered by the matching tool with respect to all those discovered. Using the notation of Table 9.1, the precision is defined as

$$Precision = \frac{TP}{TP + FP}$$

An 100% precision means that all the matches discovered by the tool are relevant. In the particular example of Fig. 9.8, both tools achieve a 100% precision:

$$Precision_{COMA++} = \frac{9}{9+0} = 100\% \qquad Precision_{SF} = \frac{7}{7+0} = 100\%$$

[Recall] *Recall* is another broadly used metric. It computes the proportion of matches discovered by the tool with respect to all the relevant matches. It is defined by the formula

$$Recall = \frac{TP}{TP + FN}$$

A 100% recall means that all relevant matches have been found by the tool. For the scenario of Fig. 9.8, COMA++ has discovered 9 matches but missed 4 relevant matches. These missed matches are the false negatives. SF, on the other hand, discovered 7 relevant matches out of the 13. These results give the following recall values:

$$Recall_{COMA++} = \frac{9}{9+4} = 69\% \qquad Recall_{SF} = \frac{7}{7+6} - 54\%$$

[F-measure] *F-measure* is a trade-off between precision and recall. It is defined as follows:

$$f - measure(\beta) = \frac{(\beta^2 + 1) \times Precision \times Recall}{(\beta^2 \times Precision) + Recall}$$

The β parameter regulates the respective influence of precision and recall. It is often set to 1 to give the same weight to these two evaluation measures. Back to our running example, using a β equal to 1, the f-measure values obtained for COMA++ and SF are, respectively, as follows:

$$f - measure_{COMA++} = \frac{2 \times 1 \times 0.69}{1 + 0.69} = 82\%$$

and

$$f - measure_{SF} = \frac{2 \times 1 \times 0.54}{1 + 0.54} = 70\%$$

[Fallout] Another metric that is often used in the literature is the fallout [Euzenat et al., 2006] [Ferrara et al., 2008]. It computes the rate of incorrectly discovered matches out of the number of those nonexpected ones. Intuitively, it measures the probability that a irrelevant match is discovered by the tool. The fallout is defined by the following formula:

$$Fallout = \frac{FP}{FP + TN}$$

In the running example of Fig. 9.8, the number of nonexpected, i.e., irrelevant, matches equals 253 (there exist a total of 266 possible matches including the 13 that are relevant). However, since neither tool discovered any irrelevant match, their fallout equals to 0%.

$$Fallout_{COMA++} = \frac{0}{0 + 253} = 0\% \qquad Fallout_{SF} = \frac{0}{0 + 253} = 0\%$$

The matching benchmark XBenchMatch [Duchateau et al., 2007] and the ontology alignment API [Euzenat, 2004] are based on the above metrics to evaluate the effectiveness of matching tools. They assume the availability of the expected set of matches through an expert user. Based on that set and the matches that the matching tool produces, the various values of the metrics are computed.

A limitation of the above metrics is that they do not take into consideration any postmatch user effort, for instance, tasks that the user may need to do to guide the matching tool in the matching process, or any iterations the user may perform to verify partially generated results.

Measuring the quality of mappings turns out to be more challenging than measuring the quality of the matches. The reason is that it requires comparisons among mappings, which is not a straightforward task. Finding whether a generated mapping belongs to the set of expected mappings requires a comparison between this mapping and every other mapping in that set. This comparison boils down to query equivalence. Apart from the fact that query equivalence is a hard task per se, it is also the case that a transformation described by a mapping may be also implemented through a combination of more than one different mapping. This means that it is not enough to compare with individual mappings only, but combinations of mappings should also be considered. For this reason, direct mapping comparison has typically been avoided as evaluation method of mapping tools. Researchers have instead opted for a comparison of the results of the mappings, e.g., the target instances.

Nevertheless, the precision, recall, and the f-measure can be used to evaluate the large class of tools that do not differentiate among the matching and the mapping process but consider the whole task as a monolithic procedure. Spicy [Bonifati et al., 2008a] is an example of such tools, as it pipelines a matching module and a mapping generation module and allows the mapping designer to reiterate between the two processes to improve the quality of the generated mappings. In Spicy, the mapping tasks were designed in such a way that the source always contains a mapping that covers the entire target, meaning that no subset of the target schema remains unmapped. The set of mapping scenarios in the system are built in such a way that for a target schema, the correct set of matches that will generate a given predetermined mapping is internally identified. These matches are called the *ideal match* $\mathcal{M}_{id}$. At this point, the mapping generation algorithm can be run, and a single transformation, T_{best}, i.e., the mapping that has the best scores in terms of instance similarity (cfr. next section for details), can be generated. Then, the matches $\mathcal{M}_{T_{best}}$ on which this mapping is based upon are identified. In the ideal case, these matches are the same as the ideal match $\mathcal{M}_{id}$. The quality of the tool can be measured in terms of precision and recall of $\mathcal{M}_{T_{best}}$ with respect to $\mathcal{M}_{id}$. However, Spicy reports quality only in terms of precision. The reason is that in all cases, the tool returns a number of matches that is equal to the size of the target, as mentioned above. As a consequence, precision and recall are both equal to the number of correct matches in $\mathcal{M}_{T_{best}}$ over the size of the target, which means that either precision or recall suffices to characterize the quality of the generated mappings.

The cases in which the source does not contain a mapping that covers the entire target are more complex and have not so far been addressed. It is believed that the most general case in which the target schema is not entirely covered by the mapping entails a new class of mapping tasks in which the target instance is partially filled with data exchanged with the source and partially filled with its own data.

The problem of characterizing mappings in a quantitative way has also been studied [Fagin et al., 2009b] through the notion of *information loss*, which is introduced to measure how much a schema mapping deviates from an ideal invertible mapping. An invertible mapping is a mapping that given the generated target instance can be used to regenerate the original source instance. A first definition of invertibility has considered only constants in the source instance and constants alongside labeled nulls in the target (cfr. [Fagin et al., 2011]). Labeled nulls are generated values for elements in the target that require a value, but the mapping provides no specification for that value. In the inversion, these labeled nulls can propagate in the source instance, resulting into an instance that has less information that the original one. To capture in a precise way such an information loss, the notion of maximum extended recovery has been introduced for tgds with disjunction and inequalities [Fagin et al., 2009b]. This new metric clearly identifies a viable approach to precisely compare schema mappings, but the full potential of this metric in benchmarking mapping tools still remains to be explored.

Another step toward the design of meaningful and high-quality schema mappings has been tackled recently [Alexe et al., 2010a] by using a *MapMerge* operator to merge multiple small mappings into large ones. The evaluation of such an operator is done by using a novel similarity metric that is able to capture the extent to which data associations are preserved by the transformation from a source to a target instance. The metric depends on the natural associations that exist among data values in the source instance, discovered by looking at the schema structures and by following the schema referential integrity constraints. The idea behind the metric is that these associations must be preserved by the transformation that the mapping describes.

7.3 Quality of the Generated Target Instance

In systems that do not differentiate between the matching and the mapping task, an alternative to measuring precision, recall, or f-measure would be preferable. One such approach is to use the final expected result of the mapping process, which is the actual target instance generated by the transformation described by the mappings. This kind of evaluation is also useful in cases where one needs to avoid comparisons between mappings for reasons like those provided earlier. The expected target instance is typically provided by an expert user. Once the expected target instance is available, the success of a mapping task can be measured by comparing it to the actual target instance produced by the generated mappings. The approach constitutes an appealing verification and validation method, mainly due to its simplicity.

The comparison between the actual and the expected target instance can be done by considering an ad hoc similarity function, such as *tree edit distance*, or by employing a general-purpose comparison technique [Bonifati et al., 2008a]. Defining such a customized comparison technique is a promising direction for future developments in this area. The Spicy system offers a comparison method based on circuit theory [Bonifati et al., 2008a], called *structural analysis*. Figure 9.9 shows an example of a circuit generated by the tree representation of a schema, as shown on the left-hand side. The circuit is based on building blocks corresponding to atomic attributes. More specifically, for each intermediate node n in the schema tree, a resistance value $r(n)$ is defined. Such a value cannot be based on instances, since intermediate nodes of the tree represent higher structures, but it is rather based on the topology of the tree. In particular, $r(n) = k \times level(n)$, where k is a constant multiplicative factor, and $level(n)$ is the *level* of n in the tree, defined as follows: (1) leaves have level 0 (2) an intermediate node with children $n_0, n_1, \ldots n_k$ has level $max(level(n_0), level(n_1), \ldots level(n_k)) + 1$.

The complete circuit is defined by means of a *circuit mapping function*, $circ(t)$ over a tree t. For a leaf node A, $circ(A)$ is defined by mapping a sampled attribute to a circuit. Intuitively, $circ(A)$ is assembled by assigning a set of features to a number of resistors and voltage generators. For a tree t rooted at node n with children $n_0, n_1, \ldots n_k$, $circ(t)$ is the circuit obtained by connecting in parallel

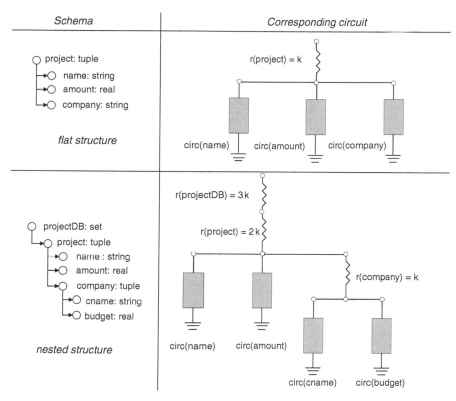

Fig. 9.9 Examples of circuits for flat and nested structures

$circ(n_0), circ(n_1), \dots circ(n_k)$ between ground and an intermediate circuit node n_{top}, and then adding a resistor of value $r(n)$ from node n_{top} to the output. Examples of such transformation are illustrated in Fig. 9.9. Note that the circuit mapping function makes the resulting circuits isomorphic to the original trees.

In Spicy, similarly to the *opaque* schema matching [Kang and Naughton, 2003], labels are ignored by the circuit mapping function, and values are basically treated as uninterpreted strings. Furthermore, values correspond to alphanumeric data in the underlying Spicy data model. The circuit features discussed above reflect this choice. However, the circuit model is sufficiently flexible to allow the treatment of special data, like large texts or multimedia, as discussed in other orthogonal usage of circuits [Palmer and Faloutsos, 2003].

Given two trees t_1 and t_2, a measure of their similarity can be computed by mapping t_1 and t_2 to the corresponding circuits, $circ(t_1)$, $circ(t_2)$, as depicted in Fig. 9.9, solving the two circuits to determine their currents and voltages, and choosing a number of descriptive features of the corresponding circuits, $f_0, f_1, \dots f_i$. A notion of *comparator* for each feature f_i as a module that computes the index of similarity Δ_i between the two structures with respect to feature f_i is defined in Spicy as follows: $\Delta_i = abs(f_i(circ(t_1)) - f_i(circ(t_2)))/f_i(circ(t_1))$. Finally, the overall similarity of the two trees is computed based on the values of $\Delta_0, \Delta_1, \dots \Delta_i$ [Bonifati et al., 2008a].

The quality of the target instance is also an important factor in the case of ETL systems. For these systems, the quality is typically determined by the *data freshness*, the *resiliency to occasional failures*, and the *easy of maintenance* [Simitsis et al., 2009]. Data freshness means that the effect of any modification in the source instance is also implemented in the target. Resiliency to failures measures whether different transformation routes or recovery procedures can guarantee that in case that a part of the transformation fails, the data that was to be generated can be generated either through different routes or by repetition of the failed procedure. Finally, the maintainability is affected, among others, by the simplicity of the transformation. A simple ETL transformation is more maintainable, whereas in a complex transformation it is more difficult to keep track of the primitive transformations that take place. Occasionally, the *compliance to business rules* is also one of the considered factors for measuring the quality of an ETL system.

7.4 Data Examples

Generating the expected target instance for evaluating a mapping system may not always be the most desired method. The size of the target schema may be prohibitively large, and its generation at mapping design time may not be feasible. Even if its generation is possible, due to its size, even an expert mapping designer may find hard to understand the full semantics of the generated transformation, since it is practically impossible to always obtain a full view of the target data. The generated mappings between a source and the target schema may also be numerous, ambiguous, and complicated to a degree that the designer is not able to understand what and how some target data was created from data in the source. To cope with these issues and help the designer in quickly and fully understanding the semantics of the mapping-system-generated transformations and validate them, carefully selected representative samples of the target instance can be used. Samples of the expected target instance can be used to drive the mapping process, while samples of the generated target instance can be used to communicate to the designer the semantics of the mappings the system has generated.

The importance of data examples in mapping generation has long ago been recognized [Yan et al., 2001]. In the specific work, each mapping is considered a transformation query and is interpreted as an indirectly connected graph $G = (N, E)$, where the set of nodes N is a subset of the relations of the source schema and the set of edges E represents conjunctions of join predicates on attributes of the source relations. Typically, joins are inner joins, but they can also be considered as outer joins or combinations of inner and outer joins. Given a query graph G, the *full* and the *possible* data associations can be computed. A data association is a relation that contains the maximum number of attributes whose data are semantically related through structural or constraint, e.g., foreign key, constructs. A full data association of G is computed by an inner join query over G, and it involves all nodes in G. Given an induced, connected subgraphs of G, a data association can be constructed in the same way, but since it is based on a subgraph of G, the data association is referred to as a possible association. Full and possible data associations can be leveraged to understand what information needs to be included in a mapping.

From a different perspective, one could think of a wizard or a debugging tool that allows to better understand the semantics of the mappings by illustrating the flow of tuples from source to target in a schema mapping task. The notion of *routes* [Chiticariu and Tan, 2006] captures this idea and is useful in the mapping debugging process to understand the behavior of mappings. Routes can be created between original source and target instances or between illustrative data examples. Ultimately, routes can be used in conjunction with data examples to help the user dig in the semantics of a mapping.

To understand what a data example represents, assume a mapping generation situation with a source schema S, a target schema T, and a set of mappings Σ. It is said that a data example (I, J) is satisfied by the set of mappings Σ, denoted as $(I, J) \models \Sigma$, if I is a fraction of an instance of S, J is a fraction of an instance of T, and there is a mapping $m \in \Sigma$ such that $m(I) = J$. Such a data example is called a *positive* data example. If I is a fraction of an instance of S, J is a fraction of an instance of T, but $(I, J) \not\models \Sigma$, then the data example is called *negative*. Positive examples are used to illustrate intended transformed data in the instance, while negative examples can be used to describe undesired mapping transformations.

In the special case that the data J of a data example (I, J) is a universal solution (cfr. [Bonifati et al., 2011]), the example is called a *universal data example*. Universal data examples are of major importance due to their generality. A recent study [Alexe et al., 2010b] has highlighted that if the only kind of mappings considered are source-to-target tgds, a mapping can be characterized by a finite set of positive and negative data examples if and only if the source and the target schema contain only unary relation symbols. Nevertheless, the study has also shown that the universal examples may characterize the entire class of local-as-view [Lenzerini, 2002] source-to-target tgds.

In short, data examples have already found their way into mapping systems as a way of helping the designer understand and refine the generated mappings [Alexe et al., 2008a] and in certain cases select a subset of those mappings that the mapping system produces [Yan et al., 2001]. They can also become an asset in mapping system evaluation as indicated by some first efforts toward this direction [Alexe et al., 2010b]. In particular, the mapping system Clio is employing debugging tools like Routes [Chiticariu and Tan, 2006] to build a mapping designer evaluation framework that is based on data examples. There are still many challenging research issues around that topic, for instance, a deeper study of the use of positive, negative, and universal examples.

7.5 *Quality of the Generated Target Schema*

When the mapping system is used to create an integrated (or target) schema, a technique to evaluate the quality of the system is to measure the quality of the generated integrated schema. This can be done mainly by measuring its relationship to the schema that the designer had in mind to create, i.e., the intended integrated schema. The relationship can be measured in terms like the amount of information in the source schema that is also described in the integrated schema, the difference in the schema structures, etc. Three metrics have been recently proposed: the *completeness*, *minimality*, and *structurality*.

Completeness. Let Si_{tool} represent the target schema generated by the mapping tool and Si_{int} the intended target schema that models the integration. The notation $|S|$ is used to refer to the number of elements in a schema S. The *completeness* [Batista and Salgado, 2007] is a metric in the range of 0 to 1, which intuitively measures how many of the concepts that can be modeled by the source schema(s) can also be modeled by the target schema, i.e., the integration. More formally,

$$Completeness = \frac{|S_{tool} \cap S_{int}|}{|S_{int}|}$$

Minimality. The *minimality* [Batista and Salgado, 2007] is another metric also in the range of 0 to 1, which indicates the redundancy that may appear in the integrated schema. The higher the minimality, the lower the redundancy. Minimality is defined by the following expression, which basically calculates the percentage of extra elements in the integrated schema produced by the mapping tool with respect to the intended instance. In particular:

$$Minimality = 1 - \frac{|S_{tool}| - |S_{tool} \cap S_{int}|}{|S_{int}|}$$

Structurality. The *structurality* has been introduced [Duchateau, 2009] to intuitively measure the *qualities of the structure an object possesses.*[6] In the case of schemas, this notion is translated to the set of ancestors of a schema structure. In other words, the structurality measures whether the elements of the generated and the intended schema contain the same set of ancestors. To compute structurality, the schemas are viewed as trees. Let S_{int} and S_{gen} denote the intended and the generated target schema, respectively. Assume also that in the tree representation of a schema S, $P_S(e)$ is the set of elements in the path from the root to the element e, exclusively. The structurality of an element e is defined as follows:

$$Structurality(e) = \max\left(0, \frac{\alpha|P_{S_{int}}(e) \cap P_{S_{gen}}(e)| - (|P_{S_{gen}}(e)| - |P_{S_{int}}(e) \cap P_{S_{gen}}(e)|)}{\alpha|P_{S_{int}}(e)|}\right)$$

Intuitively, the formula checks that an element shares most ancestors both in the generated and intended integrated schemas. Besides, it takes into account the insertion of incorrect ancestors in the generated integrated schema. Note that the

---

[6] http://en.wiktionary.org/wiki/structurality.

structurality of an element e of the intended schema that does not appear in the schema generated by the tool is zero. The parameter α is a constant factor that allows higher importance to be given to ancestors that have been created in the generated schema, as opposed to those that have not. Since the number of ancestors P_{gen} may be large, an element structurality may become negative, which explains the existence of the max function in the above formula. A negative value would be difficult to interpret by end users, as this is the case for the overall measure when dealing with matching quality.

The structurality of a schema S_{gen} generated by the mapping tool is the average of the structuralities of the individual elements in the intended schema, i.e.,

$$Structurality \; of \; S_{gen} = \frac{\sum_{e \in S_{int}} Structurality(e)}{|S_{int}|}$$

The completeness, minimality, and structurality metrics can be combined into a weighted sum to provide an overall metric for the proximity of the generated schema and the intended scheme, i.e.,

$$Proximity = w_1 * Completeness + w_2 * Minimality + w_3 * Structurability$$

with $w_1 + w_2 + w_3 = 1$.

To illustrate the above metrics, consider the abstract schema shown on the left-hand side of Fig. 9.10, and assume that it is the schema generated by the mapping tool. The schema that was intended to be created is the one on the right-hand side of the same figure. The number of common schema elements between these two schemas are 6, thus, $Completeness = \frac{6}{7}$ and $Minimality = 1 - \frac{8-6}{7} = \frac{5}{7}$. Assuming an α factor with value 2, the structuralities of the elements of the intended schema are illustrated in Table 9.2. According to these values, the structurality of the generated schema with respect to the intended schema is $\frac{1+1+1+0+\frac{1}{4}+\frac{1}{2}}{6} = 0.625$. Giving equal weight to completeness, minimality, and structurality, the overall proximity of the generated schema to the intended is as follows: $\frac{0.86+0.71+0.625}{3} = 0.73$.

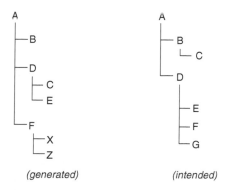

(generated)   (intended)

Fig. 9.10 An abstract example of a schema generated by a mapping tool (*left*) and the intended

Table 9.2 Element structuralities for the intended schema of Fig. 9.10

Element	P_{int}	P_{gen}	Element structurality
B	A	A	$\max(0, \frac{2\times1-(1-1)}{2\times1}) = 1$
D	A	A	$\max(0, \frac{2\times1-(1-1)}{2\times1}) = 1$
E	A,D	A,D	$\max(0, \frac{2\times2-(2-2)}{2\times2}) = 1$
G	A,D	Ø	$\max(0, \frac{2\times0-(0-0)}{2\times2}) = 0$
C	A,B	A,D	$\max(0, \frac{2\times1-(2-1)}{2\times2}) = \frac{1}{4}$
F	A,D	A	$\max(0, \frac{2\times1-(1-1)}{2\times2}) = \frac{1}{2}$

There has been an interesting set of experimental results [Duchateau, 2009] on computing the above metrics using a number of different datasets with the two popular matching systems: COMA++ [Aumueller et al., 2005] and Similarity Flooding [Melnik et al., 2002]. The former system builds integrated schemas using an ASCII-tree format (then converted into XSD using a script [Duchateau et al., 2007]), while the latter system directly generates an XSD integrated schema. The matches discovered by the tools before building the integrated schema have not been checked. The experiments include a dataset extracted from the XCBL[7] and OAGI[8] collections, a dataset on university courses provided by the Thalia benchmark [Hammer et al., 2005], a Biology dataset from Uniprot[9] and GeneCards,[10] a currency and sms dataset,[11] and a university department dataset [Duchateau et al., 2008]. These datasets present various features that reflect real-world scenarios. For instance, the biology dataset contains a specific vocabulary that is not usually found in common dictionaries. The dataset about university courses describes a case in which many schemas have to be integrated. A part of the experimental results obtained from that effort is illustrated in Fig. 9.11. It has been noticed that the tools can obtain a high completeness in most cases, mainly because the tools promote precision during the matching phase. On the contrary, the minimality is more difficult to achieve, since it depends on the recall. Finally, structurality is mostly preserved because the tools try to keep the same structure that they find in the source schemas.

8 Conclusion

We have presented a retrospective on key contributions in the area of evaluating matching and mapping tools. Schema matching and mapping is a relatively new area that has received considerable attention in the last few years. Since these

---

[7] www.xcbl.org.

[8] www.oagi.org.

[9] http://www.ebi.uniprot.org/support/docs/uniprot.xsd.

[10] http://www.geneontology.org/GO.downloads.ontology.shtml.

[11] www.seekda.com.

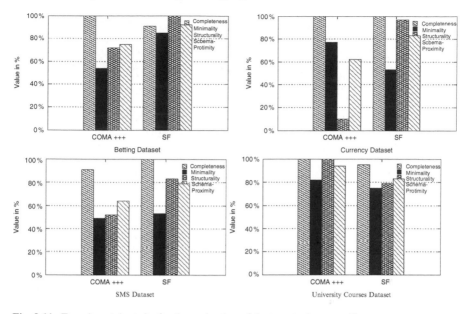

Fig. 9.11 Experimental results for the evaluation of the target schema quality

notions may not have yet matured in the minds of researchers and of the commercial developers and users, and to avoid confusions, we have first attempted to provide a complete description of the architectural components, tasks, and goals of matching and mapping tools. Then, we have motivated the importance of evaluation methods and benchmarks for researchers, developers, businesses, and users.

Schema matching is a topic that has been extensively studied. There is already a long list of research prototypes and tools. Since the matching task involves semantics, evaluating the correctness of the output of a matching tool is a task requiring human intervention. The major issue in all these matching cases is deciding what is the correct answer, i.e., the intended matches. This is a challenging task since, due to the semantic heterogeneity, different perspectives may give different answers. Evaluation techniques for matching tasks have focused on the development of metrics that will allow a common evaluation base and effective communication of the evaluation results. We have provided a description of these metrics and have highlighted features and limitations.

Schema mapping seems to be a problem for which there is still some confusion as to what constitutes a mapping tool, what is its input, in what form, and what is its output. Different research prototypes and commercial tools have followed different approaches, something that makes their direct comparison and evaluation difficult. We have attempted to provide a definition of what a mapping tool is and the parameters one should consider when evaluating such tools. We have highlighted the lack of evaluation standards and have provided a complete picture of what an evaluation standard (or benchmark) should contain, alongside existing efforts toward the creation of such a standard.

Mapping tools have been mainly designed for data exchange. Nevertheless, they have been extensively used in integration systems for constructing an integrated global schema. Based on this dimension, we have also provided a number of metrics for measuring the success of the schema integration task performed by mapping tools.

Acknowledgements We are grateful to B. Alexe, L. Chiticariu, A. Kementsietsidis, E. Rahm, and P. Shvaiko for their valuable comments and suggestions.

References

Abiteboul S, Hull R, Vianu V (1995) Foundations of databases. Addison-Wesley, MA

Alexe B, Chiticariu L, Miller RJ, Tan WC (2008a) Muse: Mapping understanding and deSign by example. In: ICDE. IEEE Computer Society, Washington, DC, pp 10–19

Alexe B, Tan WC, Velegrakis Y (2008b) Comparing and evaluating mapping systems with STBenchmark. Proc VLDB 1(2):1468–1471

Alexe B, Tan WC, Velegrakis Y (2008c) STBenchmark: Towards a benchmark for mapping systems. Proc VLDB 1(1):230–244

Alexe B, Hernandez M, Popa L, Tan WC (2010a) MapMerge: Correlating independent schema mappings. Proceedings of VLDB, vol 3(1). VLDB Endowment, pp 81–92

Alexe B, Kolaitis PG, Tan W (2010b) Characterizing schema mappings via data examples. In: PODS. ACM, NY, pp 261–272

Altova (2008) MapForce. http://www.altova.com

Atzeni P, Torlone R (1995) Schema translation between heterogeneous data models in a lattice framework. In: Data semantics conference. Chapman & Hall, London, pp 345–364

Aumueller D, Do HH, Massmann S, Rahm E (2005) Schema and ontology matching with COMA++. In: SIGMOD. ACM, NY, pp 906–908

Barbosa D, Mendelzon AO, Keenleyside J, Lyons KA (2002) ToXgene: A template-based data generator for XML. In: SIGMOD. ACM, NY, p 616

Batini C, Lenzerini M, Navathe SB (1986) A comparative analysis of methodologies for database schema integration. ACM Comp Surv 18(4):323–364

Batista M, Salgado A (2007) Information Quality Measurement in Data Integration Schemas. In: Workshop on Quality in Databases, pp 61–72

Bergamaschi S, Domnori E, Guerra F, Orsini M, Lado RT, Velegrakis Y (2010) Keymantic: Semantic keyword based searching in data integration systems. Proceedings of VLDB, vol 3(2), pp 1637–1640

Bernstein PA, Melnik S (2007) Model management 2.0: Manipulating richer mappings. In: SIGMOD. ACM, NY, pp 1–12

Bernstein PA, Giunchiglia F, Kementsietsidis A, Mylopoulos J, Serafini L, Zaihrayeu I (2002) Data management for peer-to-peer computing: A vision. In: WebDB, pp 89–94

Bertinoro (ed) (2007) Bertinoro workshop on information integration, www.dis.uniroma1.it/~lenzerin/INFINT2007

Bohme T, Rahm E (2001) XMach-1: A benchmark for XML data management. In: BTW. Springer, London, pp 264–273

Bonifati A, Chang EQ, Ho T, Lakshmanan LV, Pottinger R (2005) HePToX: Marrying XML and heterogeneity in your P2P databases. In: VLDB. VLDB Endowment, pp 1267–1270

Bonifati A, Mecca G, Pappalardo A, Raunich S, Summa G (2008a) Schema mapping verification: The spicy way. In: EDBT. ACM, NY, pp 85–96

Bonifati A, Mecca G, Pappalardo A, Raunich S, Summa G (2008b) The spicy system: Towards a notion of mapping quality. In: SIGMOD. ACM, NY, pp 1289–1294

Bonifati A, Chang EQ, Ho T, Lakshmanan LVS, Pottinger R, Chung Y (2010) Schema mapping and query translation in heterogeneous P2P XML databases. VLDB J 19(2): 231–256

Bonifati A, Mecca G, Papotti P, Velegrakis Y (2011) Discovery and correctness of schema mapping transformations. In: Bellahsene Z, Bonifati A, Rahm E (eds) Schema matching and mapping. Data-Centric Systems and Applications Series. Springer, Heidelberg

Bressan S, Dobbie G, Lacroix Z, Lee M, Li YG, Nambiar U, Wadhwa B (2001) X007: Applying 007 benchmark to XML query processing tool. In: CIKM. ACM, NY, pp 167–174

Carey MJ (2006) Data delivery in a service-oriented world: The BEA aquaLogic data services platform. In: SIGMOD. ACM, NY, pp 695–705

ten Cate B, Chiticariu L, Kolaitis P, Tan WC (2009) Laconic schema mappings: Computing core universal solutions by means of SQL queries. Proc VLDB 2(1):1006–1017

Chiticariu L, Tan WC (2006) Debugging schema mappings with routes. In: VLDB. VLDB Endowment, pp 79–90

Do HH, Rahm E (2002) COMA – A system for flexible combination of schema matching approaches. In: VLDB. VLDB Endowment, pp 610–621

Do HH, Melnik S, Rahm E (2002) Comparison of schema matching evaluations. In: Web, web-services, and database systems. ACM, NY, pp 221–237

Do HH, Melnik S, Rahm E (2003) Comparison of schema matching evaluations. In: Revised papers from the NODe 2002 web and database-related workshops on web, web-services, and database systems. Springer, London, pp 221–237

Doan A, Domingos P, Halevy AY (2001) Reconciling schemas of disparate data sources: A machine-learning approach. In: SIGMOD. ACM, NY, pp 509–520

Doan A, Madhavan J, Domingos P, Halevy AY (2004) Ontology matching: A machine learning approach. In: Handbook on ontologies. Springer, Heidelberg, pp 385–404

Duchateau F (2009) Towards a generic approach for schema matcher selection: Leveraging user pre- and post-match effort for improving quality and time performance. PhD thesis, Universite Montpellier II - Sciences et Techniques du Languedoc

Duchateau F, Bellahsene Z, Hunt E (2007) XBenchMatch: A benchmark for XML schema matching tools. In: VLDB. VLDB Endowment, pp 1318–1321

Duchateau F, Bellahsene Z, Roche M (2008) Improving quality and performance of schema matching in large scale. Ingenierie des Systemes d'Information 13(5):59–82

Euzenat J (2004) An API for ontology alignment. In: ISWC, pp 698–712

Euzenat J, Shvaiko P (2007) Ontology matching. Springer, Heidelberg

Euzenat J, Mochol M, Shvaiko P, Stuckenschmidt H, Svab O, Svatek V, van Hage WR, Yatskevich M (2006) Results of the ontology alignment evaluation initiative. In: Proceedings of the 1st International Workshop on Ontology Matching (OM-2006)

Fagin R, Kolaitis PG, Popa L (2003) Data exchange: Getting to the core. In: PODS. ACM, NY, pp 90–101

Fagin R, Kolaitis PG, Miller RJ, Popa L (2005) Data exchange: Semantics and query answering. Theor Comp Sci 336(1):89–124

Fagin R, Haas LM, Hernandez M, Miller RJ, Popa L, Velegrakis Y (2009a) Clio: Schema mapping creation and data exchange. In: Borgida A, Chaudhri V, Giorgini P, Yu E Conceptual modeling: Foundations and applications. Springer, Heidelberg, pp 198–236

Fagin R, Kolaitis PG, Popa L, Tan WC (2009b) Reverse data exchange: Coping with nulls. In: PODS. ACM, NY, pp 23–32

Fagin R, Kolaitis P, Popa L, Tan W (2011) Schema mapping evolution through composition and inversion. In: Bellahsene Z, Bonifati A, Rahm E (eds) Schema matching and mapping. Data-Centric Systems and Applications Series. Springer, Heidelberg

Ferrara A, Lorusso D, Montanelli S, Varese G (2008) Towards a benchmark for instance matching. In: Proceedings of the 3rd International Workshop on Ontology Matching (OM-2008)

Fletcher GHL, Wyss CM (2006) Data mapping as search. In: EDBT. Springer, Heidelberg, pp 95–111

Giunchiglia F, Shvaiko P, Yatskevich M (2004) S-Match: An algorithm and an implementation of semantic matching. In: ESWS. Springer, Heidelberg, pp 61–75

Giunchiglia F, Shvaiko P, Yatskevich M (2005) S-Match: An algorithm and an implementation of semantic matching. In: Dagstuhl seminar proceedings semantic interoperability and integration 2005

Giunchiglia F, Yatskevich M, Avesani P, Shvaiko P (2009) A large dataset for the evaluation of ontology matching. Knowl Eng Rev 24(2):137–157

Halevy AY, Ives ZG, Suciu D, Tatarinov I (2003) Schema mediation in peer data management systems. In: Proceedings of international conference on data engineering (ICDE), pp 505–516

Hammer J, Stonebraker M, Topsakal O (2005) THALIA: Test harness for the assessment of legacy information integration approaches. In: ICDE, pp 485–486

Heinzl S, Seiler D, Unterberger M, Nonenmacher A, Freisleben B (2009) MIRO: A mashup editor leveraging web, grid and cloud services. In: iiWAS. ACM, NY, pp 17–24

IBM (2006) Rational data architect. www.ibm.com/software/data/integration/rda

Ioannou E, Nejdl W, Niederée C, Velegrakis Y (2010) On-the-fly entity-aware query processing in the presence of linkage. Proceedings of VLDB, vol 3(1). VLDB Endowment, pp 429–438

Kang J, Naughton JF (2003) On schema matching with opaque column names and data values. In: SIGMOD. ACM, NY, pp 205–216

Kopcke H, Rahm E (2010) Frameworks for entity matching: A comparison. DKE 69(2):197–210

Lee Y, Sayyadian M, Doan A, Rosenthal A (2007) eTuner: Tuning schema matching software using synthetic scenarios. VLDB J 16(1):97–122

Legler F, Naumann F (2007) A classification of schema mappings and analysis of mapping tools. In: Proceedings BTW Conf., Aachen, pp 449–464

Lenzerini M (2002) Data integration: A theoretical perspective. In: PODS. ACM, NY, pp 233–246

Lerner BS (2000) A model for compound type changes encountered in schema evolution. TPCTC 25(1):83–127

MacKenzie IS, Sellen A, Buxton W (1991) A comparison of input devices in elemental pointing and dragging tasks. In: CHI. ACM, NY, pp 161–166

Madhavan J, Bernstein PA, Rahm E (2001) Generic schema matching with cupid. In: VLDB. Morgan Kaufmann, CA, pp 49–58

Mecca G, Papotti P, Raunich S (2009) Core schema mappings. In: SIGMOD. ACM, NY, pp 655–668

Melnik S, Garcia-Molina H, Rahm E (2002) Similarity flooding: A versatile graph matching algorithm and its application to schema matching. In: ICDE. IEEE Computer Society, Washington, DC, pp 117–128

Microsoft (2005) Visual studio. Msdn2.microsoft.com/en-us/ie/bb188238.aspx

Miller RJ, Haas LM, Hernandez MA (2000) Schema mapping as query discovery. In: VLDB. Morgan Kaufmann, CA, pp 77–88

Mork P, Seligman L, Rosenthal A, Korb J, Wolf C (2008) The harmony integration workbench. JODS 11:65–93

Naumann F, Ho CT, Tian X, Haas LM, Megiddo N (2002) Attribute classification using feature analysis. In: ICDE. IEEE Computer Society, Washington, DC, p 271

Okawara T, Morishima A, Sugimoto S (2006) An approach to the benchmark development for data exchange tools. In: Databases and applications. ACTA Press, CA, pp 19–25

Palmer C, Faloutsos C (2003) Electricity based external similarity of categorical attributes. In: Proceedings of PAKDD. Springer, Heidelberg, pp 486–500

Popa L, Velegrakis Y, Miller RJ, Hernandez MA, Fagin R (2002) Translating web data. In: VLDB. VLDB Endowment, pp 598–609

Rahm E, Bernstein PA (2001) A survey of approaches to automatic schema matching. VLDB J 10(4):334–350

Runapongsa K, Patel JM, Jagadish HV, Al-Khalifa S (2002) The Michigan benchmark: A microbenchmark for XML query processing systems. In: EEXTT. Springer, London, pp 160–161

Schmidt AR, Waas F, Kersten ML, Carey MJ, Manolescu I, Busse R (2002) XMark: A benchmark for XML data management. In: VLDB. VLDB Endowment, pp 974–985

Simitsis A, Vassiliadis P, Dayal U, Karagiannis A, Tziovara V (2009) Benchmarking ETL workflows. In: TPCTC. Springer, Heidelberg, pp 199–220

Smith K, Morse M, Mork P, Li M, Rosenthal A, Allen D, Seligman L (2009) The role of schema matching in large enterprises. In: CIDR

Stylus Studio (2005) XML Enterprise Suite. www.stylusstudio.com

Transaction Processing Performance Council (2001) TPC-H Benchmark. Tpc.org

Van-Risbergen C (1979) Information retrieval, 2nd edn. Butterworths, London

Velegrakis Y (2005) Managing schema mappings in highly heterogeneous environments. PhD thesis, University of Toronro

Wun A (2009) Mashups. In: Encyclopedia of database systems. Springer, Heidelberg, pp 1696–1697

Yan L, Miller RJ, Haas LM, Fagin R (2001) Data-driven understanding and refinement of schema mappings. In: Proceedings of SGMOD conf. ACM, NY, pp 485–496

Yao B, Ozsu T, Khandelwal N (2004) XBench benchmark and performance testing of XML DBMSs. In: Proceedings of international conference on data engineering (ICDE). IEEE Computer Society, Washington, DC, pp 621–633

Yatskevich M (2003) Preliminary evaluation of schema matching systems. Tech. Rep. DIT-03-028, University of Trento

Chapter 10
Tuning for Schema Matching

Zohra Bellahsene and Fabien Duchateau

Abstract Schema matching has long been heading towards complete automation. However, the difficulty arising from heterogeneity in the data sources, domain specificity or structure complexity has led to a plethora of semi-automatic matching tools. Besides, letting users the possibility to tune a tool also provides more flexibility, for instance to increase the matching quality. In the recent years, much work has been carried out to support users in the tuning process, specifically at higher levels. Indeed, tuning occurs at every step of the matching process. At the lowest level, similarity measures include internal parameters which directly impact computed similarity values. Furthermore, a common filter to present mappings to users are the thresholds applied to these values. At a mid-level, users can adopt one or more strategies according to the matching tool that they use. These strategies aim at combining similarity measures in an efficient way. Several tools support the users in this task, mainly by providing state-of-the-art graphical user interfaces. Automatically tuning a matching tool at this level is also possible, but this is limited to a few matching tools. The highest level deals with the choice of the matching tool. Due to the proliferation of these approaches, the first issue for the user is to find the one which would best satisfies his/her criteria. Although benchmarking available matching tools with datasets can be useful, we show that several approaches have been recently designed to solve this problem.

Z. Bellahsene (✉)
University of Montpellier II, 34000 Montpellier, France
e-mail: bella@lirmm.fr

F. Duchateau
CWI, Amsterdam, The Netherlands
e-mail: fabien@cwi.nl

Z. Bellahsene et al. (eds.), *Schema Matching and Mapping*, Data-Centric Systems
and Applications, DOI 10.1007/978-3-642-16518-4_10,
© Springer-Verlag Berlin Heidelberg 2011

1 Introduction

The gap between manual schema matching and semi-automatic schema matching
has been filled in early, especially because of the need to handle large schemas
and to accelerate the matching process [Carmel et al., 2007]. The next step towards
automatic schema matching is mainly motivated by the lack of human experts, for
instance in dynamic environments. In all cases, tuning is mainly required to improve
quality results and/or time performance. We illustrate this statement with Fig. 10.1,
on which four schema matchers (YAM, COMA, Similarity Flooding and YAM with
tuning) have been run on the same scenario. Only one of them has been tuned and
this plot compares the number of user interactions to obtain a 100% F-measure manually. In brief, a user interaction is a user (in)validation for a given pair of schema
elements [Bellahsene et al., 2011]. When a tool discovers many relevant correspondences, the user has less interactions to correct and find the missing ones. The plot
clearly shows that the tuned matcher improves quality and consequently reduces
post-match effort.

Tuning, either automatic or manual, is performed during the pre-match phase of
the schema matching process. The main motivation for tuning a schema matcher
deals with the difficulty to know in advance, even for a human expert, the best configuration of the parameters for a given set of schemas. The heterogeneity, structure
and domain specificity encompassed in every set of schemas to be matched make it
more difficult for a schema matcher to achieve acceptable results in all cases. Thus,
tuning enables schema matchers to provide flexibility and customization to cope
with the different features of each set of schemas.

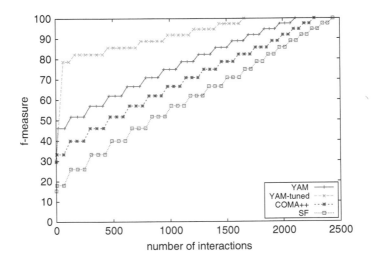

Fig. 10.1 A tuned matcher mainly improves matching quality

However, tuning the parameters to fulfil this goal is not an easy task for the user. Indeed, it has recently been pointed out that the main issue is how to select the most suitable similarity measures to execute for a given domain and how to adjust the multiple parameters [Lee et al., 2007]. Due to the numerous possible configurations of the parameters, it is not possible to try them all. Besides, they require specific knowledge from the users. Let us imagine that a user has to choose one similarity measure for matching his/her schemas and to assign a threshold to this measure. Selecting the appropriate similarity measure first implies that the user is a domain expert. Further, assigning the threshold means that the user has some background knowledge about the chosen measure, e.g., its value distribution.

One of the ten challenges for ontology matching focuses on the tuning issue [Shvaiko and Euzenat, 2008]. Authors claim that this tuning is splitted in three categories: (1) matcher selection, (2) matcher tuning and (3) combination strategy of the similarity measures. In the first category, we distinguish manual selection from automatic selection. In the former, evaluation of different matchers and benchmarking tools facilitate the choice of a matcher for a given task [Yatskevich, 2003, Do et al., 2002, Duchateau et al., 2007, Ferrara et al., 2008]. On the contrary, there exist a few tools that automatically select and build a schema matcher according to various parameters (YAM [Duchateau et al., 2009a,b]). The second category is mainly dedicated to tools such as eTuner [Lee et al., 2007], which automatically tunes a schema matcher with its best configuration for a given set of schemas. Any schema matcher which provides the possibility to change manually the value of one or more of its parameters also falls in this catagory. The last category gathers the matchers which provide a manual combination of similarity measures (e.g., COMA++ [Aumueller et al., 2005], BMatch [Duchateau et al., 2008b]) and those which automatically combines these measures (SMB [Anan and Avigdor, 2008] and MatchPlanner from Duchateau [2009]). Note that in the rest of this chapter, we consider that the combination strategy is one parameter that can be tuned. In other words, the third category is merged into the second one.

The rest of the chapter is a survey about most popular parameters in schema matching and the tuning systems. We have gathered these parameters according to the entities against which they are applied: input data, similarity measures, combination of similarity measures and finally the matcher. This means that a tool may be described at different levels, according to the parameters that they enable to tune. Thus, the chapter is organized as follows: Section 2 covers the main notions about tuning. We then present the different parameters that one might face when using a matcher. These parameters have been sorted in four categories: in Sect. 3, we present the parameters related to input data and user preferences. Then, we describe in Sect. 4 low-level parameters involved in the schema matching process, namely those dealing with the similarity measures. One level higher, we find parameters which aim at combining the similarity measures. They are presented in Sect. 5. The highest level is the matcher selection and the involved parameters are discussed in Sect. 6. Finally, we conclude and we outline perspectives in Sect. 7.

2 Preliminaries

For many systems, tuning is an important step to obtain expected results or to optimize either matching quality or execution time. In the schema matching context,
this statement is easily checkable due to the large amount and the diversity of available parameters provided by schema matchers. We now formalize the problem of
tuning a schema matcher. As depicted by Fig. 10.2, the schema matching process
requires as inputs at least two schemas, and optional *parameters* which can be given
a *value*. These values belong to a specific *domain*. We mainly distinguish three types
of domains:

- A finite (multi-)valued set, e.g., a list of synonyms <(*author, writer*), ..., (*book,
  volume*)>
- An unordered discrete domain, e.g., mapping cardinality can be *1:1, 1:n, n:1*, or
  n:m
- An ordered continuous domain, e.g., a threshold for a similarity measure in the
  range [0, 1]

Similarly to Lee et al. [2007], we call *knob* a parameter with an associated value.
However, we do not restrict knobs to have values from a finite valued set. Here are
examples of knobs: *(mapping cardinality, 1:1)* and *(threshold$_{trigrams}$, 0.15)*.

More formally, we define $S = < s_1, s_2, \ldots, s_n >$ the set of input schemas
that the user wants to match. The parameters are represented by the set $P = < p_1,
p_2, \ldots, p_k >$. The value domains are gathered in a set $D = < d_1, d_2, \ldots, d_n >$
where each $d_i \in D$ is a set $< value_{i1}, value_{i2}, \ldots, value_{it} >$. Finally,
$K = < k_1, k_2, \ldots, k_l >$ stands for the set of knobs or the configuration of a
schema matcher. With these definitions, we propose a *Match* function which uses
any schema matcher with a configuration k to match a set of schemas s. The output
of the *Match* function with the configuration k is a set of correspondences m_k.

$$Match(s, k) = m_k$$

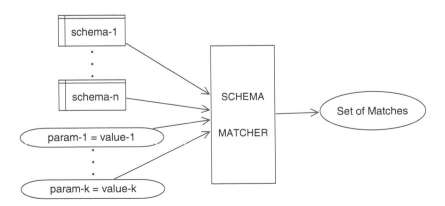

Fig. 10.2 Inputs and outputs of the schema matching process

As described in Bellahsene et al. [2011], it is possible to measure the quality of this set of correspondences, e.g., precision, recall and F-measure. We note *Fmes* the F-measure applied to a set of correspondences m_k.

$$Fmes(m_k) := [0, 1]$$

Thus, an optimal tuning k in this context consists of finding a configuration function ζ applied to parameters and domains so that the output of the schema matcher m_k is optimal given the input schemas. In other words, the configuration of the knobs would be perfectly tuned to achieve the best matching quality. That is, changing the value of any knob would decrease the matching quality.

Given that $\zeta(s, p, d) = k$ and $Match(s, k) = m_k$,
$\nexists z = \zeta(s, p, d)$ and $Match(s, z) = m_z$ with $Fmes(m_z) > Fmes(m_k)$.

Likely, the measure of satisfaction over the ouput deals with quality (F-measure). But it is also possible to tune a schema matcher to optimize time performance, for instance with decision trees [Duchateau et al., 2008a].

In the next sections, we discuss the different parameters that one may face with when using a schema matcher, based on these definitions.

3 Input and Data Parameters

In this section, we gather the data and input parameters that one may have to configure when using a schema matcher. We do not consider that the input schemas belong to the tuning parameters. Indeed, a set of input schemas is compulsory to run the matcher. Thus, this section is dedicated to parameters that may side along with the input schemas (e.g., expert correspondences, data instances) or parameters related to techniques used by the matcher (e.g., machine learning, external resources used by a similarity measure). Indeed, most of these parameters directly affect the quality or the time performance. Deciding whether to provide any of them, as well as the choice of the parameters' values, is inherent to the tuning phase. The section is organized according to the type of parameters. First, data parameters include expert feedback. Such a reliable knowledge aims at improving the matching quality by reusing entities that have been checked by a domain expert. This feedback, as well as data instances, is often combined with machine learning techniques to exploit them. These machine learning techniques hold various parameters to be efficient and/or flexible, and we study them in the second part. The third category gathers external resources, which mainly consist of providing an ontology or dictionary. Finally, due to the complexity of the matching process and the design of numerous matchers, there exist very specific parameters that one may only face by using a given tool.

3.1   Expert feedback

Expert feedback mainly consists of correct mappings between the schemas to be matched. These mappings can be seen as a bootstrap for the schema matcher, i.e., knowledge is taken as input by machine learning algorithms to classify schema instances. It may be a compulsory parameter such as in LSD/Glue [Doan et al., 2001, 2003] and APFEL [Ehrig et al., 2005].

Conversely, providing mappings is an extra option to improve matching quality with tools such as YAM. As explained in Duchateau et al. [2009a,b], each schema is built with a given "design methodology" (e.g., naming labels using underscores between tokens, using labels from an ontology). Consequently, by providing correct mappings, the system is able to infer, during the learning process, which similarity measures are the most efficient between elements of the mappings. Since a schema designer mainly keeps the same "design methodology" to build the whole (sub)schema, the similarity measures which have been detected as efficient with the correct mappings may also be efficient to discover new mappings.

Other tools have been designed to store correspondences and reuse them later [Madhavan et al., 2005]. This is called a *reuse strategy* in matchers such as COMA++ [Aumueller et al., 2005] or Quickmig [Drumm et al., 2007]. Actually, these tools are able to derive new correspondences when different successive matching processes involve the same schema. This feature is specifically useful when one of the schemas has been modified.

3.2   Machine Learning Parameters

Many schema matchers (partly) rely on machine learning techniques to discover correspondences between schemas. We distinguish two use cases of machine learning techniques: (1) as a similarity measure or (2) as a "matcher" to combine measures.

3.2.1   Parameters at the Similarity Measure Level

In most cases, these learning techniques are applied against schema instances as part of a similarity measure. We can cite many works, which have at least one such measure [Drumm et al., 2007, Li and Clifton, 2000, Berlin and Motro, 2002, Hernandez et al., 2002, Doan et al., 2003, Dhamankar et al., 2004].

The most common machine learning parameter deals with the training data. First, a suitable set of training data is a crucial issue common for all machine learning approaches. Second, users also have to cope with the number of training data. Matching tools are either provided with a knowledge base, thus enabling the storage and reuse of these data or the tools do not require too many training data to be

Table 10.1 Impact of the number of training data on the matching quality with Apfel's decision tree

Dataset	Number of training data	Precision	Recall	F-measure
Russia	20	83%	48%	60%
	50	82%	47%	60%
	150	72%	59%	65%
Biblio	20	01%	28%	01%
	50	46%	25%	32%
	150	63%	38%	47%

efficient, since this woud not be realistic. For example, if a user needs to match 100 data sources, (s)he can manually find the mappings for a few data sources and LSD discovers the others for the remaining sources [Doan et al., 2001]. Due to the availability of training data and the classifier used, tuning this parameter is complicated. To illustrate this, we have partly reproduced a table from Ehrig et al. [2005], shown as Table 10.1. We have limited this excerpt to two matching datasets (*Russia* and *biblio*) and to one Apfel's classifier (the decision tree). It depicts how the number of training data has a significant impact on the matching quality (in terms of precision, recall and F-measure). For instance, we notice that providing 20 training data in the *Russia* dataset enables the best precision (83%). This precision value tends to decrease with more training data. On the contrary, using 20 training data with the *biblio* dataset is clearly not sufficient.

Not only the number of training data may be crucial, but their validity also. For instance, APFEL [Ehrig et al., 2005] uses both positive and negative examples for training its classifiers. In this context, it is easier to provide sufficient training data to the system: authors explain that an initial matcher performs a matching over sample data and let users rate the discovered correspondences. The rated list of correspondences is then given as input to APFEL. From this list, the tools determines heuristic weights and threshold levels using various machine learning techniques, namely decision trees, neural networks, and support vector machines.

Another work aims at classifying candidate correspondences (either as relevant or not) by analysing their features [Naumann et al., 2002]. The features represent boolean properties over data instance, such as presence of delimiters. Thus, selecting an appropriate feature set is a first parameter to deal with. The choice of a classifier is also important, and authors propose, by default, the Naive Bayes classifier for categorical data and quantile-based classifier for numerical data.

Similarity measures based on machine learning may not always stand for the most effective. The ASID matcher [Bozovic and Vassalos, 2008] considers its Naive Bayes classifier (against schema instances) as a less credible similarity measure, which is applied after user (in)validation of initial results provided by more reliable measures (Jaro and TF/IDF). We think that this credibility of machine learning-based similarity measures heavily depends on the quality of their training data.

3.2.2 Parameters at the Matcher Level

The second category of matchers use machine learning techniques to combine similarity measures. However, they share almost the same parameters than the first category.

SMB [Anan and Avigdor, 2008] is based on the *Boosting* algorithm. In addition to training data, this approach also needs two parameters. The former is a hypothesis space, which is in this case a pair of similarity measures chosen among a pool. It appears that the similarity measures that perform well when used alone are mainly not included in the hypothesis space when combined with another one. The latter is an error measure, which aims at both stopping the algorithm (when the computed error value reaches a threshold, 0.5 by default) and selecting at each iteration the similarity measure which produced less errors. The authors have noticed that this error value is quickly reached, and therefore have added a pre-processing step to remove all pairs of schema elements that have been classified as irrelevant by all classifiers.

In YAM [Duchateau et al., 2009a,b], the number of training data, extracted from a knowledge base, is either provided by users or chosen according to empirical evaluation results. This tool can also be trained with similar schemas. This means that users may already have schemas that have been matched and could be reused to improve the results. Similarly, authors indicate that the schemas belong to either the same domain (e.g., biology, business) or share some features (e.g., degree of heterogeneity, nested structure).

3.3 External Resources

External resources have long been useful to bring reliable knowledge into the schema matching process. In addition to the availability and security issues, user should check the adequacy of the resource content for the given matching task and its integration within the matcher. Different types of resources are accepted by schema matchers. The simplest one is a list of similar labels, also called list of synonyms. COMA++ [Aumueller et al., 2005] and Porsche [Saleem et al., 2008] let users fill in these resources. List of abbreviations are very common to extend the labels of ambiguous schema elements, such as in COMA++ [Aumueller et al., 2005].

Another type of external resources is the domain ontology, used by Quickmig [Drumm et al., 2007] for instance. Similarly, Porsche [Saleem and Bellahsene, 2009] is enhanced by data mining techniques applied to many domain ontologies to extract mini-taxonomies, that are finally used to discover complex mappings.

The Wordnet dictionary [Wordnet, 2007] is also used in different fashions: it facilitates the discovery of various relationships (e.g., synonyms, antonyms) in approaches such as YAM [Duchateau et al., 2009a,b] and S-MATCH/S-MATCH++ [Giunchiglia et al., 2004, Avesani et al., 2005]. A dictionary can also become the core of the system against which all schema elements are matched, as performed by AUTOPLEX/AUTOMATCH [Berlin and Motro, 2001, 2002].

3.4   *Other Input Parameters*

Due to their diversity and their internal algorithms, schema matchers may have very specific parameters and/or user preferences. Here, we propose to detail some of them.

In Drumm et al. [2007], the Quickmig approach requires users to fill in a *questionnaire*. It then uses the answers to reduce the size of input schemas based on user domain knowledge. This parameter is useful when only a subpart of schemas needs to be matched or when dealing with large schemas.

Although most schema matchers implicitly promote precision, YAM [Duchateau et al., 2009a,b] is the first tool that enables users to tune *a preference towards precision or recall*. This choice affects the machine learning process by avoiding the discovery of irrelevant mappings or by preventing the missing of relevant ones. As explained by the authors, promoting precision (respectively recall) often has a negative impact on recall (respectively precision). Figure 10.3 depicts the evolution of precision, recall and F-measure averaged for 150 datasets when the weight applied to false negatives increases (thus promoting recall). It appears that F-measure slightly increases by 7% while recall value improves up to 20% to the detriment of precision. Approaches that use a threshold to select correspondences also have a means of promoting recall by lowering the value of this threshold.

In Anchor-PROMPT [Noy and Musen, 2001], authors have chosen to compare paths of schema elements. As a consequence, specific parameters are used, such as *the maximum length of a path, the number of elements involved in an equivalence group*, etc. End-users may have to understand the basics of Anchor-PROMPT algorithm to be able to tune its parameters correctly.

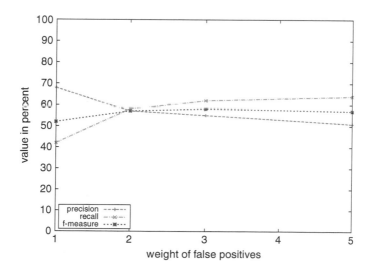

Fig. 10.3 Impact on the matching quality when promoting recall with YAM

To the best of our knowledge, AgreementMaker [Cruz et al., 2007, 2009] is the only tool that enables users to select a type of cardinality to be discovered. Given two input schemas, mapping cardinality is either *1:1*, *1:n*, *n:1* or *n:m*. In a *1:1* configuration, the matcher is limited to discover mappings between one element of the first schema and one element in the other schema. Only a few matchers emphasize the complex mappings such as *n:m*, in which any number of elements in both schemas can be involved in a mapping.

3.5 Conclusion

In this section, we have mainly presented user inputs, i.e., optional preferences and parameters applied to data. To sum up, the quality can be improved by using *external resources* and *expert feedback*. Several tools are based on *machine learning techniques* either as a similarity measure (mostly at the instance level) or as a means of combining the results of similarity measures. In both cases, training data is a crucial issue. Finally, many tools propose preferences or options which add more flexibility or may improve the matching quality. The next section focuses on the parameters at the similarity measure level.

4 Similarity Measures Parameters

Similarity measures are the basic components of schema matchers. They can be used as individual algorithms or combined with an aggregation function. Consequently, they may have internal parameters. In most cases, schema matchers do not enable users to tune such low-level parameters. Another parameter applied to similarity measures is the threshold. It filters the pair of schema elements in different categories (e.g., is a correspondence, or should apply another type of similarity measure) based on the output of the similarity measures. The last part of this section is dedicated to parameters specific to one or several matchers.

4.1 Internal Parameters

Similarity measures takes as input two schema elements, and it outputs a similarity between them. This similarity value may be a numerical value (e.g., a distance, a real in the range [0, 1]) or a relationship (e.g., equivalence, generalization). Similar to black-box algorithms, similarity measures can have internal parameters which impact the output. Due to the numerous available similarity measures, we do not intend to describe all of them with their parameters. Thus, we focus on two simple examples to illlustrate various types of such internal parameters.

The first example is the Levenhstein distance [Levenshtein, 1966] between two character strings. It computes the minimal number of operations costs needed to transform one source string into the target string, where an operation is an insertion, deletion or substitution of a single character. Each operation may have a different cost. For instance, a substitution can have a cost equal to 2, while insertions and deletions may cost 1. Users can tune these costs according to their needs.

Between the two string *dept* and *department*, one requires six character insertions to transform *dept* into *department*. If an insertion costs 1, then the Levenhstein distance between both strings is 6.

The second similarity measure that we study is Jaro Winkler [Winkler, 1999]. This measure is also terminological and it compares two character strings. It extends Jaro measure by taking into account the order of the characters of both strings. Furthermore, it promotes higher similarity values between strings which share similar prefixes. Consequently, it includes two parameters. The first one is the length of the prefix substring while the second represents a constant scaling factor for how much the score is adjusted upwards for having common prefixes.

For further reading, we advise you to check the following list of resources [Cohen et al., 2003, Euzenat et al., 2004]. Several packages also describe similarity measures and their parameters, for instance SecondString[1] or SimMetrics.[2]

4.2   Thresholds

Most similarity measures are normalized to return a value in the range [0, 1]. Among all candidate pairs of schema elements, selecting the ones to propose as mappings can be performed with a threshold. That is, all candidate pairs whose similarity value (from one measure or resulting from a combination of several measures) is above a given threshold become mappings. Many tools [Avesani et al., 2005, Madhavan et al., 2001, Duchateau et al., 2008b, Drumm et al., 2007] have a threshold for selecting mappings. In most cases, a default value for the threshold is provided with the tool, e.g., 0.6 for the string-matching threshold in S-Match [Giunchiglia et al., 2007]. COMA++ [Aumueller et al., 2005] includes a threshold often combined with a *top-K* strategy (i.e., the best *K* correspondences are returned) and a *MaxDelta* strategy (i.e., the best correspondence is returned with the closest ones, whose score only differs by a *Delta* tolerance value). Conversely, APFEL [Ehrig et al., 2005] is a machine learning-based tools which features an automatic threshold tuning.

As the value distribution is very different from a similarity measure to another, a schema matcher can have one specific threshold for each similarity measure. This is the case with MatchPlanner [Duchateau et al., 2008a]. The extended version of this matcher enables the automatic learning of these thresholds, thanks to

---

[1] SecondString (May 2010): http://sourceforge.net/projects/secondstring/.

[2] SimMetrics (May 2010): http://www.dcs.shef.ac.uk/~sam/stringmetrics.html.

machine learning techniques [Duchateau, 2009]. Similarly, Anchor-PROMPT [Noy and Musen, 2001] automatically computes the threshold values by averaging all similarity scores obtained on different runs with various parameter configurations.

In a broader way, authors of [Melnik et al., 2002] discuss the notion of filters to select the mappings. These filters include not only the thresholds, but also constraints between elements (types and cardinality) and a selection function.

Note that the threshold may be a parameter applied to a global similarity value, i.e., different similarity values are aggregated into a global one (given a strategy, see Sect. 5) and the threshold represents the decision-maker for accepting the pair of schema elements as a correspondence or not.

4.3 *Various*

Contrary to most aggregation-based approaches, Similarity Flooding/Rondo [Melnik et al., 2002, 2003] uses a graph propagation mechanism to refine similarities between schema elements. Thus, it holds specific parameters. The first one is fixpoint formula, which enables the computation of updated similarities and the end of execution of the propagation. Different fixpoint formulas have been tested and evaluated in Melnik et al. [2002]. In addition, several filters are proposed to select among all candidate pairs the ones that Rondo displays as mappings. Constraints (on cardinality and types) or thresholds are examples of filters.

For a given schema element, we do not know in advance to how many elements it should be matched [Avigdor, 2005]. However, approaches such as COMA++ [Aumueller et al., 2005] or iMAP [Dhamankar et al., 2004] can display the top-K correspondences (for future interactive mode), thus enabling users to disambiguate complex correspondences. Other works have been specifically designed to discover complex mappings, such as Porsche [Saleem and Bellahsene, 2009].

4.4 *Conclusion*

This section describes the parameters related to similarity measures. Although they have a significant impact, *parameters inside the similarity measures* are often set to default values. Schema matching tools let users tune the *thresholds*, which is a traditional decision maker for deciding what happens to a pair of schema elements. Finally, we have detailed *specific parameters* that users have to understand before optimizing the matchers. In the next section, we reach one level up by studying the parameters related to the combination of similarity measures.

5   Parameters for Combining Similarity Measures

At a higher level, schema matchers have to combine the results computed by different similarity measures. This enables an increase of the matching quality in most cases. However, the method for combining these results is crucial to derive high-quality mappings. The matcher first normalizes all similarity values. Different strategies are adopted to fulfil this goal. The first part of this section describes these different strategies. Several tools have been designed to enhance the interactivity with users for selecting the best strategy. These tools are presented in the second part of this section. Finally, we focus on a specific strategy which is widely used by matchers: the linear regression. It mainly encompasses weights to reflect each similarity measure's influence when combining them.

5.1   Strategy for Combining Similarity Measures

As many schema matchers use different similarity measures (based on string-matching, semantic, linguistics, structure, etc.), they need to adopt a strategy for combining these measures. In most cases, schema matchers combine the results computed by similarity measures, after a normalization step of the values (e.g., in the range $[0, 1]$).

One of the simplest method to combine similarity values is the average function, used by tools such as ASID [Bozovic and Vassalos, 2008] or BMatch [Duchateau et al., 2008b]. Aggregating the similarity values using weights reflects the impact of each measure in the matching process. In other words, it is possible to promote measures that are based on reliable resources (e.g., dictionaries, ontologies) by assigning them a high weight (see Sect. 5.2 for more details).

More complex strategies are found within COMA++ [Aumueller et al., 2005] in which similarity measures, types of nodes along with context, and fragments (parts) of the schema can be tuned. These strategies are then applied to the matrix built by COMA++ to deduce the correspondences that are displayed to the user. The three main combination steps are aggregation (e.g., *weighted, max* or the default *average*), direction (e.g., *unidirectional* or *stable marriage*), and selection (e.g., *threshold, maxN*) [Do and Rahm, 2002]. A strategy is built by choosing a value for each of these three steps. Figure 10.4 depicts an overview of COMA++ graphical interface for selecting a strategy. We also notice that a strategy may be performed on specific elements of the schemas (nodes, leaves, etc.).

MatchPlanner is a schema matcher based on decision trees to combine similarity measures. Although it has been extended by machine learning techniques to generate these decision trees [Duchateau, 2009], users can provide their own decision trees to the system [Duchateau et al., 2008a]. There is no weight on the measures, but their order and position in the decision tree are crucial. Manually designing such decision trees is interesting when one wants to promote time performance or use a specific similarity measure.

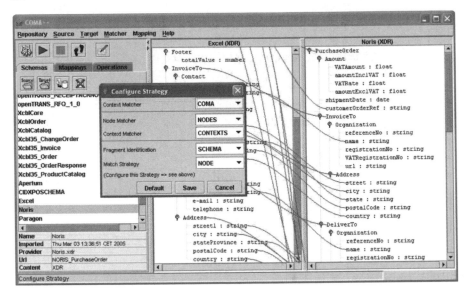

Fig. 10.4 COMA++ user interface for selecting combination strategy

In SMB [Anan and Avigdor, 2008], the output of a weak similarity measure (called *first-line matcher*) is combined with a decision maker (or *second-line matcher*) to discover correspondences. The combination strategy depends on the decision maker, which can be *Maximum Weighted Bipartite Graph* algorithm, *Stable Marriage*, etc.

In YAM [Duchateau et al., 2009a,b], the combination of similarity measures is performed by a machine learning classifier. Authors consider that any classifier is a matcher since it classifies pairs of schema elements as relevant or not. Thus, the combination of the similarity measures depends on the type of classifier (decision tree, Bayes network, neural network, etc.).

To sum up, many tools have designed their own strategies to combine similarity measures. However, most of them are based on weighted functions that the users may have to tune.

5.2 Weights in Formulas

Previously, we have detailed different types of strategies. One of the most common strategy in the matching community is the linear regression to aggregate values computed by similarity measures. In that case, the weights given to each measure is important according to the domain and the schemas to be matched. For instance, if a domain ontology is available, one may decide to give a high weight to the measures, which are able to use this ontology. However, tuning these weights manually still requires user expertise.

A simple example of aggregation function is demonstrated with BMatch [Duchateau et al., 2008b] or Cupid [Madhavan et al., 2001]. Their authors aggregate the results of terminological measure with the ones computed by a structural measure by varying the weights applied to each measure ($\frac{1}{2}$ and $\frac{1}{2}$, $\frac{1}{3}$ and $\frac{2}{3}$, etc.).

In most tools, default values are given to these weights. They are mainly the results of intensive experiments. For example, the default weights of COMA++'s *name* and *data type* similarity measures are 0.7 and 0.3, respectively [Do and Rahm, 2002]. As explained in Glue [Doan et al., 2003] or APFEL [Ehrig et al., 2005], it is possible to tune the weights of an aggregation function automatically, thanks to machine learning techniques.

To help tuning the weights in aggregating functions, we discuss the iMAP approach [Dhamankar et al., 2004]. This matcher mainly provides a new set of machine learning-based measures for discovering specific types of complex mappings (e.g., *name* is a concatenation of *firstname* and *lastname*). It also includes an explanation module to clarify why a given correspondence has been discovered to the detriment of another candidate. For instance, this module is able to describe that a string-matching classifier has a strong influence for a discovered correspondence. Thus, user can use this feedback to decrease the weight of this classifier.

5.3 Supporting Users to Revise Strategies

Although most matchers simply provide a graphical user interface to visualize the results, recent works have pointed out a need for selecting the best strategy. For instance, including some mechanisms to easily update the weights of a function so that users can directly analyse impacts of these changes.

Here, we describe recent works that aim at supporting users during the tasks of selecting appropriate similarity measures and combining them. To combine them efficiently, weights have to be efficiently tuned. To support users during these tasks, two tools have been designed: AgreementMaker and Harmony. Whatever the technique they use (interactions with users or strategy filters), they enable a revision of the current strategy by adding, removing or modifying parameters and similarity measures involved in the combination. We further describe each of these tools in the rest of this part.

5.3.1 AgreementMaker

The originality of AgreementMaker [Cruz et al., 2007, 2009] is the capability of matching methods combination. Moreover, it provides facilities for tuning manually the quality of matches. Indeed, one of the interesting features of AgreementMaker is a comprehensive user interface supporting both advanced visualization techniques and a control panel that drives the matching methods. This interface, depicted by Fig. 10.5, provides the user facilities to evaluate the matching process, thus enabling the user to be directly involved in the loop and evaluation strategies.

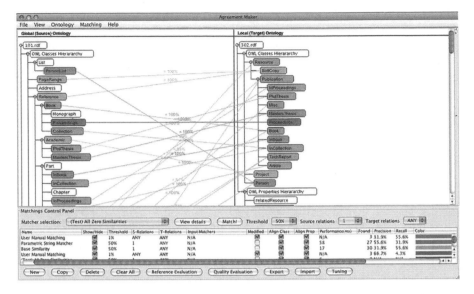

Fig. 10.5 AgreementMaker user interface for testing and comparing combination strategies

AgreementMaker provides a combination strategy based on the linear interpolation of the similarity values. The weights can be either user assigned or evaluated
through automatically determined quality measures. The system allows for serial
and parallel composition where, respectively, the output of one or more methods
can be used as input to another one, or several methods can be used on the same
input and then combined.

5.3.2 Harmony

Harmony schema matcher [Mork et al., 2008, Smith et al., 2009] combines multiple matcher algorithms by using a vote merger. The vote merging principle is
a weighted average of the match scores provided by each match voter. A match
voter provides a confidence score for each pair of schema elements to be matched.
Then, Similarity Flooding strategy [Melnik et al., 2002] is applied to adjust the
confidence scores based on structural information. Thus, positive confidence scores
propagate up the graph. An interesting feature of Harmony lies in its graphical user
interface for viewing and modifying the discovered schema correspondences. This
allows to assist the users to focus their attention on different ways. This assistance
is done through a filter, which is a predicate that is evaluated against each candidate
correspondence. Harmony supports two kinds of filters. The first kind named *link
filters* depends on the characteristics of a candidate correspondence. For example,
applying the confidence filter will have an effect to graphically display those correspondences, whose match score falls within the specific range of values. The second
one named *node filters* is related to a schema element characteristics. This kind of

filters includes a depth and a sub-tree filter. For example, in Entity Relationship schemas, entities appear at level 1, whereas attributes are at level 2. In this case, by using the depth filter with value *1*, the user may focus on matching entities, while the sub-tree filter is useful in tree based model such as XML schemas.

5.4   Discovering the Best Configuration

The previous section gathers tools that support users to manually find the best strategy, i.e., the best method for combining similarity measures and its optional parameters such as weights. This last part is dedicated to the tools that automatically discover the best strategy: eTuner and YAM.

5.4.1   eTuner

eTuner [Lee et al., 2007] is not a schema matching tool, but it aims at automatically tuning them. It proceeds as follows: from a given schema, it derives many schemas which are semantically equivalent. The mappings between the initial schema and its derivations are stored. Then, a given matching tool (e.g., COMA++ or Similarity Flooding) is applied against the schemas and the results is compared with the stored set of mappings. This process is repeated until an optimal parameters configuration of the matching tool is found, i.e., the mappings discovered by the matching tool are mostly similar to those stored. eTuner strongly relies on the capabilities of the matching tool that it tunes. In most experiments, eTuner is able to improve matching quality by 1 to 15% compared to the tools with their default configuration.

5.4.2   YAM

Similar to MatchPlanner, YAM [Duchateau et al., 2009a,b] takes some user inputs and it uses them to produce a schema matcher. Although MatchPlanner is limited to combine the similarity measures with a decision tree, YAM is able to combine them, thanks to any machine learning classifier. All low-level parameters such as weights and thresholds are therefore automatically tuned during the learning process. The combination of similarity measures only depends on the type of classifier selected by YAM. For instance, Fig. 10.6a, b depict two techniques for combining similarity measures. The first one is based on a decision tree while the second one uses NNge. With the decision tree, each pair of schema elements is matched with similarity measures from the root until a leaf node is reached, indicating whether the pair is a correspondence (T) or not (F). The value of the previously computed similarity measure is used to decide which edge (and consequently which similarity measure) should be executed next. Combining with a decision tree enables a sparing of resources since all similarity measures may not be computed for a given pair of

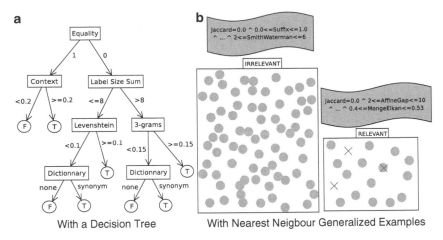

Fig. 10.6 YAM: Examples of combination of similarity measures

schema elements. On the contrary, NNge classifier builds groups of nearest neighbour pairs of schema elements and then finds the best rule, expressed by boolean logic, for each group. YAM currently includes 20 classifiers from the Weka library [Garner, 1995]. According to [Duchateau, 2009], experiments show that the tuned matchers produced by YAM are able to improve F-measure by 20% over traditional approaches. Datasets mainly include average schemas from various domains, but also two datasets involving large schemas. Similar to most machine learning-based approaches, authors have noticed the fact that the results may vary according to training data, hence the need to perform different runs during experiments.

5.5 Conclusion

In this section, we have described the *different strategies* to combine similarity measures and to tune them, mainly their *weights*. Fortunately, there exist several tools to help users revising or selecting the strategies. *Visual tools* support users for manually configuring these strategies, mainly thanks to state-of-the-art GUI. Finally, we have explored *automatic approaches* that are able to discover and tune the best strategy. In the following section, we are still heading one level higher. Indeed, the first choice of a user deals with the matching tool.

6 Matcher Selection

The selection of a schema matcher is obviously not a parameter: it does not fit with the definitions provided in Sect. 2. But this is likely meta-tuning since one first needs to choose a schema matcher before tuning its parameters and using it. Furthermore, some recent challenges directly refer to this issue [Shvaiko and Euzenat, 2008]. The selection of a schema matcher may be guided by the results that it obtains using some benchmarking tools. In addition, a few recent works have been proposed to automatize this matcher selection. We describe each of them in the rest of this section.

6.1 AHP

Authors of Malgorzata et al. [2006] have proposed to select a relevant and suitable matcher for ontology matching. They have used Analytic Hierarchical Process (AHP) to fulfil this goal. They first define characteristics of the matching process divided into six categories (inputs, approach, usage, output, documentation and costs). Users then fill in a requirements questionnaire to set priorities for each defined characteristic. Finally, AHP is applied with these priorities and it outputs the most suitable matcher according to user requirements. This approach has two drawbacks: (1) there is no experiment demonstrating its effectiveness and (2) currently there does not exist a listing of all characteristics for all matching tools. Thus, the user would have to manually fill in these characteristics.

6.2 RiMOM

RiMOM [Li et al., 2009] is a multiple strategy dynamic ontology matching system. Different matching strategies are applied to a specific type of ontology information. Based on the features of the ontologies to be matched, RiMOM selects the best strategy (or strategy combination) to apply. When loading the ontologies, the tool also compute three feature factors. The underlining idea is that if two ontologies share similar feature factors, then the strategies that use these factors should be given a high weight when computing similarity values. For instance, if the *label meaningful* factor is low, then the *Wordnet-based strategy* will not be used. Each strategy produces a set of correspondences, and all sets are finally aggregated using a linear interpolation method. A last strategy dealing with ontology structure is finally performed to confirm discovered correspondences and to deduce new ones. Contrary to other approaches, RiMOM does not rely on machine learning techniques. It is quite similar to the AHP work by selecting an appropriate matcher based on input's features. RiMOM participated to the 2009 OAEI campaign [Zhang et al., 2009]. Results show that the tool performed well in different tracks (anatomy, benchmark, instance matching). For instance, it achieves F-measures above 75% for all datasets in the instance matching track.

6.3 YAM

Yet another matcher (YAM) [Duchateau et al., 2009a,b] enables the generation of *à la carte* schema matchers according to user requirements. It uses a knowledge base that includes a (possibly large) set of similarity measures and machine learning classifiers. All classifiers are trained with scenarios from this knowledge base (and optionally provided by the users). Their individual results (precision, recall and F-measure), are computed and according to the adopted strategy, the classifier that achieves the best quality is selected as schema matcher. The strategy mainly depends on user inputs. For instance, if (s)he wants to promote recall, then the classifier with the best recall value is returned. If the user has provided expert mappings, then YAM selects as the schema matcher the classifier that obtains the best F-measure on this set of expert mappings.

6.4 SMB

In Anan and Avigdor [2008], the authors propose a machine learning approach, SMB. It uses the Boosting algorithm to classify the similarity measures, divided into first-line and second-line matchers. The Boosting algorithm consists in iterating weak classifiers over the training set while re-adjusting the importance of elements in this training set. Thus, SMB automatically selects a pair of similarity measures as a matcher by focusing on harder training data. An advantage of this algorithm is the important weight given to misclassified pairs during the training. Although this approach makes use of several similarity measures, it mainly combines a similarity measure (first-line matcher) with a decision maker (second-line matcher). Empirical results show that the selection of the pair does not depend on their individual performance.

6.5 STEM

In a broader way, the STEM framework [Köpcke and Rahm, 2008] identifies the most interesting training data set which is then used to combine matching strategies and tune several parameters such as thresholds. First, training data is generated, either manually (i.e., an expert labels the entity pairs) or automatically (at random, using static-active selection or active learning). Then, similarity values are computed using pairs in the training data set to build a similarity matrix between each pair and each similarity measure. Finally, the matching strategy is deduced from this matrix, thanks to supervised learned algorithm. The output is a tuned matching strategy (how to combine similarity measures and tune their parameters). The framework enables a comparative study of various similarity measures (e.g., Trigrams, Jaccard) combined with different strategies (e.g., decision tree, linear regression) whose parameters are either manually or automatically tuned.

6.6   Conclusion

This last section underlines the fact that selecting an appropriate schema matching tool is the first issue to be considered. A few works have been proposed in this domain, which is recognized as one of the ten matching challenges for the next decade [Shvaiko and Euzenat, 2008]. If we exclude the *AHP* approach, for which no experiment is provided, the remaining tools are all based on machine learning techniques. This is an interesting feature since more datasets with correct correspondences are becoming available. However, discovering the features of a dataset to determine the most appropriate tool could be a challenging task.

7   Conclusion

In this chapter, we have provided an overview about what has been done for tuning schema matchers. At first, schema matchers enabled users to configure some of their low-level parameters (e.g., thresholds). They mainly allow to filter or select the output (the set of mappings). The next step deals with parameters for combining similarity measures. They add more flexibility and the set of discovered mappings depends on the configuration of these parameters. More recently, some works went up one level further by selecting the appropriate matcher for a given matching task. These tools lessen the burden of the user by automatically tuning most of the low-level parameters.

In the meanwhile, much effort has also been spent to integrate user preferences or input data parameters. Most of them are based on machine learning techniques so that schema instances or expert feedback can be used in the process. The integration of such parameters is often an extra means for improving matching quality. User preferences such as the promotion of precision or recall let users choose how they intend to manage post-match effort. These options are also interesting in contexts, where high dynamicity leads to a quick evolution of data sources, thus implying that a high precision is preferred. On the contrary, recall can be promoted when data sources are going to be fully integrated and manually checked.

Although a default configuration should still be proposed with a matcher, we believe that we are heading towards a specific configuration of a schema matcher for a given matching task. Namely, various properties of the matching scenario can be computed by the tool. The latter can then deduce, based on previous experiments or properties values, the best configuration. Visual tools have a strong impact on the manual post-match effort. By displaying the results of different matching strategies, one has sufficient information to check and (in)validate the mappings. Combined with user preferences, these tools would clearly reduce manual post-match effort. To the best of our knowledge, there are currently no works which study the impact of the tuning (during pre-match effort) over matching quality (and post-match effort). A balanced effort between parameters that would bring significant impact on the matching quality given a matching task might be further investigated.

Acknowledgements We thank our reviewers for their comments and corrections on this chapter. We are also grateful to colleagues who have accepted the publication of pictures from their tools.

References

Anan M, Avigdor G (2008) Boosting schema matchers. In: OTM '08: Proceedings of the OTM 2008 confederated international conferences, CoopIS, DOA, GADA, IS, and ODBASE 2008. Part I on on the move to meaningful internet systems. Springer, Heidelberg, pp 283–300. doi:http://dx.doi.org/10.1007/978-3-540-88871-0_20

Aumueller D, Do HH, Massmann S, Rahm E (2005) Schema and ontology matching with COMA++. In: ACM SIGMOD. ACM, NY, pp 906–908

Avesani P, Giunchiglia F, Yatskevich M (2005) A large scale taxonomy mapping evaluation. In: ISWC 2005, Galway, pp 67–81

Avigdor G (2005) On the cardinality of schema matching. In: OTM workshops, pp 947–956

Berlin J, Motro A (2001) Automated discovery of contents for virtual databases. In: CoopIS. Springer, Heidelberg, pp 108–122

Berlin J, Motro A (2002) Database schema matching using machine learning with feature selection. In: CAiSE. Springer, London, pp 452–466

Bellahsene Z, Bonifati A, Duchateau F, Velegrakis Y (2011) On evaluating schema matching and mapping. In: Bellahsene Z, Bonifati A, Rahm E (eds) Schema matching and mapping. Data-694 Centric Systems and Applications Series. Springer, Heidelberg

Bozovic N, Vassalos V (2008) Two-phase schema matching in real world relational databases. In: ICDE Workshops, pp 290–296

Carmel D, Avigdor G, Haggai R (2007) Rank aggregation for automatic schema matching. IEEE Trans Knowl Data Eng 19(4):538–553. doi:http://dx.doi.org/10.1109/TKDE.2007.1010

Cohen W, Ravikumar P, Fienberg S (2003) A comparison of string distance metrics for name-matching tasks. In: Proceedings of the IJCAI-2003. http://citeseer.ist.psu.edu/cohen03comparison.html

Cruz IF, Sunna W, Makar N, Bathala S (2007) A visual tool for ontology alignment to enable geospatial interoperability. J Vis Lang Comput 18(3):230–254

Cruz IF, Antonelli FP, Stroe C (2009) Agreementmaker: Efficient matching for large real-world schemas and ontologies. Proc VLDB Endow 2(2):1586–1589

Dhamankar R, Lee Y, Doan A, Halevy A, Domingos P (2004) iMAP: Discovering complex semantic matches between database schemas. In: ACM SIGMOD. ACM, NY, pp 383–394

Do HH, Rahm E (2002) COMA – A system for flexible combination of schema matching approaches. In: VLDB. VLDB Endowment, pp 610–621

Do HH, Melnik S, Rahm E (2002) Comparison of schema matching evaluations. In: Web, web-services, and database systems workshop. Springer, London, pp 221–237

Doan A, Domingos P, Halevy AY (2001) Reconciling schemas of disparate data sources – A machine learning approach. In: ACM SIGMOD. ACM, NY, pp 509–520

Doan A, Madhavan J, Dhamankar R, Domingos P, Halevy AY (2003) Learning to match ontologies on the semantic web. VLDB J 12(4):303–319

Drumm C, Schmitt M, Do HH, Rahm E (2007) Quickmig: Automatic schema matching for data migration projects. In: CIKM. ACM, NY, pp 107–116. doi:http://doi.acm.org/10.1145/1321440.1321458

Duchateau F (2009) Towards a generic approach for schema matcher selection: Leveraging user pre- and post-match effort for improving quality and time performance. PhD thesis, Université Montpellier II – Sciences et Techniques du Languedoc. http://tel.archives-ouvertes.fr/tel-00436547/en/

Duchateau F, Bellahsene Z, Hunt E (2007) Xbenchmatch: A benchmark for xml schema matching tools. In: VLDB. VLDB Endowment, pp 1318–1321

Duchateau F, Bellahsene Z, Coletta R (2008a) A flexible approach for planning schema matching algorithms. In: OTM Conferences (1), Springer, Heidelberg, pp 249–264

Duchateau F, Bellahsene Z, Roche M (2008b) Improving quality and performance of schema matching in large scale. Ingénierie des Systèmes d'Information 13(5):59–82

Duchateau F, Coletta R, Bellahsene Z, Miller RJ (2009a) (not) yet another matcher. In: CIKM ACM, Hong Kong, pp 1537–1540

Duchateau F, Coletta R, Bellahsene Z, Miller RJ (2009b) Yam: A schema matcher factory. In: CIKM ACM, Hong Kong, pp 2079–2080

Ehrig M, Staab S, Sure Y (2005) Bootstrapping ontology alignment methods with APFEL. In: ISWC, ACM, NY, pp 1148–1149

Euzenat J, et al (2004) State of the art on ontology matching. Tech. Rep. KWEB/2004/D2.2.3/v1.2, Knowledge Web

Ferrara A, Lorusso D, Montanelli S, Varese G (2008) Towards a benchmark for instance matching. In: Shvaiko P, Euzenat J, Giunchiglia F, Stuckenschmidt H (eds) OM. CEUR-WS.org, CEUR workshop proceedings, vol 431. http://dblp.uni-trier.de/db/conf/semweb/om2008.html#FerraraLMV08

Garner SR (1995) Weka: The waikato environment for knowledge analysis. In: Proceedings of the New Zealand computer science research students conference, pp 57–64

Giunchiglia F, Shvaiko P, Yatskevich M (2004) S-Match: An algorithm and an implementation of semantic matching. In: European semantic web symposium. ACM, NY, pp 61–75

Giunchiglia F, Shvaiko P, Yatskevich M (2007) Semantic matching: Algorithms and an implementation. Tech. rep., DISI, University of Trento. http://eprints.biblio.unitn.it/archive/00001148/

Hernandez MA, Miller RJ, Haas LM (2002) Clio: A semi-automatic tool for schema mapping (software demonstration). In: ACM SIGMOD, Madison

Köpcke H, Rahm E (2008) Training selection for tuning entity matching. In: QDB/MUD, VLDB, Auckland, pp 3–12

Lee Y, Sayyadian M, Doan A, Rosenthal A (2007) etuner: Tuning schema matching software using synthetic scenarios. VLDB J 16(1):97–122

Levenshtein V (1966) Binary codes capable of correcting deletions, insertions and reversals. Sov Phys Dokl 10:707

Li J, Tang J, Li Y, Luo Q (2009) Rimom: A dynamic multistrategy ontology alignment framework. IEEE Trans Knowl Data Eng 21(8):1218–1232. DOI http://dx.doi.org/10.1109/TKDE.2008.202

Li WS, Clifton C (2000) Semint: a tool for identifying attribute correspondences in heterogeneous databases using neural networks. Data Knowl Eng 33(1):49–84. DOI http://dx.doi.org/10.1016/S0169-023X(99)00044-0

Madhavan J, Bernstein PA, Rahm E (2001) Generic schema matching with cupid. In: VLDB. Morgan Kaufmann, CA, pp 49–58

Madhavan J, Bernstein PA, Doan A, Halevy AY (2005) Corpus-based schema matching. In: International conference on data engineering. IEEE Computer Society, Washington, DC, pp 57–68

Malgorzata M, Anja J, Jérôme E (2006) Applying an analytic method for matching approach selection. In: Shvaiko P, Euzenat J, Noy NF, Stuckenschmidt H, Benjamins VR, Uschold M (eds) Ontology matching. CEUR-WS.org, CEUR workshop proceedings, vol 225. http://dblp.uni-trier.de/db/conf/semweb/om2006.html#MocholJE06

Melnik S, Garcia-Molina H, Rahm E (2002) Similarity flooding: A versatile graph matching algorithm and its application to schema matching. In: ICDE. IEEE Computer Society, Washington, DC, pp 117–128

Melnik S, Rahm E, Bernstein PA (2003) Developing metadata-intensive applications with rondo. J Web Semant I:47–74

Mork P, Seligman L, Rosenthal A, Korb J, Wolf C (2008) The harmony integration workbench. J Data Semant 11:65–93

Naumann F, Ho CT, Tian X, Haas LM, Megiddo N (2002) Attribute classification using feature analysis. In: ICDE. IEEE Computer Society, Washington, p 271

Noy N, Musen M (2001) Anchor-PROMPT: Using non-local context for semantic matching. In: Proceedings of IJCAI 2001 workshop on ontology and information sharing, Seattle, pp 63–70

Saleem K, Bellahsene Z (2009) Complex schema match discovery and validation through collaboration. In: OTM Conferences (1). Springer, Heidelberg, pp 406–413

Saleem K, Bellahsene Z, Hunt E (2008) Porsche: Performance oriented schema mediation. Inf Syst 33(7–8):637–657

Shvaiko P, Euzenat J (2008) Ten challenges for ontology matching. In: OTM Conferences (2). Springer, Heidelberg, pp 1164–1182

Smith K, Morse M, Mork P, Li M, Rosenthal A, Allen D, Seligman L (2009) The role of schema matching in large enterprises. In: CIDR, Asilomar

Winkler W (1999) The state of record linkage and current research problems. In: Statistics of Income Division, Internal Revenue Service Publication R99/04

Wordnet (2007) http://wordnet.princeton.edu

Yatskevich M (2003) Preliminary evaluation of schema matching systems. Tech. Rep. DIT-03-028, Informatica e Telecomunicazioni, University of Trento

Zhang X, Zhong Q, Shi F, Li J, Tang J (2009) Rimom results for OAEI 2009. http://oaei.ontologymatching.org/2009/results/

Index

Z. Bellahsene et al. (eds.), *Schema Matching and Mapping*, Data-Centric Systems
and Applications, DOI 10.1007/978-3-642-16518-4,
© Springer-Verlag Berlin Heidelberg 2011

Printed by Publishers' Graphics LLC
MLSI130426.15.16.183